Lecture Notes in Computer Science 4383

Commenced Publication in 1973
Founding and Former Series Editors:
Gerhard Goos, Juris Hartmanis, and Jan van Leeuwen

Editorial Board

Eyal Bin   Avi Ziv   Shmuel Ur (Eds.)

Hardware and Software, Verification and Testing

Second International Haifa Verification Conference, HVC 2006
Haifa, Israel, October 23-26, 2006
Revised Selected Papers

 Springer

Volume Editors

Eyal Bin
Avi Ziv
Shmuel Ur
IBM Labs, Haifa University
Mount Carmel, Haifa 31905, Israel
E-mail: {bin,aziv,ur}@il.ibm.com

Library of Congress Control Number: 2007920490

CR Subject Classification (1998): D.2.4-5, D.2, D.3, F.3

LNCS Sublibrary: SL 2 – Programming and Software Engineering

ISSN   0302-9743
ISBN-10   3-540-70888-X Springer Berlin Heidelberg New York
ISBN-13   978-3-540-70888-9 Springer Berlin Heidelberg New York

Springer is a part of Springer Science+Business Media

springer.com

© Springer-Verlag Berlin Heidelberg 2007
Printed in Germany

Typesetting: Camera-ready by author, data conversion by Scientific Publishing Services, Chennai, India
Printed on acid-free paper   SPIN: 12019380   06/3142   5 4 3 2 1 0

Preface

The Haifa Verification Conference 2006 took place for the second year in a row at the IBM Haifa Research Lab and at the Haifa University in Israel during October 23–26, 2006. The verification conference was a three-day, single-track conference followed by a one-day tutorial on PSL.

This Haifa Verification Conference was established to bring together researchers from two different disciplines, hardware verification and software testing. The use of similar techniques among the two communities enabled the conference to help generate a unique synergy that fortifies both groups. This year, we had two traditional tracks, hardware verification and software testing, in addition to a new track dedicated to tools in these areas.

The conference emphasized applicability to real-world challenges, which was vital to the many attendees coming from industry. The conference hosted two internationally recognized individuals as keynote speakers. Randal E. Bryant, Dean and University Professor from the School of Computer Science at Carnegie Mellon University gave a talk on "System Modeling and Formal Verification with UCLID" and Michael Jackson from the University of Newcastle gave a talk on "Testing the Machine in the World." The numerous invited speakers presented topics of great interest to the audience. Just some of these outstanding speakers included Cindy Eisner in the hardware verification track, Alon Gluska and Andrew Piziali in the tools track, and Mauro Pezze and Nir Shavit in the software testing track. The prize for Best Paper was awarded to Stefan Staber, Gerschwin Fey, Roderick Bloem and Rolf Drechsler from Graz University of Technology and the University of Bremen, for their paper titled "Automatic Fault Localization for Property Checking."

Thirty-three papers from ten countries were submitted, including Israel, Finland, India, the Czech Republic, Germany, China, USA, Spain, France, and Switzerland. The papers were reviewed by the Program Committee and additional referees, with an average of 3.6 reviews per paper. Of the papers submitted, 15 were accepted. The acceptance was based on the score received, the reviewer's confidence and the final decisions of the Organizing Committee. The keynote speakers and the invited speakers were encouraged to submit papers as well. This volume is composed of the papers accepted by the committee and the invited papers. This volume also includes an abstract of the conference panel on the "Unpaved Road between Hardware Verification and Software Testing Techniques" moderated by Shmuel Ur.

This year's conference included a number of new initiatives. A Web application was adopted to enable the online submission and review of papers. A ten-minute multimedia clip was produced to provide an overview of the activities in the conference. The clip covered recent news highlights in verification from around the world and gave viewers a short virtual tour of Haifa through scenes from around the city. The conference also included a tool exhibition where leading EDA companies presented their products. The conference organizers initiated a 'speed networking' session; based on the original idea of speed dating, this activity helped foster introductions and collaboration among individuals attending the event.

Attendance at the conference was very high throughout the four conference days, with more than 250 participants from several different countries. The facilities provided by the IBM Haifa Research Labs and the Caesarea Edmond Benjamin de Rothschild Foundation Institute for Interdisciplinary Applications of Computer Science (C.R.I.) were remarked upon very favorably by the attendees, as was the proficiency of the administrative assistants.

We would like to thank our sponsors, IBM and CRI, the Organizing Committee, and the Program Committee. Our appreciation goes out to the administrative assistants, especially Vered Aharon from IBM and Rona Perkis from CRI. Special thanks to Shai Halevi, Iliya Kalderon, Ido Levy, and Valentin Mashiah for their important help with the submission and review Web application. We also wish to thank the communications team for their important role: Ettie Gilead, Chani Sacharen, Yair Harry, Tamar Dekel, Hanan Singer and Anne Lustig-Picus. Many thanks to Tsvi Kuflik for his vital help with the proceedings. We would also like to extend special thanks all the authors who contributed their work.

It is our hope that the enthusiasm and value generated by this conference will lead to many other interesting events in the growing fields addressed by the hardware verification and software testing communities.

We would like also to thank Dana Fisman for giving the tutorial on PSL.

October 2006   Eyal Bin

Organization

The Haifa Verification Conference 2006 was organized by:

General Chair and Program Chair

Eyal Bin (bin@il.ibm.com)

Verification Conference Organizing Committee

Eyal Bin (bin@il.ibm.com)
Gadiel Auerbach (gadiel@il.ibm.com)
Laurent Fournier (laurent@il.ibm.com)
Moshe Levinger (levinger@il.ibm.com)
Shmuel Ur (ur@il.ibm.com)
Yaniv Eytani (ieytani@cslx.haifa.ac.il)
Yaron Wolfsthal (wolfstal@il.ibm.com)
Karen Yorav (yorav@il.ibm.com)
Avi Ziv (aziv@il.ibm.com)

Verification Track Co-chairs

Laurent Fournier, IBM Haifa Labs, Israel (laurent@il.ibm.com)
Karen Yorav, IBM Haifa Labs, Israel (yorav@il.ibm.com)

Tools Track Co-chairs

Avi Ziv, IBM Haifa Labs, Israel (aziv@il.ibm.com)
Gadiel Auerbach, IBM Haifa Labs, Israel (gadiel@il.ibm.com)

Software Testing Track Chair

Shmuel Ur, IBM Haifa Labs, Israel (ur@il.ibm.com)

PSL Tutorial Track Chair

Gadiel Auerbach, IBM Haifa Labs, Israel (gadiel@il.ibm.com)

Program Committee

Aarti Gupta, NEC Labs America (agupta@nec-labs.com)
Abraham Kandel, University of South Florida, USA (kandel@cse.usf.edu)
Alessandro Cimatti, IRST - Istituto per la Ricerca Scientifica e Tecnologica, Italy
    (cimatti@itc.it)
Amos Noy, Cadence (amos@cadence.com)
Andrew Piziali, Cadence (andy@cadence.com)
Assaf Schuster, Technion Institute, Haifa, Israel (assaf@cs.technion.ac.il)
Avi Ziv, IBM Haifa Labs, Israel (aziv@il.ibm.com)
Bernd Finkbeiner, Universität des Saarlandes , Germany (finkbeiner@cs.uni-sb.de)
Cindy Eisner, IBM Haifa Labs, Israel (EISNER@il.ibm.com)
Daniel Kroening, Computer Systems Institute, ETH Zuerich
    (kroening@handshake.de)
Dominique Borrione, Laboratoire TIMA (Dominique.Borrione@imag.fr)
Eitan Farchi, IBM Haifa Labs, Israel (farchi@il.ibm.com)
Erich Marschner, Cadence (erichm@cadence.com)
Eyal Bin, IBM Haifa Labs, Israel (bin@il.ibm.com)
Fabio Somenzi, University of Colorado (fabio@Colorado.EDU)
Gadiel Auerbach, IBM Haifa Labs, Israel (GADIEL@il.ibm.com)
Geert Janssen, IBM T.J. Watson Research Center (geert@watson.ibm.com)
Holger Hermanns, Saarland University, Germany (hermann@cs.uni-sb.de)
Ilan Harris, University of California, Irvine (harris@ics.uci.edu)
Jason Baumgartner, IBM Austin (baumgarj@us.ibm.com)
Joao Lourenco, University Nova de Lisboa (Joao.Lourenco@di.fct.unl.pt)
Jong-Deok Choi, IBM Research, USA (jdchoi@us.ibm.com)
Karen Yorav, IBM Haifa Labs, Israel (YORAV@il.ibm.com)
Ken McMillan, Cadence (mcmillan@cadence.com)
Kerstin Eder, University of Bristol (eder@cs.bris.ac.uk)
Klaus Havelund, NASA's Jet Propulsion Labratory (Klaus.Havelund@jpl.nasa.gov)
Laurent Fournier, IBM Haifa Labs, Israel (LAURENT@il.ibm.com)
Lyes Benalycherif, STMicroelectronics (Lyes.Benalycherif@st.com)
Mark Last, Ben Gurion University, Israel (mlast@bgumail.bgu.ac.il)
Mauro Pezze, Universita degli Studi di Milano, Bicocca (pezze@disco.unimib.it)
Moshe Levinger, IBM Haifa Labs, Israel (LEVINGER@il.ibm.com)
Ofer Strichman, Technion, Israel (ofers@ie.technion.ac.il)
Orit Edelstein, IBM Haifa Labs, Israel (edelstein@il.ibm.com)
Orna Kupferman, Hebrew University, Israel (orna@cs.huji.ac.il)
Pablo P. Sanchez, University of Cantabria (sanchez@teisa.unican.es)
Paul Strooper, University of Queensland, Australia (pstroop@itee.uq.edu.au)
Roderick Bloem, Graz University of Technology (Roderick.Bloem@ist.TUGratz.at)
Scott Stoller, SUNY Stony Brook, USA (stoller@cs.sunysb.edu)
Serdar Tasiran, Koç University, Turkey (stasiran@ku.edu.tr)
Sharad Malik, Princeton University (sharad@princeton.edu)
Shmuel Ur, IBM Haifa Labs, Israel (UR@il.ibm.com)

Tao Xie, North Carolina State University, USA (taoxie@acm.org)
Tsvi Kuflik, University of Haifa, Israel (tsvikak@mis.hevra.haifa.ac.il)
Warren Hunt, University of Texas, Austin (hunt@cs.utexas.edu)
Willem Visser, NASA, USA (wvisser@email.arc.nasa.gov)
Wolfgang Roesner, IBM Austin, USA (wolfgang@us.ibm.com)
Yaron Wolfsthal, IBM Haifa Labs, Israel (wolfstal@il.ibm.com)
Ziyad Hanna, Intel Israel (ziyad.hanna@intel.com)

Additional Referees

Ali Bayazit
Allon Adir
Andreas Griesmayer
Benny Godlin
Calogero Zarba
Georg Weissenbacher
Hana Chockler
Jörn Guy Süß
Klaus Draeger
Marco Roveri
Margaret Wojcicki
Mark Moulin
Nicolas Blanc
Orna Raz
Philippe Georgelin
Rachel Tzoref
Stefan Staber
Yarden Nir-Buchbinder
Yoad Lustig
Zhaohui Fu

Table of Contents

Software Testing Track

Model Checking PSL Using HOL and SMV

Thomas Tuerk[1,*], Klaus Schneider[1], and Mike Gordon[2]

[1] Reactive Systems Group
Department of Computer Science, University of Kaiserslautern
P.O. Box 3049, 67653 Kaiserslautern, Germany
http://rsg.informatik.uni-kl.de
[2] University of Cambridge Computer Laboratory
William Gates Building, JJ Thomson Avenue, Cambridge CB3 0FD, United Kingdom
http://www.cl.cam.ac.uk

Abstract. In our previous work, we formally validated the correctness of a translation from a subset of Accellera's Property Specification Language (PSL) to linear temporal logic (LTL) using the HOL theorem prover. We also built an interface from HOL to the SMV model checker based on a formal translation of LTL to ω-automata. In the present paper, we describe how this work has been extended and combined to produce a model checking infrastructure for a significant subset of PSL that works by translating model checking problems to equivalent checks for the existence of fair paths through a Kripke structure specified in higher order logic. This translation is done by theorem proving in HOL, so it is proven to be correct. The existence check is carried out using the interface from HOL to SMV. Moreover, we have applied our infrastructure to implement a tool for validating the soundness of a separate PSL model checker.

1 Introduction

The Property Specification Language (PSL) [1] is an industrial-strength temporal logic. It was developed by the Functional Verification Technical Committee of Accellera based on IBM's Sugar language [3] and has now become an IEEE standard. It is designed both for formal verification and for simulation and has been described as the most popular property specification language in industry [10].

The linear time subset of PSL is a complex language that includes many special cases with subtle semantics. It is well known how LTL can be translated to equivalent ω-automata [30,9,13,12,23], but PSL additionally provides a reset (abort) operator whose semantics has been the subject of debate. In order to study the impact of different kinds of abort operators on the complexity of the translation and verification, a logic RLTL [2] was introduced that extends LTL by a reset operator. It turned out that, in the worst case, Version 1.01 of PSL lead to a non-elementary blow-up in the translation to ω-automata. For this reason, the semantics of PSL's reset operator were changed in Version 1.1 (the current

---

* This work has been done while this author visited the University of Cambridge Computer Laboratory.

E. Bin, A. Ziv, and S. Ur (Eds.): HVC 2006, LNCS 4383, pp. 1–15, 2007.

version). Thus, a significant subset of PSL can now be translated to RLTL. A further translation from RLTL to LTL has already been presented in [2].

Because of the subtle semantics of PSL, it is non-trivial to ensure that implementations accurately reflect the official language standard. Thus, we feel that there is value in using automated formal methods to reason about the semantics of PSL in general, and to verify model checking algorithms for this logic. PSL has already been deeply embedded in HOL [15] and a translation from a significant subset of PSL to ω-automata via RLTL and LTL has been verified [26,25]. However, in this previous work only the correctness of these translations has been proved.

In this paper, we use revised versions of the correctness translation theorems to create PSL implementation infrastructure directly on top of the formalisation of the standard PSL semantics. Model checking problems for PSL can be handled fully automatically. We have used this infrastructure to build a specific tool to check the accuracy of an implementation of PSL used by IBM's RuleBase CTL model checker. We were able to detect an incorrectness (unknown to us, but known to IBM) in the implementation of clocked aborts (they are treated as synchronous but should have been asynchronous).

Our infrastructure includes formal translators, implemented by theorem-proving in HOL, from the linear time fragment of PSL to LTL and from LTL to ω-automata. Although these are based on previous work, they were largely rewritten so that they could be turned into a new automatic tool for translating PSL to automata. To check the existence of fair paths, we use a link from HOL to SMV. This is based on Schneider's earlier work, though we changed from a shallow to a deep embedding of LTL in HOL and modified many details. Model checking problems for PSL can be translated, using theorem proving, to equivalent checks for the existence of fair paths through a Kripke structure. A proof of the correctness of the emptiness check is created by these translation procedures. The resulting check is finally performed by SMV [19].

The rest of this paper is organised as follows. The formalisms we use are explained in the next section. We then briefly sketch translations between them. In Section 4, we describe the infrastructure and in Section 5, we outline its application to build a tool to validate the handling of PSL by RuleBase. Finally, we draw some conclusions and show directions for future work.

2   Basic Notions

Temporal logics like LTL, RLTL and PSL use propositional logic to describe (static) properties of the current point of time. The semantics of temporal properties is based on sequences of points of time called *paths*, which are usually defined by transition systems. Thus, we first define propositional logic, paths and transition systems in this section. Then, the logics LTL, RLTL, and PSL are presented. Finally, ω-automata are introduced.

Definition 1 (Propositional Logic). *Let $\mathcal{V}$ be a set of variables. Then, the set of propositional formulas over $\mathcal{V}$ (short $\mathsf{prop}_\mathcal{V}$) is recursively given as follows:*

- *each variable $v \in \mathcal{V}$ is a propositional formula*
- *$\neg\varphi \in \mathsf{prop}_\mathcal{V}$, if $\varphi \in \mathsf{prop}_\mathcal{V}$*
- *$\varphi \wedge \psi \in \mathsf{prop}_\mathcal{V}$, if $\varphi, \psi \in \mathsf{prop}_\mathcal{V}$*

An assignment *over $\mathcal{V}$ is a subset of $\mathcal{V}$. In our context, assignments are also* called *states. The set of all states over $\mathcal{V}$, which is the power set of $\mathcal{V}$, is denoted by $\mathcal{P}(\mathcal{V})$. The semantics of a propositional formula with respect to a state s is given by the relation $\models_{\mathsf{prop}}$ that is defined as follows:*

- *$s \models_{\mathsf{prop}} v$ iff $v \in s$*
- *$s \models_{\mathsf{prop}} \neg\varphi$ iff $s \not\models_{\mathsf{prop}} \varphi$*
- *$s \models_{\mathsf{prop}} \varphi \wedge \psi$ iff $s \models_{\mathsf{prop}} \varphi$ and $s \models_{\mathsf{prop}} \psi$*

If $s \models_{\mathsf{prop}} \varphi$ holds, then the assignment s is said to satisfy *the formula φ.*

We use the operators $\vee$, $\rightarrow$ and $\leftrightarrow$ and the constants true and false as syntactic sugar with their usual meaning.

A finite word v over a set Σ of length $|v| = n+1$ is a function $v : \{0, \ldots n\} \rightarrow \Sigma$. An infinite word v over Σ is a function $v : \mathbb{N} \rightarrow \Sigma$ and its length is denoted by $|v| = \infty$. The set Σ is called the *alphabet* and the elements of Σ are called *letters*. The finite word of length 0 is called the *empty word* (denoted by ε). For reasons of simplicity, $v(i)$ is often denoted by v^i for $i \in \mathbb{N}$. Using this notation, words are often given in the form $v^0 v^1 v^2 \ldots v^n$ or $v^0 v^1 \ldots$. The set of all finite and infinite words over Σ is denoted by Σ^* and Σ^ω, respectively.

Counting starts from zero, i.e. v^{i-1} refers to the i-th letter of v. Furthermore, $v^{i\cdots}$ denotes the suffix of v starting at position i, i.e. $v^{i\cdots} = v^i v^{i+1} \ldots$ for all $i < |v|$. The finite word $v^i v^{i+1} \ldots v^j$ is denoted by $v^{i\cdots j}$. Notice that in case $j < i$, the expression $v^{i\cdots j}$ evaluates to the empty word ε. For two words v_1, v_2 with $v_1 \in \Sigma^*$, we write $v_1 v_2$ for their concatenation. The union $v_1 \cup v_2$ of two words v_1, v_2 with $|v_1| = |v_2|$ over sets is defined as the word v with $|v| = |v_1| = |v_2|$ and $v^j = v_1^j \cup v_2^j$ for all $j < |v|$. Analogously, the intersection $v_1 \cap v_2$ of v_1 and v_2 is defined. We write l^ω for the infinite word v with $v^j = l$ for all j.

2.1 Kripke Structures

Systems used with model checking techniques are usually given as labelled transition systems that are often called Kripke structures. In this paper, we use symbolically represented Kripke structures as usual in symbolic model checking.

Definition 2 (Symbolically Represented Kripke Structures). *A symbolically represented Kripke structure $\mathcal{K}$ over a set of variables $\mathcal{V}$ is a tuple $\mathcal{K} = (\mathcal{I}, \mathcal{R})$ such that*

- *$\mathcal{I}$ is a propositional formula over $\mathcal{V}$*
- *$\mathcal{R}$ is a propositional formula over $\mathcal{V} \cup \{\mathsf{X}v \mid v \in \mathcal{V}\}$*

A path p *through* $\mathcal{K} = (\mathcal{I}, \mathcal{R})$ *is an infinite word over* $\mathcal{V}$ *such that for all* i, *the relation* $p^i \cup \{Xv \mid v \in p^{i+1}\} \models_{\mathsf{prop}} \mathcal{R}$ *holds. A path* p *is called* initial, *iff* $p^0 \models_{\mathsf{prop}} \mathcal{I}$ *holds. A path is called* fair *according to some propositional formula* f, *called the* fairness condition, *iff infinitely many letters of* p *satisfy the fairness condition, i. e. iff the set* $\{i \mid p^i \models_{\mathsf{prop}} f\}$ *is infinite. The set of all initial paths through* $\mathcal{K}$ *is denoted by* $\mathsf{IPath}(\mathcal{K})$. *The set of all initial paths that satisfy all fairness constraints in the set* fc *is denoted by* $\mathsf{IPath}_{\mathsf{fair}}(\mathcal{K}, fc)$.

According to this definition, the new variable Xv is used to denote the value of the variable v at the next state. It is often convenient to evaluate a whole propositional formula instead of just one variable at the next state, so the **X** operator is introduced as a shorthand for replacing every occurrence of a variable v by Xv in a propositional formula. Similarly, **X** is also used to replace every variable v in a set by Xv.

2.2   Linear Temporal Logic (LTL)

Linear Temporal Logic (LTL) has been proposed for the specification of reactive systems by Pnueli in [20]. LTL essentially consists of propositional logic enriched with the temporal operators X and $\underline{\mathsf{U}}$. The formula $X\varphi$ means that the property φ holds at the next point of time, $\varphi \underline{\mathsf{U}} \psi$ means that φ holds until ψ holds and that ψ eventually holds.

Definition 3 (Syntax of Linear Temporal Logic (LTL)). *The set* $\mathsf{ltl}_\mathcal{V}$ *of* LTL *formulas over a given set of variables* $\mathcal{V}$ *is defined as follows:*

- $p \in \mathsf{ltl}_\mathcal{V}$ *for all* $p \in \mathsf{prop}_\mathcal{V}$
- $\neg\varphi,\ \varphi \wedge \psi \in \mathsf{ltl}_\mathcal{V}$, *if* $\varphi, \psi \in \mathsf{ltl}_\mathcal{V}$
- $X\varphi,\ \varphi \underline{\mathsf{U}} \psi \in \mathsf{ltl}_\mathcal{V}$, *if* $\varphi, \psi \in \mathsf{ltl}_\mathcal{V}$

Further temporal operators can be defined as syntactic sugar, for example, $F\varphi := (\mathsf{true}\ \underline{\mathsf{U}}\ \psi)$, $G\varphi := \neg F\neg\varphi$, $\varphi\ \mathsf{U}\ \psi := \varphi \underline{\mathsf{U}} \psi \vee G\varphi$, and $\varphi\ \mathsf{B}\ \psi := \neg(\neg\varphi)\ \underline{\mathsf{U}}\ \psi$. LTL with the operators $\underline{\mathsf{U}}$ and X is, however, already expressively complete with respect to the first order theory of linear orders [23].

Definition 4 (Semantics of Linear Temporal Logic (LTL)). *For* $b \in \mathsf{prop}_\mathcal{V}$ *and* $\varphi, \psi \in \mathsf{ltl}_\mathcal{V}$ *the semantics of* LTL *with respect to an infinite word* $v \in \mathcal{P}(\mathcal{V})^\omega$ *and a point of time* $t \in \mathbb{N}$ *is given as follows:*

- $v \models_{\mathsf{ltl}}^t b$ *iff* $v^t \models_{\mathsf{prop}} b$
- $v \models_{\mathsf{ltl}}^t \neg\varphi$ *iff* $v \not\models_{\mathsf{ltl}}^t \varphi$
- $v \models_{\mathsf{ltl}}^t \varphi \wedge \psi$ *iff* $v \models_{\mathsf{ltl}}^t \varphi$ *and* $v \models_{\mathsf{ltl}}^t \psi$
- $v \models_{\mathsf{ltl}}^t X\varphi$ *iff* $v \models_{\mathsf{ltl}}^{t+1} \varphi$
- $v \models_{\mathsf{ltl}}^t \varphi \underline{\mathsf{U}} \psi$ *iff* $\exists k.\ k \geq t \ \wedge\ v \models_{\mathsf{ltl}}^k \psi \ \wedge\ \forall j.\ t \leq j < k \rightarrow v \models_{\mathsf{ltl}}^j \varphi$

A word $v \in \mathcal{P}(\mathcal{V})^\omega$ *satisfies a* LTL *formula* $\varphi \in \mathsf{ltl}_\mathcal{V}$ *(written as* $v \models_{\mathsf{ltl}} \varphi$*) iff* $v \models_{\mathsf{ltl}}^0$ φ; *a Kripke structure* $\mathcal{K}$ *satisfies* φ *(denoted* $\mathcal{K} \models_{\mathsf{ltl}} \varphi$*) iff all paths* $v \in \mathsf{IPath}(\mathcal{K})$ *satisfy* φ.

2.3 Reset Linear Temporal Logic (RLTL)

To evaluate a formula $\varphi \; \underline{U} \; \psi$, one has to consider a (potentially infinite) prefix of a path, namely the prefix up to a state where $\neg(\varphi \wedge \neg\psi)$ holds. As simulations may stop before that prefix is completely examined, the evaluation of formulas could be incomplete, and is thus aborted. In order to return a definite truth value, abort operators are introduced. The logic RLTL [2] extends LTL with an abort operator called ACCEPT. This operator aborts the evaluation and accepts a path, if a boolean condition is detected.

Definition 5 (Syntax of Reset Linear Temporal Logic (RLTL)). *The following mutually recursive definitions introduce the set* rltl$_\mathcal{V}$ *of RLTL formulas over a given set of variables* $\mathcal{V}$*:*

- *each propositional formula* $p \in$ prop$_\mathcal{V}$ *is a RLTL formula*
- $\neg\varphi$, $\varphi \wedge \psi \in$ rltl$_\mathcal{V}$, *if* $\varphi, \psi \in$ rltl$_\mathcal{V}$
- $X\varphi$, $\varphi \; \underline{U} \; \psi \in$ rltl, *if* $\varphi, \psi \in$ rltl$_\mathcal{V}$
- $\mathsf{ACCEPT}(\varphi, b) \in$ rltl$_\mathcal{V}$, *if* $\varphi \in$ rltl$_\mathcal{V}$, $b \in$ prop$_\mathcal{V}$

Definition 6 (Semantics of Reset Linear Temporal Logic (RLTL)). *The semantics of* LTL *is defined with respect to a word v and a point of time t. To define the semantics of* RLTL*, an acceptance condition $a \in$ prop$_\mathcal{V}$ and a rejection condition $r \in$ prop$_\mathcal{V}$ are needed in addition. These conditions are used to capture the required information about* ACCEPT *operators in the context of the formula. Thus, for $b \in$ prop$_\mathcal{V}$ and $\varphi, \psi \in$ rltl$_\mathcal{V}$, the semantics of* RLTL *with respect to an infinite word $v \in \mathcal{P}(\mathcal{V})^\omega$, acceptance/rejection conditions $a, r \in$ prop$_\mathcal{V}$ and a point of time $t \in \mathbb{N}$ is defined as follows:*

- $\langle v, a, r\rangle \models_{\mathsf{rltl}}^t b$ *iff* $v^t \models_{\mathsf{prop}} a$ *or* $(v^t \models_{\mathsf{prop}} b$ *and* $v^t \not\models_{\mathsf{prop}} r)$
- $\langle v, a, r\rangle \models_{\mathsf{rltl}}^t \neg\varphi$ *iff* $\langle v, r, a\rangle \not\models_{\mathsf{rltl}}^t \varphi$
- $\langle v, a, r\rangle \models_{\mathsf{rltl}}^t \varphi \wedge \psi$ *iff* $\langle v, a, r\rangle \models_{\mathsf{rltl}}^t \varphi$ *and* $\langle v, a, r\rangle \models_{\mathsf{rltl}}^t \psi$
- $\langle v, a, r\rangle \models_{\mathsf{rltl}}^t X\varphi$ *iff* $v^t \models_{\mathsf{prop}} a$ *or* $(\langle v, a, r\rangle \models_{\mathsf{rltl}}^{t+1} \varphi$ *and* $v^t \not\models_{\mathsf{prop}} r)$
- $\langle v, a, r\rangle \models_{\mathsf{rltl}}^t \varphi \; \underline{U} \; \psi$

  iff $\exists k. \; k \geq t \; \wedge \; \langle v, a, r\rangle \models_{\mathsf{rltl}}^k \psi \; \wedge \; \forall j. \; t \leq j < k \rightarrow \langle v, a, r\rangle \models_{\mathsf{rltl}}^j \varphi$
- $\langle v, a, r\rangle \models_{\mathsf{rltl}}^t \mathsf{ACCEPT}(\varphi, b)$ *iff* $\langle v, a \vee (b \wedge \neg r), r\rangle \models_{\mathsf{rltl}}^t \varphi$

A word $v \in \mathcal{P}(\mathcal{V})^\omega$ satisfies a RLTL *formula $\varphi \in$ rltl$_\mathcal{V}$ (written as $v \models_{\mathsf{rltl}} \varphi$) iff $\langle v, \mathsf{false}, \mathsf{false}\rangle \models_{\mathsf{rltl}}^0 \varphi$ holds; a Kripke structure $\mathcal{K}$ satisfies φ (denoted $\mathcal{K} \models_{\mathsf{rltl}} \varphi$) iff all paths $v \in$ IPath$(\mathcal{K})$ satisfy φ.*

2.4 Accellera's Property Specification Language

PSL is a standardised industrial-strength property specification language [1] chartered by the Functional Verification Technical Committee of Accellera. The Sugar language [3] was chosen as the basis for PSL. The Language Reference Manual for PSL Version 1.0 was released in April 2003. Finally, in June 2004, Version 1.1 [1] was released, where some anomalies (like those reported in [2]) were corrected.

PSL is designed as an input language for formal verification and simulation tools as well as a language for documentation. Therefore, it has to be as readable as possible, and at the same time, it must be precise and highly expressive. In particular, PSL contains features for simulation like finite paths, features for hardware specification like clocked statements and a lot of syntactic sugar.

PSL consists of four layers: The Boolean layer, the temporal layer, the verification layer and the modelling layer. The *Boolean layer* is used to construct expressions that can be evaluated in a single state. The *temporal layer* is the heart of the language. It is used to express properties concerning more than one state, i. e. temporal properties. The temporal layer is divided into the *Foundation Language* (FL) and the *Optional Branching Extension* (OBE). FL is, like LTL, a linear time temporal logic. In contrast, OBE is essentially the branching time temporal logic CTL [11], which is widely used and well understood. The *verification layer* has the task of instructing tools to perform certain actions on the properties expressed by the temporal layer. Finally, the *modelling layer* is used to describe assumptions about the behaviour of inputs and to model properties that cannot be represented by formulas of the temporal layer or auxiliary hardware that is not part of the design. PSL comes in four flavours, corresponding to the hardware description languages SystemVerilog, Verilog, VHDL and GDL. These flavours provide a syntax for PSL that is similar to the syntax of the corresponding hardware description language.

In this paper, only the Boolean and the temporal layers will be considered. Furthermore, mainly the formal syntax of PSL is used, which differs from the syntax of all four flavours. However, some operators are denoted slightly differently to the formal syntax to avoid confusion with similar LTL operators.

In this paper, only the linear temporal logic FL is considered. It consists of:

- propositional operators
- future temporal (LTL) operators
- a clocking operator for defining the granularity of time, which may vary for subformulas
- Sequential Extended Regular Expressions (SEREs), for defining finite regular patterns, together with strong and weak promotions of SEREs to formulas and an implication operator for predicating a formula on match of the pattern specified by a SERE
- an abort operator

Due to lack of space, only the subset of FL that is interesting for the translation will be presented (e.g. clocks are eliminated using standard rewriting rules). Note that we do not handle SEREs yet.

As described in Version 1.1 of the PSL standard, two special states $\top$ and $\bot$ are needed to define the formal semantics of FL. The state $\top$ satisfies every propositional formula, even the formula false, and state $\bot$ satisfies no propositional formula, even the formula true is not satisfied. Using these two special states, the semantics of a propositional formula $\varphi \in \mathsf{prop}_\mathcal{V}$ with respect to a state $s \in \mathcal{P}(\mathcal{V}) \cup \{\top, \bot\}$ is defined as follows:

- $\top \models_{\mathsf{xprop}} \varphi$
- $\bot \not\models_{\mathsf{xprop}} \varphi$
- $s' \models_{\mathsf{xprop}} \varphi$ iff $s' \models_{\mathsf{prop}} \varphi$ for $s' \in \mathcal{P}(\mathcal{V})$, i.e. for $s' \notin \{\top, \bot\}$

For a given set of variables $\mathcal{V}$, the set of *extended states over* $\mathcal{V}$ is denoted by $\mathcal{XP}(\mathcal{V}) := \mathcal{P}(\mathcal{V}) \cup \{\top, \bot\}$. The definition of the formal syntax of PSL uses a special function for words over these extended states. For finite or infinite words $w \in \mathcal{XP}(\mathcal{V})^* \cup \mathcal{XP}(\mathcal{V})^\omega$, the word $\overline{w}$ denotes the word over states that is obtained from w by replacing every $\top$ with $\bot$ and vice versa, i.e. for all $i < |w|$, the following holds:

$$\overline{w}^i := \begin{cases} \bot & : \text{if } w^i = \top \\ \top & : \text{if } w^i = \bot \\ w^i & : \text{otherwise} \end{cases}$$

Using these extended states and words over these states, the formal syntax and semantics of SERE-free, unclocked FL (which we call SUFL) is defined as follows.

Definition 7 (Syntax of SUFL). *The set of* SUFL *formulas* $\mathsf{sufl}_\mathcal{V}$ *over a given set of variables* $\mathcal{V}$ *is defined as follows:*

- $p, p! \in \mathsf{sufl}_\mathcal{V}$, *if* $p \in \mathsf{prop}_\mathcal{V}$
- $\neg\varphi \in \mathsf{sufl}_\mathcal{V}$, *if* $\varphi \in \mathsf{sufl}_\mathcal{V}$
- $\varphi \wedge \psi \in \mathsf{sufl}_\mathcal{V}$, *if* $\varphi, \psi \in \mathsf{sufl}_\mathcal{V}$
- $\underline{\mathsf{X}}\varphi, \varphi \underline{\mathsf{U}} \psi^1 \in \mathsf{sufl}_\mathcal{V}$, *if* $\varphi, \psi \in \mathsf{sufl}_\mathcal{V}$
- $\varphi\ \mathsf{ABORT}\ b \in \mathsf{sufl}_\mathcal{V}$, *if* $\varphi \in \mathsf{sufl}_\mathcal{V}$, $b \in \mathsf{prop}_\mathcal{V}$

Definition 8 (Semantics of SUFL). *For propositional formulas* $b \in \mathsf{prop}_\mathcal{V}$ *and* SUFL *formulas* $\varphi, \psi \in \mathsf{sufl}_\mathcal{V}$, *the semantics of* SUFL *with respect to a finite or infinite word* $v \in \mathcal{XP}(\mathcal{V})^* \cup \mathcal{XP}(\mathcal{V})^\omega$ *is defined as follows:*

- $v \models_{\mathsf{sufl}} b$ *iff* $|v| = 0$ *or* $v^0 \models_{\mathsf{xprop}} b$
- $v \models_{\mathsf{sufl}} b!$ *iff* $|v| > 0$ *and* $v^0 \models_{\mathsf{xprop}} b$
- $v \models_{\mathsf{sufl}} \neg\varphi$ *iff* $\overline{v} \not\models_{\mathsf{sufl}} \varphi$
- $v \models_{\mathsf{sufl}} \varphi \wedge \psi$ *iff* $v \models_{\mathsf{sufl}} \varphi$ *and* $v \models_{\mathsf{sufl}} \psi$
- $v \models_{\mathsf{sufl}} \underline{\mathsf{X}}\varphi$ *iff* $|v| > 1$ *and* $v^{1..} \models_{\mathsf{sufl}} \varphi$
- $v \models_{\mathsf{sufl}} \varphi \underline{\mathsf{U}} \psi$ *iff* $\exists k.\, k < |v|$ *s.t.* $v^{k..} \models_{\mathsf{sufl}} \psi$ *and* $\forall j.\, j < k$ *implies* $v^{j..} \models_{\mathsf{sufl}} \varphi$
- $v \models_{\mathsf{sufl}} \varphi\ \mathsf{ABORT}\ b$ *iff either* $v \models_{\mathsf{sufl}} \varphi$ *or*
  $\exists j. j < |v|$ *s.t.* $v^j \models_{\mathsf{sufl}} b$ *and* $v^{0..j-1}\top^\omega \models_{\mathsf{sufl}} \varphi$

A word v *satisfies a* SUFL *formula* φ *iff* $v \models_{\mathsf{sufl}} \varphi$ *holds; a Kripke structure* $\mathcal{K}$ *satisfies* φ *(denoted* $\mathcal{K} \models_{\mathsf{sufl}} \varphi$*) iff all paths* $v \in \mathsf{IPath}(\mathcal{K})$ *satisfy* φ.

Some standard syntactic sugar is defined for SUFL:

- $\varphi \vee \psi := \neg(\neg\varphi \wedge \neg\psi)$
- $\varphi \rightarrow \psi := \neg\varphi \vee \psi$
- $\varphi \leftrightarrow \psi := (\varphi \rightarrow \psi) \wedge (\psi \rightarrow \varphi)$
- $\mathsf{X}\varphi := \neg\underline{\mathsf{X}}\neg\varphi$

- $\mathsf{F}\varphi := \mathsf{true}\ \underline{\mathsf{U}}\ \varphi$
- $\mathsf{G}\varphi := \neg\mathsf{F}\neg\varphi$
- $\varphi\ \mathsf{U}\ \psi^2 := \varphi \underline{\mathsf{U}} \psi \vee \mathsf{G}\varphi$
- $\varphi\ \mathsf{B}\ \psi^3 := \neg(\neg\varphi \underline{\mathsf{U}} \psi)$

---

[1] Written as $\varphi\ \mathsf{U}\ \psi$ in [1].
[2] Written as $[\varphi\ \mathsf{W}\ \psi]$ in [1].
[3] Written as $[\varphi\ \mathsf{BEFORE!\_}\ \psi]$ in [1].

All SUFL operators correspond to RLTL operators. A difference from RLTL is that SUFL is able, in addition, to consider finite paths. Thus, for a propositional formula b, a strong variant $b!$ is introduced that does not hold for the empty word ε, while every propositional formula b holds for the empty word. Analogously, $\underline{X}$ is introduced as a strong variant of X. The semantics of $\underline{X}$ requires that a next state exists, while $X\varphi$ trivially holds if no next state exists. For the remaining temporal operator $\underline{U}$, a weak variant U is already available in RLTL. Apart from finite paths, the meaning of the FL operators is the same as the meaning of the corresponding RLTL operators. The role of the two special states $\top, \bot$ is played by the acceptance/rejection conditions of RLTL.

2.5 ω-Automata

ω-automata were introduced by J. R. Büchi in 1960 [7]. They are similar to finite state automata as introduced by Kleene in 1956 [18]. While finite state automata decide whether a finite word belongs to some language, ω-automata decide this property for infinite words. There are different kinds of ω-automata and some of slightly different definitions. In this paper, we will use a symbolic representation of nondeterministic ω-automata, which is closely related to the formalism of automaton formulas described in previous work [23]. For conciseness, some details in this paper have been simplified.

Definition 9 (Symbolic Representation of ω-Automata). *A symbolically represented nondeterministic or universal ω-automaton over a set of variables $\mathcal{V}$ is a tuple $(\mathcal{Q}, \mathcal{I}, \mathcal{R}, l)$ such that*

- $\mathcal{Q} \subseteq \mathcal{V}$ *is a finite set of state variables,*
- $\mathcal{I}$ *and $\mathcal{R}$ represent a Kripke structure over $\mathcal{V}$ and*
- l *is a LTL formula over $\mathcal{V}$ called* acceptance condition.

Symbolically represented nondeterministic ω-automata are often written in the form $\mathcal{A}_{\exists}(\mathcal{Q}, \mathcal{I}, \mathcal{R}, l)$, universal ones are denoted by $\mathcal{A}_{\forall}(\mathcal{Q}, \mathcal{I}, \mathcal{R}, l)$. A run of some input $i \in \mathcal{P}(\mathcal{V} \setminus \mathcal{Q})^\omega$ through $\mathfrak{A} := \mathcal{A}_{\exists/\forall}(\mathcal{Q}, \mathcal{I}, \mathcal{R}, l)$ is an infinite word $r \in \mathcal{P}(\mathcal{Q})^\omega$ such that $i \cup r$ is a path through the Kripke structure represented by $(\mathcal{I}, \mathcal{R})$. The input i satisfies the ω-automaton (denoted by $i \models_{\mathsf{omega}} \mathcal{A}_{\exists/\forall}(\mathcal{Q}, \mathcal{I}, \mathcal{R}, l)$) iff for at least one run / all runs r of i through $\mathfrak{A}$ the path $r \cup i$ satisfies l. For inputs that contain state variables, this definition is extended by restricting the inputs: $i \models_{\mathsf{omega}} \mathfrak{A} := i \cap (\mathcal{V} \setminus \mathcal{Q})^\omega \models_{\mathsf{omega}} \mathfrak{A}$. As usual, a Kripke structure $\mathcal{K}$ satisfies $\mathfrak{A}$ (denoted $\mathcal{K} \models_{\mathsf{omega}} \mathfrak{A}$) iff all paths $i \in \mathsf{IPath}(\mathcal{K})$ satisfy $\mathfrak{A}$.

An ω-automaton $\mathfrak{A} := \mathcal{A}_{\exists/\forall}(\mathcal{Q}, \mathcal{I}, \mathcal{R}, l)$ is called total, iff for all $i, i' \subseteq \mathcal{V} \setminus \mathcal{Q}$, $s \subseteq \mathcal{Q}$ a state $s' \subseteq \mathcal{Q}$ exists such that $i \cup s' \models_{\mathsf{prop}} \mathcal{I}$ and $i \cup s \cup \mathbf{X}i' \cup \mathbf{X}s' \models_{\mathsf{prop}} \mathcal{R}$ holds. $\mathfrak{A}$ is called deterministic iff for all i, i', s an unique s' with these properties exists.

For all input paths there is exactly one run through a deterministic automaton. Thus, the semantics of $\mathcal{A}_{\exists}(\mathcal{Q}, \mathcal{I}, \mathcal{R}, l)$ and $\mathcal{A}_{\forall}(\mathcal{Q}, \mathcal{I}, \mathcal{R}, l)$ coincide for deterministic automata. Therefore, the notation $\mathcal{A}_{\det}(\mathcal{Q}, \mathcal{I}, \mathcal{R}, l)$ is used as well in the deterministic case.

3   Translations

As already mentioned, all operators of the sublanguage SUFL of PSL correspond
to RLTL operators. As shown in previous work [26,25] these correspondences lead
to a very simple translation procedure from SUFL on infinite words to RLTL.

However, during this translation not only the formula itself but also the input
words have to be translated, because in contrast to RLTL, inputs for PSL may
contain the special states $\top$ and $\bot$. The translation used considers only *infinite
proper words* [17]. An *infinite proper word* over $\mathcal{V}$ is an infinite word $v \in \mathcal{XP}(\mathcal{V})^\omega$
such that $\forall j.\ v^j = \top \longrightarrow v^{j+1} = \top$ and $\forall j.\ v^j = \bot \longrightarrow v^{j+1} = \bot$ hold.

The set of all infinite proper words over $\mathcal{V}$ is denoted by $\mathcal{XP}(\mathcal{V})^{\omega^{\top\bot}}$. At first
glance, it may seem to be a restriction to consider only proper words, however,
this is not the case. Special states are just an auxiliary means used to explain
the semantics; they do not occur in practise and proper words are sufficient to
explain the semantics.

Theorem 1. *With the definitions of Figure 1, the following are equivalent for
all $f \in \mathsf{sufl}_\mathcal{V}$, all infinite proper words $v \in \mathcal{XP}(\mathcal{V})^{\omega^{\top\bot}}$ and all $t, b \notin \mathcal{V}$:*

- $v \models_{\mathsf{sufl}} f$
- $\langle \mathsf{RemoveTopBottom}(t, b, v), t, b \rangle \models^0_{\mathsf{rltl}} \mathsf{PSL\_TO\_RLTL}\ f$
- $\mathsf{RemoveTopBottom}(t, b, v) \models_{\mathsf{rltl}} \mathsf{ACCEPT}(\mathsf{REJECT}((\mathsf{PSL\_TO\_RLTL}\ f), b), t)$

If v does not contain $\top$ and $\bot$, i. e. in case $v \in \mathcal{P}(\mathcal{V})^\omega$, this can be simplified to:

$$v \models_{\mathsf{sufl}} \varphi \Longleftrightarrow v \models_{\mathsf{rltl}} \mathsf{PSL\_TO\_RLTL}(\varphi)$$

$$\mathsf{RemoveTopBottom}(t, b, v)^j := \begin{cases} \{t\} & : \textit{if } v^j = \top \\ \{b\} & : \textit{if } v^j = \bot \\ v^j & : \textit{otherwise} \end{cases}$$

```
function PSL_TO_RLTL(Φ)
    case Φ of
        b               : return b;
        b!              : return b;
        ¬φ              : return ¬PSL_TO_RLTL(φ);
        φ ∧ ψ           : return PSL_TO_RLTL(φ) ∧ PSL_TO_RLTL(ψ);
        Xφ              : return X(PSL_TO_RLTL(φ));
        φ U ψ           : return PSL_TO_RLTL(φ) U PSL_TO_RLTL(ψ);
        φ ABORT b       : return ACCEPT(PSL_TO_RLTL(φ), b);
    end
end
```

Fig. 1. Translation of SUFL to RLTL

After the translation to RLTL, the formula can easily be translated further to
LTL. This translation step is due to [2].

Theorem 2 (Translation of RLTL to LTL). *With the definition of Figure 2, the following holds for all infinite words $v \in \mathcal{P}(\mathcal{V})^\omega$, all acceptance / rejection conditions $a, r \in \mathsf{prop}_\mathcal{V}$, all RLTL formulas $\varphi \in \mathsf{rltl}_\mathcal{V}$ and all points of time $t \in \mathbb{N}$:*

$$\langle v, a, r \rangle \models^t_{\mathsf{rltl}} \varphi \Longleftrightarrow v \models^t_{\mathsf{ltl}} RLTL\_TO\_LTL(a, r, \varphi)$$

Obviously, this can be instantiated to:

$$v \models_{\mathsf{rltl}} \varphi \Longleftrightarrow v \models_{\mathsf{ltl}} RLTL\_TO\_LTL(\mathsf{false}, \mathsf{false}, \varphi)$$

> **function** $RLTL\_TO\_LTL(a, r, \Phi)$
>   **case** Φ **of**
> b : **return** $a \vee (b \wedge \neg r)$;
> $\neg\varphi$: **return** $\neg RLTL\_TO\_LTL(r, a, \varphi)$;
> $\varphi \wedge \psi$: **return** $RLTL\_TO\_LTL(a, r, \varphi) \wedge RLTL\_TO\_LTL(a, r, \psi)$;
> $\mathsf{X}\varphi$: **return** $a \vee \big(\mathsf{X}(RLTL\_TO\_LTL(a, r, \varphi)) \wedge \neg r\big)$;
> $\varphi \underline{\mathsf{U}} \psi$: **return** $RLTL\_TO\_LTL(a, r, \varphi) \underline{\mathsf{U}} RLTL\_TO\_LTL(a, r, \psi)$;
> $\mathsf{ACCEPT}(\varphi, b)$: **return** $RLTL\_TO\_LTL(a \vee (b \wedge \neg r), r, \varphi)$;
>   **end**
> **end**

Fig. 2. Translation of RLTL to LTL

$\mathsf{lPath}(\mathcal{K}) \subseteq \mathcal{P}(\mathcal{V})^\omega$ holds for all Kripke structures $\mathcal{K}$ over $\mathcal{V}$. This leads to the following corollary.

Corollary 1 (Direct translation of PSL to LTL). *For all $f \in \mathsf{sufl}_\mathcal{V}$ and all Kripke structures $\mathcal{K}$ over $\mathcal{V}$ the following holds:*

$$\mathcal{K} \models_{\mathsf{sufl}} f \Longleftrightarrow \mathcal{K} \models_{\mathsf{ltl}} RLTL\_TO\_LTL(\mathsf{false}, \mathsf{false}, PSL\_TO\_RLTL(f))$$

It remains to translate LTL to ω-automata. It is well known how this can be achieved [30,5,13,9,12]. In this work, we use an algorithm by Klaus Schneider [22,23] to translate LTL to the symbolic representation of ω-automata introduced above. This algorithm is very similar to the one used in [27] to translate LTL to alternating ω-automata.

Theorem 3 (Translation of LTL to ω-automata). *For all LTL formulas $\Phi \in \mathsf{LTL}_\mathcal{V}$ and $(Q, \mathcal{I}, \mathcal{R}, \mathcal{F}, p) := \mathsf{TopProp}_\sigma(\Phi)$, where $\mathsf{TopProp}$ is defined as in Figure 3, the following holds:*

- *for $\sigma = \mathsf{true}$ and all $v \in \mathcal{P}(\mathcal{V})^\omega$, the following holds:*

$$v \models_{\mathsf{ltl}} \Phi \Longleftrightarrow v \models_{\mathsf{omega}} \mathcal{A}_\exists(Q, \mathcal{I} \wedge p, \mathcal{R}, \bigwedge_{\xi \in \mathcal{F}} \mathsf{GF}\,\xi)$$

- *for $\sigma = \mathsf{false}$ and all $v \in \mathcal{P}(\mathcal{V})^\omega$, the following holds:*

$$v \models_{\mathsf{ltl}} \neg\Phi \Longleftrightarrow v \models_{\mathsf{omega}} \mathcal{A}_\exists(Q, \mathcal{I} \wedge \neg p, \mathcal{R}, \bigwedge_{\xi \in \mathcal{F}} \mathsf{GF}\,\xi)$$

function $\mathsf{TopProp}_\sigma(\varPhi)$

   case $\varPhi$ **of**

     p : **return** $(\{\}, \mathsf{true}, \mathsf{true}, \{\}, p)$;

     $\neg\varphi$: $(Q_\varphi, \mathcal{I}_\varphi, \mathcal{R}_\varphi, \mathcal{F}_\varphi, p_\varphi) := \mathsf{TopProp}_{\neg\sigma}(\varphi)$;

                        return $(Q_\varphi, \mathcal{I}_\varphi, \mathcal{R}_\varphi, \mathcal{F}_\varphi, \neg p_\varphi)$;

     $\varphi \wedge \psi$: **return** $\mathsf{TopProp}_\sigma(\varphi) \times \mathsf{TopProp}_\sigma(\psi)$;

     $\mathsf{X}\varphi$: $(Q_\varphi, \mathcal{I}_\varphi, \mathcal{R}_\varphi, \mathcal{F}_\varphi, p_\varphi) := \mathsf{TopProp}_\sigma(\varphi)$;

                        $q := \mathsf{new\_var}$;

                        return $(Q_\varphi \cup \{q\}, \mathcal{I}_\varphi, \mathcal{R}_\varphi \wedge (q \leftrightarrow \mathsf{X}p_\varphi), \mathcal{F}_\varphi, q)$;

     $\varphi \mathbin{\underline{\mathsf{U}}} \psi$: $(Q_\varPhi, \mathcal{I}_\varPhi, \mathcal{R}_\varPhi, \mathcal{F}_\varPhi, p_\varphi \wedge p_\psi) := \mathsf{TopProp}_\sigma(\varphi) \times \mathsf{TopProp}_\sigma(\psi)$;

                        $q := \mathsf{new\_var}$;

                        $\mathcal{R}_Q := q \leftrightarrow (p_\psi \vee (p_\varphi \wedge \mathsf{X}q))$;

                        $\mathcal{F}_Q :=$ **if** σ **then** $\{q \vee p_\psi\}$ **else** $\{\}$;

                        return $(Q_\varPhi \cup \{q\}, \mathcal{I}_\varPhi, \mathcal{R}_\varPhi \wedge \mathcal{R}_Q, \mathcal{F}_\varphi \cup \mathcal{F}_Q, q)$;

   end

 end

Fig. 3. Translation of LTL to ω-automata [22,23]

4 Infrastructure

The HOL System [14,16] is an interactive theorem prover for higher order logic. In this work the HOL4 implementation is used. The version of higher order logic used in HOL is predicate calculus with terms from the typed lambda calculus [8]. The interactive front-end of HOL is the functional programming language ML, in which terms and theorems of the logic, proof strategies and logical theories are implemented. This language is used to implement the translations described here and also to interface to SMV.

In earlier work, Gordon deeply embedded PSL in HOL [15], Schneider created a shallow embedding of symbolically represented ω-automata and a shallow embedding of LTL and verified a translation between these two embeddings [24]. Also, we have previously deeply embedded RLTL, LTL and symbolically represented ω-automata, and verified the translations described in Sec. 3 [25,26]. However, no automatic translations or other parts that could be used for tools existed.

In this work, we describe such tools. In particular, we have implemented validating compilers for all the translations described here, i.e. we have implemented ML-functions that translate an LTL term to an ω-automaton and also produce a correctness proof of the generated automaton. Thus, possible bugs in these implementations may only lead to exceptions and failing translations, but no wrong results can be produced. In addition, we have implemented validating compilers to convert model checking problems for SUFL and LTL to check the existence of fair paths through a Kripke structure. For example, we can translate the check $\mathcal{K} \models_{\mathsf{sufl}} f$ to a Kripke structure M and a set of propositional formulas fc such that $\mathcal{K} \models_{\mathsf{sufl}} f \iff \mathsf{IPath}_{\mathsf{fair}}(M, \mathsf{fc}) = \emptyset$ holds. This emptiness check can be handled by CTL model checkers that can handle fairness. In this work, we use the model checker SMV [19] and reuse an interface already developed in previous work [24]. However, interfaces to other model checkers can easily be added.

As a result of this work, we can perform model checking for SUFL using HOL and SMV. Assuming that SMV and HOL are correct, we have high confidence that the whole tool is correct, since only the interface between HOL and SMV is not verified and this interface is very small and simple.

Provably correct SUFL model checking is interesting in its own right as SUFL is a significant subset of PSL and PSL is difficult to model check. PSL is a complex language, so errors in designing and implementing model checking procedures for it are potentially very easy to make. However, the main purpose of the work reported here is to create a library of theorems and ML functions as a basis for building special purpose tools. One example of such an tool is described in the next section. This enables implementers of PSL tools to validate their code on concrete examples with respect to the Version 1.1 PSL semantics.

5   Application: Validating a Translator from **PSL** to **CTL**

Our tool aims to validate how IBM's model checker RuleBase [4] handles PSL. RuleBase checks if a Kripke structure $\mathcal{K}$ satisfies a PSL specification f, by translating the specification f to a total transition system $\mathcal{T} = (\mathcal{Q}, \mathcal{I}, \mathcal{R})$ and a CTL formula of the form $\mathsf{AG}\,p$ with propositional p. This translation is a blackbox to us. Then $\mathcal{K}\,\|\,\mathcal{T} \models_{\mathsf{CTL}} \mathsf{AG}\,p$ is checked. Neither CTL semantics nor this combination of $\mathcal{K}$ and $\mathcal{T}$ are explained here, but note that $\mathcal{K}\,\|\,\mathcal{T} \models_{\mathsf{CTL}} \mathsf{AG}\,p$ is equivalent to $\mathcal{K} \models \mathcal{A}_\forall(\mathcal{Q}, \mathcal{I}, \mathcal{R}, \mathsf{G}\,p)$. Thus, given $f, \mathcal{Q}, \mathcal{I}, \mathcal{R}$ and p one would like to automatically prove

$$\forall \mathcal{K}.\ \mathcal{K} \models_{\mathsf{omega}} \mathcal{A}_\forall(\mathcal{Q}, \mathcal{I}, \mathcal{R}, \mathsf{G}\,p) \iff \mathcal{K} \models_{\mathsf{sufl}} f.$$

We are able to solve this problem for all SUFL formulas f with the library we have developed. Moreover, clock operators can also be handled, since they can be considered as syntactic sugar and eliminated by rewrite rules [1]. Thus only regular expressions can not be handled. However, we have a preprocessing step that tries to eliminate regular expressions by rewriting them to SUFL formulas. Regular expression strictly increase the expressiveness of FL [28,29,25]. Thus, we can not eliminate all of them. But luckily we can eliminate most of the regular expressions occurring in practise.

It is of course vital to anybody using RuleBase with PSL specifications, that the translation to CTL model checking is sound. However, we think our work should be of interest to implementers of other model checking tools also. Note that neither IBM's translation nor our tool can handle full FL. Nevertheless, the intersection between the subsets that our tool can handle and RuleBase can handle is big enough to be interesting.

To implement a tool to solve the translation validation problem using our library, formal translation (implemented by theorem proving) is used to convert a PSL formula f to an equivalent LTL formula l. Then the quantification over the models $\mathcal{K}$ is replaced by quantification over all paths i, which is equivalent for this problem. $\mathcal{A}_\forall(\mathcal{Q}, \mathcal{I}, \mathcal{R}, \mathsf{G}\, p)$ is then translated to a deterministic automaton $\mathcal{A}_{\mathsf{det}}(\mathcal{Q}_{\mathsf{det}}, \mathcal{I}_{\mathsf{det}}, \mathcal{R}_{\mathsf{det}}, \mathsf{G}\, p_{\mathsf{det}})$, which is possible because the input automaton is total [23]. Thus, the original problem is equivalent to

$$\forall i. \; i \models_{\mathsf{omega}} \mathcal{A}_\forall(\mathcal{Q}_{\mathsf{det}}, \mathcal{I}_{\mathsf{det}}, \mathcal{R}_{\mathsf{det}}, \mathsf{G}\, p_{\mathsf{det}}) \iff i \models_{\mathsf{ltl}} l.$$

This is in turn equivalent to $(\mathcal{I}_{\mathsf{det}}, \mathcal{R}_{\mathsf{det}}) \models_{\mathsf{ltl}} \mathsf{G}\, p_{\mathsf{det}} \leftrightarrow l$. Thus, the library can be used to translate the original problem to a LTL model checking problem, which can be solved using the techniques described in Section 4. Moreover, all steps needed for this translation to a LTL model checking problem are formally verified in HOL. Therefore, we have an automatic tool to prove the correctness of the translation for concrete examples.

We have validated several examples provided by IBM. Most of these examples can be verified in a few minutes, some take several hours. However, the determinisation of the input automaton leads to an exponential blowup. Thus, small PSL formulas may lead to huge model checking problems. However, we have been able to show that the tool we developed is able to handle non toy examples. Moreover, we have been able to detect an error in the translation of the ABORT operator under clocks using it (though, unknown to us, this problem was already known to the RuleBase developers).

6   Conclusions and Future Work

We have developed a library that allows us to handle a significant subset of PSL using HOL and SMV. There are theorems about PSL and especially about translations between PSL, LTL and ω-automata, and also ML-functions that solve common problems automatically. Model checking problems of SUFL and LTL can be tackled using these automatic procedures. However, the main purpose of the library is to provide a basis to build tools that can handle special PSL problems.

We used the library to validate the handling of PSL by RuleBase. We were able to show that our tool could handle interesting examples. Moreover, we were even able to detect an error in IBM's procedure.

A lot of implementation details could be improved. However, the main challenge will be to extend the subset of PSL. Adding regular expression strictly increases the expressiveness such that the resulting subset of PSL can no longer be translated to LTL [28,29,25]. However, it is possible to translate PSL directly to ω-automata. There is an approach by Bustan, Fisman and Havlicek [6] which translates PSL to alternating ω-automata. Another approach by Zaks and Pnueli [21] translates PSL to symbolically represented automata. It would be interesting to use this work to verify a direct translation to symbolically described nondeterministic ω-automata using HOL.

Acknowledgements

Thomas Tuerk's visit to Cambridge is partly supported by an IBM Faculty Award to Mike Gordon and partly by EPSRC grant GR/T06315/01. The problem of checking conformance of the PSL-to-CTL translation used by RuleBase with the semantics of PSL in the official standard was originally formulated by Cindy Eisner and Dana Fisman of IBM, and we thank them for much helpful advice and for supplying examples.

References

1. ACCELLERA. Property specification language reference manual, version 1.1. http://www.eda.org, June 2004.
2. ARMONI, R., BUSTAN, D., KUPFERMAN, O., AND VARDI, M. Resets vs. aborts in linear temporal logic. In *Conference on Tools and Algorithms for the Construction and Analysis of Systems (TACAS)* (Warsaw, Poland, 2003), H. Garavel and J. Hatcliff, Eds., vol. 2619 of *LNCS*, Springer, pp. 65–80.
3. BEER, I., BEN-DAVID, S., EISNER, C., FISMAN, D., GRINGAUZE, A., AND RODEH, Y. The temporal logic Sugar. In *Conference on Computer Aided Verification (CAV)* (Paris, France, 2001), vol. 2102 of *LNCS*, Springer, pp. 363–367.
4. BEER, I., BEN-DAVID, S., EISNER, C., GEIST, D., GLUHOVSKY, L., HEYMAN, T., LANDVER, A., PAANAH, P., RODEH, Y., RONIN, G., AND WOLFSTHAL, Y. RuleBase: Model checking at IBM. In *Conference on Computer Aided Verification (CAV)* (Haifa, Israel, 1997), O. Grumberg, Ed., vol. 1254 of *LNCS*, Springer, pp. 480–483.
5. BURCH, J., CLARKE, E., McMILLAN, K., DILL, D., AND HWANG, L. Symbolic model checking: 10^{20} states and beyond. In *Symposium on Logic in Computer Science (LICS)* (Washington, D.C., June 1990), IEEE Computer Society, pp. 1–33.
6. BUSTAN, D., FISMAN, D., AND HAVLICEK, J. Automata construction for PSL. Technical Report MCS05- 04, The Weizmann Institute of Science, Israel, 2005.
7. BÜCHI, J. On a decision method in restricted second order arithmetic. In *International Congress on Logic, Methodology and Philosophy of Science* (Stanford, CA, 1960), E. Nagel, Ed., Stanford University Press, pp. 1–12.
8. CHURCH, A. A formulation of the simple theory of types. *Journal of Symbolic Logic 5* (1940), 56–68.
9. DANIELE, M., GIUNCHIGLIA, F., AND VARDI, M. Improved automata generation for linear temporal logic. In *Conference on Computer Aided Verification (CAV)* (Trento, Italy, 1999), N. Halbwachs and D. Peled, Eds., vol. 1633 of *LNCS*, Springer, pp. 249–260.
10. DeepChip survey on assertions. http://www.deepchip.com/items/dvcon04-06.html, June 2004.
11. EMERSON, E., AND CLARKE, E. Using branching-time temporal logic to synthesize synchronization skeletons. *Science of Computer Programming 2*, 3 (1982), 241–266.
12. GASTIN, P., AND ODDOUX, D. Fast LTL to Büchi automata translation. In *Conference on Computer Aided Verification (CAV)* (Paris, France, 2001), vol. 2102 of *LNCS*, Springer, pp. 53–65.
13. GERTH, R., PELED, D., VARDI, M., AND WOLPER, P. Simple on-the-fly automatic verification of linear temporal logic. In *Symposium on Protocol Specification, Testing, and Verification (PSTV)* (Warsaw, June 1995), North Holland.
14. GORDON, M. HOL: A machine oriented formulation of higher order logic. Tech. Rep. 68, Computer Laboratory, University of Cambridge, May 1985.
15. GORDON, M. PSL semantics in higher order logic. In *Workshop on Designing Correct Circuits (DCC)* (Barcelona, Spain, 2004).

16. GORDON, M., AND MELHAM, T. *Introduction to HOL: A Theorem Proving Environment for Higher Order Logic.* Cambridge University Press, 1993.

17. HAVLICEK, J., FISMAN, D., AND EISNER, C. Basic results on the semantics of Accellera PSL 1.1 foundation language. Technical Report 2004.02, Accellera, 2004.

18. KLEENE, S. Representation of events in nerve nets and finite automata. In *Automata Studies*, C. Shannon and J. McCarthy, Eds. Princeton University Press, Princeton, NJ, 1956, pp. 3–41.

19. MCMILLAN, K. *Symbolic Model Checking.* Kluwer, Norwell Massachusetts, 1993.

20. PNUELI, A. The temporal logic of programs. In *Symposium on Foundations of Computer Science (FOCS)* (New York, 1977), vol. 18, IEEE Computer Society, pp. 46–57.

21. PNUELI, A., AND ZAKS, A. PSL model checking and run-time verification via testers. In *FM* (2006), J. Misra, T. Nipkow, and E. Sekerinski, Eds., vol. 4085 of *Lecture Notes in Computer Science*, Springer, pp. 573–586.

22. SCHNEIDER, K. Improving automata generation for linear temporal logic by considering the automata hierarchy. In *International Conference on Logic for Programming, Artificial Intelligence, and Reasoning (LPAR)* (Havanna, Cuba, 2001), vol. 2250 of *LNAI*, Springer, pp. 39–54.

23. SCHNEIDER, K. *Verification of Reactive Systems – Formal Methods and Algorithms.* Texts in Theoretical Computer Science (EATCS Series). Springer, 2003.

24. SCHNEIDER, K., AND HOFFMANN, D. A HOL conversion for translating linear time temporal logic to omega-automata. In *Higher Order Logic Theorem Proving and its Applications (TPHOL)* (Nice, France, 1999), Y. Bertot, G. Dowek, A. Hirschowitz, C. Paulin, and L. Théry, Eds., vol. 1690 of *LNCS*, Springer, pp. 255–272.

25. TUERK, T. A hierarchy for Accellera's property specification language. Master's thesis, University of Kaiserslautern, Department of Computer Science, 2005.

26. TUERK, T., AND SCHNEIDER, K. From PSL to LTL: A formal validation in HOL. In *International Conference on Theorem Proving in Higher Order Logics (TPHOL)* (Oxford, UK, 2005), J. Hurd and T. Melham, Eds., vol. 3603 of *LNCS*, Springer, pp. 342–357.

27. VARDI, M. Branching vs. linear time: Final showdown. In *Conference on Tools and Algorithms for the Construction and Analysis of Systems (TACAS)* (Genova, Italy, 2001), T. Margaria and W. Yi, Eds., vol. 2031 of *LNCS*, Springer, pp. 1–22.

28. WOLPER, P. Temporal logic can be more expressive. In *Symposium on Foundations of Computer Science (FOCS)* (New York, 1981), IEEE Computer Society, pp. 340–348.

29. WOLPER, P. Temporal logic can be more expressive. *Information and Control 56*, 1-2 (1983), 72–99.

30. WOLPER, P., VARDI, M., AND SISTLA, A. Reasoning about infinite computations paths. In *Symposium on Foundations of Computer Science (FOCS)* (New York, 1983), IEEE Computer Society, pp. 185–194.

Using Linear Programming Techniques for Scheduling-Based Random Test-Case Generation

Amir Nahir, Yossi Shiloach, and Avi Ziv

IBM Research Laboratory in Haifa, Israel
{nahir, shiloach, aziv}@il.ibm.com

Abstract. Multimedia SoCs are characterized by a main controller that directs the activity of several cores, each of which controls a stage in the processing of a media stream. Stimuli generation for such systems can be modeled as a scheduling problem that assigns data items to the processing elements of the system. Our work presents a linear programming (LP) modeling scheme for these scheduling problems. We implemented this modeling scheme as part of SoCVer, a stimuli generator for multimedia SoCs. Experimental results show that this LP-based scheme allows easier modeling and provides better performance than CSP-based engines , which are widely used for stimuli generation.

1 Introduction

Functional verification is widely acknowledged as one of the main challenges of the hardware design cycle [1,2]. During the last few years, complex hardware designs have shifted from custom ASICs toward SoC (system on a chip)-based designs, which include ready-made components (cores). SoC-based designs are dominant in multimedia applications. Many consumer products of this type, such as digital cameras, web cameras, and DVD recorders and players, share a common base structure. They include several cores, such as DSPs, encoders, and decoders, which communicate through shared memory (or memories) and a main microprocessor that controls and coordinates the entire system.

The verification of SoC-based designs for multimedia applications incorporates several challenges. Foremost is the need to verify the integration of several previously designed cores in a relatively short time period. Typically, the system's embedded software is not fully written until fairly late in the development cycle. Although several cores can work concurrently in such systems, the system's functionality enforces temporal constraints on the order in which the cores carries out their tasks. This serves to compound the challenges faced.

Simulation is the main functional verification vehicle for large and complex designs, such as multimedia SoCs [2]. Therefore, test case generation plays a central role in this field. In recent years, technology has shifted towards constraint-based modeling of the generation task and generation schemes driven by solving Constraint Satisfaction Problems (CSP) [3]. In fact, leading verification environments, such as Specman [4] and Vera [5], and stimuli generation tools use CSP solvers as the base for the generation engine.

E. Bin, A. Ziv, and S. Ur (Eds.): HVC 2006, LNCS 4383, pp. 16–33, 2007.

Stimuli generation for multimedia SoCs often involves determining the time at which various cores in the system process input items and transfer these items from the system's inputs to its outputs [6]. These scheduling problems can be modeled as constraint satisfaction problems and solved using CSP solvers. In [6] we presented a modeling scheme that does this and a tool named SoCVer, which implements the scheme to generate high-quality stimuli for multimedia SoCs.

Scheduling problems appear in many places, such as scheduling jobs in a computer system to maximize CPU utilization, and scheduling machine operation in a factory to minimize operation costs. These types of problems also receive a lot of attention in the research community [7]. While CSP can be used to model and solve scheduling problems, other techniques such as linear programming (LP) are considered more efficient in solving these problems [7]. With LP, the scheduling problem is modeled as a set of linear inequalities whose solution provides the required scheduling information.

In this paper, we provide a scheme for modeling the scheduling problem for multimedia SoCs as a mixed integer program. While this modeling scheme borrows ideas from traditional linear programming modeling techniques for scheduling problems, it provides a new modeling framework. This new modeling framework is designed to address the specific characteristics that are unique to stimuli generation [3]. These characteristics include soft constraints that improve the quality of the generated stimuli and the need to provide random solutions. These two unique characteristics are handled in our modeling scheme via the LP objective function.

We implemented the proposed scheme as an alternative modeling scheme in SoCVer and combined it with a commercial solver to create an LP-based generation engine. We used a DVD Player SoC to compare this LP-based generation engine to the CSP-based engine described in [6]. The comparison shows that the LP-based engine has several advantages over the CSP-based engine. First, LP-based modeling is more natural and more expressive than CSP-based modeling. Second, the optimizations used by the LP solver enabled the LP-based engine to generate stimuli faster and with a higher success rate.

The rest of the paper is organized as follows: Section 2 describes a DVD Player SoC that is used as a running example. Section 3 presents the main challenges in stimuli generation for the DVD Player SoC. In Section 4, we provide a brief introduction to mixed integer programming and its main applications. In Section 5, we describe our LP-based modeling framework. In Section 6, we compare the LP-based and CSP-based solution schemes. Conclusions and directions for future work are presented in Section 7.

2   The DVD Player SoC Example

We used a DVD Player SoC to demonstrate our LP modeling technique. Our example focuses on the 'Play' operation for an MPEG-2 video stream. To clarify the system's complexity, we provide a brief description of the MPEG-2 format, as well as the DVD Player SoC's internal blocks and functions. The details provided here set the background required to properly understand the examples given in Section 5. We omitted many additional details about the DVD player's functionality for the sake of simplicity.

2.1   MPEG-2 Format

MPEG-2 is a standard for the coding of moving pictures and associated audio [8]. One of the main goals of this standard is to define the way data is compressed to minimize the storage space required to hold the pictures. For this purpose, the standard defines three possible ways to encode a single picture (frame):

- Intraframe (denoted 'I') - contains complete information that enables the decoding of the frame independently of other frames. This encoding method provides the lowest compression.
- Predicted frame (denoted 'P') – tells the DVD player how to decode the frame based on the most recently decoded intraframe or predicted frame. Using this method, the frame contains only the data that relates to how the picture has changed from the previous intraframe.
- Bidirectional frame (denoted 'B') - to decode this type of frame, the player must have information from the surrounding intraframes or predicted frames. Using data from the closest surrounding frames, it uses interpolation to calculate the position and color of each pixel.

An MPEG-2 video stream is a sequence of 'I', 'P', and 'B' frames. Usually, the sequence of encoded frames appears as follows: 'IPBB-PBB-PBB-IPBB'. (The hyphens are only inserted for clarity — they are not part of the standard.) This kind of sequence is displayed in the following order: 'IBBP-BBP-BBP-IBBP'.

Figure 1 clarifies the MPEG-2 encoding standard: the three images in the top row show a scene in which a car travels from left to right, revealing and hiding the background view as it moves. The frames below each image show how the image is encoded in MPEG-2. The leftmost frame is an 'I' frame and shows the entire image. The rightmost frame is a 'P' frame, which includes motion vectors that describe the motion of the car and some background details required to fill in the space created by the car's movement. The frame in the middle is a 'B' frame, based on the two adjacent frames. Using additional data provided within the 'B' frame, the middle image on the top row can be recreated.

2.2   DVD Player SoC

The DVD player's main tasks are to read the data from storage (DVD drive, hard drive), decode the MPEG-2 encoded movie, and turn it into a standard composite video signal. In addition to decoding the movie, the DVD player decodes the movie's soundtrack and subtitles (if requested). The DVD Player SoC is depicted in Figure 2.

In our example, the DVD player's actions are coordinated by a central controller. This controller takes user actions delivered through the remote control or control panel ('Play', 'Pause', 'Fast Forward', etc.) and implements them in

'I' Frame   'B' Frame   'P' Frame

Fig. 1. MPEG-2 illustration

the software as a sequence of commands issued by the controller to the various modules.

The DVD player is composed of several internal modules (or cores):

- Input Stream Reader (ISR) - one of the DVD player's peripheral modules, which reads the data stream from the DVD drive or hard drive.
- Demultiplexer (DeMux) - receives the stream read by the ISR and converts it into video images, audio track, and subtitles.
- MPEG Decoder Unit (MDU) - decodes the video images.
- Video Display Unit (VDU) - the DVD's output unit. The VDU converts the images created by the MDU into the display format (termed fields). Each decoded image is converted into two fields. Whenever the VDU has no new fields to display, the controller instructs the VDU to display the last two fields again, causing the image in the viewer's screen to freeze.

In addition to the main cores described above, the DVD Player SoC contains several other sub-units. For example, the VDU contains a sub-unit called VDU-Next, which assists the VDU in improving image quality. VDU-Next processes the field that will be processed by the VDU at the following time-tick, unless this field belongs to a different scene. Note that VDU-Next is idle whenever the VDU is idle, but this only occurs at the beginning of operation. Figure 3 shows an example of two scenes handled by the VDU and VDU-Next, where F_j^i denotes the j'th field of the i'th scene.

Each of the processed items (frames or fields) is stored in a main memory module. To have one of the modules process an item, the controller first sets the module to the required processing mode. The module then reads the item from

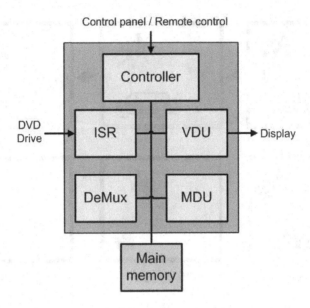

Fig. 2. DVD Player SoC structural block diagram

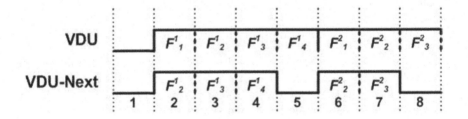

Fig. 3. Handling two scenes by the VDU and VDU-Next

memory, processes it, and stores it back in memory. Figure 4 depicts the data flow within the DVD player when it plays an MPEG-2 video stream.

3   Stimuli Generation for the DVD Player SoC

One of the main challenges in the verification of multimedia SoCs, such as the DVD Player SoC presented in the previous section, is the generation of interesting scenarios that verify the interactions between the various cores in the design. Controlling the various cores in the SoC and synchronizing their operation is done via the SoC's main controller. Therefore, generating stimuli in the form of "software" to the main controller is the best method for achieving high quality stimuli [6].

With this generation scheme, the role of the stimuli generator is to convert a set of operations in the test template file (e.g., "play - stop - play" for a DVD

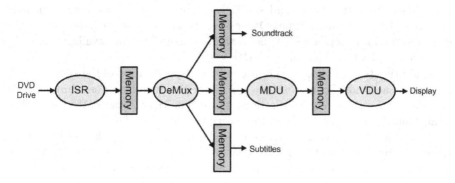

Fig. 4. 'Play MPEG-2' data flow within the DVD player

Player SoC) into commands given by the main controller to the various cores in the SoC. These commands are, in fact, the driving element of the test, as opposed to traditional verification environments where the test is primarily driven by the system's input.

To perform the operations requested by the user, the main controller needs to activate the various cores in a specific order, with many constraints defining when each core should start and finish its operation. In addition, the main controller must manage the shared workspaces through which the cores communicate and ensure that each work space is used properly (e.g., a data item is not over-written before being consumed).

All of this can be translated into a scheduling problem that organizes the operation of the various cores in the system and allocates areas in the shared workspaces for the storage of data items. A solution for the scheduling problem must adhere to many constraints. Some of these constraints are general and typical to many scheduling problems. Examples are:

- The processing start-time of a data item in a specific core is constrained to be greater than the processing end-time of this data item in the previous core, as determined by the operation flow. In addition, in the time between the end of processing in the previous core and beginning of processing in the current core, the data item is stored in an entry in the shared workspace.
- The duration required to process a data item in a given core is expressed as constraints relating the processing end-time and start-time of the data item within the core. In contrast, no constraint is placed on the duration of time a data item remains in a shared workspace, other than requiring that its end-time be greater than its start-time.

Other constraints are imposed by the specific settings or behavior of the Design Under Verification (DUV). The most prominent constraint of this kind is mutual exclusion. This constraint indicates that each core can process only a single data item at a time, and similarly, a shared workspace entry can hold only one data item at a time. Other such behaviors can include the VDU's unique behavior of repeating old fields when no new fields are available, and the dependency of VDU-Next on the VDU.

In addition to the constraints imposed by the specification of the system, users can specify additional constraints as part of the test template. For example, users can add a constraint requiring at least three time-ticks between the entry-time of an input item to the MDU and its entry-time to the VDU.

To increase the quality of the generated test cases, expert knowledge of the DUV can be incorporated in the form of non-mandatory ('soft') constraints. Examples of such constraints include: requiring that the operation complete within a minimum number of time-ticks, or giving priority to an odd number of time-ticks between the entry-time of an item to the MDU and its entry-time to the VDU.

Figure 5 depicts a solution to the 'Play MPEG-2' over an 'IPBB' stream scheduling problem. On top of the basic operation, the test template contains a directive that emulates a slow down in the rate at which frames arrive at the ISR. This could represent a problem in the DVD reader. The input stream flows from the ISR, through the DeMux to the MDU, where each unit processes the frames whenever they become available. The handling by the VDU is more complex. In addition to the VDU's processing of fileds, there are other elements that affect the processing by the VDU. First, the VDU starts handling the data at the eighth time-tick because of a start-at-an-even-tick testing knowledge directive. Second, the order in which the VDU processes the fields is different from their arrival order because of the MPEG-2 reordering rule. Finally, the VDU is required to repeat some of the fields because of the slow rate of data arrival. When formulated as a CSP, such a scheduling problem consists of about 500 variables and over 3000 constraints, and takes the solver about one minute to solve. (More detailed results are presented in Section 6.)

	1	2	3	4	5	6	7	8	9	10	11	12	13	14	15	16	17	18	19	20	21	22	23
ISR	I				P				B				B										
DeMux			I			P					B				B								
MDU				I					P				B				B						
VDU								I_1	I_2	I_1	I_2	I_1	I_2	I_1	I_2	B_1	B_2	B_1	B_2	B_1	B_2	P_1	P_2

Fig. 5. 'Play MPEG-2' over an 'IPBB' stream scheduling solution

In previous work [6], we described SoCVer, a stimuli generator for multimedia SoCs. SoCVer uses a CSP modeling scheme and a CSP solver to generate high-quality stimuli for such systems. In this paper, we present a new modeling scheme based on mixed integer programming. Before describing this modeling scheme, we briefly introduce mixed integer programming.

4   Mixed Integer Programming

A Linear Program (LP) is an optimization problem, that seeks the minimization (or maximization) of a linear function, subject to linear constraints. The development of linear programming has been ranked among the most important scientific advances of the 20th century [7]. Today, linear programming is a standard tool in the use of many applications in the industry. Mixed Integer Programming (MIP), an extension of LP, requires that some of the variables are assigned integer values. In this section, we provide a brief introduction to MIP. In addition, we describe some of the applications of LP and MIP, along with the basic algorithms for solving them.

4.1   Formal Representation

As noted above, MIP requires that some of the variables be assigned integer values. In addition to the linear constraints, there may be additional restrictions requiring that some of the variables be assigned with integer values as part of the solution. Solving MIPs is an NP-Complete problem [9], hence, no known algorithm is guaranteed to solve it efficiently (i.e., in polynomial time). In its most general form, a MIP problem can be represented as:

$$Minimize \sum_{x_j \in \mathbb{Z}} c_j x_j + \sum_{y_j \in \mathbb{R}} c_j y_j$$

subject to:

$$\sum_{x_j \in \mathbb{Z}} a_{ij} x_j + \sum_{y_j \in \mathbb{R}} a_{ij} y_j \left\{ \begin{array}{c} \leq \\ \geq \\ = \end{array} \right\} b_i, \quad i = 1, \ldots m$$

The function being minimized is called the *objective function*. The restrictions are referred to as *constraints*. The size of a MIP problem is measured by three parameters: the number of constraints, the number of variables, and the number of non-zero a_{ij} coefficients in the constraints (termed *non-zeros*).

4.2   Common Uses

Linear programming, as well as its MIP extension, is commonly used in a great number of applications. Examples include:

- Scheduling of shift workers – used to enforce business rules, minimize the size of the workforce, plan the shifts (length and start hours), and maximize worker satisfaction.
- Flow problems – assists in the design of all kinds of transportation and communication networks.
- Packaging problems - used to determine the location of containers on ships.
- Time tabling – for example, used to construct a timetable for high school students.

- Resource allocation – optimally assigns resources to tasks, for example, lecture halls in a college, operating rooms in hospitals, and so forth.
- Finance – used to optimize stock portfolios, control risks, regulate markets, and so forth.

And many, many more...

4.3   Relevant Algorithms

Simplex Method. The Simplex method [10] is an algorithm used to solve continuous linear problems (i.e., all the variables can be assigned fractional values). Even though it does not adhere to integrality constraints, the Simplex method is used as an internal procedure by all IP (and MIP) solvers, and is executed thousands of times for each MIP instance. IP solvers use Simplex to test solutions for feasibility and find bounds for the objective function value. The Simplex method is an iterative procedure that begins at an arbitrary vertex of the feasible solution polytope. This vertex is the intersection of several constraints (hyperplanes). At each iteration, the Simplex method tries to improve the value of the objective function by looking at the values of all adjacent vertices, where an adjacent vertex is obtained by replacing a single constraint with another one. If one or more such vertices are found, Simplex moves to the one that offers the best improvement. In addition, the Simplex method can determine if no solution actually exists.

Branch and Bound. Branch and bound [11] is the 'classic' method for solving IPs and MIPs. This method begins by finding the optimal solution to the problem without the integrality requirements, known as the 'relaxed' problem, via standard linear optimization methods (such as the Simplex method). If the 'should-be integer' variables all have integer values, the algorithm completes. If one or more integer variables have non-integer values, the branch and bound method picks one such variable and 'branches' on it, creating two new subproblems. If the branching variable X received the value of 7.3, for example, the original problem is enriched with two new constraints: $X \geq 8$ and $X \leq 7$. Obviously, they cannot both be added to the original problem as they contradict each other. In fact, each of the two new subproblems consists of the original constraints plus one of the above new constraints. The next step is to decide which of the subproblems to solve first; this is referred as 'choosing the direction'. After deciding, the algorithm solves the subproblem and continues by choosing the next variable to branch on and the subproblem to solve (or 'which direction to go'). The entire process of roaming the space of many subproblems (all of which contain the original constraints), picking the next variable to branch, and choosing the direction to go, can be viewed as traversing a giant search tree. Even if an all-integer solution is found, the typical branch and bound algorithm continues seeking a better integer solution (in terms of objective function value). Most branch and bound computations do not achieve a global optimum, or do not know when they have achieved it. They terminate because of time or value limits, or when the gap between the current solution and the lower bound on the best possible solution is narrow enough.

Branch and Cut. The gap between the current solution and the lower bound on the best possible solution can be narrowed in two ways: by improving the objective function and by lifting the lower bound. The initial lower bound is the value of the relaxed (continuous) problem. There are, however, methods to lift the lower bound strictly above the relaxed solution value by introducing 'cuts'. A cut is an additional constraint that can decrease the space of the polytope of feasible solutions without ruling out any integer solutions. There are several techniques for obtaining such cuts. In the branch and cut algorithm [12], branching and cutting are done alternately according to a certain strategy. Usually the MIP algorithm contains many parameters that control this strategy, including the cutting method, the pivoting method (selecting the node to branch on), the branching direction method, and the termination rule. Other parameters control some other heuristics that are involved in the search for optimal solutions. All in all, when moving from LP to MIP, we move from mathematics to the mathematically assisted art of search.

5   The MIP Model

We propose a novel technique to model scheduling problems. At the heart of this technique lies the concept of processing functions. We decided to use processing functions instead of traditional LP modeling schemes for scheduling problems because they significantly simplify the representation of the constraints that are unique to our scheduling problems, as presented in Section 3. In this section, we provide a detailed description of this modeling scheme. We start by describing our modeling framework, then show how this framework can be used to model temporal constraints and address the specific characteristics of stimuli generation.

5.1   Modeling Framework

To explain the concept of a processing function, we must first provide several related definitions. We use the term 'job' when referring to the processing of an input item by one of the DUV's cores or the storing of an input item in a shared work space [6]. Note that in Operations Research (OR) vocabulary, jobs are sometimes referred to as processes. For each job, we want to describe the time-ticks at which this job is active. For example, in Figure 5, the job in which the ISR processes the first I-frame is active at the first two time-ticks of the test.

To achieve the above, we allocate a vector of variables, each representing the processing state of the job at a different time-tick. That is, $Process[i]$ denotes a variable that indicates if a job is active at time-tick i. We term such a vector the $Process$ function of the job.

To ease the modeling of the scheduling problem and assist the solver in efficiently finding a solution, in addition to the processing function, we use three more functions: *Start*, *End*, and *Spike*.

The *Start* function and *End* function are monotonically non-decreasing functions. Both functions start at 0. The *Start* function changes to 1 when the job begins processing and the *End* function changes to 1 immediately after the job ends. Both functions maintain the value 1 from the point of change through the remainder of time. Note that the *Process* function is defined as the difference between the *Start* function and the *End* function. The *Spike* function is only active at the first time-tick of the job's processing and can be expressed by the formula:

$$\forall t, Spike[t] = Start[t] - Start[t-1]$$

All variables defined so far, as well as the variables that will be defined later, are indicator variables, and thus can only be assigned a value of 0 or 1. To enhance solver performance, we relax some of these requirements and allow the solver to assign some of the variables values in the range $[0, 1]$. This relaxation does not affect the solution because relations among the variables implicitly force the solver to assign them with integer values.

Figure 6 depicts an example of the four indicator functions of a single job. The processing time of the job is between time-ticks three and five. The *Start* function changes its value to 1 at time-tick three, and the *End* function changes its value at time-tick six; both functions remain high thereafter. In contrast, the *Spike* function is high only at time-tick three.

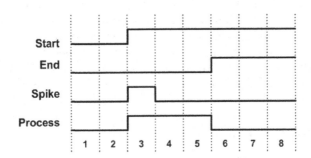

Fig. 6. An example of indicator functions for a single job

5.2 Temporal Scheduling Constraints

Based on the framework defined in the previous subsection, we can formulate various temporal relations between different jobs. In [13,14,15], thirteen fundamental relationships between jobs are defined. All of these relationships can be easily expressed as linear constraints within our framework. For example:

- Job *A* *equals* Job *B* - means Job *A* is active at the same time as Job *B*. This relationship is expressed within our framework using the constraint:

$$\forall t, Process_A[t] = Process_B[t],$$

where $Process_A$ and $Process_B$ denote the $Process$ function of jobs A and B, respectively.

- Job A *meets* Job B - means Job B starts immediately after Job A completes. The constraint for this relationship is:

$$\forall t, End_A[t] = Start_B[t].\tag{1}$$

- Job A *overlaps* Job B means that during at least one time-tick, both jobs are active. To express this relationship, we define an auxiliary function in the following manner:

$$M_{A,B}[t] = \min(Process_A[t], Process_B[t]),$$

where the minimum operator is implemented using a set of constraints. The relationship itself is expressed using:

$$\sum_t M_{A,B}[t] \geq 1.$$

On top of the relative temporal relationships, absolute constraints can also be expressed within our framework. For example, "the MDU starts processing the I-frame at time-tick five" is simply expressed by the constraint:

$$Spike_{(MDU,I-frame)}[5] = 1.$$

These constraints, which are related to the state of a single job, can be easily extended to constraints related to the state of a resource. For example, "ISR is busy at time-tick three" can be expressed by the constraint:

$$\sum_{j \in ISR} Process_j[3] \geq 1,$$

where $j \in ISR$ denotes that job j is processed by the ISR.

5.3   Domain Specific Constraints

In addition to the generic temporal constraints presented above, scheduling problems for multimedia SoCs contain numerous other constraints that are specific for this domain. These constraints can also be easily handled by our modeling framework. The mutual exclusion constraint requiring that each agent processes at most a single data item at any given time-tick can be simply expressed as the set of equations:

$$\forall Agent \ A, \quad \forall t, \ \sum_{j \in A} Process_j[t] \leq 1$$

In a similar fashion, constraints for managing the shared workspaces are expressed as the set of equations:

$$\forall Shared \ Workspace \ S, \quad \forall t, \ \sum_{j \in S} Size(j) \cdot Process_j[t] \leq Alloc(S)$$

where $Size(j)$ denotes the size of the input item handled by job j and $Alloc(S)$ denotes the amount of memory allocated for shared workspace S. Note that both $Size(j)$ and $Alloc(S)$ are known prior to the MIP formulation.

Optional jobs are another unique characteristic of our scheduling problems. Optional jobs are jobs that could potentially be performed during the execution of the test case, but we cannot determine whether they'll be performed at the stage of problem formulation [6]. To handle the optional jobs, we add an additional indicator variable for each optional job. This variable serves as an existence indicator. That is, if the job executes, the solver sets the variable to 1, otherwise to 0. In addition, we replace the following equation used to constrain the job processing time for mandatory jobs:

$$\sum_t Process_j[t] = P_j,$$

with this equation:

$$\sum_t Process_j[t] = P_j \cdot E_j,$$

where P_j is the processing time of job j and E_j is the existence indicator. Therefore, if the solver determines that the optional job exists, the equation is essentially the same as the equation for mandatory jobs. If the job doesn't exist, the job receives no processing time.

5.4   Stimuli Generation Requirements

The goal of constraint problem solvers is to find a solution that satisfies the constraints or, more commonly, to find a solution that minimizes an objective function. The requirements from a constraint solver for random stimuli generation are somewhat different [3]. Stimuli generators are required to generate many different solutions from the same test specification. Therefore, they are required to generate random solutions. In addition, instead of the traditional objective function that indicates the quality of a solution, stimuli generators use soft constraints that represent testing knowledge. Adding these soft constraints to the constraint problem improves the quality of the solution and thus the quality of the generated test.

Traditional MIP solution techniques are not designed to address randomness and soft constraints, and commercial MIP solvers do not have such capabilities. We developed two novel techniques that utilize the objective function to add the required capabilities to our framework.

Soft constraints are constraints the solver tries to fulfill if possible, but their fulfillment is not mandatory. To handle soft constraints, we add indicator variables to each soft constraint, indicating whether this soft constraint is violated. For example, the constraint Job A meets Job B of Eq. 1 is replaced by the soft constraint

$$\forall t, End_A[t] = Start_B[t] + S_j^+[t] - S_j^-[t],$$

where $S_j^+[t]$ and $S_j^-[t]$ are the soft constraint indicator variables of soft constraint j at time t. If the soft constraint is fulfilled and Job A meets Job B, the equation holds by setting the indicator variables to 0. However, if Job A does not meet Job B, by setting $S_j^+[\cdot]$ and / or $S_j^-[\cdot]$ to 1 at the time ticks where the original constrint fails, the soft constraint equations still hold. These soft constraint indicator variables are also added to the objective function with a penalty factor. That is, the objective function will be of the form:

$$\ldots + P_j \cdot \sum_t (S_j^+[t] + S_j^-[t]) + \ldots,$$

where P_j is the penalty factor of soft constraint j. The higher the penalty factor, the bigger the incentive of the solver to fulfill the soft constraint.

To add randomness, we randomly select a set of variables from the MIP and add these variables to the objective function. When the MIP solver tries to minimize the objective function, it tries to set the value of these variables to 0. A specific selection of the variables that are added to the objective function direct the solver into a different area in the solution space. Because the variables that are added to the objective function are selected randomly, each activation of the solver generates a different random solution. Our experimental results show that this technique indeed provides solutions that are significantly different from each other. We are currently investigating how this technique compares with techniques that are used to add randomness to CSP solvers.

6   Experimental Results

We implemented the framework described in Section 5 for the DVD Player SoC described in Section 2 as an alternative generation engine in SoCVer [6]. We compared this new generation engine with the CSP-based generation engine described in [6]. The results of this comparison are presented in this section and show that the MIP-based framework is better than the CSP-based framework. Note that the results are not limited to performance, but include other criteria such as expressiveness and scalability.

6.1   Expressiveness

In general, CSP is not limited to linear constraints, making it more flexible. On the other hand, the ability to use a large number of variables and constraints in the MIP formulation provides a better means to express temporal relationships. For example, consider the temporal rule stating that the VDU must remain active after its initial activation. In the CSP framework, this rule requires the addition of CSP variables related to the VDU's state over time, and complex constraints linking the *start* and *end* variables with the new *state* variables. In the MIP framework, the rule is simply expressed as:

$$\forall t \quad \sum_{j \in VDU} Process_j[t] \geq \sum_{j \in VDU} Process_j[t-1].$$

A more complicated example is the relationship between the VDU and its sub-unit VDU-Next. Recall that VDU-Next assists the VDU by processing the field that will be processed by the VDU at the following time-tick, unless the field belongs to a different scene (as illustrated in Figure 3). In the CSP framework, this rule requires the addition of multiple constraints over both *state* and *start-end* variables. In addition, specially tailored constraints guarantee that the jobs executed concurrently by the VDU and VDU-Next are of the same scene. In the MIP framework, we model this relationship using a set of constraints:

$$\forall t \quad \sum_{\substack{j \in VDU-Next \\ j \in Scene_i}} Process_j[t] = \min\left(\sum_{\substack{j \in VDU \\ j \in Scene_i}} Process_j[t], \quad \sum_{\substack{j \in VDU \\ j \in Scene_i}} Process_j[t+1] \right).$$

Additional constraints determining the correct placement of jobs are based on the temporal relationships described in Section 5.2.

6.2   Performance

We compared several characteristics of the CSP and MIP constraint problems related to the same user request. The comparison was based on four different tests, of varying levels of difficulty. Table 1 summarizes this comparison. For each user request and each framework, the table shows the size of the constraint problem in terms of the number of variables and constraints, the density factor, the average time needed to solve the problem, and the success rate of each solver. The density factor, an additional parameter for the complexity of the constraint problem, is defined as the ratio between the sum of constraint degrees and the product of the number of variables with the number of constraints.

The four user requests used for testing involve playing a short scene of four frames (the first two test cases) and seven frames (the last two test cases). The number of simulation time-ticks allocated for each test case is indicated by the second parameter of the test name. For example, the first test case is allocated 18 time-ticks. Note that DUV-related rules require the use of all time-ticks.

The experiments were conducted on a Linux platform running on an Intel Pentium 4, 3.6 GHz processor, with 2 GB memory. For the CSP framework, we used an in-house solver designed for stimuli generation. This solver is used by several other stimuli generation tools [16,17]. For the MIP framework, we used ILOG's CPLEX 10.0 solver [18].

The table shows that the number of variables in the MIP framework is much larger than the number of variables in the CSP framework. In fact, it is roughly the same as the number of variables in the CSP framework multiplied by the number of time-ticks allocated for the solution. The number of MIP constraints is also much larger than that of the CSP framework, by a factor of five to seven. In spite of the big difference in problem sizes, the table clearly shows that the average time needed to obtain a successful solution in the MIP framework is much smaller, ranging from a factor of 20 for small problems, to about five for the larger problems.

There are several reasons for the big difference in performance. First, MIP solvers are based on highly efficient algorithms designed to deal with linear

Table 1. Experimental results

Test Name	Framework	Variables	Constraints	Density factor (x10⁻³)	Success Rate	Time to success
Play(IPBB,18)	CSP	552	3077	7.43	100%	40.76
	LP	9412	14429	0.59	100%	1.73
Play(IPBB,23)	CSP	582	3260	7.52	90%	129.42
	LP	12002	18469	0.46	100%	18.99
Play(IPBBPBB,28)	CSP	945	7562	4.82	90%	529.99
	LP	25410	39225	0.22	100%	90.75
Play(IPBBPBB,33)	CSP	975	7795	4.88	40%	2181.20
	LP	29920	46265	0.18	100%	400.08

constraints, while CSP solvers rely on more general, and less efficient, algorithms because of the general nature of the constraints they need to handle. Second, MIP solvers tend to fail (i.e., not find a solution in a bounded time) less often than CSP solvers, as indicated by the sixth column in Table 1.

6.3 Scalability

The size of the problem, expressed by the number of variables and constraints, grows fast in both frameworks with the number of jobs and time-ticks allocated for the test case. In the CSP framework, the number of variables is $O(jobs + time)$ and the number of constraints is $O(jobs^2)$, while in the MIP framework, there are $O(jobs \cdot time)$ variables and constraints. While the MIP problem grows quickly, its density decreases, as can be seen in the fifth column of Table 1 and Figure 7. For the CSP framework, the density decreases with the number of

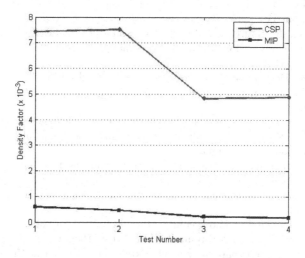

Fig. 7. Density factor for the CSP and MIP frameworks

jobs, but increases slightly with the allocation of additional time-ticks. Overall, in both frameworks, increasing problem size in terms of jobs and time-ticks has a significant effect on solver performance. This increase in problem size also has a significant effect on the ability of the CSP solver to find a solution within a bounded time.

7   Conclusions

We present a novel modeling scheme based on linear programming techniques for scheduling problems. This new modeling scheme is designed to fit the unique characteristics of stimuli generation, by providing random solutions and handling soft constraints. Combining this modeling scheme with a commercial LP solver provides a generation engine that is more expressive and outperforms generation engines based on traditional CSP modeling.

We are looking into several interesting issues regarding the use of linear programming techniques for stimuli generation. First, we are investigating the amount of randomness provided by the LP solvers using the proposed modeling scheme and the effects of the solver's parameters on randomness. Another intriguing issue is the combination of LP techniques and CSP techniques in the same generation engine and solver. We consider this a research topic that can significantly improve generation capabilities, and more generally, enhance the ability to solve more complex constraint problems.

References

1. Bergeron, J.: Writing Testbenches: Functional Verification of HDL Models. Kluwer Academic Publishers (2000)
2. Wile, B., Goss, J.C., Roesner, W.: Comprehensive Functional Verification - The Complete Industry Cycle. Elsevier (2005)
3. Bin, E., Emek, R., Shurek, G., Ziv, A.: Using a constraint satisfaction formulation and solution techniques for random test program generation. IBM Systems Journal **41**(3) (2002) 386–402
4. Planitkar, S.: Design verification with e. Prentice Hall (2003)
5. Haque, F., Michelson, J., Khan, K.: The Art of Verification with Vera. Verification Central (2001)
6. Nahir, A., Ziv, A., Emek, R., Keidar, T., Ronen, N.: Scheduling-based test-case generation for verification of multimedia SoCs. In: Proceedings of the 43rd Design Automation Conference. (2006)
7. Hillier, F., Lieberman, G.: Introduction to Operations Research. McGraw-Hill Higher Education (2005)
8. ISO/IEC 13818-1: Generic coding of moving pictures and associated audio information (2000)
9. Karp, R.M.: Reducibility among combinatorial problems. In Miller, R.E., Thatcher, J.W., eds.: Complexity of Computer Computation. Plenum (1972) 85–103
10. Dantzig, G.: Linear Programming and Extensions. Princeton University Press, Princeton, N.J. (1963)

11. Land, A.H., Doig, A.G.: An automatic method for solving discrete programming problems. Econometrica **28** (1960) 497–520
12. Crowder, H., Padberg, M.W.: Solving large-scale symmetric travelling salesman problems to optimality. Management Science **26**(5) (1980) 495–509
13. Allen, J.F.: Maintaining knowledge about temporal intervals. Communications of the ACM **11**(26) (1983) 832–843
14. Ladkin, P.B., Maddux, R.D.: On binary constraint problems. Journal of the ACM **41** (1994) 435–469
15. Vilain, M., Kautz, H.: Constraint propagation algorithms for temporal reasoning. In: Proceedings of the Fourth National Conference on Artificial Intelligence. (1986) 377–382
16. Emek, R., Jaeger, I., Naveh, Y., Bergman, G., Aloni, G., Katz, Y., Farkash, M., Dozoretz, I., Goldin, A.: X-Gen: A random test-case generator for systems and SoCs. In: IEEE International High Level Design Validation and Test Workshop. (2002) 145–150
17. Adir, A., Almog, E., Fournier, L., Marcus, E., Rimon, M., Vinov, M., Ziv, A.: Genesys-Pro: Recent advances in test-program generation for functional processor verification. IEEE Design & Test of Computers **26**(2) (2004) 84–93
18. ILOG: Ilog cplex - high performance software for mathematical programming and optimization. (http://www.ilog.fr/products/cplex/index.cfm)

Extracting a Simplified View of Design Functionality Based on Vector Simulation

Onur Guzey[1], Charles Wen[1], Li-C. Wang[1], Tao Feng[2], Hillel Miller[3], and Magdy S. Abadir[4]

[1] University of California, Santa Barbara
[2] Cadence Desing Systems, Inc
[3] Freescale Semiconductor Israel
[4] Freescale Semiconductor

Abstract. This paper presents a simulation-based methodology for extracting a simplified view of design functionality from a given module. Such a simplified design view can be used to facilitate test pattern justification from the outputs of the module to the inputs of the module. In this work, we formulate this type of design simplification as a learning problem. By developing a scheme for learning word-level functions, we point out that the core of the problem is to develop an efficient Boolean learner. We discuss the implementation of such a Boolean learner and compare its performance with the one of best-known learning algorithms, the Fourier analysis based method. Experimental results are presented to illustrate the implementation of the simulation-based methodology and its usage for extracting a simplified view of Open RISC 1200 datapath.

1 Introduction

Generating functional tests for a complex design can be a challenging task. For processor verification, Random Test Program Generation (RTPG) is an effective way to overcome the complexity [1]. In a recent work, the authors in [2] proposed a learning-guided functional test pattern generation methodology. The main idea of the methodology is illustrated in Figure 1.

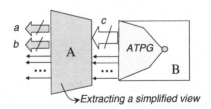

Fig. 1. Extracting a simplified view for module A to facilitate test pattern justification

Suppose our goal is to produce a test at the inputs of module A, for a target contained in module B. The task is divided into two parts. First a sequential ATPG is applied on module B to obtain a test at the inputs of the module. Then,

E. Bin, A. Ziv, and S. Ur (Eds.): HVC 2006, LNCS 4383, pp. 34–49, 2007.

this test is *justified* to the inputs of module A by working on a *simplified view* of the module. The objective of using such a simplified view is to avoid the complexity of ATPG search in module A. A simplified view allows us to potentially find a *short-cut* to map the test from the outputs of the module to its inputs. The authors in [2] proposed to use *statistical regression* on input-output simulation data of module A and extract a *polynomial equation* as the simplified model for the input-output behavior of the module. However, statistical regression might not work well on discrete and Boolean data.

The limitation of using statistical regression to extract a simplified view was recognized in [3]. The authors in [3][4] then proposed separated learning methods for learning bit-level logic functions and word-level arithmetic functions. These methods were developed for constructing a simplified hybrid design view such that (1) the view allows test justification to be done without ATPG search in module A, and (2) the view approximates as closely as possible to the original functionality of the module.

Although the objective of extracting a simplified view is clear in the context of Figure 1, in all previously proposed methods, the idea of "a simplified view" has not been explicitly defined and explored. Previous methods try to learn from the simulation data and develop a model that is as complete as possible to the input-output behavior of the module. This can be an unrealistic goal. In theory, it is unrealistic to expect that a good approximation of the entire functionality of a design can always be learned based on input-output simulation data. As a result, the performance of those methods on some cases can be quite unpredictable.

In this work, we propose a new method for extracting a simplified view from a module. Our method achieves the intended *design simplification* by giving two restrictions in the simulation-based learning: (1) We restrict the class of word-level functions that can be learned. (2) We impose a bound on the complexity of the Boolean functions that can be learned. Because of these restrictions, our method does not intend to learn the complete functionality of a module. Instead, it only tries to extract part of the functionality that fits within the capacity of the learning scheme. This is quite different from the previous methods and allows a more robust extraction methodology to be implemented.

In this work, we focus on developing the core engine for extracting a simplified view. Application of the simplified view in test pattern justification is not addressed here, partly due to space limitation. In addition, such an application has been discussed in previous works [2][3][4]. Although we spend most of the paper discussing the learning algorithms for extracting a simplified view, we emphasize that this work is only the first step to develop a robust functional test pattern generation methodology illustrated in Figure 1 and proposed in [4].

Because a simplified view by nature is incomplete, test justification may not always succeed through this view. Therefore, the proposed methodology in [4] is not a complete solution but a complementary solution to the existing test generation flow based on deterministic search or on random test program construction. Moreover, because the extraction method is simulation-based, the internal complexity of module A is unimportant, as long as the module can be efficiently

simulated. This allows the proposed method to be built on top of existing simulation framework, which can be a crucial consideration in practice.

The rest of the paper is organized as the following. Section 2 briefly discusses
the background of this work. Section 3 presents an efficient Boolean learning
algorithm. Section 4 explains how Boolean learning can be extended to work in
the hybrid domain. Section 5 discusses word-level learning which is a required
component for hybrid learning. Section 6 presents experimental results with
hybrid learning. Section 7 concludes the paper.

2   Background

Refer to Figure 1 again. Suppose our goal is to extract a simplified view based
on a given word-level function "$c = a + b$." Module A may perform many other
functions but we are interested in only extracting the view based on the addition
function. Module A may be a sequential circuit. To simplify the problem, we
assume a known initial state to begin with and the input-output behavior to be
learned is based on a fixed number of timeframes. For some designs, the simplified
view may target input-output behavior across a fixed number of timeframes.
For others, we may fix the input values across multiple timeframes and target
on input-output behavior when the output values stabilize. In both cases, we
essentially turn the problem of learning a sequential design into a problem of
learning a combinational function.

Given three numbers a_1, b_1, c_1, if we know the representation method, i.e. 2's
complement or 1's complement, it is easy to check if $c_1 = a_1 + b_1$. Because
there are only a few popular representation schemes, we can try them one by
one to see if $c_1 = a_1 + b_1$ holds for a particular scheme. Because given the
word-level data (a_1, b_1, c_1), it is easy to check if the data match to the addition
function or not, the problem of extracting a simplified view with $c = a + b$
becomes the problem of deciding all combinations of the bit-level inputs (over
the fixed number of timeframes) where the addition function is performed. This
is a *Boolean learning* problem.

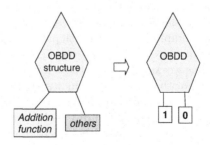

Fig. 2. Boolean learning for extracting a simplified view

Figure 2 illustrates why the core of the problem is Boolean learning. In the
figure, the Boolean function is represented as an Ordered Binary Decision Diagram (OBDD) [5]. In Boolean learning, our goal is to learn a Boolean function

$y = f(x_1, \ldots, x_n)$ based on simulation of a number of input vectors. On a given vector, the output y takes value of 0 or 1. In Figure 2, on a given bit vector, the output y takes two values: "is performing an addition function" and "is not performing an addition function." To decide on this value (for a given bit vector on the bit-level inputs), we can try a few numbers (on the word-level inputs) to obtain data $(a_1, b_1, c_1), \ldots, (a_k, b_k, c_k)$. If all of them are consistent with the same addition function, then we can be pretty sure that the y value should be the "addition function." Otherwise, it is not. In this way, we turn the problem into a Boolean learning problem.

If we are given a set of predefined word-level functions $\{A_1, \ldots, A_m\}$, then the problem becomes learning a $(m+1)$-logic-value function. Again, for every bit vector sampled, we can try a few numbers to obtain data $(a_1, b_1, c_1), \ldots, (a_k, b_k, c_k)$. Then, we need to be able to decide if any A_i function is consistent with the data or not. Moreover, we should have at most one A_i that is consistent with the data presented. This constrains the set of word-level functions that can be defined, i.e. they should be easily *differentiable* based on a limited number of sampled data. We note that for many commonly implemented logic and arithmetic functions, they are easily differentiable. This point will be clarified when the discussion moves to word-level arithmetic learning later.

Regardless if we are trying to extract a simplified view based on a single given arithmetic function or a set of arithmetic functions, having an efficient Boolean learning method is at the core of the extraction problem. The problem of learning Boolean functions has been studied extensively since the pioneer work of L. Valiant [6] and is at the core of machine learning research [7]. Valiant defined a theoretical framework called *Probably Approximately Correct* (PAC) model. In this model, a learned function g approximates a target Boolean function f with an error probability $\epsilon \to 0$. Except for some special cases, most problems formulated in Boolean learning were considered not efficiently *PAC-learnable* [8][9], which usually involves proving that those problems are NP-hard.

It is important to note that in our work we are not trying to solve a Boolean learning problem in PAC sense. PAC learning of Boolean functions has been proved to be a computationally difficult problem. In our application, we do not intend to learn a complete Boolean function and hence, we avoid solving such a difficult problem. Our method emphasizes more on computational efficiency. Given a resource limitation, our objective is to extract as much information as possible from the simulation data. The learning may focus on learning the Boolean function in a particular sub-space while ignoring other sub-spaces due to resource limitations.

Refer back to the example of extracting a simplified view based on a given addition function. Suppose that to have module A to perform addition, we have to set 30 control lines into particular values and all other combinations enable the module to perform other functions. Then, when these control lines are randomly sampled, it is unlikely that the particular combination of values are sampled. As a result, we may not have any sampled data that indicate that module A is performing an addition function. Consequently, no simplified view can be extracted and we may conclude that module A does not perform addition.

The above example illustrates that corner cases are not learned in the extraction process. This is an important feature of the methodology, where those cases are ignored and in a sense, the design is simplified. Because the methodology is based on sampling, only "simple" functionality will be seen in the simulation data. This simplicity is defined based on how easily it is to sample the input values to observe a particular function.

Although our method is not to learn complete Boolean functions, for comparison purpose we implemented one of the most effective algorithms proposed for learning Boolean functions, the Fourier analysis based learning method [10]. The algorithm attempts to approximate the coefficients in the Fourier representation of a target function. Fourier representation of a Boolean function has 2^n terms but in some cases the behavior of the function can be approximated without calculating all terms in the transform. The authors in [10] describe an algorithm that estimates all coefficients larger than a given threshold value θ. For certain types of functions Fourier based learning perform quite well. For example, using Fourier based learning, any constant-depth, polynomial-size circuit can be PAC-learned in run time bounded by $O(n^{poly-log(n)})$ [10]. This is the only sub-exponential bound known for learning this family of circuits. A practical application of the algorithm was reported in a recent paper [11].

3   OBDD-Based Learning

To learn Boolean functions, we work with the OBDD representation. We first restrict the number of nodes in each layer to be smaller than or equal to a given number U. This number U controls the *capacity* of the learning machine. Figure 3 illustrates the basic idea in the algorithm.

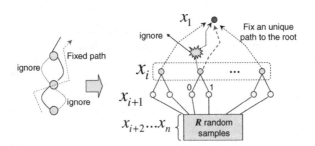

Fig. 3. Construction of a new layer

Suppose that we are learning a function of n input variables ordered as $x_1, x_2, \ldots, x_n$. Suppose that the learner has constructed the OBDD up to the variable x_i and in the layer, there are $d_i \leq U$ nodes with label x_i. Figure 3 depicts the method to construct the nodes in the x_{i+1}th layer.

On variables $x_{i+1}, \ldots, x_n$, R (uniformly) random postfix vectors are drawn. For a node labeled x_i and for each postfix vector, we follow a *unique path* from the node to the root. In order to define the unique path from every node to the root, every time the learner merges two nodes, it randomly picks an edge to its parent and ignores the other edge. Then, every node has a unique edge to its parent and hence, a unique path to the root. After this process, each x_i node is associated with R vectors whose x_i value remain undetermined. We then expand these R vectors into two sets of R vectors by filling x_i with 1 and with 0. As illustrated in the figure, on the layer x_{i+1} we have $2 * d_i$ nodes and each node is associated with R random vectors. Then, we simulate these $2 * d_i * R$ sampled vectors to obtain their output values.

The result of simulation is a set of $2d_i$ vectors $\{\overrightarrow{v_1}, \overrightarrow{v_2}, \ldots, \overrightarrow{v_{2d_i}}\}$. Each $\overrightarrow{v_j}$, $1 \le j \le 2d_i$, is an R-bit wide vector. For any pair $\overrightarrow{v_j}, \overrightarrow{v_k}$, we need to determine if $\overrightarrow{v_j} = \overrightarrow{v_k}$. If they are, we merge the two corresponding nodes into one node. This checking and merging can be done by first sorting the $2d_i$ vectors and then, scan the sorted result to merge nodes.

The basic algorithm has two important parameters, U and R. U determines the maximum number of nodes allowed in any level of the decision diagram. If there are more than U nodes at a particular level, some of these nodes are merged by relaxing the merging rule until there are less than U nodes. This can be done by checking $\|v_j \oplus v_k\| \le h$ for a given $h = 1, 2, \ldots$. On a given h, to check across all pairs of vectors is expensive. Hence, we only check for each v_j against $w = 10, 20, \ldots$ vectors that are closest to it in the sorted list. The parameter U has a direct impact on the memory requirement and run-time of the algorithm. If the actual OBDD satisfies the width constraint given by U, U does not have any effect on the learning result. We note that those nodes merged with others because of exceeding the width constraint can be viewed as those nodes (functional sub-spaces) ignored in learning.

How a learned OBDD can differ from the actual OBDD for the function to be learned? Given a prefix α on input variables $x_1, \ldots, x_i$, let f_α denote the restricted function $f(x_1, \ldots, x_i = \alpha)$. A learned OBDD can differ from the actual OBDD in two ways, as illustrated in Figure 4.

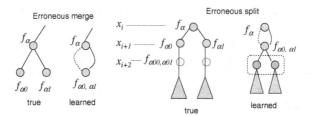

Fig. 4. A learned OBDD may differ from the actual OBDD in two possible ways

– (**Erroneous merge**). In the actual OBDD, $f_{\alpha 0}$ and $f_{\alpha 1}$ are two separated nodes. In the learned OBDD, they are merged into the same node (as a result, it disappears in the final OBDD structure). This is due to the lack of a witness vector to differentiate the two restricted functions during the sampling of random vectors. Hence, the learner may conclude, based on what it sees on the simulation result, that $f_{\alpha 0} = f_{\alpha 1}$.

- (**Erroneous split**). An erroneous merge may cause an erroneous split as shown in the figure. For example, in the actual OBDD, there are no nodes that correspond to the variable x_{i+2}. However, because the learner erroneously merged $f_{\alpha 0}$ and $f_{\alpha 1}$ into $f_{\{\alpha 0, \alpha 1\}}$, when it tries to decide on the variable x_{i+2}, it may see samples to differentiate $f_{\{\alpha 0, \alpha 1\} 0}$ from $f_{\{\alpha 0, \alpha 1\} 1}$. This is because $f_{\alpha 00} \neq f_{\alpha 11}$ and $f_{\alpha 10} \neq f_{\alpha 01}$. But after the erroneous merge, the learner would not know that the difference is actually caused by x_{i+1} and not by x_{i+2}.

We note that in our algorithm, erroneous merges are possible but erroneous split is avoided by following a unique path from each node to the root during sampling. Because of this feature, we can prove that a learned OBDD is always smaller in size than the actual OBDD. When they are in the same size, they are equivalent. The proof is omitted due to space limitation. This is a desired property of the algorithm because with a larger R, a learned OBDD cannot become smaller in size. If R is large enough, we ensure that the actual OBDD can be eventually learned.

3.1   Experimental Results

To assess the effectiveness of our Boolean learning algorithm, we compare its performance to the Fourier analysis based learning method. The performance is evaluated based on combinational benchmark circuits. The reader may wonder why we chose combinational circuits for evaluation while our objective is to learn complex sequential designs. There are two reasons. Firstly, both Boolean learning algorithms are for learning Boolean functions. There is no notion of time in these algorithms. To be applied on a sequential design, as mentioned before, we would need timeframe expansion. Hence, there is no real advantage to evaluate the performance on sequential designs than on combination circuits. For simplicity, we took combinational circuits for the evaluation. Secondly, as far as a learning algorithm concerns, it only sees the input-output behavior of a black box. Hence, it is the complexity of this IO behavior that matters. Internal complexity is irrelevant. Hence, we can think of a combinational circuit as an example where the IO behavior is of the particular function but the internal implementation can be as complex as we want. From this perspective, the combinational circuits represent difficult enough cases to compare the performance of the two algorithms.

Two obvious criteria to evaluate the performance of a learning algorithm is its run-time and learning accuracy. Run-time can be divided into *learning time* spent by the learner and *simulation time* spent by the simulator. The learner is integrated with a commercial Verilog simulator.

For learning accuracy, we define two metrics. Let $\|OBDD\|$ denote the number of min-terms in the function represented by the $OBDD$. The *learning error* between a learned OBDD $obdd$ and its actual OBDD $OBDD$ can be defined as $\varepsilon = \|obdd \oplus OBDD\|/2^n$ where n is the number of input variables. Because we do not know $OBDD$, we often estimate the *empirical learning error* based on a set of randomly-produced m input patterns. We denote this empirical error ε_m.

In the experiments, ε_m is calculated based on randomly generated $10k$ input vectors. Let M_0 be the number of vectors that the actual function gives output 1 and the learned OBDD reports output 0. Let M_1 be defined reversely. Define $\varepsilon_0 = M_0/10k$ and $\varepsilon_1 = M_1/10k$. We calculate the empirical learning error $\varepsilon_{10k} = \frac{\varepsilon_0 + \varepsilon_1}{2}$.

Table 1. Results of OBDD learning

Circuit	t_{avg}	#nodes	Accu.	Circuit	t_{avg}	#nodes	Accu.
c432	1	280	99.77%*	c499	12	3458	99.3%*
c880	2	181	99.98%*	c2670	8	28	98.14%
c1908	3	633	99.76%*	c5315	67	1519	94.61%
c3540	48	6770	95.02%*	c7552	44	362	99.52%
c6288**	2	227	100%	too_large	38	5290	98.5%
Average simulation time per output: 873s							

t_{avg}: average learning times across all outputs (in secs), excluding simulation

#nodes: average # of OBDD nodes (learned) over all outputs

Accu.: average empirical accuracy $(1 - \varepsilon_{10k})$ over all outputs

*Accuracy computed based on actual error ε, against actual OBDDs

**c6288: only the 8 most significant bits

Table 1 shows the experimental results for the proposed algorithm. In Table 2 we also present results obtained by an implementation of the Fourier analysis based learning method. In Table 1 we used sample size limit $R = 512$ and OBDD width bound $U = 2048$. To be consistent in Fourier learning, in Table 2, the coefficient bound θ is set at $\theta = 0.06$ for all experiments. We selected this number based on running several preliminary experiments on various benchmarks and observing the performance of the learner. For Fourier learning since we do not have the actual Fourier representation, all accuracy results are empirical.

Experimental results show that the learning accuracy of our Boolean learner is comparable to or better than Fourier analysis based learning method.

3.2   Experimental Results in the Restricted Input Space

When the OBDD width bound U is reached, some nodes are merged with others even though they represent different sub-functions. Figure 5 illustrates the situation. The ignored nodes represent sub-spaces ignored in learning. In Table 1 above, we do not differentiate between the sub-space being learned and the sub-space being ignored. Each learned OBDD is treated as the representation for the entire space during the evaluation of the empirical error ε_{10k}. We can focus the evaluation on the sub-space that is actually learned and report accuracy result based on the sub-space only. Table 3 shows the result for every output of the example c3540.

The unrestricted accuracy is calculated based on the entire space. The restricted accuracy is calculated based on the sub-space being learned. The ratio

Table 2. Results of Fourier learning

Circuit	t_{avg}	#$Coffs$	Accu.	Circuit	t_{avg}	#$Coffs$	Accu.
c432	33	53	69.10%	c499	5	1	99.00%
c880	21	29	85.00%	c2670	175	4	90.5%
c1908	5	8	99.70%	c5315	115	37	87.00%
c3540	18	31	85.6%	c7552	277	26	89.4%
c6288**	121	47	74.71%	too_large	15	19	49.9%
Average simulation time per output: 824s							

t_{avg}: average learning times across all outputs (in secs), excluding simulation

#$Coffs$: average # of Fourier coefficients (learned) over all outputs

Accu.: average empirical accuracy $(1 - \varepsilon_{10k})$ over all outputs

Accu.: ε_{10k} computed based on 10k randomly generated input vectors

**c6288: only the 8 most significant bits

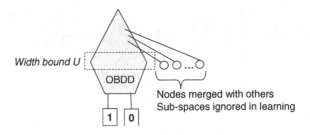

Fig. 5. Sub-spaces ignored in learning due to OBDD width constraint U

of the learned sub-space to the entire space is also reported as a percentage. It is interesting to observe that in the learned sub-space, high accuracy can be achieved. However, in some cases the learned sub-space is quite small. Achieving high learning accuracy in the sub-space being actually learned is a desired result

Table 3. Learning accuracy within restricted input-space for individual c3540 outputs

	Unrestricted Accu.	Restricted Accu.	% of learned space		Unrestricted Accu.	Restricted Accu.	% of learned space
1	100	100	100	12	99	99	20.5
2	100	100	100	13	100	100	100
3	99.5	100	99.5	14	100	100	100
4	100	100	100	15	100	100	100
5	100	100	100	16	97.5	99	35.7
6	99	99	73.7	17	93.5	100	31.3
7	97.5	100	100	18	94.5	100	37.2
8	100	100	100	19	98.5	99	20.2
9	100	100	100	20	97.5	99.5	42.9
10	100	100	100	21	55	95	2.3
11	97.5	100	76.2	22	54	97.5	4.5

for our learning method. As emphasized before, we do not intend to learn the entire function. With a resource constraint U, we care more about the learning effectiveness in the sub-space that is actually being sampled and learned.

4 Extending Boolean Learning to Hybrid Domain

In this section we extend the Boolean learner to work with word-level variables. Suppose $x_1, \ldots, x_n$ are bit-level inputs and $op_1, \ldots, op_m$ are word-level inputs. Let *out* be the word-level output. To apply the learner, we order these inputs as $x_1, \ldots, x_n, op_1, \ldots, op_m$ and the decision graph is constructed with all the Boolean variables first.

Let α be a prefix vector on the bit-level input variables, which leads to a node f_α in the learned OBDD. Essentially, the learner checks if $f_{\alpha 0}() = f_{\alpha 1}()$ by drawing R sample vectors. In Boolean learning, the results are two R-bit vectors and the learner believes $f_{\alpha 0}() = f_{\alpha 1}()$ if the two vectors are the same. In word-level learning, each vector consists of R k-bit numbers where k is the number of bits in *out*. Again, the learner believes $f_{\alpha 0}() = f_{\alpha 1}()$ if two vectors are the same. The difference between comparisons made for Boolean and hybrid learning is illustrated in Figure 6.

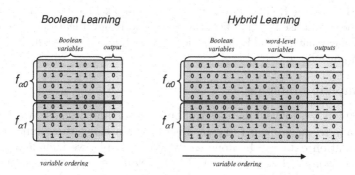

Fig. 6. Illustration of difference between Boolean and hybrid learning

When the learner stops at the $(n+1)$th layer, there may be more than two nodes in the layer. Hence, the result is an ordered *multi-terminal* decision diagram (OMDD). Each terminal node represents a unique function h where $out = h(op_1, \ldots, op_m)$. After building the OMDD we can then use word-level learning methods to extract the functionality of each terminal individually.

With some of the terminal nodes, word-level learning may fail to decide the functionality because of its complexity. Then, those nodes are ignored in learning. In word-level learning, we apply two methods: (1) template matching and (2) polynomial interpolation. The capacity of the word-level learner is limited by the availability of predefined functions in the template library and by the highest degree number allowed in the polynomial representation. In other words, the total number of word-level functions recognized by the word-level learner is limited. Because of this, the learner can perform efficiently.

One interesting thing to note is that the capacity of the word-level learner does not affect bit-level learning. When the learner works on the Boolean variables $x_1, \ldots, x_n$, it does not need to know what word-level functions are available for matching. The word-level learning only applies after the bit-level learning completes the decision graph up to the $n + 1$ layer.

5   Learning Word-Level Functions

In this section, two word-level learning methods are presented. Template matching and polynomial interpolation are selected because they can learn restricted set of functions with high accuracy. Additionally both of these methods generate results that can be easily used for justification. We accept the fact that these methods may fail if the target functions are very complicated. In the section 6 we show that these methods can be powerful enough to extract most of the functionality of a practical design with high accuracy.

The capacity of the word-level learner is limited by the availability of the functions in the template library and the polynomial representation. Many functions may fall out of this scope. However, we do not want to go for a more complicated learning method, for example neural network with Radial Basis Functions (RBFN) [12]. Using RBFN may learn more complex functions but the results may not be easily used in justification. In our word-level learning method, improving the capacity of the learner is done by adding more predefined functions in the template library.

5.1   Template Matching

Some common word-level functions can be seen in many designs. We use a template library to include such known functions. Matching these functions with given simulation data can be done easily. For example, we include all bit-wise logical operations such as bit-wise AND, OR, NOR, etc. as well as simple arithmetic functions like addition, subtraction, multiplication, and division. In addition, high-degree polynomials can be included to take care of special cases that are out of the scope of polynomial representation.

As mentioned before, all functions in the template should be easily differentiable by checking with a small number of simulation samples. This means that we cannot have two functions that are too similar to be added to the template. The similarity of two functions can be defined based on drawing, for example, 100 random inputs to the functions. If their outputs are all the same, they are too similar. From this perspective, we see that most of the commonly implemented word-level functions are not similar. An example of a pair of similar functions can be an adder and an adder with exception control. For most inputs, these two adders behave the same. Only some special inputs cause the exception handling in the second adder to activate and produce non-addition outputs. Then, these two adders may not be easily differentiable by random sampled inputs.

5.2   Multivariate Polynomial Interpolation

Multivariate polynomial interpolation is the process of determining polynomials over several variables from their values at selected points. Any multivariate polynomial with degree lower than a predetermined value, d, can be learned from a relatively small number of observations. Methods for interpolating dense polynomials have been known for a long time, yet development of methods for efficiently interpolating sparse multivariate polynomials have been more recent [13][14].

Assuming d is the maximum degree of any variable in the polynomial. A polynomial can have up to $(d+1)^n$ terms where n is the number of variables. If the number of terms in the polynomial is close to this limit it is called a dense polynomial, otherwise it is a sparse polynomial. We use capital letters for variables and non-capital letters for value assignments. $x_{n,0}$ denotes a particular random value assigned to the nth variable. We will describe a sparse interpolation algorithm and discuss its implementation but before that dense univariate interpolation, which is used in sparse multivariate case, is summarized.

In dense univariate interpolation, a polynomial with a single variable is interpolated from its values at $d+1$ distinct points. Lets call the values of the variable chosen $x_1 \ldots x_{d+1}$ and the polynomial's values $p_1 \ldots p_{d+1}$. Coefficients of the polynomial, $c_0 \ldots c_d$ can be found by solving the following Vandermonde system:

$$c_0 + c_1 x_1 + \ldots + c_d(x_1)^d = p_1$$
$$c_0 + c_1 x_2 + \ldots + c_d(x_2)^d = p_2$$
$$\vdots$$
$$c_0 + c_1 x_{d+1} + \ldots + c_d(x_{d+1})^d = p_{d+1}$$

This system is non-singular if values $x_1 \ldots x_{d+1}$ are distinct.

Sparse interpolation algorithm works by starting with a single variable and introducing a new variable at each stage. The first stage is the same as the dense univariate interpolation. At each stage variables that have not been processed stay the same. First $P(X_1 x_{(2,0)}, \ldots x_{(n,0)})$ is determined. This requires $d+1$ values which are results of the assignments, $P(x_{(1,0)}, x_{(2,0)}, \ldots x_{(n,0)}) \ldots P(x_{(1,d)}, x_{(2,0)}, \ldots x_{(n,0)})$. From these values we can interpolate the polynomial $P(X_1, x_{1,0}, x_{2,0}, \ldots x_{n,0})$ using univariate dense interpolation.

Assume that first i stages have been completed and we are ready to determine the polynomial $P(X_1 \ldots X_i, X_{i+1}, x_{(i+2,0)} \ldots x_{(n,0)})$. We choose i values for the first i variables, $Y_i = x_{(1,k)}, \ldots x_{(i,k)}$. We also choose $d+1$ values for the variable we are working on, $Z_i = x_{(i,1)} \ldots x_{(i,d+1)}$. For each of these $d+1$ assignments we calculate a polynomial by interpolating following values:

$$P(1, \ldots 1, x_{(i+2,0)} \ldots x_{(n,0)})$$
$$P(x_{(1,k)}, \ldots x_{(i,k)}, x_{(i,1)}, x_{(i+2,0)} \ldots x_{(n,0)})$$
$$P((x_{(1,k)})^2, \ldots (x_{(i,k)})^2, (x_{(i,1)})^2, x_{(i+2,0)} \ldots x_{(n,0)})$$
$$\vdots$$
$$P((x_{(1,k)})^T, \ldots (x_{(i,k)})^T, (x_{(i,1)})^T, x_{(i+2,0)} \ldots x_{(n,0)})$$

We solve the transposed Vandermonde system these values form to get the polynomial $P(X_1 \ldots X_i, x_{(i+1,1)}, x_{(i+2,0)} \ldots x_{(n,0)})$. If the same steps are followed for the other d values in Z_i we will have $d+1$ such polynomials. These polynomials may look like:

$$c_{(1,1)}P_1(X_1 \ldots X_i) + \ldots + c_{(t,1)}P_t(X_1 \ldots X_i)$$
$$\vdots$$
$$c_{(1,d+1)}P_1(X_1 \ldots X_i) + \ldots + c_{(t,d+1)}P_t(X_1 \ldots X_i)$$

where $c_{(1,d+1)}$ is the coefficient of polynomial P_1 for $x_{(i+1,d+1)}$. Notice that there are a total of t such polynomials because we assume the polynomial is sparse an has less than maximum number of terms possible.

Key point of the algorithm is noticing that in these $d+1$ polynomials each coefficient can be regarded as a different polynomial. For example coefficient $c_{(1,1)}$ is the value of the univariate polynomial in X_{i+1} with assignment $x_{(i+1,1)}$. Since we have $d+1$ such coefficient values we can use univariate interpolation to derive a polynomial. After all t polynomials are determined then we can get $P(X_1 \ldots X_i, X_{i+1}, x_{(i+2,0)} \ldots x_{(n,0)})$.

Although basic algorithms are summarized here, there are more issues that cannot be discussed because of space constraints, for a more throughout discussion on polynomial interpolation interested readers are directed to [15][14][16].

6   Hybrid Experimental Results

In this section, we illustrate an application of the hybrid learner for automatic extraction of a simplified view on OpenRISC 1200 datapath [17]. OpenRISC 1200 is an open source processor core. The current design is a 32-bit scalar RISC with Harvard micro architecture and a 5-stage integer pipeline supporting 52 core instructions.

The ALU performs arithmetic, logic, comparison and shift/rotate operations. Based on its instruction set architecture (ISA), we know that 30 core instructions can produce signal activities on the ALU. The ALU module has 120 inputs and contains a 32-bit output bus *out*. The 120 inputs contain three 32-bit buses to take three operands op_1, op_2, op_3. The remaining 24 input bits are control signals.

Table 4. Learning result for RISC 1200 ALU module

	Empirical learning accuracy
Word-level evaluation metric $(1 - \varepsilon_{2k})$	83.7%
Bit-level evaluation metric $(1 - \varepsilon_{2k})$	95.6%

For the Boolean part we set $U = 2048$. For the experiment, $R = 512$ and $R = 64$ gave the same results. For the word-level part first we do polynomial interpolation with $d = 3$. Next step is template matching which filters out bitwise

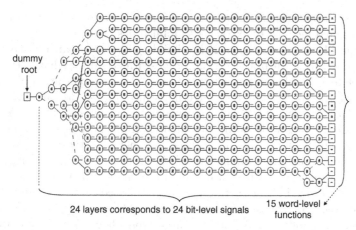

dummy
root

24 layers corresponds to 24 bit-level signals

15 word-level
functions

Fig. 7. Execution paths of ALU, automatically extracted

operations. For word-level output variables we calculate two different empirical learning accuracy numbers, one based on treating all 32 bit outputs as a whole (word-level accuracy) and the other based on treating all 32 bit outputs individually (bit-level accuracy). Table 4 shows learning results including both word-level and bit-level empirical accuracy.

Figure 7 shows the OMDD result on the ALU, where the functionality consists of 15 word-level functions. 5 of these were extracted through polynomial interpolation and others are through template matching. The run-time was about 2.5 minutes and more than 2 minutes were spent in simulation. It is interesting to note that the ALU actually can perform additional custom-defined complex functions. However, those complex functions are left out in this simplified view.

7   Conclusion

This paper presents a simulation-based method for extracting a simplified view from a design. At the core of this method we implement an OBDD-based Boolean learning engine. The capacity of the Boolean learner is restricted by a width bound U. This limits the functions that can be completely sampled and learned, and also constrains the learner to work on only a sub-space when the function to be learned is too complex. The Boolean learner is integrated with a word-level learner that is based on template matching and polynomial interpolation. The word-level learner does not intend to learn all word-level functions. Our goal is to learn commonly used functions. The capacity of the arithmetic learner can be extended by adding the more pre-defined functions in the template.

We provide experimental results to show that the Boolean learner can handle complex Boolean functions well, based on a number of combinational benchmarks. Hybrid learning is naturally built on top of the Boolean learning. We applied hybrid learning to extract a simplified view on the datapath of Open RISC 1200 processor. Although this is a rather simple design, compared to industrial high-performance processors, the result serves as a proof of concept for the proposed method to extract a simplified design view.

The hybrid learner serves as a critical building block for realizing the methodology proposed in [4] in practice. The proposed method may have other applications yet to be explored. However, the most obvious application of using the simplified view is to facilitate test pattern justification as illustrated in Figure 1. For that purpose, we need to develop several other components: (1) A sequential data mining engine is needed to identify input-output signals at certain timeframes, which should then be learned together with the proposed method. This data mining engine should serve as the front-end of the learning method in this work which has no notion of time in learning. (2) An interface to integrate a sequential ATPG with test justification based on the simplified design view is required. (3) Justification of values assigned to multiple outputs based on multiple learned models needs further elaboration when some of them are word-level outputs and some of them are bit-level outputs. Moreover, we will need to demonstrate that the overall methodology works well on complex sequential designs while sequential ATPG does not. We plan to pursue these directions in the immediate future.

References

1. A. Aharon, D. Goodman, M. Levinger, Y. Lichtenstein, Y. Malka, C. Metzger, M. Molcho, and G. Shurek, "Test Program Generation for Functional Verification of PowerPC Processors in IBM," Proc. *DAC*, pp. 279-285, 1995.
2. L. Chen, S. Ravi, A. Raghunathan, and S.Dey, "A Scalable Sofware-Based Self-Test Methodology for Programmable Processors," Proc. Design Automation Conf, Anaheim, pp. 548-553, 2003.
3. C. Wen, L.-C. Wang, K.-T. Cheng, W.-T. Liu, and C.-C. Chen, "On A Software-Based Self-Test Methodology and Its Application," Proc. VLSI Test Symp., Palm Springs, pp. -, 2005.
4. C. Wen, L. Wang and K.-T. Chang, "Simulation-Based Functional Test Generation for Embedded Processors," to be accepted in *IEEE Transaction on Computer*, 2006.
5. R.E. Bryant. "Symbolic Boolean Manipulation with Ordered Binary- Decision Diagrams," ACM Computing Surveys vol.24, no.3,pp 293318, 1992
6. L. Valiant, "A theory of the learnable," Communications of the ACM, vol. 27, no.11, pp.1134-1142, 1984.
7. M. J. Kearns, and U. V. Vazirani. *An Introduction to Computational Learning Theory*. The MIT Press, 1994.
8. M. Kearns, M. Li, L. Pitt and L. Valiant, "On the learnability of Boolean formulae," Proc. 19th Symp. on Theory of Computing, pp. 285-295, 1987.
9. M. Kearns, and L. Valiant, "Learning Boolean formulae or finite automata is as hard as factoring," Technical Report TR-14-88, Harvard University, 1988
10. N. Linial, Y. Mansour, and N. Nisan. Constant depth circuits, Fourier transform, and learnability. *J. of ACM*, 40(3), pp. 607-620, 1993.
11. Y. Mansour. Implementation Issues in the Fourier Transform Algorithm. *Machine Learning*, 40, pp. 5-33, 2000.

12. J. Park and I. W. Sandberg, "Universal approximation using radial-basis-function networks," Neural Computation, vol. 3, num. 2, pp. 246–257, 1991
13. M. Ben-Or and P. Tiwari, "A deterministic algorithm for sparse multivariate polynomial interpolation," Proc. 12th ACM Symp. Theory Comput.,pp. 301–309, 1988.
14. R. Zippel, "Interpolating polynomials from their values," J. Symb. Comput. vol.9, no.3, pp. 375-403, 1990
15. George M. Phillips *Interpolation and Approximation by Polynomials*. Springer-Verlag, 2003
16. J. Schwartz, "Fast probabilistic algorithms for verification of polynomial identities," Jour. ACM, vol.27, no.4, pp.701-717, 1980.
17. OpenRISC 1200 at http://www.opencores.org/

Automatic Fault Localization for Property Checking[*]

Stefan Staber[1], Görschwin Fey[2], Roderick Bloem[1], and Rolf Drechsler[2]

[1] Graz University of Technology, 8010 Graz, Austria
[2] University of Bremen, 28359 Bremen, Germany

Abstract. We present an efficient, fully automatic approach to fault localization for safety properties stated in linear temporal logic. We view the failure as a contradiction between the specification and the actual behavior and look for components that explain this discrepancy. We find these components by solving the satisfiability of a propositional Boolean formula. We show how to construct this formula and how to extend it so that we find exactly those components that can be used to repair the circuit for a given set of counterexamples. Furthermore, we discuss how to efficiently solve the formula by using the proper decision heuristics and simulation based preprocessing. We demonstrate the quality and efficiency of our approach by experimental results.

1 Introduction

When a design does not fulfill its specification, debugging begins. There is little tool support for fault localization and correction, although industrial experience shows that it takes more time and effort than verification does.

In this paper we propose an approach for automatic localization of fault candidates for sequential circuits at the gate or HDL level for safety properties. The diagnosis uses a set of counterexamples that is obtained from either a formal verification tool or a simulator with functional checkers. Our approach builds on model based diagnosis [21]. A failure is seen as a discrepancy between the required and the actual behavior of the system. The diagnosis problem is then to determine those components that explain the discrepancy, when assumed that they are incorrect.

In [12], it is shown that for certain degenerate cases of sequential circuits, model based diagnosis marks all components as possible faults. Perhaps for this reason, there is little work on model-based diagnosis for sequential circuits, with the exception of [19], which does not take properties into account and has a different fault model than we do. Our experimental results show, however, that such degenerate cases rarely happen and that model based diagnosis can be used successfully in the sequential case.

Previous work in both the sequential and combinatorial case has assumed that a failure trace is given and the correct output for the trace is provided by the user. In our approach, instead of requiring a fixed error trace, we only assume that a specification is given in *Linear Temporal Logic* (LTL) [20]. Counterexamples to a specification can be extracted automatically and the user does not need to provide the correct output: the necessary constraints on the outputs are contained in the specification.

---

[*] This work was supported in part by the European Union under contract 507219 (PROSYD).

E. Bin, A. Ziv, and S. Ur (Eds.): HVC 2006, LNCS 4383, pp. 50–64, 2007.

We formulate the diagnosis problem as a SAT problem. Our construction is closely related to that used in Bounded Model Checking (BMC) [5]. In our setting, a counterexample of length k is given. As in BMC, we unroll the circuit to length k and build a propositional formula to decide whether the LTL property holds. If we fix the inputs in the unrolled circuit to the values given in the counterexample and assert that the property holds, we arrive at a contradiction. The problem of diagnosis is the problem of resolving this contradiction.

To resolve the contradiction, we extend the model of the circuit. We introduce a set of predicates which assert that a component functions incorrectly. If an *abnormal predicate* is asserted, the functional constraints between inputs and outputs of the component are suspended. The diagnosis problem is to find which abnormal predicates need to be asserted in order to resolve the contradiction.

We can further restrict the set of satisfying assignments by requiring that the output of a gate must depend functionally on the inputs and the state of the circuit. Thus, we require the existence of a combinatorial correction. This allows us to extract a suggestion of the proper behavior of the suspect component from the satisfying assignments.

To improve the performance of the algorithm, we have experimented with decision heuristics for the SAT solver. In our setting a small set of decision variables suffices to imply the values of all other variables. Restricting the decision variables to this set leads to a considerable speedup and allows us to handle large and complex designs.

The search space can be further pruned by applying a simulation based preprocessing step. By calculating sensitized paths, the set of candidate error sites is pruned first. Only those components identified as candidates during the preprocessing step have to be considered during SAT based diagnosis.

The paper is structured as follows. In Section 2, we give an overview of related work. Section 3 gives the foundation of our approach and presents how we perform fault localization. The applicability of the approach on the source level is shown in Section 4. Then, Section 5 gives experimental evidence of the usability of our approach and we conclude in Section 6.

2   Related Work

There is a large amount of literature on diagnosis and repair. Most of it is restricted to combinatorial circuits. Also, much of it is limited to *simple faults* such as a forgotten inverter, or an AND gate that should be an OR. Such faults are likely to occur, for example, when a synthesis tool makes a mistake when optimizing the circuit. The work in [25] and [7] on diagnosis on the gate level, for example, combine both limitations.

Wahba and Borrione [26] treat sequential circuits on the gate level, but limit themselves to simple faults. The fault model of [13] is more general, and it addresses sequential circuits, but assumes that the correct outputs are given. Its technical approach is also quite different from ours.

Ali et al. proposed a SAT based diagnosis approach for sequential equivalence checking [3] and debugging combinational hierarchical circuits [2]. But the technique was only applied on the gate level and under the assumption that correct output values for counterexamples are given.

Both [10] and [29] work on the source code level (for hardware and programs, respectively). Both are based on the idea of comparing which parts of the code are exercised by similar correct and incorrect traces.

Only a few approaches have been proposed that are dedicated to fault localization or correction for property checking. In [9] a simulation based approach is presented which is less accurate than ours. Also, they do not consider functional consistency constraints. We use this simulation based technique as a preprocessing step to prune the number of components considered during diagnosis. In [14,23] a game based approach is presented which locates a fault and provides a new function as a correction for a faulty component. Because it computes a repair, this approach is far less efficient than the one presented here.

3   Diagnosis for Properties

In this section we describe our approach. In 3.1 we give a description of the basic algorithm. We describe extensions of the algorithm for runtime and accuracy improvements in Section 3.2, 3.3, and 3.4. We conclude this section with a discussion in 3.5.

3.1   Computing Fault Candidates

In this section, we describe how to find fault candidates in a sequential circuit. To simplify our explanation, we assume that the components of the circuit are gates, that is, a fault candidate is always a single gate. We will return to the question of the proper definition of components in Section 4. We furthermore assume that the correct specification is given as a (single) LTL formula.

We proceed in four steps:

1. Create counterexamples,
2. build the unrolling of the circuit, taking into account that some components may be incorrect,
3. build a propositional representation of the property, and
4. use a SAT solver to compute the fault candidates.

The counterexamples to the property can be obtained using model checking or using dynamic verification. It is advantageous to have many counterexamples available as this increases the discriminative power of the diagnosis algorithm. Techniques for obtaining multiple counterexamples in model checking have been studied in [8,11]. We will, however, first focus on the case where one counterexample (of length k) is present. We assume that the counterexamples are finite, that is, we ignore the liveness part of the specification.

The purpose of steps 2 and 3 is to construct a propositional formula ψ such that the fault candidates can easily be extracted from the satisfying assignments for ψ. As explained before, the procedure is closely related to BMC, and we will pay attention specifically to the differences.

Unrolling the Circuit. We will assume that the reader knows how a propositional logic formula is obtained by unrolling the circuit. Let n be the number of gates in the circuit (before unrolling) and let $\varphi_{i,t}$ be the propositional representation of the behavior of gate i at time frame t. Then, $\bigwedge_{t \in \{0,\ldots,k-1\}} \bigwedge_{i \in \{0,\ldots,n-1\}} \varphi_{i,t}$ is the (standard) length-k temporal unrolling of the circuit.

In order to perform diagnosis, we introduce n new propositional variables, ab_0 through ab_{n-1}. We replace the description of gate i at time frame t by the formula $\varphi'_{i,t} = (\neg ab_i \rightarrow \varphi_{i,t})$. Intuitively, if ab_i is asserted, gate i may be incorrect, and we do not make any assumptions on its behavior at any time frame. If ab_i is not asserted, the gate works as required. Now assume that we have just one counterexample and we use the formula ξ to represent that the inputs of the unrolled circuit are as prescribed by our counterexample. Then the description of the unrolling is given by

$$\varphi' = \xi \wedge \bigwedge_{t \in \{0,\ldots,k-1\}} \bigwedge_{i \in \{0,\ldots,n-1\}} \varphi'_{i,t} \, .$$

Building the Property. Next, we explain how to construct the propositional formula χ representing the specification.

Suppose a partial specification of the system is given in a LTL formula f. For each subformula g of f and for every time frame t we introduce a new propositional variable $v_{g,t}$. These variables are related to each other and to the variables used in the unrolling of the circuit as follows. For the temporal connectives, we use the well-known expansion rules [15], which relate the truth value of a formula to the truth values of its subformulas in the same and the next time frame. For instance, $G f = f \wedge X G f$ and $F f = f \vee X F f$. The Boolean connectives used in LTL are trivially translated to the corresponding constructs relating the propositional variables. Finally, the truth value of atomic proposition p at time frame t is equal to the value of the corresponding variable in the unrolling of the circuit. The final requirement is that the formula is not contradicted by the behavior of the circuit. That is, $v_{f,0}$, the variable corresponding to the specification in time frame 0, is true.

Propositional Formula. Note that if we combine the description of the counterexample, the circuit, and the specification and we assume that all abnormal predicates are false, we arrive at a contradiction. Let $\zeta_0 = \bigwedge_{i=0}^{n-1} \neg ab_i$, then $\varphi' \wedge \chi \wedge \zeta_0$ is contradictory.

A diagnosis is obtained by asking which abnormal predicates can resolve the contradiction. For instance, for single fault candidates, let $\zeta_1 = \bigvee_{i=0}^{n-1} \bigwedge_{j \neq i} \neg ab_j$ guarantee that at most one abnormal predicate is true and let $\psi = \varphi' \wedge \chi \wedge \zeta_1$. If a is a satisfying assignment for ψ, and a asserts ab_i, then i is a fault candidate.

Multiple counterexamples can be used to reduce the number of diagnosed components: only an explanation that resolves the conflict for all counterexamples is a fault candidate. The propositional formula corresponding to this problem consists of one unrolling of the circuit for each counterexample. All sets of variables are disjoint, the abnormal predicates, which are shared, are an exception.

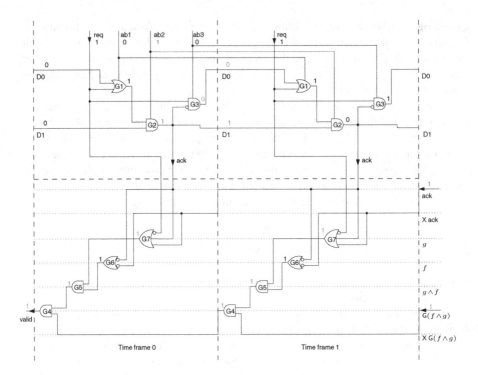

Fig. 1. Circuit with gate G2 as diagnosis ($g = \neg\text{req} \vee \text{ack} \vee \text{X ack}$, $f = \neg\text{ack} \vee \neg\text{X ack}$)

Example. In the following we illustrate the process using a simple arbiter with input req and output ack. The arbiter is supposed to acknowledge each request either instantaneously or in the next clock tick, but it may not emit two consecutive acknowledgements. In LTL, the specification reads

$$G((\neg\text{req} \vee \text{ack} \vee \text{X ack}) \wedge (\neg\text{ack} \vee \neg\text{X ack})).$$

Let D0 and D1 be latches. Latch D0 remembers whether there is a pending request, and D1 remember whether an acknowledge has occurred in the last step. The arbiter is defined by the following equations: $\text{ack} = (\text{D0} \vee \text{req}) \wedge \text{D1}$, $next(\text{D0}) = \text{req} \wedge \neg\text{ack}$, and $next(\text{D1}) = \text{ack}$. Furthermore, the initial values of D0 and D1 are 0. Note that the circuit contains a fault: ack should be $G1 \wedge \neg\text{D1}$ (see Figure 1).

The shortest counterexamples to the property have length two. For example, if we have requests in the first two time frames, ack is 0 in both frames, which violates the specification.

Figure 1 shows the unrolled circuit combined with the unrolled LTL specification. The abnormal predicates can remove the relation between the input and the output of a gate. For instance, the clauses for gate G2 are equivalent to $\neg\text{ab}_2 \rightarrow (G2 \leftrightarrow (G1 \wedge D1))$. Nothing is ascertained about the case where ab_2 is true.

The gates below the horizontal dashed line correspond to the unrolled formula. The signal corresponding to the truth of the specification is labeled "valid". For every time frame, the outputs of the gates in the unrolled formula correspond to a subformula of the specification. In the figure, the labels on the dashed horizontal lines indicate which subformula is represented by a gate output.

It is easily seen that valid is zero when two requests occur and all abnormal signals are set to zero. (Please ignore the gray numbers.) Note that signals corresponding to the valuation of ack and $G(f \wedge g)$ in time frame 2 are inputs (bottom right). The fact that the specification is false can be derived regardless of the values of these signals, since the counterexample is finite.

The question we pose the SAT solver is whether there is a consistent assignment to the signals that makes the specification true and sets only one of the abnormal predicates to true. One solution to this question is shown in gray in the figure. Gate G2 is assumed to be incorrect (as expected). For the circuit to be correct, it could return 1 in time frame 0 and 0 in time frame 1. The corresponding value suggested by this satisfying assignment is that G2 should be 0 when G1 is 1 and D1 is 0, and 0 when both inputs to the gate are 1.

The contradiction cannot be explained by setting ab_1 or ab_3 to true, which means that G2 is our only fault candidate.

3.2 Functionality Constraints

There is another satisfying assignment to the example just discussed: let G2 be 0 in the first step and 1 in the second. Note that there is no combinational correction to the circuit that implements this repair, as the inputs and states in both steps would be the same, but the output of G2 is required to be different.

In fact, the approach may find diagnoses for which there is no combinational repair. It may even find diagnoses when the specification is not realizable as a circuit. (A similar observation is made in [28] for multiple test cases). We will now show that by adding Ackermann constraints to our propositional formula we can guarantee that for any diagnosis there is a fix that makes the circuit correct for at least the given set of counterexamples.

Let us say that a gate g is *repairable* if there is a Boolean function $b(i, s)$ in terms of the inputs and the state such the circuit adheres to the specification when g is replaced by $b(i, s)$. That is, a gate is repairable if we can fix the circuit by replacing the gate by some new cone of combinational logic.

We say that g is *repairable with respect to* C, where C is a set of sequences of inputs, if there is a Boolean function $b(i, s)$ such that none of the sequences in C are a counterexample to the property when g is replaced by $b(i, s)$.

Given a set of counterexamples C, the *Ackermann constraint* for a gate g says that for any (not necessarily distinct) pair of counterexamples c_1, c_2 and any pair of time steps i, j, if the state and the inputs of the circuit in time step i of counterexample c_1 equal the state and the inputs in time step j of counterexample c_2, then the output of g is the same in both steps.

Ackermann constraints can easily be added to the propositional formula by adding a number of clauses that is quadratic in the cumulative length of the counterexamples and linear in the number of gates.

We have the following result.

```
 1  function staticDecision
 2    for i := 1 to A.size
 3      let ab be the variable A[i];
 4      if ab == UNDECIDED then
 5        ab := 1;
 6        return DECISION_DONE;
 7      else if ab == 1 then
 8        for t := 0 to k − 1
 9          if H(ab)[t] == UNDECIDED
10            H(ab)[t] := 0;
11            return DECISION_DONE;
12    return SATISFIED;
```

Fig. 2. Pseudocode of the static decision strategy

Theorem 1. *In the presence of Ackermann constraints, given a set of counterexamples C, any gate that is a diagnosis is repairable for C.*

It can be argued that our choice of what constitutes a repairable gate is somewhat arbitrary. Alternative definitions, however, are handled just as easily. For instance, one could require that a fix is a replacement by a single gate with the same inputs. The Ackermann constraints would change correspondingly. On the other extreme, one could allow any realizable function, in which case the Ackermann constraints would require that the output is equal if all the inputs in the past have been equal.

3.3 SAT Techniques

In practice, one wants all fault candidates, not just one. This can be achieved efficiently by adding blocking clauses [17] to the SAT instances stating that the abnormal predicates found thus far must be false. Note that we do not add the full satisfying assignment as a blocking clause, but just the fact that some abnormal predicates must be false, to exclude all other valuations of this assignment.

The efficiency of the SAT solver can be drastically improved using a dedicated decision strategy similar to [24]. By default, the solver performs a backtrack search on all variables in the SAT instance. In our case all variable values can be implied when the abnormal predicates and the output values of gates asserted as abnormal are given, since the inputs of the unrolled circuit are constraint to values given by the counterexample. Therefore, we apply a static decision strategy that decides abnormal predicates first and then proceeds on those gates that are asserted abnormal starting at time frame 0 up to time frame $k − 1$.

Figure 2 shows the pseudo code for this decision strategy. The vector A contains all abnormal predicates. This vector is searched until a predicate ab with an undecided value is found. If no value was assigned, the predicate is set to 1 (Lines 4-6). Due to the construction of the SAT instance, this assignment implies the value 0 for all other abnormal predicates. If the first assigned predicate has value 1, the output variable of the gate influenced by ab is considered (Lines 7-11). The hash H maps abnormal predicates to output variables of gates. $H(ab)$ returns a vector of k propositional variables. Variable $H(ab)[t]$ represents the output of the gate that is asserted abnormal by ab at time frame t. Thus, the first gate with unknown output value that is asserted abnormal is set to the value 0. Gates in earlier time frames are considered first. If no unassigned variable is found, a satisfying assignment was found (Line 12). Note that only one value of each variable has to be assigned in the decision strategy because the other value is implied by failure driven assertions [16]. Note also that $H(ab)[t]$ is a list in the general case because we consider multiple counterexamples and components instead of gates, i.e. each abnormal predicate may correspond to multiple gates as explained in Section 4. In our implementation this list is searched for the first gate that is undecided.

The experiments show a significant speed up when this strategy is applied. We have not yet experimented with constraint replication, but this can obviously be used in our setting, especially when multiple counterexamples are present.

3.4   Simulation Based Preprocessing

When all gates or components of a circuit are considered as potential diagnoses the search space is very large. A first obvious method to reduce this search space is a cone-of-influence analysis or the calculation of a static slice. As a result, only those components that drive signals considered in the property are contained in the SAT instance.

Furthermore, we apply a simulation based preprocessing step [25,9] to further reduce the number of components that have to be considered during diagnosis. Given a counterexample, all values are simulated on the unrolled circuit and the property in a linear time traversal. Then, starting at the output of the property, sensitized paths are traced towards the inputs and state at time frame 0 of the circuit [1]. This relies on the notion of controlling values of inputs for gates that determine the value of the output, e.g. the value 0 (1) is the controlling value for an AND gate (OR gate). First, the output is marked. Then, inputs with controlling values are marked recursively. If no input is controlling all inputs are marked recursively. Only components on a sensitized path are candidates for diagnoses. When using multiple counterexamples only components marked by each counterexample are candidates. Under a single failure assumption this procedure does not change the solution space for diagnosis, because changing a component that is not on a sensitized path cannot change the output value of the property.

The experimental results show that the overhead of this linear time preprocessing step is low. This step can prune the search space and, by this, reduces the overall run time.

3.5   Discussion

Just like multiple counterexamples, stronger specifications reduce the number of diagnoses. When more properties are considered, the constraints on the behavior are tightened. This observation is supported by our experiments.

In practical applications a hint how to repair the faulty behavior at a particular component is useful. The satisfying assignments not only provide diagnoses, but also the values that the faulty components should have. Thus, a correction is determined for the scenarios defined by the counterexamples.

Debugging the property – that might be faulty in practice – is also possible using the same approach. In this case abnormal predicates are associated to components of the property instead of the circuit.

The extension to liveness properties does not seem to be simple. In model checking, the counterexample to a liveness property is "lasso-shaped": after some initial steps, it enters an execution that repeats infinitely often. It is very easy to remove such a counterexample by changing any gate that breaks the loop without violating the safety part of the property. The recent observation that liveness properties can be encoded as safety [4] does not seem to affect this observation as it merely encodes the loop in a different way. Note however, that on an implementation level one probably has bounds on the response time and liveness can thus be eliminated from the specification, at least for the purpose of debugging.

4   Source Level Diagnosis

The previous section describes our approach by means of sequential circuits on the gate level. In this section we show the applicability of the approach on the source level. An expression on the source level may correspond to multiple gates. Therefore a single fault on the source level may correspond to multiple faults on the gate level. To avoid multiple fault diagnosis on the gate level, we can shift the diagnosis process to the source level and do not care about the gate level representation. Another possibility is to keep the information between source level and gate level and use it for the diagnosis process.

We present two principal techniques to calculate diagnoses at the source code level, discuss their advantages and point out the differences between them. Both techniques have been implemented for an evaluation.

4.1   Instrumentation Approach

The instrumentation approach directly includes the abnormal predicates in the source code of the design, this means components and reported diagnoses are parts of the source code.

We modify the design by introducing new primary inputs for abnormal predicates. Then, each component is enclosed by an if-statement that allows to override the value that is internally calculated by an arbitrary value from another new primary input. For example, when we consider the assignment c = (a && !b) as a component, we replace it by

```
c = if(ab) then new_input else (a && !b).
```

In this implementation the mapping between source and gate level is not important. This makes the approach very easy to implement on top of an existing model checker.

The choice of components only depends on the instrumentation of the source code and can be adjusted to meet particular needs. Our choice regards any expression as a component, including right-hand sides of assignments and branching conditions.

We implemented the instrumentation approach on top of the VIS model checker [6]. We used two Perl scripts to instrument the Verilog design and the LTL property. We used the BMC package of VIS to generate counterexamples. As SAT solver for computing the diagnoses, we used zchaff [18] enhanced with the static decision heuristic discussed in Section 3.5. In the current version of the implementation multiple counterexamples need multiple calls to the SAT solver.

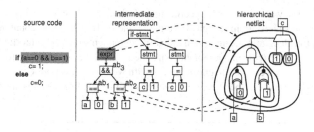

Fig. 3. Source code link in the Hierarchical Approach

4.2 Hierarchical Approach

In the second approach, the hierarchy that is induced by the syntactical structure of the source code is included in the gate level representation of the design and the property. This allows us to link the gate level to the source code.

The link between source code and gate level model is established during synthesis. Figure 3 shows this procedure. An *Abstract Syntax Tree* (AST) is created from the source code at first. Then, the AST is traversed and directly mapped to gate level constructs. During this mapping, the gates that correspond to certain portions of the source code can be identified. Thus, the AST induces regions at the gate level. These regions are grouped hierarchically.

Components are identified based on this representation. Each region corresponds to a component. E.g., the expression $(a==1)$ && $(b==0)$ corresponds to three components: $(a==1)$, $(b==0)$, and the complete expression. We introduce a single abnormal predicate for each region. All gates that do not belong to a lower region in the hierarchy are associated to this abnormal predicate. In the example the predicates ab_1, ab_2, and ab_3 are introduced.

Although this approach requires a modified synthesis tool, the diagnosis engine can take advantage of the hierarchical information. For instance, a correction of a single expression may not be possible but changing an entire module may rectify all counterexamples. When this hierarchy information is encoded in the diagnosis problem, a single fault assumption still returns a valid diagnosis.

The granularity of the diagnosis result can also be influenced. For example, we may choose only source level modules as components to retrieve coarse diagnoses, or, in contrast, we may consider all subexpressions and statements as components for a fine grained diagnosis result.

Finally, hierarchical information can be used to improve the performance of the diagnosis engine [2]. First, a coarse granularity can be used to efficiently identify possibly erroneous parts of the design. Then, the diagnosis can be carried out at a finer granularity with higher computational cost to calculate more accurate diagnoses for the previously diagnosed components.

The implementation of the hierarchical approach uses a modified version of the synthesis tool vl2mv from VIS and an induction-based property checker. The design *and* the property were described in Verilog. As a result, each can be considered during diagnosis. This environment can use multiple counterexamples for diagnosis and simulation based preprocessing. The property checker is based upon a version of zchaff that

Table 1. Results for weak vs. strong specification (Columns 1,2, and 3: name of the design, number of gates and registers in design; Columns 4 and 5: length of the counterexample and time in seconds to calculate it; Column 6: number of components on source level; Column 7 and 8: results for static slice (percentage numbers are the ratio of the result to the total number of components); Columns 9 and 10: diagnosis results with weak specification; Columns 11 and 12: diagnosis results with strong specification, Column 13 time to solve SAT instance for a single and all diagnoses

Circuit			BMC		Diagnosis							
						slice		weak		strong		
Prop	gates	registers	len	time	#cmp	#cmp	%	#cmp	%	#cmp	%	time
b01_e1, *pOverfl*	98	7	5	0.01	40	32	80	8	20	5	13	0.04, 0.10
b02_e1, *pAltOut*	46	4	5	0.02	20	20	100	6	30	5	25	0.01, 0.02
b03_e1, *pGrantInv*	387	30	4	0.01	50	49	98	10	20	7	14	0.01, 0.14
b09_e1, *pLoadOld*	398	28	21	0.13	33	22	67	14	42	6	18	0.38, 0.83
b10_e1, *pRx2Tx*	318	20	7	0.02	61	53	87	16	26	10	16	0.73, 0.96
b11_e1, *pRsum*	770	31	6	0.17	44	39	89	16	36	9	20	0.11, 0.39
b13_e1, *pRelease*	505	53	5	0.11	96	72	75	6	6	3	3	1.88, 1.94
VsaR_e1, *pInv*	2956	154	15	0.5	56	50	89	14	25	8	14	1.99, 5.87

supports incremental SAT [27] and is enhanced with the static decision heuristic. During diagnosis, one SAT instance is created that includes a copy of the design for each counterexample. We use the incremental interface of zchaff to calculate all diagnoses.

5   Experimental Results

For the experimental data, we used benchmarks provided with VIS. We manually introduced a bug in each of the designs by changing an operator or a constant. In the following, we will show how specific the diagnosis is and we will show the benefit of the modified decision heuristics and simulation based preprocessing. We are currently using two implementations, one for the instrumentation approach and one for the hierarchical approach. This is the reason that the designs in the two tables are not the same.

5.1   Accuracy

Diagnosis Results and Strong Specification. For the analysis of the accuracy of the diagnosis we first consider the results of the instrumentation approach. We used a Pentium IV (Hyperthreading, 2.8 GHz, 3GB, Linux) for the experiments.

Table 1 contains the obtained experimental results. Since a verification engineer would only consider the expressions for debugging that are in the cone of influence of the failing property, we have calculated a static slice. For the diagnosis process we first used a weak specification, namely only the property which failed during bounded model checking. As shown in the table, the diagnosis results with the weak specification are far better than the slicing results. We repeated the experiments with a stronger specification. We added between three and ten additional properties to the property that failed during bounded model checking. With a stronger specification the number of diagnoses were reduced for every example, and for some examples results were significantly better. The small number of diagnoses underlines the usefulness of our approach to fault localization.

Table 2. Diagnosis results for multiple counterexamples and Ackermann constraints

Circuit					Diagnosis							
						slice	single		four		Ackermann	
Prop	gates	registers	len	#cmp	#cmp	%	#cmp	%	#cmp	%	#cmp	%
am2910_p1_e1, pEntry5	2257	102	5	227	205	90	66	29	36	15	36	15
am2910_p2_e1, pStackPointer	2290	102	5	230	87	37	37	16	26	11	26	11
bpbs_p1_e1, pValidTransition	1640	39	2	127	102	80	15	11	13	10	13	10
bpbs_p1_e2, pValidTransition	1640	39	2	127	102	80	15	11	4	3	4	3
counter_e1, pCountValue	25	7	3	11	10	90	4	36	4	36	1	9
FPMult_e1, pLegalOperands	973	69	4	119	105	88	3	2	3	2	3	2
FPMult_e2, pLegalOperands	973	69	4	119	105	88	54	45	47	39	47	39
gcd_e1, pReadyIn22Cyc	634	51	22	87	68	78	45	51	35	40	35	40
gcd_e2, pReadyIn22Cyc	634	51	22	87	68	78	34	39	32	36	32	36
gcd_e1, pBoth	634	51	23	87	71	81	46	52	36	41	36	41
gcd_e2, pBoth	634	51	23	87	71	81	33	37	33	37	33	37
gcd_e1, pThree	634	51	23	87	71	81	33	37	23	26	23	26
gcd_e2, pThree	634	51	23	87	71	81	39	44	22	25	22	25

Case Study. This example shows the difference in accuracy between two specifications for example b09.

The original functionality of example b09 is a serial to serial converter. As a fault, we negated the condition of an if-statement. The resulting circuit violates the property that describes that in a certain state an input register must be zero. When we perform diagnosis using only the failing property, 14 components are identified.

The converter has four states: INIT, RECEIVE, EXECUTE, and LOAD_OLD. There are specific transitions that are possible between the states, for example from the INIT mode we must only reach the RECEIVE mode. If the permitted transitions between the states are included in the specification, the number of diagnoses is only six.

For the diagnosis corresponding to the actual fault we can conclude out of the new value that we have to invert the if-condition. One diagnosis is located in the branch of the if assignment that is executed because of the faulty if-condition. The suggested value for the input register is zero, as it is required in the property. The property that failed is an implication. In four of the six remaining diagnoses, the new values for the suspended components set the antecedent of the implication to false and therefore the property is satisfied.

Multiple Counterexamples and Ackermann Constraints. Table 2 shows the influence of multiple counterexamples and Ackermann constraints on the diagnosis results. The implementation of these features demands full access to the generation of the SAT instance. We therefore integrated them in the hierarchical environment as explained in Section 4.2. Experiments were carried out on an AMD Athlon 3500+ (Linux, 2.2GHz, 1 GB, Linux).

The columns provide the same data as the previous table. Besides diagnosis results for static slicing, we report results for using a *single* counterexample, *four* counterexamples and four counterexamples together with *Ackermann* constraints. The use of multiple counterexamples can significantly improve the diagnosis result. In all but two cases the number of diagnoses was reduced.

Table 3. Run times for the different approaches (using four counterexamples)

	BMC	Diagnosis								
		zchaff default			static			simulation+static		
Circuit, *Property*	time	time	#cmp	#dec	time	#cmp	#dec	time	#cmp	#dec
am2910_p1_e1, *pEntry5*	0.54	11.87	205	165,247	2.63	205	8,047	1.62	69	7,855
am2910_p2_e1, *pStackPointer*	0.01	0.40	87	3,848	0.31	87	989	0.28	52	916
bpbs_p1_e1, *pValidTransition*	0.06	0.19	102	2,819	0.20	102	302	0.13	19	266
bpbs_p1_e2, *pValidTransition*	0.03	0.16	102	1,805	0.14	102	110	0.11	5	87
counter_e1, *pCountValue*	<0.01	0.01	10	259	0.01	10	131	<0.01	9	130
FPMult_e1, *pLegalOperands*	0.04	0.41	105	397	0.19	105	60	0.15	5	60
FPMult_e2, *pLegalOperands*	0.04	2.27	105	17,540	1.14	105	8,440	0.95	76	7,320
gcd_e1, *pReadyIn22Cyc*	18.7	1057.21	68	3,271, 957	53.98	68	479,526	54.35	67	479,525
gcd_e2, *pReadyIn22Cyc*	22.07	351.16	68	1,022,573	19.65	68	115,519	18.59	63	112,833
gcd_e1, *pBoth*	32.24	2213.35	71	3,468,162	91.74	71	425,438	90.08	67	425,436
gcd_e2, *pBoth*	24.20	453.83	71	1,058,165	55.23	71	237,104	50.19	59	232,334
gcd_e1, *pThree*	42.74	1626.07	71	2,617,354	201.76	71	723,180	198.44	65	730,191
gcd_e2, *pThree*	35.50	498.99	71	1,278,064	1306.90	71	3,586,181	1307.80	71	3,586,181

In contrast, Ackermann constraints do not yield the same improvement. Only in one case the number of diagnoses was reduced and the algorithm returned exactly the real error site. The overhead in runtime is quite high for Ackermann constraints. We observed an increase by up to a factor of 60 especially on large instances. Thus, Ackermann constraints should only be applied in a second stage of the diagnosis process due to their low influence on the accuracy.

5.2 Runtime

In Section 3 we suggested two techniques to improve the runtime of the overall algorithm: a static decision strategy for the SAT solver and the use of a simulation based preprocessing step. Both techniques were implemented within the hierarchical framework. Due to page limitation, we only report experimental results for the use of four counterexamples without Ackermann constraints in Table 3. The table shows runtimes for the different approaches. Additionally, the number of components considered during SAT based diagnosis (this is not the number of components returned as diagnoses that is shown in Table 2) and the number of decisions made by the SAT solver are reported.

The runtime decreases drastically when the static decision heuristic is applied. This is due to the reduction of the number of decisions that have to be done by the SAT solver. The only exception is the last benchmark, but when using only one counterexample the runtime was only 9.91 seconds at the cost of a lower accuracy (see above). Usually, the runtime does not exceed the time for BMC much — even when four counterexamples are applied for diagnosis. Here, incrementally applying more and more counterexamples as suggested in [22] can yield an even shorter runtime. The use of the simulation based preprocessing step also saves some runtime in those cases were the number of components considered during SAT based diagnosis can be reduced significantly. On the other hand the overhead is quite low when no components can be pruned.

The creation of counterexamples dedicated for diagnosis may improve the diagnosis results. This hypothesis is strengthened by following experimental results. We did 1000 diagnosis runs with 4 randomly chosen counterexamples on am2910_e1 for the property *pEntry5*. The number of diagnoses varied from 28 to 90 and the runtime varied between 1.75 and 3.75 seconds. Usually, a better diagnosis accuracy also had a shorter runtime.

In summary, the runtime was reduced drastically by the proposed techniques and makes the effort of diagnosis comparable to that of BMC.

6   Conclusions

We have presented an approach to automatically locate design faults at the gate level or the source code level. The approach handles safety properties written in LTL. A propositional logic formula is built in such a way that diagnoses can be derived from its satisfying assignments. We have shown how to extend the formula to make sure that a diagnosed component is actually repairable for the given input sequences.

We have proposed two techniques to implement the approach. One is easy to implement on top of an existing model checker, the other allows the diagnosis engine to exploit hierarchical information. We have shown that the use of multiple counterexamples and more comprehensive specifications provides a more accurate diagnosis result. We have drastically improved the efficiency of the approach by using a dedicated search strategy for the SAT solver and shown its applicability with experimental results.

Some ideas for future work have been discussed already. Furthermore, we would like to further investigate in how far the techniques presented here can be used to find faults in the specification rather than the system. Finally, we would like to attempt to use these ideas on models of a C program, and we would like to try the approach for all possible counterexamples, thus making it complete, by using quantified Boolean formulas.

References

1. M. Abramovici, P.R. Menon, and D.T. Miller. Critical path tracing - an alternative to fault simulation. In *Design Automation Conf.*, pages 214–220, 1983.
2. M.F. Ali, S. Safarpour, A. Veneris, M.S. Abadir, and R. Drechsler. Post-verification debugging of hierarchical designs. In *Int'l Conf. on CAD*, pages 871–876, 2005.
3. M.F. Ali, A. Veneris, S. Safarpour, R. Drechsler, A. Smith, and M.S.Abadir. Debugging sequential circuits using Boolean satisfiability. In *Int'l Conf. on CAD*, pages 204–209, 2004.
4. A. Biere, C. Artho, and V. Schuppan. Liveness checking as safety checking. *Electronic Notes in Theoretical Computer Science*, 66(2), July 2002. Formal Methods for Industrial Critical Systems (FMICS'02).
5. A. Biere, A. Cimatti, E. Clarke, and Y. Zhu. Symbolic model checking without BDDs. In *Fifth International Conference on Tools and Algorithms for Construction and Analysis of Systems (TACAS'99)*, pages 193–207, Amsterdam, The Netherlands, March 1999. LNCS 1579.
6. R. K. Brayton et al. VIS: A system for verification and synthesis. In T. Henzinger and R. Alur, editors, *Eighth Conference on Computer Aided Verification (CAV'96)*, pages 428–432. Springer-Verlag, Rutgers University, 1996. LNCS 1102.
7. P.-Y. Chung, Y.-M. Wang, and I. N. Hajj. Diagnosis and correction of logic design errors in digital circuits. In *Design Automation Conference (DAC'03)*, pages 503–508, 2003.
8. G. Fey and R. Drechsler. Finding good counter-examples to aid design verification. In *MEMOCODE*, pages 51–52, 2003.

9. G. Fey and R. Drechsler. Efficient hierarchical system debugging for property checking. In *Workshop on Design and Diagnostics of Electronic Circuits and Systems (DDECS'05)*, pages 41–46, 2005.

10. A. Groce. Error explanation with distance metrics. In *International Conference on Tools and Algorithms for Construction and Analysis of Systems (TACAS'04)*, pages 108–122, Barcelona, Spain, March-April 2004. LNCS 2988.

11. A. Groce, D. Kroening, and F. Lerda. Understanding counterexamples with explain. In R. Alur and D. Peled, editors, *Sixteenth Conference on Computer Aided Verification (CAV'04)*, pages 453–456. Springer-Verlag, Berlin, July 2004. LNCS 3114.

12. W. Hamscher and R. Davis. Diagnosing circuits with state: An inherently underconstrained problem. In *Proceedings of the Fourth National Conference on Artificial Intelligence (AAAI'84)*, pages 142–147, 1984.

13. S.-Y. Huang and K.-T. Cheng. Errortracer: Design error diagnosis based on fault simulation techniques. *IEEE Trans. on CAD*, 18(9):1341–1352, 1999.

14. B. Jobstmann, A. Griesmayer, and R. Bloem. Program repair as a game. In K. Etessami and S. K. Rajamani, editors, *17th Conference on Computer Aided Verification (CAV'05)*, pages 226–238. Springer-Verlag, 2005. LNCS 3576.

15. Z. Manna and A. Pnueli. *The Temporal Logic of Reactive and Concurrent Systems *Specification**. Springer-Verlag, 1991.

16. J.P. Marques-Silva and K.A. Sakallah. GRASP: A search algorithm for propositional satisfiability. *IEEE Trans. on Comp.*, 48(5):506–521, 1999.

17. K. L. McMillan. Applying SAT methods in unbounded symbolic model checking. In E. Brinksma and K. G. Larsen, editors, *Fourteenth Conference on Computer Aided Verification (CAV'02)*, pages 250–264. Springer-Verlag, Berlin, July 2002. LNCS 2404.

18. M. Moskewicz, C. F. Madigan, Y. Zhao, L. Zhang, and S. Malik. Chaff: Engineering an efficient SAT solver. In *Proceedings of the Design Automation Conference*, pages 530–535, Las Vegas, NV, June 2001.

19. B. Peischl and F. Wotawa. Modeling state in software debugging of VHDL-RTL designs — a model based diagnosis approach. In *Automated and Algorithmic Debugging (AADE-BUG'03)*, pages 197–210, 2003.

20. A. Pnueli. The temporal logic of programs. In *IEEE Symposium on Foundations of Computer Science*, pages 46–57, Providence, RI, 1977.

21. R. Reiter. A theory of diagnosis from first principles. *Artificial Intelligence*, 32:57–95, 1987.

22. A. Smith, A. Veneris, and A. Viglas. Design diagnosis using Boolean satisfiability. In *ASP Design Automation Conf.*, pages 218–223, 2004.

23. S. Staber, B. Jobstmann, and R. Bloem. Finding and fixing faults. In D. Borrione and W. Paul, editors, *13th Conference on Correct Hardware Design and Verification Methods (CHARME '05)*, pages 35–49. Springer-Verlag, 2005. LNCS 3725.

24. O. Strichman. Accelerating bounded model checking of safety properties. *Formal Methods in System Design*, 24(1):5–24, January 2004.

25. A. Veneris and I. N. Hajj. Design error diagnosis and correction via test vector simulation. *IEEE Trans. on CAD*, 18(12):1803–1816, 1999.

26. A. Wahba and D. Borrione. Design error diagnosis in sequential circuits. In *Correct Hardware Design and Verification Methods (CHARME'95)*, pages 171–188, 1995. LNCS 987.

27. J. Whittemore, J. Kim, and K. Sakallah. SATIRE: A new incremental satisfiability engine. In *Proceedings of the Design Automation Conference*, pages 542–545, Las Vegas, NV, June 2001.

28. F. Wotawa. Debugging hardware designs using a value-based model. *Applied Intelligence*, 16:71–92, 2002.

29. A. Zeller and R. Hildebrandt. Simplifying and isolating failure-inducing input. *IEEE Transactions on Software Engineering*, 28(2):183–200, February 2002.

Verification of Data Paths Using Unbounded Integers: Automata Strike Back

Tobias Schuele and Klaus Schneider

Reactive Systems Group, Department of Computer Science, University of Kaiserslautern
P.O. Box 3049, 67653 Kaiserslautern, Germany
{Tobias.Schuele,Klaus.Schneider}@informatik.uni-kl.de
http://rsg.informatik.uni-kl.de

Abstract. We present a decision procedure for quantifier-free Presburger arithmetic that is based on a polynomial time translation of Presburger formulas to alternating finite automata (AFAs). Moreover, our approach leverages the advances in SAT solving by reducing the emptiness problem of AFAs to satisfiability problems of propositional logic. In order to obtain a complete decision procedure, we use an inductive style of reasoning as originally proposed for proving safety properties in bounded model checking. Besides linear arithmetic constraints, our decision procedure can deal with bitvector operations that frequently occur in hardware design. Thus, it is well-suited for the verification of data paths at a high level of abstraction.

1 Introduction

Hardware verification is usually performed at the level of propositional logic which is self-evident if the system to be verified is given as a netlist of gates. Using propositional logic as the basic formalism allows one to perform a symbolic state space exploration of the system by means of binary decision diagrams (BDDs), or to apply bounded model checking procedures that make use of sophisticated SAT solvers. However, while both approaches have been successfully used for the verification of control-flow intensive systems, large data paths are still hardly tractable using most symbolic model checkers. To solve this problem, various approaches have been proposed such as abstract interpretation, symmetry reduction, partial order reduction, and many others that aim at fighting the state explosion problem.

Another approach to verify data-flow intensive systems is the use of more powerful base logics. This is particularly interesting if the system is given at a higher level of abstraction than gate level, where more complex operations are available. Regarding the verification of data paths, such a logic should at least contain operations for integer arithmetic. However, due to the undecidability of full arithmetic, this either requires the use of interactive theorem provers or to consider decidable fragments such as Presburger arithmetic [1]. In recent years, decision procedures for such decidable logics have attained increasing interest, not only as stand-alone procedures, but also as the basis for combined decision procedures. For instance, the UCLID system [2] that is based on a combination of the theory of uninterpreted functions with equality, Presburger arithmetic, and the theory of arrays has been successfully used for the verification of complex micro-processors.

E. Bin, A. Ziv, and S. Ur (Eds.): HVC 2006, LNCS 4383, pp. 65–80, 2007.
© Springer-Verlag Berlin Heidelberg 2007

In this paper, we present yet another procedure for checking satisfiability of quantifier-free Presburger arithmetic formulas. Our method is based on the translation of Presburger formulas to finite automata as originally proposed in [3] and enhanced for example in [4,5,6]. It is sometimes argued that automata-based decision procedures for Presburger arithmetic are in general less efficient than other approaches such as integer linear programming and Fourier-Motzkin variable elimination [7]. Indeed, none of the benchmarks used in [8] could be solved using the LASH tool [9] that is based on the method presented in [5]. However, such comparisons certainly depend on the type of automata formulas are translated to and on the underlying decision procedures for propositional logic (BDDs vs. SAT solvers).

In contrast to previous approaches, our method employs alternating finite automata (AFAs) which can be viewed as a generalization of nondeterministic automata. As a major advantage of AFAs, our method can benefit from sophisticated SAT solvers that are state-of-the-art in many areas. In particular, the equational structure of AFAs allows us to unwind their transition relations efficiently which is useful for checking emptiness (a formula is unsatisfiable iff the language of the corresponding automaton is empty). However, simply unwinding an AFA only yields a semi-decision procedure that can be used to prove satisfiability of a formula, but not to prove its unsatisfiability. To solve this problem, we use an inductive style of reasoning that has been originally proposed for checking safety properties in bounded model checking.

As another advantage, our approach can be easily extended to deal with more powerful logics. Regarding the verification of data paths, we consider an extension of Presburger arithmetic by bitvector operations, since these operations frequently occur in hardware design. For example, the ALUs of most microprocessors support arithmetic as well as bitwise operations. While such an extension is straightforward in practice, it has considerable impact on the complexity of the decision procedures: We show that the satisfiability problem of Presburger arithmetic with bitvector operations cannot be reduced to a polynomial sized satisfiability problem of propositional logic. For this reason, we use an inductive approach and do not rely on a polynomial upper bound on the size of the constructed formulas as in [8]. Finally, it should be mentioned that automata encode all solutions of a formula which makes it easy to find the smallest one.

There has been much work on decision procedures for Presburger arithmetic. A comparison of different approaches can be found in [10,11,7]. The construction of deterministic finite automata (DFAs) from linear arithmetic constraints is described in detail in [5]. However, the proposed algorithms perform an explicit enumeration of the state space. A symbolic encoding using BDDs is presented in [7,12]. From a practical point of view, our method is most closely related to the approach presented in [8] that also makes use of SAT solvers. The idea is to reduce the infinite domain of Presburger formulas to a finite one by computing bounds on the size of the solutions. In contrast to our approach, however, it cannot directly deal with bitvector operations as described above. Strichman [13] presents another SAT based decision procedure that is based on Fourier-Motzkin elimination. In the worst case, this approach leads to a SAT problem that is doubly exponential in the size of the formula. Finally, Kroening et. al [14] propose an abstraction-based procedure that combines a SAT solver with a theorem prover in order to successively generate approximations of the original formula.

The outline of the paper is as follows: after briefly describing AFAs and Presburger arithmetic in the next section, we present the corresponding translation in Section 3. Then, we describe our approach for checking emptiness of AFAs and discuss the effect of introducing bitvector operations (Section 4). Experimental results are given in Section 5, and finally, we conclude with a summary and directions for future work.

2 Foundations

2.1 Alternating Finite Automata

Alternating finite automata (AFAs) [15,16,17,18] and also Boolean automata [19,20,21] are a natural generalization of nondeterministic finite automata (NFAs) in the sense that the next state is not just chosen from a set of states, but determined by a propositional formula[1]. Recall that an NFA is a tuple $(Q, \Sigma, \delta, q_0, F)$, where Q is the set of states, Σ is the alphabet, $\delta : Q \times \Sigma \rightarrow \mathscr{P}(Q)$ is the transition function, q_0 is the initial state, and $F \subseteq Q$ is the set of final states. A word $aw \in \Sigma^+$ is accepted in a state $q \in Q$ iff there exists at least one successor state $q' \in \delta(q, a)$ such that w is accepted in q' (the empty word is accepted in q iff $q \in F$). More formally, we recursively define $\mathsf{acc}(q, aw) :\Leftrightarrow \exists q' \in \delta(q, a).\mathsf{acc}(q', w)$. Since there are only finitely many states, the existential[2] acceptance condition of NFAs can be replaced by a disjunction, i.e., $\mathsf{acc}(q, aw) :\Leftrightarrow \bigvee_{q' \in \delta(q,a)} \mathsf{acc}(q', w)$. AFAs extend this idea to allow arbitrary propositional formulas in place of the disjunctions found in NFAs: Instead of a set of successor states, each state has an associated formula that characterizes its acceptance condition. Thus, to decide whether a word is accepted in a state, one simply evaluates the associated formula.

An AFA can be formally defined as follows, where we use Boolean variables not only to represent the states, but also to encode the alphabet, i.e., we assume that a letter is a vector of Boolean values:

Definition 1 (Alternating Finite Automaton (AFA)). *An alternating finite automaton is a tuple (Q, V, δ, I, F), where*

- *Q is the set of state variables,*
- *V is the set of input variables,*
- *$\delta : Q \rightarrow \mathsf{Prop}(Q \cup V)$ is the transition function that associates with each state variable a propositional formula over the variables $Q \cup V$,*
- *$I \in \mathsf{Prop}(Q \cup V)$ is the initial formula over the variables $Q \cup V$, and*
- *$F : Q \rightarrow \mathbb{B}$ is the final function that maps state variables to the Booleans.*

In the sequel, we denote state variables by $q_0, \ldots, q_m$ and input variables by $v_0, \ldots, v_n$. Moreover, we abbreviate $\Sigma := \mathbb{B}^{|V|}$.

---

[1] Originally, the term alternation stems from the fact that existential and universal quantifiers can alternate during the course of a computation, whereas in a nondeterministic computation there are only existential quantifiers.

[2] Clearly, one can also define a dual type of automata, where a word is accepted in a state iff all of its successor states accept the remaining word. The acceptance condition of such universal automata is a conjunction of the acceptance conditions over the successor states.

This definition slightly differs from the ones found in the literature in that it provides an initial formula instead of only a single initial state. As a result, an AFA as defined above cannot accept the empty word. Moreover, we allow arbitrary propositional formulas, i.e., a variable may occur not only in positive, but also in negative form.

Definition 2 (Acceptance and Language of an AFA). *Given a propositional formula* f, *let* $f[v_i/g_i, w_j/h_j]_{0 \leq j \leq n}^{0 \leq i \leq m}$ *denote the formula obtained by simultaneously substituting the formulas* g_i *and* h_j *for the variables* v_i *and* w_j, *respectively, for* $0 \leq i \leq m$ *and* $0 \leq j \leq n$. *Given an AFA* $\mathcal{A} = (Q, V, \delta, I, F)$, *the acceptance of a word with respect to a formula* f *is defined as follows, where* $(b_0, \ldots, b_n) \in \Sigma$ *and* $w \in \Sigma^+$:

$$\mathrm{acc}(f, (b_0, \ldots, b_n)\, w) :\Leftrightarrow \mathrm{acc}(f[q_i/\delta(q_i), v_j/b_j]_{0 \leq j \leq n}^{0 \leq i \leq m}, w)$$

$$\mathrm{acc}(f, (b_0, \ldots, b_0)) :\Leftrightarrow f[q_i/F(q_i), v_j/b_j]_{0 \leq j \leq n}^{0 \leq i \leq m}$$

A word w *is accepted by* $\mathcal{A}$ *iff* $\mathrm{acc}(I, w)$ *holds. The language accepted by* $\mathcal{A}$ *is defined as* $\mathcal{L}(\mathcal{A}) := \{w \in \Sigma^* \mid \mathrm{acc}(I, w)\}$.

AFAs have the property that they are backward deterministic which means that they are deterministic if one considers them working on the input string from right to left. Thus, an AFA can also be viewed as a symbolic description of a deterministic finite automaton (DFA) accepting the reverse language. The transition relation is thereby given as an equation system, i.e., by the conjunction $\bigwedge_{q \in Q} q' \leftrightarrow \delta(q)$, where q' is the next state variable associated with q. For this reason, it is often more convenient to consider the reverse language when dealing with AFAs, which has lead to the notion of reversed AFAs [22,23,24]. In particular, when constructing AFAs for Presburger formulas, we will assume that the input is being read from right to left.

However, it should be emphasized that the order in which the input is read is mainly a matter of taste. For instance, checking whether a word is accepted by an AFA can be done in both directions with essentially the same complexity. The only difference is that when reading from right to left, we have to deal with a vector of formulas, whereas in the opposite direction it suffices to consider a single formula (cf. Definition 2). The crucial point is that AFAs have an equational structure [25], or in terms of symbolic model checking, an explicit partitioning of the transition relation. This allows us to unwind AFAs without introducing additional state variables and to employ efficient SAT solvers for checking emptiness, as mentioned in the introduction.

Given two AFAs $\mathcal{A}_1 = (Q_1, V, \delta_1, I_1, F_1)$ and $\mathcal{A}_2 = (Q_2, V, \delta_2, I_2, F_2)$, the Boolean operations are defined by the corresponding operations on the initial formulas:

- $\neg \mathcal{A}_1 := (Q_1, V, \delta_1, \neg I_1, F_1)$
- $\mathcal{A}_1 \wedge \mathcal{A}_2 := (Q_1 \cup Q_2, V, \delta_1 \cup \delta_2, I_1 \wedge I_2, F_1 \cup F_2)$
- $\mathcal{A}_1 \vee \mathcal{A}_2 := (Q_1 \cup Q_2, V, \delta_1 \cup \delta_2, I_1 \vee I_2, F_1 \cup F_2)$

It is easy to see that the Boolean operations satisfy the following equations (ϵ denotes the empty word):

- $\mathcal{L}(\neg \mathcal{A}_1) = \overline{\mathcal{L}(\mathcal{A}_1)} \setminus \{\epsilon\}$
- $\mathcal{L}(\mathcal{A}_1 \wedge \mathcal{A}_2) = \mathcal{L}(\mathcal{A}_1) \cap \mathcal{L}(\mathcal{A}_2)$
- $\mathcal{L}(\mathcal{A}_1 \vee \mathcal{A}_2) = \mathcal{L}(\mathcal{A}_1) \cup \mathcal{L}(\mathcal{A}_2)$

2.2   Quantifier-Free Presburger Arithmetic with Bitvector Operations

In this subsection, we briefly describe the syntax and semantics of quantifier-free Presburger arithmetic with bitvector operations (QFPAbit).

Definition 3 (Syntax of QFPAbit**).** *Let* $\mathcal{V} := \mathcal{V}_\mathbb{Z} \cup \mathcal{V}_\mathbb{B}$ *be a finite set of integer and Boolean variables, respectively, such that* $\mathcal{V}_\mathbb{Z} \cap \mathcal{V}_\mathbb{B} = \emptyset$ *holds. Then, the set of terms is defined as follows with* $c \in \mathbb{Z}$ *and* $x \in \mathcal{V}_\mathbb{Z}$:

$$T := c \mid x \mid T + T \mid c \cdot T \mid \overrightarrow{\neg} T \mid T \overrightarrow{\wedge} T \mid T \overrightarrow{\vee} T$$

The set of formulas is defined as follows with $p \in \mathcal{V}_\mathbb{B}$ *and* $\bowtie \in \{=, \neq, <, \leq, >, \geq\}$:

$$F := p \mid T \bowtie T \mid \neg F \mid F \wedge F \mid F \vee F$$

The semantics should be clear from the context except for the bitvector operations $\overrightarrow{\neg}$, $\overrightarrow{\wedge}$, and $\overrightarrow{\vee}$ that need some further explanation. Their semantics is based on two's complement encoding, where the value $\langle x_k \ldots x_0 \rangle_\mathbb{Z}$ of a bitvector $(x_k \ldots x_0)$ is defined as follows:

$$\langle x_k \ldots x_0 \rangle_\mathbb{Z} := -2^k x_k + \sum_{i=0}^{k-1} 2^i x_i$$

Recall that in this encoding the most significant bit can be replicated without changing the value (sign extension). Thus, the equation $\langle x_k \ldots x_0 \rangle_\mathbb{Z} = \langle x_k x_k \ldots x_0 \rangle_\mathbb{Z}$ is valid for all bitvectors $(x_k \ldots x_0)$. A term $\overrightarrow{\neg} x$ is then interpreted as $\langle \neg x_k \ldots \neg x_0 \rangle_\mathbb{Z}$, provided that $x = \langle x_k \ldots x_0 \rangle_\mathbb{Z}$ holds. Similarly, the terms $x \overrightarrow{\wedge} y$ and $x \overrightarrow{\vee} y$ are interpreted as $\langle x_k \wedge y_k \ldots x_0 \wedge y_0 \rangle_\mathbb{Z}$ and $\langle x_k \vee y_k \ldots x_0 \vee y_0 \rangle_\mathbb{Z}$, respectively. For example, as -6 is represented by the bitvector (1010), and 5 by (0101), it follows that $-6 \overrightarrow{\vee} 5$ is represented by (1111), which is the number -1. Moreover, we have $\overrightarrow{\neg} 5 = -6$.

It is well-known that a set can be defined in pure Presburger arithmetic, i.e., without extensions such as bitvector operations, iff it is ultimately periodic [26,27]. A set $Z \subseteq \mathbb{Z}$ is ultimately periodic iff there exists a $p \geq 1$ (the period) such that the following holds:

- $\exists n^+ \geq 0. \forall n \geq n^+. n \in Z \Leftrightarrow n + p \in Z$
- $\exists n^- \leq 0. \forall n \leq n^-. n \in Z \Leftrightarrow n - p \in Z$

However, this does not hold for Presburger arithmetic with bitvector operations as defined above. Consider, for example, the formula

$$\mathsf{pow2}(x) := 1 + ((x - 1) \overrightarrow{\vee} x) = 2x \wedge x > 0$$

which holds iff x is a power of two. Since the set of satisfying assignments of pow2 is not ultimately periodic, QFPAbit is strictly more expressive than pure Presburger arithmetic. In fact, QFPAbit is as expressive as the quantifier-free fragment of the weak monadic second order logic of linear order (WMSO$_<$). The proof is based on the fact that for every WMSO$_<$ formula there exists an equivalent one whose atoms express singletons, set inclusion, and the successor function. Since these atoms are definable in QFPAbit, every WMSO$_<$ formula can be translated to an equivalent QFPAbit formula.

3 Translation of Quantifier-Free Presburger Arithmetic to AFAs

The relationship between QFPAbit formulas and AFAs is established via the two's complement encoding presented in the previous subsection. For that purpose, we associate with each integer variable $x \in V_{\mathbb{Z}}$ and each Boolean variable $p \in V_{\mathbb{B}}$ exactly one input variable $v \in V$ of an AFA. A word $w \in \Sigma^+$ with

$$w = \begin{pmatrix} b_{0,k} \\ \vdots \\ b_{n,k} \end{pmatrix} \cdots \begin{pmatrix} b_{0,1} \\ \vdots \\ b_{n,1} \end{pmatrix} \begin{pmatrix} b_{0,0} \\ \vdots \\ b_{n,0} \end{pmatrix}$$

is then interpreted as the assignment $\xi_w : V \to \mathbb{Z} \cup \mathbb{B}$, where $\xi_w(x_i) := \langle b_{i,k} \ldots b_{i,0} \rangle_{\mathbb{Z}}$ for $x_i \in V_{\mathbb{Z}}$ and $\xi_w(p_i) := b_{i,k}$ for $p_i \in V_{\mathbb{B}}$. Using this encoding scheme, the i-th row encodes the value of the i-th variable, and the j-th column is read by an automaton in the j-th step. Hence, the number of variables is finite and fixed, whereas their bitwidth is also finite, but arbitrarily large.

Since we have already shown how to perform the Boolean operations on AFAs, it remains to describe the construction of automata for relations and Boolean variables. Since the latter only depend on the most significant bits of a word, they can be easily translated to an AFA by considering only the initial formula, i.e., a formula p with $p \in V_{\mathbb{B}}$ is translated to the automaton $(\emptyset, V, \emptyset, v_p, \emptyset)$ with $v_p \in V$ (the third and the fifth component are the empty set, since the domain of the corresponding functions is empty). Hence, there is no overhead for translating the propositional part of a QFPAbit formula to an AFA.

The translation of arbitrary relations is slightly more difficult. As a first step, we separate the bitvector parts from the arithmetic parts. By introducing new variables, it is straightforward to construct an equisatisfiable formula that only contains relations of either type. In the same way, relations over more than three variables can be reduced to relations over at most three variables. For instance, the formula $(x \overrightarrow{\wedge} y) + z = s$ is satisfiable iff the formula $(x \overrightarrow{\wedge} y = t) \wedge (t + z = s)$ is satisfiable. Thus, it suffices to consider the following three types of relations: $\overrightarrow{\neg} x = y$, $x \overrightarrow{\wedge} y = z$, and $x + y \leq z$. In practice, however, this is rather inefficient, since it often requires a large number of auxiliary variables. Moreover, equations must be expressed by a conjunction of inequalities. For this reason, we consider relations of the following types, where T_1 and T_2 are terms containing only bitvector operations:

$$\text{(A)} \ T_1 = T_2 \qquad \text{(B)} \ \sum_{i=0}^{n} c_i x_i = c \qquad \text{(C)} \ \sum_{i=0}^{n} c_i x_i < c$$

Equations of type (A) can be translated to an AFA with a single state variable. Initially, this variable is set to true and at each step it is checked whether the inputs satisfy the equation. If the equation is not satisfied, the state variable is set to false and keeps this value until the last letter has been read. More precisely, let T_1' and T_2' be the terms obtained by replacing all integer variables x_i with the corresponding input variables v_i. Then, the equation $T_1 = T_2$ is translated to the AFA $(\{q\}, V, \delta, I, F)$ with $\delta(q) \equiv I \equiv q \wedge (T_1' \leftrightarrow T_2')$ and $F(q) \equiv 1$ ($\equiv$ denotes equivalence of propositional formulas).

The construction of DFAs from linear arithmetic constraints over natural numbers has already been presented in [4] and extended in [5] to deal with integers. The idea is to read the input from left to right, i.e., starting with the most significant bits, and to keep track of the value of the left-hand side of an equation (inequality) as successive bits are read. Thus, each state corresponds to an integer γ that represents the current value. The next state is then defined by $\gamma' = 2\gamma + \sum_{i=0}^{n} c_i b_i$, where $(b_n, \ldots, b_0)$ is the input vector. For an equation, the final state is uniquely determined by its right-hand side, i.e., the constant c. Similarly, for an inequality, a state is final iff its value is less than c. Moreover, it was shown in [5] that there always exists an $\alpha \in \mathbb{N}$ such that $|\gamma| > \alpha$ implies $|\gamma'| > |\gamma|$. Thus, all states with $|\gamma| > |c|$ can be collapsed into a single nonaccepting state. As a result, there are only finitely many states. More precisely, the number of states is bounded by $O(\log_2 |c| \cdot \sum_{i=0}^{n} |c_i|)$ [5].

In contrast to [5], our approach is based on reading the input from right to left when considering DFAs (the corresponding AFAs still read from left to right, and thus, the most significant bits that determine the signs can be easily encoded in the initial formulas). In many cases, this allows us to detect conflicts very early. For example, given an equation $\sum_{i=0}^{n} c_i x_i = c$ with c_i even and c odd, it is clear that the least significant bit of the sum is always zero. Thus, the equation is unsatisfiable which can be detected after reading the right-most input vector. Let us first consider the translation of equations. Given a term $T = \left(\sum_{i=0}^{n} c_i x_i \right) - c$, the translation is based on the following recursion ($T \cong_k 0$ holds iff T is divisible by k):

$$T = 0 \Leftrightarrow T \cong_2 0 \wedge \lfloor T/2 \rfloor = 0 \tag{1}$$

Unwinding this equation is essentially equivalent to checking whether the bits of the sum (first conjunct) and the carry (second conjunct) are zero. Hence, by reading the input from right to left, we do not use the states of an AFA to store the current value of the sum, but to store the result of the division, i.e., the carry.

Before we can construct an AFA for an equation or inequality, we must determine the number of required state variables (since in [5] the states are represented explicitly instead of symbolically, they can be constructed on-the-fly). For that purpose, we have to compute the maximal (minimal) carry that can occur while reading a word.

Theorem 1. *Given a relation $\sum_{i=0}^{n} c_i x_i \bowtie c$ with $\bowtie \in \{=, <\}$, let $c_{\max}$ and $c_{\min}$ denote the sum of the positive and negative coefficients, respectively. Then, the following holds for the maximal carry $k_{\max}$ and the minimal carry $k_{\min}$:*

$$k_{\max} = \begin{cases} c_{\max} - 1 & \text{if } c_{\max} + c > 1 \\ -c & \text{otherwise} \end{cases} \qquad k_{\min} = \begin{cases} c_{\min} & \text{if } c_{\min} + c < 0 \\ -c & \text{otherwise} \end{cases}$$

Proof. In the worst case, either only variables with positive or with negative coefficients contribute to the carry. Hence, the sequence of maximal (minimal) carries is $x_{i+1} := f(x_i)$ starting with $x_0 := -c$, where $f(x) = \lfloor (x + A)/2 \rfloor$ for $A = c_{\max}$ ($A = c_{\min}$). Note that f is monotonic, since it is composed of the monotonic functions $\lambda x.x + A$, $\lambda x.x/2$, and $\lambda x.\lfloor x \rfloor$. Thus, the sequence is monotonically increasing if $x_0 \leq f(x_0)$ and monotonically decreasing if $x_0 \geq f(x_0)$. Moreover, f has two fixpoints, namely a greatest fixpoint $\nu x.f = A$ and a least fixpoint $\mu x.f = A - 1$. In order to determine

$k_{max} := \max\{x_i \mid i \geq 0\}$, we have to distinguish between two cases: If $x_0 < f(x_0)$, i.e., $-c < \lfloor(-c + c_{max})/2\rfloor \Leftrightarrow c_{max} + c > 1$, then $\lim_{i \to \infty} x_i = \mu x.f = A - 1$, and hence, $k_{max} = c_{max} - 1$. Otherwise, the sequence is monotonically decreasing and converges to A so that $k_{max} = x_0 = -c$. The proof for k_{min} is analog. $\square$

Thus, the number of bits required to store the carries is $m := \max(||k_{max}||, ||k_{min}||)$, where $||.|| : \mathbb{Z} \to \mathbb{N}$ yields the number of bits required to represent an integer in two's complement encoding.

Definition 4 (Translating Equations to AFAs). *Given a set of integer variables* $V_{\mathbb{Z}} = \{x_0, \ldots, x_n\}$, *let* $V := \{v_0, \ldots, v_n\}$ *be the set of input variables. Then, an equation* $\sum_{i=0}^{n} c_i x_i = c$ *is translated to an AFA* (Q, V, δ, I, F) *with* $m + 1$ *state variables* $Q = \{q_0, \ldots, q_m\}$ *such that the following holds, where* $d := \sum_{i=0}^{n} c_i v_i$:

- $\langle \delta(q_m), \ldots, \delta(q_1) \rangle_{\mathbb{Z}} = \langle q_m, \ldots, q_1 \rangle_{\mathbb{Z}} + \lfloor d/2 \rfloor$
- $\delta(q_0) \equiv (q_0 \wedge d \cong_2 0)$
- $I \equiv (\langle q_m, \ldots, q_1 \rangle_{\mathbb{Z}} - \lfloor d/2 \rfloor = 0 \wedge q_0)$
- $\langle F(q_m), \ldots, F(q_1) \rangle_{\mathbb{Z}} = -c$
- $F(q_0) = 1$

An AFA constructed according to the above definition essentially implements the successive application of Equation (1). Given a word with k letters, we obtain the following formula by unwinding the equation, where q_0 represents the conjunction of the sum bits at positions $0 \leq i < k$ and $\langle q_m, \ldots, q_1 \rangle_{\mathbb{Z}}$ the carry at step k:

$$\underbrace{T \cong_2 0 \wedge (T/2) \cong_2 0 \wedge \cdots \wedge (T/2^{k-1}) \cong_2 0}_{q_0} \wedge \underbrace{\lfloor T/2^k \rfloor = 0}_{\langle q_m, \ldots, q_1 \rangle_{\mathbb{Z}}}$$

As an example, consider the equation $2x - y = 1$. With $c_{max} = 2$ and $c_{min} = -1$ we obtain $k_{max} = 1$ and $k_{min} = -1$. Since $m = \max(||1||, ||-1||) = \max(2, 1) = 2$, a total number of three state bits are required. The reachable part of the corresponding DFA is shown in Figure 1, where dotted transitions indicate the application of the initial formula. Note that this leads to nondeterministic behavior, since one might apply the initial formula, but one might also unwind the AFA once more. However, the remaining (large) part is always deterministic.

The translation of inequalities to AFAs is very similar to the translation of equations except that we do not have to check whether all bits of the sum are zero. It suffices to check whether the carry will eventually be negative. This can be easily done by examining the most significant bit which determines the sign in two's complement encoding.

Definition 5 (Translating Inequalities to AFAs). *Given a set of integer variables* $V_{\mathbb{Z}} = \{x_0, \ldots, x_n\}$, *let* $V := \{v_0, \ldots, v_n\}$ *be the set of input variables. Then, an inequality* $\sum_{i=0}^{n} c_i x_i < c$ *is translated to an AFA* (Q, V, δ, I, F) *with* m *state variables* $Q = \{q_1, \ldots, q_m\}$ *such that the following holds, where* $d := \sum_{i=0}^{n} c_i v_i$:

- $\langle \delta(q_m), \ldots, \delta(q_1) \rangle_{\mathbb{Z}} = \langle q_m, \ldots, q_1 \rangle_{\mathbb{Z}} + \lfloor d/2 \rfloor$
- $I \equiv (\langle q_m, \ldots, q_1 \rangle_{\mathbb{Z}} - \lfloor d/2 \rfloor < 0)$
- $\langle F(q_m), \ldots, F(q_1) \rangle_{\mathbb{Z}} = -c$

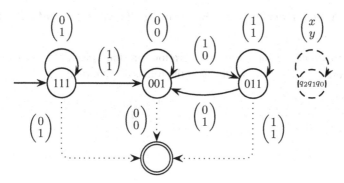

Fig. 1. Automaton for the equation $2x - y = 1$

4   Checking Emptiness of AFAs

Once we have constructed the AFA $\mathcal{A}_\varphi$ for a QFPAbit formula φ, checking satisfiability of φ amounts to checking whether the language of $\mathcal{A}_\varphi$ is empty. If so, there does not exist a satisfying assignment for φ. A straightforward way to check emptiness of an AFA is to unwind it according to Definition 2 without assigning values to the input variables. Hence, a formula is satisfiable iff there exists a $k \geq 0$ such that the formula obtained by unwinding the AFA is satisfiable. However, this only yields a semi-decision procedure that cannot be used directly to prove that a formula is unsatisfiable, since this would require infinitely many unwinding steps.

To solve this problem, we could make use of the fact that for finite state systems there always exists an upper bound on the required number of unwinding steps which is referred to as the completeness threshold in bounded model checking. In general, however, computing the completeness threshold is a nontrivial task and does not always yield a tight bound. On the other hand, regarding the special case of quantifier-free Presburger formulas, it is well-known that if a formula has a satisfying solution, there is one whose size, measured in the number of bits, is polynomially bounded in the size of the formula. This allows one to translate every quantifier-free Presburger formula to an equisatisfiable propositional formula of polynomial size [8] (in theory, this follows from the fact that deciding formulas of linear integer arithmetic is NP-complete [28]).

Unfortunately, computing an upper bound on the number of unwinding steps for checking emptiness of an AFA is hardly feasible in practice. This is due to the fact that QFPAbit is more expressive than quantifier-free Presburger arithmetic (cf. Section 2.2). In particular, if a formula contains bitvector operations, there may not even exist a polynomially sized model w.r.t. to the length of the formula. To prove this, let R_k be a family of formulas defined as follows with $k \geq 2$:

$$R_k := x > 0 \wedge \mathsf{pow2}\left(1 + \bigvee_{i=0}^{k-1} 2^i x\right) \wedge \bigwedge_{i=0}^{k-2} \bigwedge_{j=i+1}^{k-1} 2^i x \overrightarrow{\wedge} 2^j x = 0$$

Note that a formula $\mathsf{pow2}(f(x))$ can be easily translated to the equisatisfiable formula $\mathsf{pow2}(y) \wedge y = f(x)$. The models of R_k are characterized by the following lemma:

Lemma 1. *A natural number x is a model of R_k iff every k-th bit of x is one and all other bits are zero.*

Proof. The operands of the bitvector operations are multiples of x, each shifted by i bits to the left for $0 \leq i < k$, as shown in the following diagram:

x		0	x_n	$\ldots$	x_k	x_{k-1}	$\ldots$	$\ldots$	x_1	x_0	
$2x$		0	x_n	$\ldots$	x_k	x_{k-1}	$\ldots$	$\ldots$	x_1	x_0	0
					$\vdots$						
$2^{k-1}x$	0	x_n	$\ldots$	x_k	x_{k-1}	$\ldots$	$\ldots$	x_1	x_0	$\ldots$	0	0	0

First, we prove that a number $x = \langle 0, x_n, \ldots, x_0 \rangle_{\mathbb{Z}}$ is a model of R_k if $x_i = 1$ and $x_j = 0$ for all $0 \leq i, j \leq n$ such that $i \cong_k 0$ and $j \neq i$ holds. The first part of the conjunction is obviously satisfied, since the most significant bit of x is zero. The second part is also satisfied, since each column in the above diagram contains an x_i with $i \cong_k 0$. Thus, the result of the bitvector disjunction is a string of 1's and the increment of the corresponding number is a power of two. The third part of the conjunction performs a pairwise comparison of the rows to ensure that at most one bit is set in each column. Since the columns consist of exactly k elements, they cannot contain an x_i and an x_{i+k} with $i \cong_k 0$. Hence, this part is also satisfied. The reverse direction of the proof follows from the fact that this is the only assignment of the x_i's that satisfy the formula. Given an arbitrary x, we must have $x_0 = 1$ by the second part of the conjunction, $x_1 = \cdots = x_{k-1} = 0$ by the third part, and so on. $\square$

Theorem 2. *Given a satisfiable QFPAbit formula φ, the size of its smallest model, measured in the number of bits, is not polynomially bounded in the size of φ.*

Proof. Let $|\varphi|$ denote the size of a formula φ, where the size of a constant is measured in its number of bits. Then, we have $|R_k| \in O(k^3)$. Moreover, given that $p : \mathbb{N} \to \mathbb{N}$ is the sequence of prime numbers, it holds that $p(i) \sim i \cdot \ln i$ and $\prod_{i=1}^{n} p(i) \sim e^n$ [29]. We define $S_n := -2 \overrightarrow{\wedge} \bigwedge_{i=1}^{n} R_{p(i)}$ (the bitvector conjunction with -2 masks out the least significant bits) and obtain $|S_n| \in O(\sum_{i=1}^{n}(i \cdot \ln i)^3)$. Hence, the size of S_n is polynomially bounded by $O(n^4 (\ln n)^3)$. Note that a number x satisfies S_n iff every l-th bit of x is true and all other bits are zero, where $l = \prod_{i=1}^{n} p(i)$. Thus, the size of the smallest solution is $\Theta(e^n)$ which is not polynomially bounded by n. $\square$

For this reason, we use another approach which has been originally proposed for checking safety properties in bounded model checking [30]. As a major advantage, this approach uses an inductive style of reasoning and terminates as soon as possible, i.e., it does not suffer from non-tight bounds. Given a finite set of states $\mathcal{S}$, a complete transition relation $\mathcal{R} \subseteq S \times S$, and a set of initial states $\mathcal{I} \subseteq S$, let $\mathsf{path}(s_0 \ldots s_k)$ hold iff $(s_i, s_{i+1}) \in \mathcal{R}$ for all $0 \leq i < k$. Moreover, let $\mathsf{loopFree}(s_0 \ldots s_k)$ hold iff $\mathsf{path}(s_0 \ldots s_k)$ holds and $s_i \neq s_j$ for all $0 \leq i < j \leq k$. Then, the method presented in [30] aims at checking whether a property $\mathcal{P} \subseteq \mathcal{S}$ invariantly holds on all paths originating in $\mathcal{I}$ using the following induction scheme, where k denotes the induction depth:

base case: $s_0 \in \mathcal{I} \wedge \mathsf{path}(s_0 \ldots s_k) \to (\forall i.0 \leq i \leq k \to s_i \in \mathcal{P})$
induction step: $\mathsf{loopFree}(s_0 \ldots s_{k+1}) \wedge (\forall i.0 \leq i \leq k \to s_i \in \mathcal{P}) \to s_{k+1} \in \mathcal{P}$

The base case checks whether $\mathcal{P}$ holds on a path $s_0 \ldots s_k$, and the induction step checks whether this path can be extended without violating $\mathcal{P}$. Thus, $\mathcal{P}$ invariantly holds on all paths if both conditions are valid[3]. Note that the method is sound and complete for sufficiently large values of k (completeness follows simply speaking from the fact that every infinite path in a finite state system eventually contains a loop).

In order to prove that an AFA (Q, V, δ, I, F) is empty using induction, we show that the initial formula I never evaluates to true for the given assignment of the final states F, i.e., we set $\mathcal{P} := \neg I$. For that purpose, the AFA is iteratively unwound until the base case fails or the induction step holds. As mentioned previously, this does not require the introduction of new state variables due to the equational structure of AFAs. Instead, it suffices to replace the input variables with new variables at each step, since a path is uniquely determined by the read word. As a consequence, the size of the resulting formulas is reduced significantly which simplifies the check for satisfiability.

The algorithm for checking emptiness of an AFA is shown in Figure 2, where a set of paths is viewed as a tuple of propositional formulas. The current set of paths and their prefixes are stored in the list unwind. Remembering the suffixes is necessary to update the variable loopFree when a path is extended. The variable reject corresponds to the formula $\forall i.0 \leq i \leq k \rightarrow s_i \in \mathcal{P}$ of the induction scheme, where $\mathcal{P} := \neg I$. That is, reject holds iff a path and its suffixes are nonaccepting. As the first step, the algorithm checks whether I is unsatisfiable. If so, the AFA is clearly empty. Otherwise, induction is applied for increasing depths, starting with paths of length one. If the base case fails, a counterexample has been found and the algorithm returns false. Otherwise, the current set of paths is extended and the induction step is checked. If the induction step also holds, it follows that the AFA is empty. If it does not hold, the procedure is repeated for an increased induction depth.

5   Experimental Results

The approach presented in this paper has been implemented in our symbolic model checker Beryl which is part of the Averest framework[4]. We performed two sets of experiments, one with a number of benchmarks contained in Averest and one with the quantifier-free linear integer arithmetic (QF_LIA) benchmarks of the satisfiability modulo theories library (SMT-LIB) [31]. The former are given in our synchronous language Quartz and were compiled to symbolically encoded transition systems. As the base logics, our compiler supports propositional logic as well as Presburger arithmetic with bitvector operations. The generated transition systems are essentially the same for both logics, except that arithmetic operations on integers are translated to the corresponding operations on fixed sized bitvectors when using propositional logic as the base logic.

The results for the Averest benchmarks are shown in Table 1. For each benchmark we proved a liveness property (first row) and disproved a safety property (second row). All runtimes are given in seconds and were measured on a Xeon processor with 3GHz.

---

[3] As described in [30], there exists a dual type of induction scheme that can be thought of as working in the backward direction. For the sake of simplicity, however, we restrict ourselves to the forward case. Nevertheless, our implementation supports both approaches.

[4] http://www.averest.org

```
function empty(Q, V, δ, I, F)
    if ¬sat(I) then return true;
    reject := ¬I;
    unwind := cons((q₀, ..., qₘ), []);
    loopFree := true;
    loop
        // base case
        if ¬valid(reject[qᵢ/F(qᵢ)]^{0≤i≤m}) then return false;
        // unwind
        (w₀, ..., wₙ) := createFreshVariables(n + 1);
        (r₀, ..., rₘ) := head(unwind);
        (s₀, ..., sₘ) := (δ(q₀)[qᵢ/rᵢ, vⱼ/wⱼ]^{0≤i≤m}_{0≤j≤n}, ..., δ(qₘ)[qᵢ/rᵢ, vⱼ/wⱼ]^{0≤i≤m}_{0≤j≤n});
        u := unwind;
        repeat
            (t₀, ..., tₘ) := head(u);
            loopFree := loopFree ∧ ⋁ᵢ₌₀ᵐ sᵢ ⊕ tᵢ;
            u := tail(u);
        until u = [];
        unwind := cons((s₀, ..., sₘ), unwind);
        rejectNext := reject[qᵢ/sᵢ]^{0≤i≤m};
        // induction step
        if valid(loopFree ∧ reject → rejectNext) then return true;
        reject := reject ∧ rejectNext;
    end;
end;
```

Fig. 2. Algorithm for checking emptiness of an AFA using induction

A dash indicates that a benchmark could not be solved in less than ten minutes. The first two columns show the runtimes for bounded model checking (BMC) using AFAs and DFAs. The latter were constructed by the method presented in [5] and use a semi-symbolic encoding, i.e., the states are represented explicitly and the transitions symbolically by means of BDDs. Moreover, we measured the runtimes for global model checking (GMC) using DFAs (GMC is not possible for AFAs, since they do not support image computation). As can be seen, AFAs are much more efficient than DFAs for BMC, and in many cases also more efficient than GMC/DFA. For BubbleSort, however, BMC/AFA is significantly slower which is due to the fact that this benchmark requires a high bound in BMC. Finally, we verified the benchmarks using Cadence SMV and NuSMV for integers with fixed bitwidths (dynamic variable reordering was enabled). One might argue that such a comparison is like comparing apples and oranges, particularly since the results for AFAs are based on bounded model checking, while the results for SMV/NuSMV were obtained using global model checking[5]. Nevertheless,

---

[5] Unfortunately, neither SMV nor NuSMV was able to check the specifications generated by our compiler using bounded model checking, even though the specifications are simple safety and liveness properties.

Table 1. Runtimes for Averest benchmarks

Benchmark	Beryl			NuSMV				SMV			
	BMC AFA	BMC DFA	GMC DFA	8 bit	16 bit	24 bit	32 bit	8 bit	16 bit	24 bit	32 bit
BinarySearch	0,3	-	0,4	16,7	24,9	132,8	182,9	2,3	12,1	52,3	99,8
	0,2	22,4	1,0	18,7	148,1	-	-	12,6	-	-	-
BubbleSort	117,3	-	1,3	3,1	27,7	104,7	347,0	0,1	0,1	0,1	0,1
	102,6	-	19,5	9,6	-	-	-	2,4	77,6	45,3	93,3
FastMax	0,1	0,8	0,2	1,3	26,9	47,2	398,9	0,0	0,0	0,1	0,1
	0,3	1,8	1,8	3,6	-	-	-	-	-	-	-
LinearSearch	0,4	329,7	0,2	1,4	6,9	20,3	34,0	0,9	7,7	15,6	38,9
	0,1	0,1	0,3	2,2	11,8	26,1	58,1	2,2	8,4	19,4	40,8
MinMax	0,6	-	1,5	5,6	254,1	-	-	0,0	0,0	0,1	0,1
	0,3	148,9	71,4	92,4	-	-	-	104,3	-	-	-
ParallelPrefixSum	1,3	-	39,6	4,1	37,5	235,9	-	0,1	0,1	0,1	0,1
	7,3	-	-	-	-	-	-	453,7	266,5	-	-
ParallelSearch	0,2	-	8,9	1,4	8,7	11,0	40,6	1,1	1,8	5,7	29,7
	60,6	541,7	8,6	3,7	22,4	17,6	37,1	1,9	3,7	11,1	19,5
Partition	1,1	-	14,0	147,0	-	-	-	39,7	208,2	-	-
	0,4	-	116,6	256,1	-	-	-	112,1	-	-	-
SortingNetwork4	0,2	149,7	0,3	1,0	35,5	143,1	344,8	0,0	0,0	0,0	0,1
	0,1	174,7	0,9	74,5	-	-	-	-	243,5	-	-
SortingNetwork8	3,0	-	-	534,2	-	-	-	0,0	0,1	0,1	0,1
	2,1	-	-	-	-	-	-	-	-	-	-

we list the results to compare our approach with sophisticated model checkers that are frequently used in hardware verification.

The results for the SMT-LIB benchmarks are shown in Table 2, where we compared Beryl with CVC Lite 2.5[6], MathSat 3.3.1[7], and Yices 0.2[8]. We list only those benchmarks that could be solved by at least one of the tools within five minutes. As can be seen, the runtimes largely differ depending on the benchmark. For example, our approach clearly outperforms all other tools for the SIMPLEBIT_ADDER benchmarks that could be solved up to size 10 using Beryl, whereas the other tools could only solve them for size 5 (CVC Lite), 7 (MathSat), and 8 (Yices). For the FISCHER benchmarks, however, the situation is converse. These benchmarks are most efficiently solved using MathSat and Yices. For the remaining benchmarks, Beryl can in many cases compete with the best tool and is usually much faster than the slowest tool.

To check satisfiability of a formula, our implementation currently constructs an AFA $\mathcal{A}$ for the whole formula and then checks whether $\mathcal{A}$ is empty. Clearly, this is more than necessary if the result only depends on some subformulas. A better approach is to check subformulas lazily, i.e., by need. For that purpose, MathSat and Yices use an extension of the DPLL procedure for propositional logic that often allows one to restrict the search for a satisfying assignment to a small number of subformulas. As an example, given the formula $x \geq 0 \land (p \lor x + y = z)$, it suffices to prove that $x \geq 0$ is satisfiable, provided

---

[6] http://www.cs.nyu.edu/acsys/cvcl/
[7] http://mathsat.itc.it/
[8] http://yices.csl.sri.com/

Table 2. Runtimes for SMT-LIB benchmarks

Benchmark	Status	Beryl	CVC Lite	MathSat	Yices
ckt_PROP0_tf_15	sat	< 1	24.9	42.2	< 1
ckt_PROP0_tf_20	sat	< 1	-	66.0	< 1
FISCHER5-2-fair	unsat	20.1	1.3	< 1	< 1
FISCHER5-3-fair	unsat	2.3	2.9	< 1	< 1
FISCHER5-4-fair	unsat	4.2	5.4	< 1	< 1
FISCHER5-5-fair	unsat	96.9	9.6	< 1	< 1
FISCHER5-6-fair	unsat	-	15.1	< 1	< 1
FISCHER5-7-fair	unsat	-	29.5	< 1	< 1
FISCHER5-8-fair	unsat	-	67.6	1.9	< 1
FISCHER5-9-fair	unsat	-	116.4	4.1	< 1
FISCHER5-10-fair	sat	38.0	-	1.8	< 1
MULTIPLIER_2	unsat	< 1	2.3	< 1	< 1
MULTIPLIER_3	unsat	< 1	32.1	< 1	< 1
MULTIPLIER_4	unsat	< 1	172.9	1.2	< 1
MULTIPLIER_5	unsat	1.3	-	7.1	< 1
MULTIPLIER_6	unsat	5.6	-	42.1	1.0
MULTIPLIER_7	unsat	33.7	-	255.4	10.3
MULTIPLIER_8	unsat	-	-	-	54.3
MULTIPLIER_64	sat	4.3	-	< 1	< 1
MULTIPLIER_PRIME_2	sat	< 1	abort	< 1	< 1
MULTIPLIER_PRIME_3	sat	< 1	segfault	< 1	< 1
MULTIPLIER_PRIME_4	sat	< 1	wrong	< 1	< 1
MULTIPLIER_PRIME_5	sat	< 1	abort	< 1	< 1
MULTIPLIER_PRIME_6	sat	< 1	-	< 1	< 1
MULTIPLIER_PRIME_7	sat	< 1	segfault	< 1	< 1
MULTIPLIER_PRIME_8	sat	< 1	-	< 1	< 1
MULTIPLIER_PRIME_9	sat	2.2	-	< 1	< 1
MULTIPLIER_PRIME_10	sat	2.6	-	< 1	< 1
MULTIPLIER_PRIME_11	sat	3.6	-	< 1	< 1
MULTIPLIER_PRIME_12	sat	4.8	-	1.0	< 1
MULTIPLIER_PRIME_13	sat	9.9	segfault	3.2	< 1
MULTIPLIER_PRIME_14	sat	25.6	-	6.2	< 1
MULTIPLIER_PRIME_15	sat	30.6	-	21.8	< 1
MULTIPLIER_PRIME_16	sat	16.1	-	67.3	< 1
MULTIPLIER_PRIME_32	sat	2.5	segfault	< 1	< 1
MULTIPLIER_PRIME_64	sat	4.3	-	< 1	< 1
SIMPLEBITADDER_COMPOSE_2	unsat	< 1	< 1	< 1	< 1
SIMPLEBITADDER_COMPOSE_3	unsat	< 1	3.8	< 1	< 1
SIMPLEBITADDER_COMPOSE_4	unsat	< 1	51.6	1.1	< 1
SIMPLEBITADDER_COMPOSE_5	unsat	< 1	70.0	5.3	< 1
SIMPLEBITADDER_COMPOSE_6	unsat	1.2	-	26.9	< 1
SIMPLEBITADDER_COMPOSE_7	unsat	7.2	-	231.3	5.2
SIMPLEBITADDER_COMPOSE_8	unsat	23.7	-	-	94.3
SIMPLEBITADDER_COMPOSE_9	unsat	56.2	-	-	-
SIMPLEBITADDER_COMPOSE_10	unsat	115.0	-	-	-
wisa1	sat	3.4	8.8	223.5	< 1
wisa2	unsat	-	113.8	-	< 1
wisa3	sat	6.4	226.0	-	< 1
wisa4	sat	4.1	28.0	-	1.1
wisa5	unsat	-	-	-	6.1

that p has already been set to true. Of course, such a lazy decision procedure can also be used with the approach presented in this paper to check arithmetic and bitvector formulas on demand.

6 Summary and Conclusion

We proposed a decision procedure for quantifier-free Presburger arithmetic with bitvector operations. The translation to alternating automata allows us to benefit from efficient SAT solvers for checking emptiness of the automata using induction. This is necessary, since formulas of the considered logic cannot always be reduced to a propositional formula of polynomial size. The experimental results show that our approach can compete with state-of-the-art decision procedures and is sometimes even more efficient. We plan to combine the use of AFAs with quantifier elimination in order to support quantified Presburger arithmetic. For that purpose, the translation has to be extended in order to deal with congruences that occur during quantifier elimination.

References

1. Presburger, M.: Über die Vollständigkeit eines gewissen Systems der Arithmetik ganzer Zahlen, in welchem die Addition als einzige Operation hervortritt. In Leja, F., ed.: Sprawoz-danie z I Kongresu Matematyków Krajów Słowiańskich, Warszawa 1929 (Comptes–rendus du I Congrès des Mathématiciens des Pays Slaves, Varsovie 1929), Warszawa (1929) 92–101 (supplement on p. 395)
2. Lahiri, S., Seshia, S., Bryant, R.: Modeling and verification of out-of-order microprocessors in UCLID. In Aagaard, M., O'Leary, J., eds.: Conference on Formal Methods in Computer Aided Design (FMCAD). Volume 2517 of LNCS., Portland, USA, Springer (2002) 142–159
3. Büchi, J.: Weak second order arithmetic and finite automata. Z. Math. Logik Grundlagen Math. **6** (1960) 66–92
4. Boudet, A., Comon, H.: Diophantine equations, Presburger arithmetic and finite automata. In Kirchner, H., ed.: Colloquium on Trees in Algebra and Programming (CAAP). Volume 1059 of LNCS., Linköping, Sweden, Springer (1996) 30–43
5. Wolper, P., Boigelot, B.: On the construction of automata from linear arithmetic constraints. In Graf, S., Schwartzbach, M., eds.: Conference on Tools and Algorithms for the Construction and Analysis of Systems (TACAS). Volume 1785 of LNCS., Berlin, Germany, Springer (2000) 1–19
6. Klaedtke, F.: On the automata size for Presburger arithmetic. Technical Report 186, Institute of Computer Science at Freiburg University (2003)
7. Ganesh, V., Berezin, S., Dill, D.: Deciding Presburger arithmetic by model checking and comparisons with other methods. In Aagaard, M., O'Leary, J., eds.: Conference on Formal Methods in Computer Aided Design (FMCAD). Volume 2517 of LNCS., Portland, USA, Springer (2002) 171–186
8. Seshia, S., Bryant, R.: Deciding quantifier-free Presburger formulas using parameterized solution bounds. Logical Methods in Computer Science **1**(2:6) (2005) 1–26
9. Boigelot, B.: The Liège automata-based symbolic handler (LASH) (2006) http://www.montefiore.ulg.ac.be/~boigelot/research/lash/.
10. Janicic, P., Green, I., Bundy, A.: A comparison of decision procedures in Presburger arithmetic. Research Paper 872, University of Edinburgh (1997)

11. Shiple, T., Kukula, J., Ranjan, R.: A comparison of Presburger engines for EFSM reachability. In Hu, A., Vardi, M., eds.: Conference on Computer Aided Verification (CAV). Volume 1427 of LNCS., Vancouver, BC, Canada, Springer (1998) 280–292
12. Schuele, T., Schneider, K.: Symbolic model checking by automata based set representation. In Ruf, J., ed.: Methoden und Beschreibungssprachen zur Modellierung und Verifikation von Schaltungen und Systemen, Tübingen, Germany, GI/ITG/GMM, Shaker (2002) 229–238
13. Strichman, O.: On solving Presburger and linear arithmetic with SAT. In Aagaard, M., O'Leary, J., eds.: Conference on Formal Methods in Computer Aided Design (FMCAD). Volume 2517 of LNCS., Portland, USA, Springer (2002) 160–170
14. Kroening, D., Ouaknine, J., Seshia, S., Strichman, O.: Abstraction-based satisfiability solving of Presburger arithmetic. In Alur, R., Peled, D., eds.: Conference on Computer Aided Verification (CAV). Volume 3114 of LNCS., Boston, MA, USA, Springer (2004) 308–320
15. Yu, S.: Regular languages. In Rozenberg, G., Salomaa, A., eds.: Handbook of Formal Languages. Volume 1. Springer (1997) 41–110
16. Fellah, A., Jürgensen, H., Yu, S.: Constructions for alternating finite automata. International Journal of Computer Mathematics **35** (1990) 117–132
17. Fellah, A.: Equations and regular-like expressions for AFA. International Journal of Computer Mathematics **51** (1994) 157–172
18. Chandra, A., Kozen, D., Stockmeyer, L.: Alternation. Journal of the ACM **28**(1) (1981) 114–133
19. Brzozowski, J., Leiss, E.: On equations for regular languages, finite automata, and sequential networks. Theoretical Computer Science **10** (1980) 19–35
20. Leiss, E.: Succinct representation of regular languages by Boolean automata. Theoretical Computer Science **13** (1981) 323–330
21. Leiss, E.: Succinct representation of regular languages by Boolean automata II. Theoretical Computer Science **38** (1985) 133–136
22. Huerter, S., Salomaa, K., Wu, X., Yu, S.: Implementing reversed alternating finite automaton (r-AFA) operations. In Champarnaud, J.M., Maurel, D., Ziadi, D., eds.: International Workshop on Implementating Automata (WIA). Volume 1660 of LNCS., Rouen, France, Springer (1999) 69–81
23. Salomaa, K., Wu, X., Yu, S.: Efficient implementation of regular languages using r-AFA. In Wood, D., Yu, S., eds.: International Workshop on Implementing Automata (WIA). Volume 1436 of LNCS., London, Ontario, Canada, Springer (1998) 176–184
24. Salomaa, K., Wu, X., Yu, S.: Efficient implementation of regular languages using reversed alternating finite automata. Theoretical Computer Science **231**(1) (2000) 103–111
25. Tuerk, T., Schneider, K.: Relationship between alternating omega-automata and symbolically represented nondeterministic omega-automata. Internal Report 340, Department of Computer Science, University of Kaiserslautern, http://kluedo.ub.uni-kl.de (2005)
26. Bès, A.: A survey of arithmetical definability. Bulletin of the Société Mathématique Belgique (2002) 1–54
27. Bruyere, V., Hansel, G., Michaux, C., Villemaire, R.: Logic and p-recognizable sets of integers. Bulletin of the Société Mathématique Belgique **1** (1994) 191–238
28. von zur Gathen, J., Sieveking, M.: A bound on solutions of linear integer equalities and inequalities. Proceedings of the American Mathematical Society **72**(1) (1978) 155–158
29. Hardy, G., Wright, E.: An introduction to the theory of numbers. Oxford University Press (1979)
30. Sheeran, M., Singh, S., Stålmarck, G.: Checking safety properties using induction and a SAT-solver. In Hunt, W., Johnson, S., eds.: Conference on Formal Methods in Computer Aided Design (FMCAD). Volume 1954 of LNCS., Austin, Texas, USA, Springer (2000) 108–125
31. Ranise, S., Tinelli, C.: The satisfiability modulo theories library (SMT-LIB) (2006) http://goedel.cs.uiowa.edu/smtlib.

Smart-Lint: Improving the Verification Flow

Itai Yarom and Viji Patil

Intel Corporation
Itai.Yarom@Intel.com, Viji.Patil@Intel.com

Abstract. As design features increase and sizes shrink and more transistors are squeezed into a system-on-a-chip (SoC) IC, the sheer number of on-chip devices far outstrips a design team's ability to harness the full benefits of all the transistors. Furthermore, according to a Synopsys survey, one of the main reasons for bugs in first silicon designs is logic bugs. To address those needs the EDA community provides a large set of tools for the logic designer that includes simulation, formal verification and linting among others. To fully benefit from these tools, the logic design teams should use them as one environment rather than as separate tools. In this paper, we will demonstrate how this usage of linting, simulation and formal verification as one environment can provide a solution that is greater than the sum of its parts. Several groups at Intel from the Digital Enterprise Group (DEG) and the Mobility Group (MG) are reporting good results by using this flow.

1 Introduction

The complexity of designs drives the need to introduce new tools and flows for the supporting verification efforts. Those new techniques include assertion based verification (ABV) [2, 8], coverage driven verification (CDV) [1] and formal property verification (FPV). New languages and verification languages have been introduced such as Open Verification Library (OVL), SystemVerilog assertions (SVA), 'e', Vera and Property Specification Language (PSL) [3, 4, 5, 6 and 7]. Those new technologies can improve the verification flow. On the other hand, more tools and technology added to the verification flow means more work (unless they are used efficiently). We believe that front-end tools will experience the same transition as in the implementation flow. In the implementation flow we used to have several tools for different parts of the flow (e.g., synthesis, place and route, DFT, static timing). However, those tools are being replaced by one implementation tool that generates GDSII from the RTL.

In this paper we propose the first step in the direction of having one front-end tool. We present how the integration of a lint tool, with simulation and formal property verification tools can provide value that is greater than its parts. The glue between those tools is assertions. The assertions can capture the questions of structural analysis of the lint tool, and answer them using the logic verification tools (i.e., simulation and FPV).

This idea is not new. Mentor (0-in) is using assertion synthesis to verify clock domain crossing (CDC) issues [9]. Other companies use assertion promotion for

E. Bin, A. Ziv, and S. Ur (Eds.): HVC 2006, LNCS 4383, pp. 81–91, 2007.

verifying the correctness of false-paths and multi-cycle paths [10, 11, and 12]. Our contribution to the following is threefold. First, we use the assertion promotion technique to provide an enhanced verification environment, by combining the particular usages that we mentioned above. Furthermore, we extend this concept to new areas like lint violation refinement. In addition to that, we provided additional assertions to improve the existing verification flow. For example, we added a missing synchronization checker to the clock domain crossing (CDC) checkers.

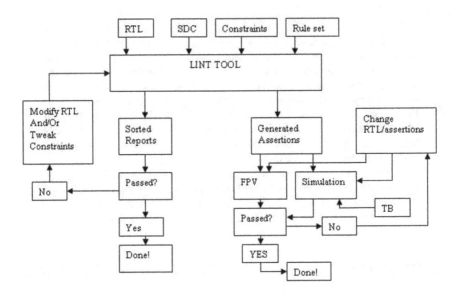

Fig. 1. The Smart-Lint flow

2 Smart-Lint

The idea of smart lint is to provide a single front-end environment like the silicon implementation environment used for backend. The silicon implementation area underwent a complete change. Several years ago we had several tools that when combined together provided the silicon implementation flow. For example, we had a synthesis tool, place and route tool, static timing analysis tool and extraction tool. However, today we have a silicon implementation environment that combines all those engines and capabilities together. We still have the above engines under the hood, but we have a common database that they all work on. And using the entire silicon implementation environment provides better performance over using each element separately. The question is how can we perform the same transition to the front-end environment?

To perform this transition we take advantage of three key tools, Lint, simulation and formal property verification (FPV). Those tools have different capabilities. The Lint understands the design structure, but it doesn't understand their behavior. The simulation and formal tools understand the design behavior, without needing to know the structure.

For example, a lint tool can detect synchronization structures, which can be as simple as a 2-FF synchronization scheme. However, it cannot verify that the target client receives all the data passing through the synchronization. This can be verified using simulation or formal techniques.

We use assertions as the glue between the lint and the simulation and the formal tools. Assertions provide the ability to ask questions on the design behavior. Returning to our example, the lint tool wants to verify the data stability passing in the 2-FF synchronizer. Therefore, it can generate an assertion that checks that the data-in of the synchronizer is stable long enough so that the data out of the synchronizer will detect it.

The smart-lint technology is independent of the lint, simulation and formal tools being used. The same technology can be used with tools from a mix of vendors. However, we believe that in the future, this kind of technology will be part of the front-end environment and will provide benefit from using one vendor environment. In the next sub-section we describe the structure of the smart-lint environment, and follow with three usages of this technique in different design areas.

2.1 Smart-Lint Implementation

There are several options on how to implement the smart-lint flow. We chose a flow that will enable us to easily plug it in our verification environment and to be able to seamlessly plug-in any Lint tool we desired (see figure 1). To achieve this we use an XML based uniform violation report format as an input for the environment. Therefore, for plugging a new Lint tool to the environment you need to provide the violations in this format. Synopsys' LEDA and Atrenta's SpyGlass have an API interface for generating reports in the desire format, which is very useful in this case. An alternative solution is to convert the lint output to the desired format, which is less convenient and adds another step to the flow.

The next step is to identify the violations that we want to further explore and what kind of checks we want to perform. For example, for missing synchronization message we want to add a checker that checks whether a synchronizer is needed. Another example can be of a checker that verifies that there is no contention on a tri-state bus.

To generate the checkers out of the violation report, the tool needs to understand where this block is placed in the verification design. Therefore, the designer provides a prefix from the top of the verification to the lint top module. This prefix is added to the signal names that appear in the violation report. The checkers can be generated as one verification module or in separate modules divided by the checkers type or by hierarchy. Dividing the checker modules can be useful for controlling which checkers we want to use. The checker files can be added to the verification environment, which can be a simulation or formal based environment. Adding the checkers to the verification environment is easy because of the full hierarchy name of the signals.

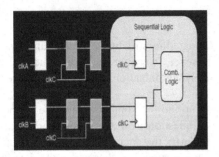

Fig. 2. An example of reconvergence of two synchronizations

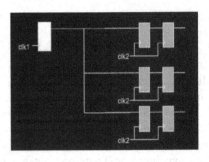

Fig. 3. Fanouts into multiple synchronizers

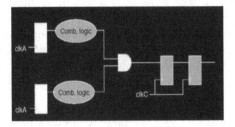

Fig. 4. An example of glitch scenario

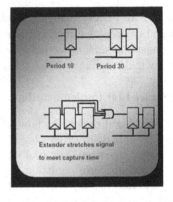

Fig. 5. An example of fast to slow clock synchronization

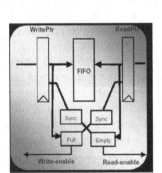

Fig. 6. An example of usage of FIFO for synchronization

2.2 Clock Domain Crossing

Typical modern chips have many clock domains, driven by SOC integration (more asynchronous clocks) and higher clock frequencies (skewed synchronous clocks).Many design teams are being forced to redesign to reduce domains and risk. Poor management of Clock-Domain Crossing (CDC) signals is a major cause of re-spins. Traditional verification techniques do not work for CDC signals. CDC problems are subtle, will occur in hardware, and are complex to debug.

Therefore there is a need to specifically verify and automate CDC verification, thereby significantly reducing the risk of CDC related silicon respins. Common CDC scenarios that need to be verified are listed:

- CDC Reconvergence: Data correlation problems in downstream logic can cause functional errors (see figure 2).
- Fanouts into multiple synchronizers: One signal that is being synchronized several times can result in correlation issues of the synchronized data (see figure 3).
- Glitch scenario: Combinational logic between flip-flops can cause a glitch to propagate into downstream logic causing functional errors (see figure 4).
- Fast to slow clock: Signal is synchronized correctly for meta-stability but can drop fast pulses from source domain. Example illustrates general data-hold check (see figure 5).
- Gray Code check: to resolve time racing between the different signals of a bus, a Gray code technique will ensure that only one bit of the bus changes at each time. Furthermore, this behavior can occur with two signals that are synchronized separately and drive the same logic (see figure 2). Other synchronization schemes include handshake and FIFO synchronization (see figure 6).

How to handle legacy code with a lot of false violations of missing synchronization? Most Lint tools that perform CDC checks (and stand alone CDC tools) use a basic control file, which is used to set controls on how to run CDC analysis. The warnings produced can help you further refine your control file and allow the tool to produce meaningful results. For example, by adding a checker that will identify signals that are not synchronized and do change. Those signals need to be synchronized. However, we don't need to use synchronization for signals that are static. To perform this check we use the assert_missing_sync checker, that checks whether a signal changes during the simulation or not. By defining this checker as a synchronizer we move the violation from the lint to the verification tools, and the verification tools notify only on the potential bugs.

To handle reconvergence and Gray code cases, using the OVL assert_one_hot checker in the following way can work (which we bundle in a new checker assert_gray_code):

```
assert_one_hot #(0,SIZE) aoh1 (clk, !rst_l,
                        decoded_bus^prev_decoded_bus);

always @(posedge clk) prev_decoded_bus<=decoded_bus;
```

For checker that there is no data lost, we use an assert_data_stable checker, that ensures that the data is stable for the desired period of clock cycles (provided as a parameter). Other checkers can be used for different synchronization algorithms, like handshake.

2.3 Lint Closure

How to automatically refine the lint violation list to show only the important violations? One of the common comments on lint tools is how can we refine the tool reports in a way they will identify the important issues. Several techniques were used, including sorting the violations in groups, different level of errors and so on. However, the solution that was often used was a human sorting the violations and marking the important ones. Can we improve this work of violation sorting?

Table 1. The checkers that can be generated automatically

Automatic Assertions	Class	Checker	Monitor	Fully automatic
Dead code	Lint	Yes	No	Yes
Bus contention	Lint	Yes	No	Yes
FSM deadlock	Lint	Yes	No	Yes
Uninitialized FSM variables	Lint	Yes	No	Yes*
Unreachable FSM states	Lint	Yes	No	Yes
Full-case synopsys pragma violation	Lint	Yes	No	Yes
Parallel-case synopsys pragma violation	Lint	Yes	No	Yes
Uninitialized memory	Lint	Yes	No	Yes
FIFO monitor	Monitor	No	Yes	No
SRAM monitor	Monitor	No	Yes	No
Missing synchronizers	CDC	Yes	Yes	Yes
Gray-code	CDC	Yes	Yes	Yes*
Handshake	CDC	Yes	Yes	Yes*
Multi-cycle path	TCV**	Yes	No	Yes
False-path	TCV**	Yes	No	Yes

* Sometimes user intervention is needed.
** Timing Constraint Verification (TCV)

Lint has a problem when coming to sort violations because it has no knowledge of the functionality of the design. Therefore, it cannot answer on questions like do we have a contention on a tri-state bus? Is this combinational loop stable? Might this unconnected net be an issue? Do I have an unknown value in one of the states of a state machine?

To answer those and other questions a verification tool is needed. For the example of the tri-state bus or other signals that have multiple drivers, we can use a checker that monitors that only one of them is active. In that way, we can identify the cases that the bus is driven by multiple drivers. Furthermore, the level of guaranty that you achieve by using simulation might not be enough, and a formal verification might help. In cases like combinational loops, you usually don't want to have any in your design to start with. However, if the combinational loop appears in a legacy design, you have to decide whether you want to make any changes to this design. Therefore, a checker that verifies whether the loops might be unstable can help you to answer this. An example of those and other checkers can be seen in Table 1.

In the end of the day, the number of violations that a designer can handle a day is limited. Getting hundreds or even thousands of violations provides you no indication on what you need to do first. However, reducing those numbers to tens of violations provides you a better understanding of the major issues in the design. What you do with the rest of the violations is up to you and it depends on schedule, is it legacy code or not and what is the level of guaranty you have with the design.

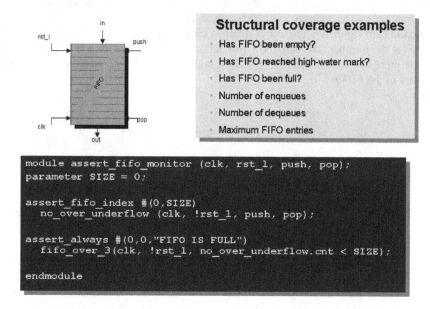

Structural coverage examples

- Has FIFO been empty?
- Has FIFO reached high-water mark?
- Has FIFO been full?
- Number of enqueues
- Number of dequeues
- Maximum FIFO entries

```
module assert_fifo_monitor (clk, rst_l, push, pop);
parameter SIZE = 0;

assert_fifo_index #(0,SIZE)
    no_over_underflow (clk, !rst_l, push, pop);

assert_always #(0,0,"FIFO IS FULL")
    fifo_over_3(clk, !rst_l, no_over_underflow.cnt < SIZE);

endmodule
```

Fig. 7. An example of FIFO structure, coverage points and monitor implementation

2.4 Structural Coverage

How would you measure the verification progress? One approach is to use functional coverage. Functional coverage uses coverage points provided by the design and the verification teams. The functional coverage points measure the types of operation that are being executed on the design. Those coverage points are defined according to the design specification. To measure and identify which structures of the design are being covered we are using the code coverage measurement. Code coverage can measure which line of code is being used, do we use all the branch options, and so on. Usually those we use both the functional and the code coverage measurements. Are those measures enough?

In order to answer the question we will use an example. We would like to verify a design that collects requests for three clients. Using the functional coverage we will measure the types of request scenarios that are being used. The code coverage will measure how well those scenarios cover the code and branches. However, how will we measure the usage of the FIFO that collects the requests? How will we measure whether the FIFO is being full or empty?

To address the following we introduce a new coverage measurement – structural coverage. The lint tools have the advantage of knowing the structure of the design. They can locate structures like memories and busses. The lint tool can help to add coverage monitors for those structures. Those monitors will provide coverage information that is based on the structure of the design and therefore we refer to them as structural coverage monitors. In cases that some of the information for the monitor cannot be extracted automatically, the user will need to fill out the missing information in the monitor. For example, a lint tool can identify a FIFO memory structure (see figure 7). The FIFO monitor checks provide coverage information that includes the numbers of read and write actions, and whether the FIFO was full. One of the pieces of information the FIFO monitor needs is to identify the pop and push signals of the FIFO.

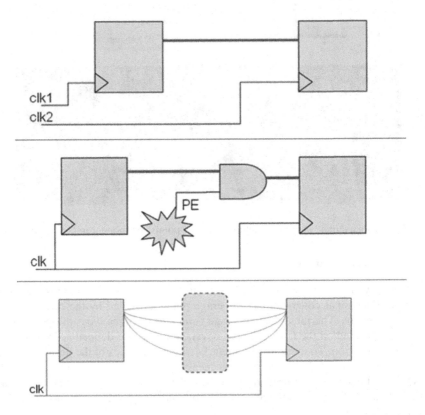

Fig. 8. Three types of timing violations: (top) is a false-path between asynchronous clock domains, (middle) is a logic false-path in the same clock domain and (bottom) is a multi-cycle path

2.5 Timing Constraint Verification

This area is one of the hot ones with a lot of companies and technology. The technology addresses two main ideas, one is generating timing constraints and the second is verifying existing constraints. As for timing constraints, there are three types as can be seen in figure 8: false-paths between asynchronous clock domains (A-FP), false-paths between synchronous clock domains (S-FP) and multi-cycle paths (MCP). It's important to note, that A-FP is correct by definition and the verification for this path is whether it's correctly synchronized. As for the S-FP and the MCP, the verification is done logically from the design behavior. The S-FP and MCP are addressed by tools available in the market, while none of the tools address the A-FP.

The lint tools are familiar with the design clocks and they can verify the correctness of the synchronization schemes. Furthermore, they can handle those issues earlier in the design flow, which helps to improve the interactions of the design and the implementation teams. Furthermore, we can use the Lint tool to generate the clock definitions and the A-FP in SDC format.

3 Experiences at Intel

The flow of smart-lint is in the implementation phases in Intel and some projects started to use it. Using the smart-lint flow enables the projects to find bugs that they wouldn't find otherwise. Furthermore, the smart-lint flow improves the effectiveness of the verification flow. For example, in a FSM a designer assumed that moving to a certain state the value of a certain signal was already set. However, the formal tool found a counter example in a special situation that this assumption wasn't correct. This kind of bug can be found using the FSM monitor. Below you can find additional two examples, of how the smart-lint flow can be used for clock domain crossing (CDC) and timing constraint verification (TCV) flows.

Example: Sunrise lake FSENG unit
Issue: There were about 1000 violations of different kinds starting from two signals, namely, protocol and mmr_proto_rst_n. Especially for the violation groups "Combinational logic before synchronizer" and "Signal feeds to the asynchronous reset port of the receiving register has no synchronizer"
Design data: mmr_proto_rst_n is intentionally OR'ed before driving the flop's reset to maintain an asynchronous assertion. However synchronous deassertion is guaranteed.

And signal protocol is static (it is a fuse option). There was a need to filter these out.

Solution: To resolve this we want to waive those signals from the report of those particular violations. Then we want to be sure that the waiver is correct. To perform both of those tasks we can use the following checkers:

```
assert_guaranty_by_design deassertion_ok (.in(mmr_proto_rst_n_in),
                                          .out(mmr_proto_rst_n));

assert_missing_sync protocol_sig (.in(protocol_in), .out(protocol),
                                  .clk(clk), .rst(!rst_1));
```

You should note that the assert_guaranty_by_design checker is assigned by the user to mark that she or he is aware of the synchronization issue. The assert_missing_sync checker is assigned automatically by the smart-lint environment. This checker makes sure that the signal in is static. Furthermore, we use those checkers to waive the CDC violations by defining them as synchronizers.

Example: ICH8, Nahum block
Issue: There were ~100K false-paths between asynchronous clocks to be verified (as reported by the static timing tool like Synopsys PrimeTime).
Solution: To resolve this we need to check that the false-paths are correctly synchronized. Therefore using Lint tool for this task is preferred. The number of violations using the Lint CDC flow was ~3K, where 1K were related to false-path and the rest were other CDC issues. To further refine the 1K CDC violations, we used the assert_missing_sync checker that removes the static signals from the violation list. This reduces the list of violation to several hundreds, which is significantly smaller compared to the original 100K.

4 Summary

The smart-lint flow provides a way to improve the lint results by reducing the number of violations to the ones that affect the chip behavior. Therefore, the smart-lint provides one of the major improvements in lint technology in several years. Furthermore, the smart-lint flow is the first step to having a unified environment for design and verification. We don't want to have a 'bunch of tools' to work with, we want an environment that will work together flawlessly. When we used the smart-lint flow in Intel, it helped to find bugs more easily and got good feedback from the users. In summary, the smart-lint flow provides benefit in concept and in practice.

Acknowledgments

I would like to thank Alex Panich who helped to implement the smart-lint environment, Michael Zuckerman who is the lint master and Shalom Bresticker for his help with the development of the paper.

References

[1] Indicators help manage coverage-driven verification, Akiva Michelson, EETimes 2005.
[2] Assertion-Based Design, Harry Foster, Adam Krolnik and David Lacey, Kluwer Academic Publishers, 2004.
[3] IEEE Open Verification Library Assertion Monitor Reference Manual, June 2003.
[4] IEEE Std 1850-2005, Property Specification Language (PSL).
[5] IEEE Std 1800-2005, SystemVerilog.
[6] eLanguage Reference manual, available at www.ieee1647.org.
[7] OpenVera Language Reference Manual, December 2003.

[8]   Synopsys Verification Methodology Manual (VMM) for SystemVerilog, Janick Bergeron, Eduard Gerny, Alan Hunter and Andrew Nightingale, Springer 2005.

[9]   Four Pillars of Assertion-based Verification, by Ping Yeung, 0-In Design Automation, DesignCon 2004.

[10] Assertion-Based Verification of Timing Exceptions, FishTail-DA/Focus Application Note 2005.

[11] Indigo RTL Analysis Datasheet, Blue Pearl Software 2006.

[12] Validation Design Constraints with Conformal Constraint Designer (CCD), CTC-2005.

Model-Driven Development with the jABC

Bernhard Steffen[1], Tiziana Margaria[2], Ralf Nagel[1], Sven Jörges[1],
and Christian Kubczak[1]

[1] Chair of Programming Systems, University of Dortmund, Germany
{steffen,nagel,joerges,kubczak}@ls5.cs.uni-dortmund.de
[2] Chair of Service and Software Engineering, University of Potsdam, Germany
margaria@cs.uni-potsdam.de

Abstract. We present the jABC, a framework for model driven application development based on Lightweight Process Coordination. With jABC, users (product developers and system/software designers) easily develop services and applications by composing reusable building-blocks into hierarchical (flow-) graph structures that are executable models of the application. This process is supported by an extensible set of plugins providing additional functionalities, so that the jABC models can be animated, analyzed, simulated, verified, executed and compiled. This way of handling the collaborative design of complex software systems has proven to be effective and adequate for the cooperation of non-programmers and technical people, and it is now being rolled out in the operative practice.

1 Lightweight Process Coordination

jABC[2] is a mature framework for service development based on Lightweight Process Coordination [29]. Predecessors of jABC have been used since 1995 to design, among others, industrial telecommunication services [30], Web-based distributed decision support systems [19], and test automation environments for Computer-Telephony integrated systems [16].

jABC allows users to easily develop services and applications by composing reusable building-blocks into (flow-) graph structures. This development process is supported by an extensible set of plugins that provide additional functionality in order to adequately support all the activities needed along the development lifecycle like animation, rapid prototyping, formal verification, debugging, code generation, and evolution. It does not replace but rather enhances other modelling practices like the UML-based RUP (Rational Unified Process, [3,15]), which are in fact used in our process to design the single components.

Lightweight Process Coordination (LPC) [29] as a service-oriented, model-driven development approach, offers a number of advantages that play a particular role when integrating off-the-shelf, possibly remote functionalities:

- **Simplicity.** jABC focuses on application experts, who are typically non-programmers. The basic ideas of our modelling process have been explained in past projects to new participants in less than one hour.

E. Bin, A. Ziv, and S. Ur (Eds.): HVC 2006, LNCS 4383, pp. 92–108, 2007.

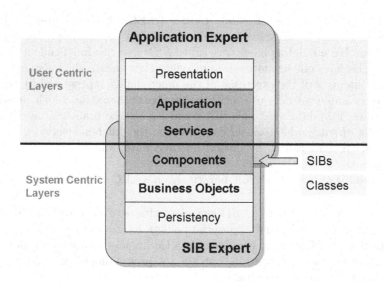

Fig. 1. Layered Architecture of jABC Applications

- **Agility.** We expect requirements, models, and artefacts to change over time, therefore the process supports evolution as a normal process phase.
- **Customizability.** The building blocks which form the model can be freely renamed or restructured to fit the habits of the application experts.
- **Consistency.** The same modelling paradigm underlies the whole process, from the very first steps of prototyping up to the final execution, guaranteeing traceability and semantic consistency.
- **Verification.** With techniques like model checking and local checks we support the user to consistently modify his model. The basic idea is to define local or global properties that the model must satisfy and to provide automatic checking mechanisms.
- **Service orientation.** Existing or external features, applications, or services can be easily integrated into a model by wrapping the existing functionality into building blocks that can be used inside the models.
- **Executability.** The model can have different kinds of execution code. These can be as abstract as textual descriptions (for example in the first animations during requirement capture), and as concrete as the final runtime implementation.
- **Universality.** Thanks to Java as largely platform-independent, object-oriented implementation language, jABC can be easily adopted in a large variety of technical contexts and of application domains.

The basic idea of Lightweight Process Coordination is to add a coordination layer to the generally well established three tier architecture. This coordination layer spans the application and services layers of Fig. 1. It is a purely model driven development layer, created and managed within a graphical interactive tool: the *Java Application Building Center* (jABC). In jABC, users build co-ordination models by arranging predefined building blocks simply by drag and drop. These basic building blocks are called *SIBs* (Service Independent Building Block). SIBs have one or more outgoing edges (*branches*), which depend on the different outcomes of the execution of the functionality represented by the SIB.

As an example we may use a SIB called `CreateBooking`, which prepares a modification in a database. This SIB could have three branches, labelled *Successful*, *DataError* and *DatabaseError*, showing the difference between a correct execution, an error caused by invalid featured data, and an error caused by a problem with the database.

Two groups of users work collaboratively on a LPC standard model:

- **SIB Experts**, who are (Java) developers with detailed knowledge about the development of SIBs and appropriate plugin interfaces, and
- **Application Experts**, who have detailed knowledge about the process or application under realization, but are not programmers and may not even have a technical background.

As shown in Fig.1, application experts model the business logic of the application from existing SIBs that correspond to components or basic services, and from instances of a special SIB used as placeholder for functionalities not yet implemented. If an application needs additional SIBs, the application expert can use the placeholder to define name, appropriate parameters and branches on his own, using the SIBCreator Plugin. Adding real functionality to the SIB is done in cooperation with the SIB expert, on the basis of the specification of the SIB and possibly also of the business logic model (called Service Logic Graph or SLG) of the application.

SIB experts take care of implementing missing SIBs, of the integration of legacy systems and components at the SIB level, and of the persistency layer.

Feature-Oriented Descriptions. The terminology SIB and SLG is taken from the context of Intelligent Networks, a successful telecommunications domain which was among the first to standardize a service-oriented architecture and development methodology [23,24], also in connection with features (here seen as basic services). In fact, the jABC methodology instantiates those concepts as follows:

Definition [Feature-oriented Description]

1. A *feature-oriented service description* of a complex service specifies the behaviours of a *base system* and a set of *optional features*.
2. The behaviour of each feature and of the basic system are given by means of Service Logic Graphs (SLGs) [24].
3. The realization of each SLG bases on a library of *reusable components* called Service Independent Building-Blocks (SIBs).
4. The feature-oriented service description includes also a set of *abstract requirements* that ensure that the intended purposes are *met*.

5. *Interactions* between features are regulated *explicitly* and are usually expressed via *constraints* in temporal logics.
6. Any *feature composition* is allowed that does not violate any constraint.

Hierarchy and Refinement. Each SLG model can be wrapped into a single coarser-grained SIB, and may be used on another hierarchical level of modelling. Similarly, each SIB can be refined into an own model, showing a more detailed view on the represented feature. This way we support both a top-down and bottom-up application modelling process.

In the remainder of the paper we present the basic components of the complete jABC toolbox. Sect. 2 and 3 give a more detailed overview of the jABC. In Sect. 4 and 5 we focus on the included verification and analysis tools (the local- and model checker). The jABC Tracer, used to animate, simulate, interpret, and debug at the coordination level is presented in Sect. 6. In Sect. 7 we present the jABC code generator, which is itself constructed by means of the jABC, as a LPC process. In Sect. 8 we discuss related approaches and in Sect. 9 we present our conclusions.

2   The Java Application Building Center

The jABC is meanwhile the fourth generation of this framework [34], with C++ precursors dating back to 1992 [33]. Thanks to Java we are largely platform independent: jABC runs wherever a JVM is available, solving this way many portability and interoperability issues of its precursors. jABC is at the same time used as a commercial product in several projects with industry, and as a teaching and experimental platform for our students. This is possible thanks to a plugin framework concept which supports the easy replacement of almost every part of the system and the easy addition of new (customer-specific) features.

Handling Basic Services. Java simplifies the handling of SIB components too - a single Java class contains all the required or optional information:

- the *name* is represented by the Java class name,
- the *parameters* are defined as the *public* fields of the class,
- the *branches* are represented by the reserved field *branches*, which can be optionally flagged as *final*,
- the *graphical representation* in the drawing canvas is the picture returned by the *getIcon()* method,
- the *online documentation* for the SIB, its parameters and branches, are retrieved via the *getTooltipText()* method, and
- optional information for animation, simulation, analysis, etc., are encapsulated with plugin-specific interfaces. For example, the interface `Tracer` consists of the defined method *onTrace()*.

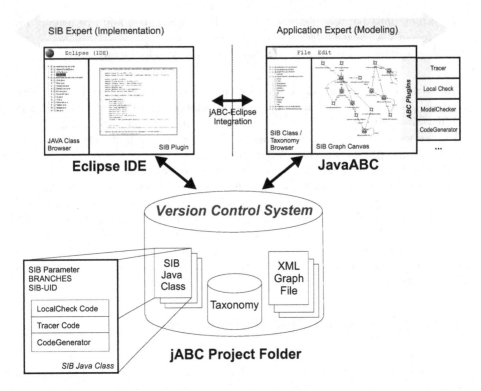

Fig. 2. jABC Big Picture

SIB Palettes as Taxonomies. At runtime, the jABC discovers and analyses the compiled SIB class files and generates a structured representation of the available SIBs for the application experts. The SIBs are presented as a taxonomy, as in Fig. 3(upper left), which shows on the canvas the model of the code generator. This taxonomy is a tree representation of a directed acyclic graph. A SIB can thus appear there several times, even with different names.

Different to standard Java classes, the physical class package of the SIB is irrelevant for the jABC: the SIB description achieves this decoupling. The jABC replaces unavailable or deleted SIB classes with the *ProxySIB*, a specific place-holder, and protects the model from information loss. If the graph is stored again, the information of the missing SIB is kept; if the SIB becomes available again, the model will automatically load the correct SIB. Even after refactoring a SIB class, older models referencing such a SIB will use the correct class.

Meaning of the Coordination Graphs. The basic jABC System does not define a standard semantics for graphs: at this point, SLGs are purely structural descriptions that can be printed, layouted, edited, but have no meaning. This meaning is given by different jABC-plugins, like the Tracer already mentioned. The Tracer interprets an SLG as a flow graph with one or more distinguished start nodes and is able to execute it. The Tracer defines an own Java interface that contains

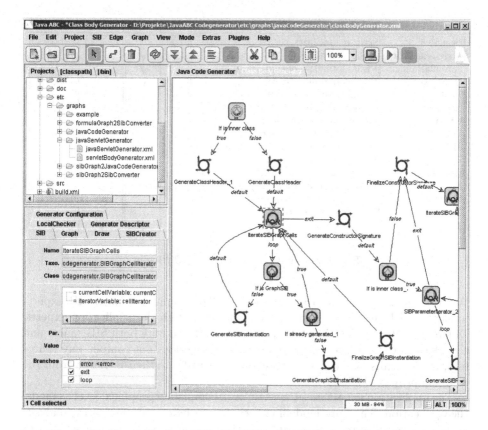

Fig. 3. Working with the jABC: Modifying the SLG of the Code Generator

all methods it can execute for a SIB. To support a Tracer execution, a SIB must implement this Tracer interface. Missing interface implementations are semantically empty, thus the corresponding plugin simply stops executing.

3   Overview of the jABC Architecture

Fig. 2 shows an overview of the complete jABC development system. The work with the jABC is organized in projects, which are seen as local storage folders. Users can define multiple projects, but only one at a time is active. A project folder contains all the elements (files and materials) needed for a model, even if not necessarily needed by the jABC. By versioning this folder with a versioning system (like CVS) it is possible to retrieve arbitrary older versions of a model and to distribute model changes to all project members. Currently, the rights and roles management within a project is delegated to the underlying versioning system.

There is no prescribed development environment for the jABC SIBs: it is possible to use any compatible Java development application (even *vi* and *javac*).

Plugin	Description	local	global	internal	interface
BeanShell	Scripting facilities	✓			✓
CodeGenerator	Model compilation		✓		✓
FormulaBuilder	Visual formula modelling		✓		✓
DBSchema	ER-diagram modelling		✓		✓
Docbook	Documentation for jABC projects	✓	✓		✓
Eclipse	Eclipse integration for jABC	✓	✓		✓
GEAR	mu-calculus Model checker		✓	✓	
jETI	Integration of remote services	✓			✓
JEEWAB	Web technologies support (e.g. J2EE)		✓		✓
jMosel	Verification with M2L		✓		✓
LearnLib	Automata Learning & Experimentation		✓		✓
LocalChecker	Local SIB verification	✓		✓	
SIBCreator	Automatic SIB generation	✓			✓
Taxonomy-Editor	SIB taxonomy customization	✓		✓	
Tracer	Model execution	✓	✓	✓	

Fig. 4. Summary of available jABC Plugins

We use Eclipse [1] because it utilizes a similar plugin approach. SIB experts implement SIB Java classes in close collaboration with the application experts. Different to the usual CVS setup, the SIB expert commits both SIB source and class files to the project repository. In fact, jABC does not compile any source files, it just scans for available SIB classfiles, which are then retrieved from the common project CVS.

The application expert uses the jABC at a completely graphical level to model the application. The pure modelling activity can be complemented by analysis, animation, verification, and execution, which come together with a set of plugins. Usually the set of plugins corresponds to the implemented interfaces in the SIBs.

In the following, we describe the central plugins, which are part of the standard jABC distribution. Fig. 4 shows a list of currently available jABC plugins, here classified according to distinguishing criteria for their nature and aim:

- SIB-level plugins are *locally scoped* in the sense that they concern single SIBs, while SLG-level plugins are *globally scoped*, since they handle whole SLGs,
- jABC *internal* plugins which are used inside the jABC, and *interface* plugins, that provide functionality that interfaces the jABC framework with other worlds, like Webservices, databases, or ERP systems like SAP.

According to the full lifecycle of applications built with the jABC, depicted in Fig. 5, we see that the jABC core, which includes the Local Checker and the Tracer plugins, is used along the full development cycle. Other plugins are more phase specific, like the ITE (Integrated Test Environment) [16] and the LearnLib [7] plugins, which focus on the runtime.

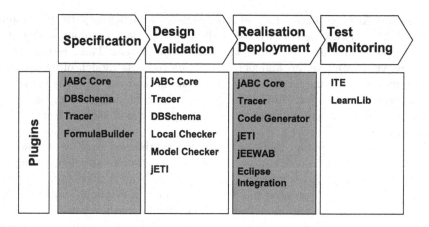

Fig. 5. Model Based Lifecycle Management in jABC

4   The LocalChecker

The LocalChecker-plugin checks whether some assertions (expressed in Java) concerning the single instance of this SIB hold. These assertions are locally specified and concern the correct use of this SIB in its immediate neighbourhood. They concern single instances of user-defined SIBs. They can be used to check the value of a SIB parameter or some conditions of a branch. While relating to many different parameters or branches of a SIB-instance at once, the assertions can be free in complexity yet always simple in the definition formalism. They are formulated in plain Java code, therefore the whole power of the Java language could be used to implement and analyse such properties.

The main advantage of using Java code for local check definitions is that it enables runtime checking of non-trivial properties of a SIB-instance, more involved than standard abstract interpretations. One could for instance need to know whether a given attribute value is contained in an external database. This can be simply solved by embedding the database query in the local check code. For many common checks relating to SIBs and their branches the corresponding rule implementation is already provided with the LocalChecker-Plugin itself, simplifying the use and helping users to reduce the amount of additional work.

As an example consider a SIB representing a table in a database: the name of this table must neither be empty nor too long, it should only consists of valid characters and may not be a reserved word of SQL. In the LocalCheck code the SIB experts test all these different criteria with corresponding Java statements and create warning or error messages, which are presented by the jABC GUI to the user and help users to correct the problems.

5   Model Debugging Via the ModelChecker

Even at an early modelling stage requirements, properties, and general frame conditions emerge which have to be fulfilled by a system or an application.

Besides very local requirements, which only relate to particular parts of a system and which can easily be checked using the LocalChecker, there are also global requirements which are associated with the entire system. These requirements are often very intuitive, are independent of the concrete model, often are part of the rules of the game for an application domain, and can be easily expressed by the application expert during the business logic modelling. E.g., in a web application a logout can only be performed if there was a login at some earlier point in time.

In the last years model checking [8,32] has established itself as a powerful approach to automatic verification of systems. It provides an effective way to determine whether a given system is consistent with a specified property. The jABC framework incorporates this technique via a core plugin called GEAR [6]. Intuitively, any system modelled as SLGs can be verified with this plugin: SLGs consist of SIBs holding labels that the model checker interprets as atomic propositions (for example the SIB names), and have edges annotated with branch names that for the model checker represent actions. Fig. 3 shows an example of such a SLG which models the core part of the jABC code generator for Java classes (see Sect. 7). Properties of such a model have to be specified using appropriate formalisms, in the case of GEAR these are temporal logics, for example CTL (Computation Tree Logic) or the modal μ-calculus [21].

GEAR augments the GUI of the jABC with specific functionalities that enable the user to:

- equip the individual SIBs of a model with atomic propositions,
- add and describe properties,
- check properties for a particular model and
- interactively investigate the error diagnosis information by playing model checking games.

As formal specifications of properties are basically formulas in a temporal logic, which are usually difficult to create and to understand without the required theoretical knowledge, GEAR provides two separate views for using the plugin.

- The *basic view* is designed for users that are unfamiliar with temporal logic-based specification formalisms. Properties here are displayed as natural language descriptions which are tagged according to their validity in the model of interest. E.g., green highlighted properties in Fig. 6 are verified and red highlighted are disproved.
- The *advanced view* addresses experts who know how to create properties using CTL or the modal μ-calculus. If the user enters a formula, its syntax tree is immediately visualized, so that all corresponding subformulae are directly visible. The user may invoke model checking for the whole formula or just for one of its subformulae - the satisfying nodes in the model are then marked accordingly. It is also possible to do *reverse checking*, by using the model checker in the opposite direction. By selecting a subset of nodes in the model of interest it is immediately possible to see which subformulae are satisfied by the selected nodes.

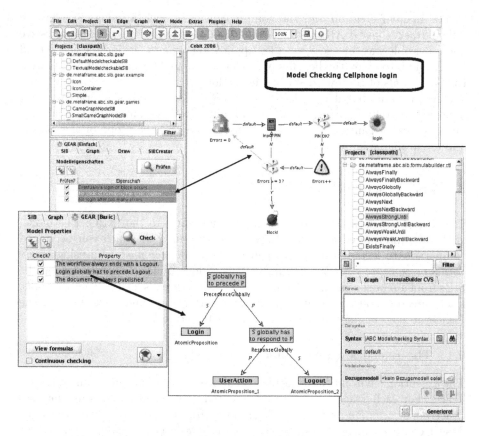

Fig. 6. Using the GEAR Model Checker and the FormulaBuilder

To further improve the accessibility of property specifications, the Formula-Builder plugin [18,17] can be used in conjunction with GEAR. With the For-mulaBuilder, also formulae can be modelled as SLGs. Fig. 6 right shows the collection of SIBs for CTL operators. Users can create such graphs also by us-ing commonly-occurring specification patterns based on a system proposed by Dwyer, Avrunin and Corbett [12,11].

Fig. 6 bottom left shows an example of pattern usage: this formula graph cor-responds to the template used for the third property checked on this graph: *No login after too many errors*. It uses the patterns *Global Precedence* and *Global Response*. The *Global Precedence* pattern expresses the following property: *Glob-ally, the occurrence of S has to be an enabling condition for the occurrence of P*. In Fig. 6 *S* and *P* are instantiated to the values *Login* resp. *Global Response*, so the whole graph models a property that uses hierarchical patterns. From this sim-ple and intuitive graph visualization the FormulaBuilder generates a mu-calculus formula that can be stored, or directly used for model checking in GEAR, for example to verify whether a web application modelled with the jABC satisfies the property.

The manual creation and the comprehension of such formulas is a known difficult task, thus GEAR and the FormulaBuilder together provide an expressive and accessible way for users, even for application experts lacking the theoretical background, to enjoy the benefits of model checking. This goes well in line with the basic goals of LPC we described in section 1.

Being a game based model checker, GEAR also supports interactive error diagnosis by computing and animating winning strategies for modal mu-calculus model checking games. Details on this use go beyond the scope of this paper, and are available in [35,31,36].

6   The Tracer

The Tracer plugin adds an execution layer for SLGs to the jABC. The model is thereby interpreted as a *directed control flow diagram* which can be traced comparable to a standard debugger in *run mode* or *step mode* and using *breakpoints* or *pause* to stop the execution. This is done by the Tracer by taking the SIBs from a model as an input to create execution threads, called *Tracer threads*. Each thread contains a number of linear execution steps and is executed by the *Execution environment* of the Tracer, as illustrated in Fig. 7(a).

6.1   The Execution Environment

The execution environment as mentioned above is a runtime environment for the Tracer. For each Tracer thread to be executed, the execution environment uses exactly one *execution stack* containing a single *execution context*. By doing so, the Tracer can execute recursive threads, as variables and invariants are available inside each context. In addition to the execution contexts bound to a single thread there are other contexts with a more global scope. They are available to different SIB instances and they can mutually communicate. Thereby, a global context could also be available through remote interfaces like RMI or JNDI, causing a communication between locally separated models or SIBs. The global execution contexts are usable for different kinds of tasks, for example a context for all available objects or one for just some special kinds of objects.

6.2   Parallel Execution

In general a SIB represents an application feature within the jABC, but it cannot modify the control flow of a modelled application. While talking about a standard SIB, all branches are treated as *alternatives*. A *ControlSIB* overwrites this default setting of a branch and allows choosing two branches in parallel, synchronizing branches, or passing messages between SIBs.

The Tracer is able to execute threads in parallel by using two *ControlSIBs*: *ForkSIB* and *JoinSIB*. A fork divides a thread in any number of subthreads which are independently executed (see Fig. 7(b)) by stopping the current thread and starting a number of new threads. The Tracer waits for each single subthread

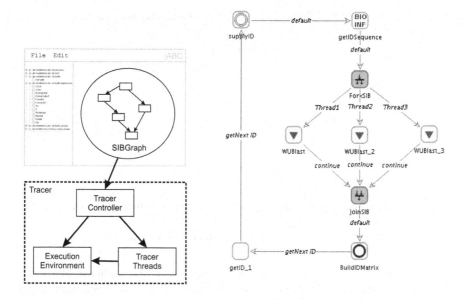

Fig. 7. The Tracer: (a) overview and (b) fork/join parallelism

to end, then the JoinSIB terminates all the subthreads and starts a new single thread to continue the execution of the whole model.

Finally, a whole model can be transformed into a single SIB, called a *Graph-SIB*. These ControlSIBs could be seen in terms of control macros, as they obfuscate complex structures to the user by building a hierarchical control structure within large models.

6.3 Remote Debugging Tool

To comfortably handle the Tracer, the *Remote debug tool* plugin provides a GUI that offers all the features of the Tracer, like starting an execution or executing only a single step. The viewed hierarchy can be chosen freely, allowing the user to control a special scope of the traced model. To visualize the tracing of a graph, the SIBs visited by the Tracer are highlighted during execution. By supporting different underlying communication protocols (like RMI, SOAP, CORBA) the debug tool truly gets "remote" and therefore it could be even used to control separate tracing processes on different machines (e.g. over the internet).

7   The Code Generator

Once a jABC application is ready for deployment, the current version of the model is often transformed into an executable and deployable piece of code in a desired programming language. This is supported by the jABC Codegenerator plugin, which currently allows generating the control flow of a model into a standard Java class or a Java servlet.

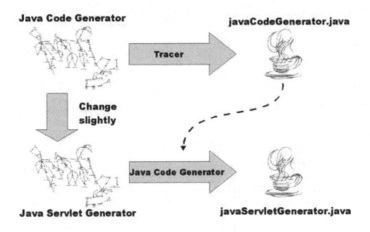

Fig. 8. The development process for the family of Code Generators

The Codegenerator is itself a direct application of the Lightweight Process Coordination approach: it was not programmed by hand, but itself modelled as a SLG within the jABC.

Already our first code generator, the generator for standard Java classes, was completely modelled using the jABC. To assure the correctness of the design, the LocalChecker and the ModelChecker were constantly used during the modelling phase. The result is a SLG that, after parameterization, generates an executable Java class from another SLG. We bootstrapped the generator by executing the model with the Tracer: the execution produces an executable Java class *of itself* - this way we obtained our first code generator as a standalone Java application.

This generator forms the basis for our family of code generators. The generator for Java servlets was achieved by slight modifications to the SLG of the initial Java class generator and subsequent code generation from this SLG via the original Java class generator. The development process for these two is depicted in Fig. 8.

Following this approach, we have a general and easy way of creating new code generators. We envisage here generating J2ME MIDlets, C++ code or even one single SIB from a whole SLG (implemented). By exploiting the advantages of the LPC approach we can profit directly from the code generators already available, achieving high reusability and increasing the efficiency of development.

8   Related Work

There are numerous powerful verification environments/tools that work at the programming language level, like SLAM, Bandera or ESC/Java[1], and others that focus for example on protocol aspects like CADP[2] or on the development of

---

[1] See the websites at http://research.microsoft.com/slam/, http://bandera.projects. cis.ksu.edu/, and http://secure.ucd.ie/products/opensource/ESCJava2/, respectively.

[2] See the website at http://www.inrialpes.fr/vasy/cadp/

embedded systems like Autofocus[3]. The jABC with its LPC approach is different from them in that it operates on a much higher level of abstraction. We will therefore concentrate the following discussion on approaches which more closely resemble this characteristic trait of the jABC.

Our way of aggressive model-driven development closely relates to the concepts of generative software development, where "a given system can be automatically generated from a specification written in one or more textual or graphical *domain-specific languages*t, as in [10]. Both concepts focus on achieving application-domain and technical flexibility. The notation for specifying a system in our approach is given through the SIBs, which can be considered a domain-specific language since they offer domain-specific functionalities both as concepts in the taxonomy and as design primitives. Thanks to taxonomies and high customizability, the user is free to resort to familiar terminology and to graphical representations that fit the specific application domain. By defining rules for local checking and model checking domain-specific error-checking can be performed, and the framework character of the jABC allows to add any domain-specific tool support by providing new plugins. Technical variability is gained among others through different code generators, which generate a running and deployable system in such a way that it fits virtually any target platform.

Another approach very close to ours is presented in [4]. This approach proposes the use of coordination contracts to promote the separation of the coordination aspects that regulate the way objects interact in a system from the way objects behave internally. As with us, their main concern is supporting evolutionary aspects of the whole system. In their work, contracts fulfill a role similar to architectural connectors: they make these coordination features available as first-class citizens, so that it is possible to treat them distinctly from the functionality of the components.

Contracts are based on superposition mechanisms [20] for supporting forms of dynamic reconfiguration of systems. These mechanisms enable contracts to be added or replaced without the need to change the objects to which they apply. CDE, an environment for developing coordination contracts in Java, is described in [13]. The CDE approach is still programming oriented: unlike our coordination graphs, contracts must be programmed; they do not (yet) support macros or hierarchy, and no automatic verification of contracts is available.

Subject-oriented design [9] is another approach comparable to LPC. The basic idea behind it is the decomposition of standard design models into smaller units called design subjects, which are very close to our SIBs. Just like SIBs, design subjects encapsulate "a single, coherent piece of functionality" [9] and may be built so that they fit the structure of application-specific requirements. Thus subject-oriented designs help to bridge the gap between requirements, which may relate to certain features, and implementation code, which may utilize object-oriented terminology. This is also achieved by our LPC approach, as it propagates a notation and the corresponding tools and framework, which explicitly can be adequately used by both non-programmers and programmers.

---

[3] See the website (in German) at http://autofocus.in.tum.de/Infos/afinfo-de.html

While the aim of most of the approaches of the five categories named above
is very similar to our LPC, their realization is quite different. They work still
at much lower level of abstraction, and they typically do not support formal
methods-based *verification mechanisms* like model checking.

9   Conclusion

In this paper we have presented the jABC Framework, which incarnates the Lightweight Process Coordination development method. We also introduced the core
plugins of the jABC (LocalChecker, the ModelChecker, the Tracer, and the Codegenerator). The set of available jABC plugins is constantly growing and covers a
broad range of topics (see [37], [28]). Besides enhancing the range of applicability,
these plugins focus on improved validation technology, like improved diagnosis for
model checking and run time verifcation based on our integrated test environment.

Several application domains have been successfully covered so far with the
jABC: complex supply chain management with IKEA [15], modelling and execution of bioinformatics workflows [27], the Semantic Web Service challenge
[22], and dataflow analysis of Java programs [26], a management framework for
remote intelligent configuration of systems [5], and an application development
platform for Galileo services [14]. These projects were very different in nature,
nevertheless we observed a surprisingly high potential of synergy, which was due
to the jABC approach.

References

1. *Eclipse Website.* http://www.eclipse.org/.
2. *jABC Website.* http://www.jabc.de.
3. *Rational Unified Process.* http://www-306.ibm.com/software/awdtools/rup/.
4. L. Andrade, J. Fiadeiro, J. Gouveia, G. Koutsoukos, A. Lopes, M. Wermelinger.
   Coordination technologies for component-based systems. In Proc. *Integrated Design
   and Process Technology*, 2002.
5. M. Bajohr, T. Margaria: *MATRICS: A Management Tool for Remote Intelligent
   Configuration of Systems*, Innovations in System and Software Engineering - a
   NASA Journal, Springer Verlag, July 2006.
6. M. Bakera and C. Renner. *GEAR - A Model Checking Plugin for the jABC framework.* http://www.jabc.de/modelchecking/.
7. T. Berg, H. Raffelt, B. Steffen: *LearnLib: A Library for Automata Learning and
   Experimentation*, Proc. FMICS'05 (ACM 10th Int. Worksh. on Formal Methods
   for Industrial Critical Systems), Sept. 2005, Lissabon (P), ACM Press.
8. E. M. Clarke, O. Grumberg, and D. Peled. *Model Checking.* MIT Press, 2001.
9. S. Clarke, W. Harrison, H. Ossher, and P. Tarr. Subject-oriented design: towards
   improved alignment of requirements, design, and code. *ACM SIGPLAN Notices*,
   34(10):325–339, 1999.
10. K. Czarnecki. Overview of generative software development. In *UPP*, pages 326–
    341, 2004.
11. M. Dwyer, G. Avrunin, J. Corbett. *Specification Patterns Website.*
    http://patterns.projects.cis.ksu.edu/.

12. M. B. Dwyer, G. S. Avrunin, and J. C. Corbett. Patterns in property specifications for finite-state verification. In Proc. *ICSE'99*, pp. 411–420, Los Alamitos, CA, 1999. IEEE CS Press.

13. J. Gouveia, G. Koutsoukos, L. Andrade, J. L. Fiadeiro. Tool support for coordination-based software evolution. Proc. *TOOLS'01: Technology of Object-Oriented Languages and Systems*, p.184, Washington DC, 2001. IEEE CS Press.

14. M. Högl, T. Margaria, B. Steffen: *The GalileoGate Solution Factory for Location-Based Integrated Services*, Proc. IDPT 2006, Int. Conf. on Integrated Design and Process Technologies, San Diego, June 2006.

15. M. Hörmann, T. Margaria, T. Mender, R. Nagel, M. Schuster, B.Steffen, H. Trinh: *The jABC Appraoch to Collaborative Development of Embedded Applications*, CCE'06, Int. Workshop on Challenges in Collaborative Engineering - State of the Art and Future Challenges on collaborative Design, Prag (CZ), April 2006 (Industry day).

16. H. Hungar, T. Margaria, B. Steffen: *Test-Based Model Generation for Legacy Systems*, Proc. IEEE ITC'03, Charlotte, 2003, IEEE CS Press, pp.971–980.

17. S. Jörges. *FormulaBuilder Website.* http://www.jabc.de/formulabuilder/.

18. S. Jörges, T. Margaria, and B. Steffen. Formulabuilder: A tool for graph-based modelling and generation of formulae. In Proc. *ICSE'06* Shanghai, May 2006.

19. M. Karusseit, T. Margaria: *Feature-based Modelling of a Complex, Online-Reconfigurable Decision Support Service*, WWV'05, 1st Int. Worksh. Automated Specif. and Verification of Web Sites, Valencia, March 2005, ENTCS N. 1132.

20. S. Katz. A superimposition control construct for distributed systems. *ACM TOPLAS.*, 15(2):337–356, 1993.

21. D. Kozen. Results on the propositional mu-calculus. *Theoretical Computer Science*, 27:333–354, 1983.

22. C. Kubczak, R. Nagel, T. Margaria, B. Steffen: *The jABC Approach to Mediation and Choreography*, Semantic Web Services Challenge 2006, Phase I-III Workshops, DERI, Stanford University, U. of Georgia, March-November 2006.

23. ITU: *General recommendations on telephone switching and signaling - intelligent network: Introduction to intelligent network capability set 1*, Recommendation Q.1211, Telecommunic. Standardization Sector of ITU, Geneva, Mar. 1993.

24. ITU-T: *Recommendation Q.1203. "Intelligent Network - Global Functional Plane Architecture"*, Oct. 1992.

25. ITU-T: *Recommendation Q.1204. "Distributed Functional Plane for Intelligent Network Capability Set 2: Parts 1-4"*, Sept. 1997.

26. A.L. Lamprecht, T. Margaria, B.Steffen: *Data-Flow Analy-sis as Model Checking within the jABC*, Proc. CC'06, 15th Int. Conf. on Compiler Construction, Vienna (A), March 2006, LNCS, 3923, Springer Verlag, pp. 101-104.

27. T. Margaria, C. Kubczak, M. Njoku, B. Steffen: *Model-based Design of Distributed Collaborative Bioinformatics Processes in the jABC*, Proc. ICECCS 2006, Stanford Univ., CA (USA), August 2006, IEEE CS Press.

28. T. Margaria, R. Nagel, B. Steffen: *Remote Integration and Coordination of Verification Tools in JETI*, Proc. IEEE ECBS 2005, April 2005, Greenbelt (USA), IEEE CS Press, pp. 431–436.

29. T. Margaria and B. Steffen. Lightweight coarse-grained coordination: a scalable system-level approach. *STTT*, 5(2-3):107–123, 2004.

30. T. Margaria, B. Steffen, M. Reitenspieß: *Service-Oriented Design: The Roots*, IC-SOC 2005: 3rd ACM SIGSOFT/SIGWEB Int. Conf. on Service-Oriented Computing, Amsterdam, Dec. 2005, LNCS 3826, pp. 450-464, Springer Verlag.

31. M. Müller-Olm and H. Yoo. Metagame: An animation tool for model-checking games. In *TACAS 04, LNCS 2988*, pages 163–167. Springer-Verlag, 2004.

32. J.-P. Queille and J. Sifakis. Specification and verification of concurrent systems in cesar. In *Proceedings of the 5th Colloquium on International Symposium on Programming*, pages 337–351, London, UK, 1982. Springer-Verlag.

33. B. Steffen, B. Freitag, A. Claßen, T. Margaria, and U. Zukowski. *Intelligent Software Synthesis in the "DaCapo" Environment* In Proc. 6th /Nordic Workshop on Programming Theory/, Aarhus (DK), October 1994, BRICS Report N. 94/6, December 1994.

34. B. Steffen, T. Margaria. METAFrame in Practice: Design of Intelligent Network Services. In *Correct System Design - Recent Insights and Advances*, LNCS N. 1710, State-of-the-Art Survey, pp. 390–415. Springer-Verlag, 1999.

35. C. Stirling and P. Stevens. Practical model-checking using games. Proc. *TACAS 98*, LNCS N.1384, pp. 85–101. Springer-Verlag, 1998.

36. W. Thomas. On the synthesis of strategies in infinite games. Proc.*STACS'95*, LNCS N.900, pp.1-13. Springer-V., 1995.

37. C. Topnik, E. Wilhelm, T. Margaria, B. Steffen: *jMosel: A Stand-Alone Tool and jABC Plugin for M2L(Str)*, Proc. SPIN'06, 13th Int. Works. on Model Checking of Software, Vienna, April 2006, LNCS 3925, Springer V., pp.293-298.

Detecting Design Flaws in UML State Charts for Embedded Software

Janees Elamkulam[1], Ziv Glazberg[2], Ishai Rabinovitz[3,*], Gururaja Kowlali[1],
Satish Chandra Gupta[1], Sandeep Kohli[1], Sai Dattathrani[1],
and Claudio Paniagua Macia[4]

[1] IBM, Bangalore, India
{janees.ek, kgururaja, satish.gupta, sandeep.kohli,
saidatta}@in.ibm.com
[2] IBM Research Lab, Haifa, Israel
glazberg@il.ibm.com
[3] Mellanox Inc., Israel
ishair@gmail.com
[4] IBM Barcelona, Spain
cpaniagua@es.ibm.com

Abstract. Embedded systems are used in various critical devices and correct functioning of these devices is crucial. For non-trivial devices, exhaustive testing is costly, time consuming and probably impossible. A complementary approach is to perform static model checking to verify certain design correctness properties. Though static model checking techniques are widely used for hardware circuit verification, the goal of model checking software systems remains elusive. However embedded systems fall in the category of concurrent reactive systems and can be expressed through communicating state machines. Behavior of concurrent reactive systems is more similar to hardware than general software. So far, this similarity has not been exploited sufficiently.

IBM[®1] Rational[®] Rose[®] RealTime (RoseRT) is widely used for designing concurrent reactive systems and supports UML State Charts. IBM RuleBase is an effective tool for hardware model checking. In this paper, we describe our experiments of using RuleBase for static model checking RoseRT models. Our tool automatically converts RoseRT models to the input for RuleBase, allows user to specify constraints graphically using a variation of sequence diagrams, and presents model checking results (counterexamples) as sequence diagrams consisting of states and events in the original UML model. The model checking step is seamlessly integrated with RoseRT. Prior knowledge of model checking or formal methods is not expected, and familiarity of UML sequence diagram is exploited to make temporal constraint specification and counterexample presentation more accessible. This approach brings the benefits of model checking to embedded system developers with little cost of learning.

---

* Ishai contributed to this research while his employment with IBM Research Lab, Haifa, Israel.

[1] IBM, Rational, and Rational Rose are trademarks or registered trademarks of IBM Corporation in the United States, other countries, or both.

E. Bin, A. Ziv, and S. Ur (Eds.): HVC 2006, LNCS 4383, pp. 109–121, 2007.

1   Introduction

Adherence of a system implementation to its requirement is demonstrated by running a set of test cases. However, this can only prove presence of features and not absence of defects. In case of concurrent systems, depending upon the sequence of events, there is potential for problems such as race conditions, dead locks, and live locks. To verify absence of these defects, an exhaustive set of test cases have to be designed, which is a daunting task and prone to errors. But these defects can't be tolerated in mission critical systems for medical, automotive, and military industry.

Researchers have tried to solve this problem by applying Static Model Checking [14] techniques. Tools such as SPIN [24], SMV [35] either require an abstract model of the system in a propriety language, or try to extract an abstract model from source code. Both these techniques have limitations. In case of former, specialized skills are needed for defining an abstract model in a tool specific language, and there is a danger of the model specifications becoming outdated as the system implementation evolves. In case of latter, it is extremely hard for a tool to extract accurate and complete model specification out of the source code. Incapability to construct accurate yet manageable-size abstractions of the software and keeping it consistent with the implementations are among the key hurdles in widespread adoption of software model checking.

IBM Rational Rose RealTime (RoseRT) [25] presents an unique opportunity to bring model checking techniques to embedded system development. It is an advanced UML [8] modeling tool for soft real time systems, and widely used in industry for designing software for commercial embedded devices. The system behavior is specified through a collection of communicating state machines (UML State Charts). RoseRT generates the code from the model, but user can execute and debug at the model level – that is, the model is the code – therefore there is no disparity between the model specification and system implementation. Nor is the possibility of extracting incomplete model specification from the implementation. The fact that a RoseRT model is complete and correct representation of the underlying system provides the needed advantage, at least in the embedded software domain, for overcoming above mentioned hurdles.

We observe that concurrent reactive systems are more similar to hardware than common software. Typically, in software systems, a relatively small set of variables change in every cycle, but in hardware, all variables may change in every cycle. Similarly, in communicating state machines for concurrent reactive systems, all machines may change their states in every cycle. Due to this similarity, we believe that hardware model checking techniques are more likely to succeed on these systems. Therefore for our experiments, we use IBM RuleBase [2,4], a model checking tool for hardware circuits, for model checking RoseRT models.

In the rest of this paper, we first provide an overview of our tool (Section 2), and describe experimental results (Section 3). Later we discuss related research (Section 4) and draw some conclusions (Section 5).

2   Connecting RoseRT and RuleBase

RoseRT models consist of state machines that communicate with each other by passing messages. These communicating state machines embody the concurrent reactive

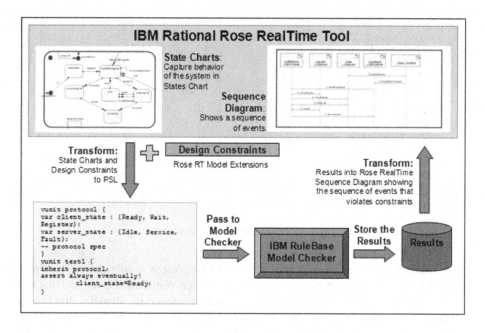

Fig. 1. Modeling checking RoseRT models using RuleBase

behavior of an embedded device. Typically, these devices must adhere to a set of constraints, e.g., no sequence of events should cause a deadlock (a deadlock occurs when two or more state machines are stuck in their respective states waiting for a message from each other). Any failure to follow these constraints is potentially a design flaw. A mechanism must be provided to specify the constraints. We achieve that by providing a graphical interface in RoseRT for specifying design constraints, and by extending RoseRT model definition to include these constraints.

Our tool transforms a RoseRT model (which now includes constraints) to Property Specification Language (PSL) [26], a language understood by RuleBase. RuleBase performs model checking and generates results indicating event sequences that violate the design constraints. These results are automatically correlated to the states and events in the original model, and transformed into sequence diagrams to expose the problems and present them to the user. In this section, we explain each of these steps (Figure 1) in details with the help of client-server protocol [9] example.

The client-server example has two state machines, one each for the client and the server, and they are connected via a two-way FIFO communication channel (Figure 2). The Client state machine has 3 states: Ready, Wait and Register. The Server state machine also has 3 states: Idle, Service and Fault. A state machine changes the state either upon receiving a message or due to internal events (such as server completing a request or detecting a fault). When an internal event occurs, a state machine may also send out a message. The state transition is represented by an arc and the arcs are tagged with the messages. Reception of a message is represented by plus sign (+m), and dispatch of a message is represented by a minus sign (-m).

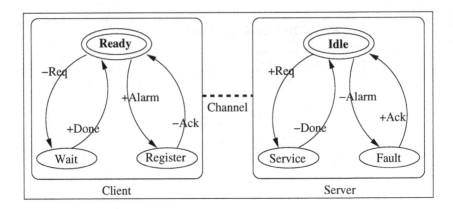

Fig. 2. Client and Server state machines

Initially, the client is in the Ready state and the server is in Idle state. The Client can send a request (Req) to the Server, and enter to the Wait state. Upon receiving the request, the Server goes to the Service state. When the request is completed, the Server sends a Done message to the Client and goes back to the Idle state. When the Client gets the Done message, it goes back to the Ready state.

While the server is Idle, it may detect a fault in itself. It sends an Alarm message to the Client, and enters to the Fault state. When the Client gets the Alarm message, it goes to the Register state to log the fault, and then it acknowledges the fault by sending an Ack message to the Server and goes back to Ready state. Upon receiving the acknowledgment, the Server goes to the Idle state. If any message other than the one tagged on the arcs arrives, it is ignored and the state remains unchanged. It is a simple example yet sufficient to explain various aspects of our tool. Experimental results with more complex examples are discussed in Section 3.

2.1   Constraint Specification

While examining various alternatives to specify design constraints, an important consideration is that it should be easy for users to adapt. Since users are familiar with sequence diagrams, we created simple and intuitive sequence diagram extensions (similar to Harel's Live Sequence Diagrams [21]) for defining temporal constraints and to accommodate the temporal layer of PSL. For the Client - Server example, an interesting constraint to verify would be that there are no deadlocks, or in other words "*eventually* Server state machine should come to Idle state, and Client state machine should come to Ready state". The screen dump in Figure 3 shows how a user can specify this constraint.

2.2   Transforming RoseRT Model

Our tool automatically transforms RoseRT models and constraints to PSL. Converting constraints to PSL is trivial because of the one-to-one mapping between our extensions for defining constraints and temporal layer of PSL. Converting RoseRT model requires generating PSL code for state machines and the connection channels between them. A

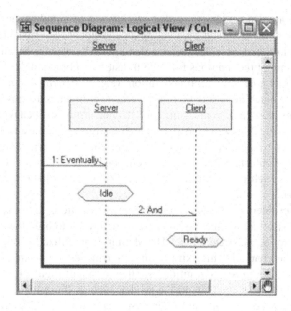

Fig. 3. Screen dump of constraints specification using Sequence Diagram extensions

state machine consists of a set of states, one of which is the initial state, and a set of
state transitions. PSL code for each state machine is generated as following:

- define a PSL variable that enumerates on all states,
- capture initial state by defining a PSL init construct,
- encode each state transition tuple ⟨ *source state*, *destination state*, *precondition*,
  action⟩ using PSL next and case constructs.

Enumerating states and defining initial state is simple (see definitions of $Server\_state$
and $init(Server\_state)$ in Figure 4). But encoding a state transition is non-trivial due
to two reasons: nondeterministic interleaving of simultaneous occurrence of multiple
preconditions, and potential effect of an action on the state of the channel. We will
explain both complexities using the Idle state in the Server state machine.

Examine Figure 2, from Idle state, two state transitions are possible. First transition is to handle requests: $\langle Idle, Service, top() == Req, dequeue()\rangle$, where $top()$
checks the type of first message in the channel's message queue, and dequeue() removes the first message of the queue. Second transition is to handle server alarms:
$\langle Idle, Fault, event(ServerAlarm), enqueue(Alarm)\rangle$, where $enqueue()$ inserts
a message in the channel's message queue. If a request comes in the channel and an
error occurs at the same time, preconditions for both state transitions become true simultaneously. Which of the two should be considered first is nondeterministic. Both
interleavings must be examined by model checker, and the PSL encoding must reflect
that. Also, actions associated with both state transitions alter the message queue in the
communication channel, and this interdependence of state machine and channel behaviors complicates the encoding logic. Therefore decoupling of these two is desired.

The first problem of nondeterministic interleaving of simultaneous occurrence of multiple preconditions is solved by creating an additional PSL variable for each state machine. This additional variable is used to distinguish between event and message triggers, and in defining preconditions for state transitions. For example, *Server_trigger* variable in Figure 4 is used by all preconditions (e.g. *S_ReqReceived*, *S_SendDone*) in the Server state machine. Using this extra variable eliminates the possibility of multiple preconditions being true at the same time. Nondeterministic behavior of the trigger is specified using PSL's assign construct, which instructs RuleBase to explore all possible interleavings by nondeterministically setting the extra variable to *event* or *msg*. Next states of various state transitions are encoded in a PSL's next construct with a case construct for each precondition (see *next(Server_state)* statement near the bottom of Figure 4).

The second problem of interdependency between actions and channel's message queue behavior is solved by having an *enqueue* definition to hold the message that an action inserts into the message queue. This definition is utilized in encoding the message queue of the channel. This extra definition achieves the desired decoupling. An example is the *S2C_enqueue* definition near the bottom of Figure 4.

Note that the define statements in the model, such as those for *C2S_dequeue* and *S2C_enqueue* can be omitted, and their usage can be replaced by full encoding of the condition. But the define statements don't increase the model size, and improve readability.

The message queue of a channel follows FIFO semantics. FIFO is encoded using following template (To handle boundary cases, FIFO definition includes two constants: `fifo(-1)!=0` and `fifo(FIFO_SIZE)=0`).

```
%for i in 0..(FIFO_SIZE-1) do
    assign init(fifo(i)) := 0;
    assign next(fifo(i)) := case
        dequeue & fifo(0)!=0 : case
            enqueue(new) & fifo(i)!=0
                & fifo(i+1)=0 : new;
            else : fifo(i+1);
        esac;
        enqueue(new) & fifo(i)=0
            & fifo(i-1)!=0 : new;
        else : fifo(i);
    esac;
%end
```

When a message is consumed from the FIFO, all other messages shift. The model for this behavior is trivial: `next(fifo(i)) := fifo(i+1)`. However this simplistic approach can not take care of all scenarios, and that is why our FIFO model template is slightly more complex, and need explanation:

– When a message is consumed (dequeue) from a non-empty FIFO, and at the same time a new message arrives (enqueue), then the last message entry is replaced by the *new* message. This behavior is captured by condition `fifo(i)!=0 & fifo(i+1)=0`, since the condition is true only for the last entry.

```
#define FIFO_SIZE 2
vunit protocol {
-- First Pass: define all variables for all
-- state machines and channels

-- define state machines, enumerate states
var Server_state : {Idle, Service, Fault};
var Client_state : {Ready, Wait, Register};

-- define triggers for all state machines
var Server_trigger   : {event, msg};
assign Server_trigger := {event, msg};
var Client_trigger   : {event, msg};
assign Client_trigger := {event, msg};

-- define events for all state machines
var Server_event    : {S_None, S_ReqFinished, S_ErrorDetetcted};
assign Server_event := {S_None, S_ReqFinished, S_ErrorDetetcted};
var Client_event    : {C_None, C_NewReq, C_AlarmRegistered};
assign Client_event := {C_None, C_NewReq, C_AlarmRegistered};

-- define FIFO msg queues for all channels between, any two state machines
var MsgQ_S2C(0..(FIFO_SIZE-1)) : {S2C_Empty, S2C_Done, S2C_Alarm};
var MsgQ_C2S(0..(FIFO_SIZE-1)) : {C2S_Empty, C2S_Req, C2S_Ack};

-- Second Pass: For all state machines, encode init states and transitions.
-- Encode all communication channels.

-- define init states for Server SM
assign init(Server_state) := Idle;

-- define preconditions for Server SM
define S_ReqReceived := (Server_state = Idle  & Server_trigger = msg
                                              & MsgQ_C2S(0) = C2S_Req);
define S_SendDone := (Server_state = Servive  & Server_trigger = event
                                              & Server_event = S_ReqFinished);
define S_SendAlarm := (Server_state = Idle    & Server_trigger = event
                                              & Server_event = S_ErrorDetetcted);
define S_AckReceived := (Server_state = Fault & Server_trigger = msg
                                              & MsgQ_C2S(0) = C2S_Ack);

-- define state transitions for Server SM
assign next(Server_state) := case
    S_ReqReceived : Service;
    S_SendDone    : Idle;
    S_SendAlarm   : Fault;
    S_AckReceived : Idle;
    else          : Server_state;
esac;

-- define enqueue actions for Server SM
define S2C_enqueue := case
    S_SendDone    : S2C_Done;
    S_SendAlarm   : S2C_Alarm;
    else          : S2C_Empty;
esac;

-- define dequeue actions for server
define C2S_dequeue := case
    S_ReqReceived : 1;
    S_AckReceived : 1;
    else          : 0;
esac;

-- skipped: client state machine, S2C and C2S channels
}
```

Fig. 4. Generated PSL for Client and Server State Machines

- When a message is dequeued, all messages shift (except for the last entry if there is also an enqueue, this is the former case). This is the trivial case.
- When there is only enqueue, the new message should be stored at the first empty FIFO entry. This is captured by condition `fifo(i)=0 & fifo(i-1)!=0`, since it is true only for the first empty entry.
- When there is no dequeue, all messages should keep their value (except the first empty entry when there is an enqueue , which is handled be previous case).

The occurrences of enqueue and dequeue in the template are replaced by appropriate enqueue definitions and preconditions. We also have a model for priority queue but we are omitting it in this paper for sake of simplicity.

The transformation of RoseRT model to PSL is done in two passes. In the first pass, all variables are generated. In second pass, remaining definitions are generated.

2.3   Executing RuleBase and Transforming Counterexample

The PSL for the state machine model and constraints is fed to RuleBase. RuleBase performs model checking. If any constraint is found to be violated, it reports a counter example exposing the offending event sequence. Our tool maps the counterexamples to the states and events in the original model and presents it as a UML sequence diagram, making it easy for user to understand the design flaw.

Model checking of the client-server state machines example discovered a deadlock, the counterexample is shown in Figure 5. A deadlock is caused when the Client sends a Req message to the Server, goes to the Wait state and waits for the Server to complete the request and send it back a Done message. Meanwhile, the Server detects an error before getting Client's Req message. It sends an Alarm message to the Client and waits for the Client to send it back an Ack message. Now both Client and Server state machines are waiting for a message from each other.

3   Experimental Results

We performed model checking on some of the benchmarks [22]: Client Server protocol, ATM machine, ATM machine with an error, and Railway Crossing. The results are shown in Table 1. We checked for liveliness property for each test case:

- Client Server: Eventually, Client and State will return to Ready and Idle states respectively.
- ATM: Eventually ATM will return to Idle state. We also introduced an error in the ATM UML models by removing a message that needed to be passed. Model checking found a counter example where due to that error, ATM will never return to Idle state.
- General Railroad Crossing (GRC): We checked two liveliness properties. The first set of data are for checking that *when a train is crossing a track, the gates should be closed*. The second set of data are for checking *eventually a train will pass and not get blocked*.

For each test case, Table 1 shows: the size of the BDD in the last model checking iteration, the size of state space, total BDD nodes allocated while model checking (includes

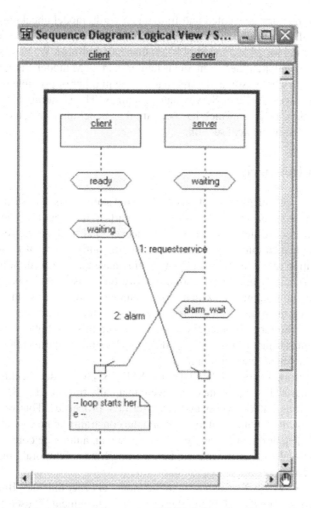

Fig. 5. Screen dump of model checking results, IBM RuleBase has discovered a deadlock in the Client Server state machines

Table 1. Model checking results on benchmarks

Benchmark	UML Model Complexity				Model Checking Complexity				
	State m/c's	States	Trans-itions	Trigg-ers	BDD Size	State Space	Nodes Allocated	Memory (MB)	User Time(s)
Client Server	2	6	8	4	67	53056	5657	38	0.85
ATM Machine	2	10	15	9	27	800	2778	38	0.54
ATM Error	2	10	15	9	28	672	4752	38	0.77
Railroad 1	4	24	31	11	673	$9.47*10^{10}$	727518	52	13.21
Railroad 2	4	24	31	11	673	$9.47*10^{10}$	727153	52	24.89

all iterations), memory consumed and time taken while model checking. All of these are indicative of the complexity of model and the design constraint being examined.

Model checking for all test cases took less than half a minute. We were surprised that model checking our Client Server model is harder than ATM model, though it is smaller than ATM model. The reason is that there are more number of possible interleaving of events and messages in Client Server state machines. The General Railroad Crossing is a more complex example which has been used as benchmark in some of the related research discussed in the next section.

4   Related Research

There have been several attempts of model checking state charts. Not surprisingly, all of them follow the same basic idea: translate state charts to the input language for a model checker, specify constraints, run the model checker, and analyze the results. Though the level of sophistication of each step varies significantly. Some of these approaches require translation to be done manually, and some have automated it. Some allow constraints to be specified graphically, some require the constraints to be written in the model checker input language (which requires understanding of the language as well as the conversion internals, even if it is automated). Some expects users to analyze the counterexample produced by model checker, and map this symbolic result to the state charts and events (which is not easy), while some does this mapping automatically. We describe here the most relevant literature.

Chan's [11] work was one of the first to use SMV [35] for model checking a variant of Harel's state charts [19]. The state charts were manually translated to SMV, and model checking was done for robustness and safety-critical properties. This work lies at one end of spectrum where both input to SMV and the constraints to be validated were hand crafted. TABU [3], at the other end of spectrum, had an automatic conversion of UML state charts to SMV and had a wizard to help writing Linear Temporal Logic properties. It showed the counterexample in a tabular form.

Just like SMV, VIS [10] is also a symbolic model checker that uses Binary Decision Diagrams (BDDs). The STATEMATE Verification Environment [7] used VIS for model checking STATEMATE [20] charts. Alur [1] used BDD package from VIS for model checking hierarchical state machines. Shen [41] used Abstract State Machine (ASM) model checker, which is based on SMV, for model checking UML state charts and OCL constraints, and presented counterexample in a tabular form.

SPIN [24] is another favorite model checker. Mikk's [36] tool automatically translated STATEMATE models to Promela, the input language for SPIN. Results were mapped back to original specifications and presented in non-graphical form. Latella [32] used SPIN but targeted UML state charts. The translation was automatic but handled only one state machine (authors claimed that it can be easily extended to handle multiple state machines). vUML [34] automated the translation of UML state charts to Promela and performed deadlock detection. HUGO [29] automatically translated UML state chart and fed it to SPIN and UPPAAL [31] model checkers. Constraints had to be specified in Promela. A textual counterexample trace was generated with the help of printf statements embedded in the Promela code. Darvas [15] also used SPIN on UML models. The counterexample was presented as message sequence chart, but not mapped back to original model.

Apart from SMV and SPIN, there are attempts to use other model checker such as converting STATEMATE charts to Esterel [40], UML state charts to Jack [18], and an Eclipse plug-in [6] using BLAST model checker [23].

There is also a body of work on formal semantics for state charts [30,33,39] and temporal constraints [17]. And there have been efforts for making temporal logic [5] specification more accessible by providing graphical interfaces [21,27,28,37].

We believe that for model checking to become popular, a tool must have following characteristics: automatic translation of state charts to input language for model checker, graphical and way of defining constraints, translation of counterexample back to the original model, and displaying it using common notations such as UML sequence diagrams. Essentially model checking should be invisible to the user and should be available at a click of a button. Currently available tools described in this section does not have all of these characteristics.

5   Conclusions and Future Work

The work presented here exploits the similarities of hardware circuits and embedded systems by seamlessly integrating IBM RuleBase to IBM Rational RoseRT. We support graphical way of specifying constraints and automatic translation of UML state charts and constraints to RuleBase input without requiring user intervention, and display counterexamples as sequence diagrams using states and events in the original UML model. This approach reduces the needed learning time, and brings down the complexity below the threshold for widespread adoption of model checking.

Our sequence diagram modifications for constraint definition is similar to Harel's Live Sequence Diagram (LSC) [21]. An alternative approach is to use OCL [38] as done by Flake [16]. A suitable mix of both needs to be explored that combines mathematical rigor of OCL with the intuitiveness of LSC. Another dimension of future work is to perform model checking at various levels of state machine hierarchy instead of attempting to flatten the state charts without state space explosion [42]. The abstraction at a given level of the hierarchy might lead to false positive due to some combination of events that are not possible if the details from the lower levels of the hierarchy are considered. Therefore, when model checking results into a spurious counterexample, the abstraction should be refined. Only the compound states relevant to the counterexample can be flattened and model checking can be performed again. We plan to explore this approach with an expectation that it will lead to further improvements. We also plan to explore the possible ways of handling models that have C/C++ code embedded as actions.

References

1. Alur, R., Yannakakis, M.: Model checking of hierarchical state machines. ACM Transactions on Programming Languages and Systems 23(3) (2001) 273–303
2. Barner, S., Glazberg, Z., Rabinovitz, I.: Wolf - bug hunter for concurrent software using formal methods. In: Proc. of 17th International Conference on Computer Aided Verification, Lecture Notes in Computer Science. Volume 3576., Springer (2005) 153–157

3. Beato, M.E., Barrio-Solórzano, M., Quintero, C.E.C., de la Fuente, P.: UML automatic verification tool with formal methods. Electronic Notes in Theoretical Computer Science **127**(4) (2005) 3–16

4. Beer, I., Ben-David, S., Eisner, C., Landver, A.: RuleBase: an industry-oriented formal verification tool. In: Proc. of the 33rd Design Automation Conference. (1996) 655–660

5. Bellini, P., Mattonlini, R., Nesi, P.: Temporal logics for real-time system specification. ACM Computing Surveys **32**(1) (2000) 12–42

6. Beyer, D., Henzinger, T.A., Jhala, R., Majumdar, R.: An Eclipse plug-in for model checking. In: Proc. of 12th International Workshop on Program Comprehension (IWPC2004), IEEE Computer Society (2004) 251–255

7. Bienmüller, T., Damm, W., Wittke, H.: The STATEMATE verification environment – making it real. In: Proc. of 12th International Conference on Computer Aided Verification, Lecture Notes in Computer Science. Volume 1855., Springer (2000) 561–567

8. Booch, G., Rumbaugh, J.E., Jacobson, I.: Unified Modeling Language User Guide. Addison-Wesley (1999)

9. Brand, D., Zafiropulo, P.: On communicating finite-state machines. Journal of the Association for Computing Machinery **30**(2) (1983) 323–342

10. Brayton, R.K., Hachtel, G.D., Sangiovanni-Vincentelli, A.L., Somenzi, F., Aziz, A., Cheng, S.T., Edwards, S.A., Khatri, S.P., Kukimoto, Y., Pardo, A., Qadeer, S., Ranjan, R.K., Sarwary, S., Shiple, T.R., Swamy, G., Villa, T.: VIS: a system for verification and synthesis. In: Proc. of 8th International Conference on Computer Aided Verification, Lecture Notes in Computer Science. Volume 1102., Springer (1996) 428–432

11. Chan, W., Anderson, R.J., Beame, P., Burns, S., Modugno, F., Notkin, D., Reese, J.D.: Model checking large software specifications. IEEE Transactions on Software Engineering **24**(7) (1998) 498–520

12. Clarke, E.M., Emerson, E.A., Sistla, A.P.: Automatic verification of finite-state concurrent systems using temporal logic specifications. ACM Trans. on Programming Languages and Systems **8**(2) (1986) 244–263

13. Clarke, E.M., Grumberg, O., Long, D.E.: Model checking and abstraction. ACM Trans. on Programming Languages and Systems **16**(5) (1994) 1512–1542

14. Clarke, E.M., Grumberg, O., Peled, D.A.: Model Checking. The MIT Press (2000)

15. Darvas, A., Majzik, I., Benyo, B.: Verification of UML statechart models of embedded systems. In: Proc. of 5th IEEE Design and Diagnostics of Electronic Circuits and Systems Workshop. (2002) 70–77

16. Flake, S., Müller, W.: A UML profile for real-time constraints with the OCL. In: Proc. of The Unified Modeling Language (UML2002), Lecture Notes in Computer Science. Volume 2460., Springer (2002) 179–195

17. Flake, S., Müller, W.: Formal semantics of static and temporal state-oriented OCL constraints. Software and System Modeling **2**(3) (2003) 164–186

18. Gnesi, S., Latella, D., Massink, M.: Model checking UML statechart diagrams using JACK. In: Proc. of 4th IEEE International Symposium on High-Assurance Systems Engineering. (1999) 46–55

19. Harel, D.: Statecharts: A visual formalism for complex systems. Science of Computer Programming **8**(3) (1987) 231–274

20. Harel, D., Naamad, A.: The STATEMATE semantics of statecharts. ACM Transactions on Software Engineering and Methodology **5**(4) (1996) 293–333

21. Harel, D., Marelly, R.: Come, Let's Play: Scenario-Based Programming Using LSCs and the Play-Engine. Springer (2003)

22. Heitmeyer, C.L., Jeffords, R.D., Labaw, B.G.: A benchmark for comparing different approaches for specifying and verifying real-time systems. In: Proc. of the 10th IEEE workshop on Real-time operating systems and software. (1993) 122–129

23. Henzinger, T.A., Jhala, R., Majumdar, R., Sutre, G.: Software verification with BLAST. In: Proc. of 10th SPIN Workshop on Model Checking Software (SPIN2003), Lecture Notes in Computer Science. Volume 2648., Springer (2003) 235–239
24. Holzmann, G.J.: The Spin Model Checker: Primer and Reference Manual. Addison-Wesley (2003)
25. IBM: Rational Rose RealTime. (http://www.ibm.com/software/awdtools/developer/technical)
26. IEEE: PSL – IEEE Standard for Property Specification Language, IEEE P1850. (http://www.eda.org/ieee-1850/)
27. Jahanian, F., Mok, A.K.: Modechart: A specification language for real-time systems. IEEE Transactions on Software Engineering **20**(12) (1994) 933–947
28. Kent, S.: Constraint diagrams: visualizing invariants in object-oriented models. In: Proc. of the 12th ACM SIGPLAN conference on Object-oriented programming, systems, languages, and applications (OOPSLA97), ACM Press (1997) 327–341
29. Knapp, A., Merz, S., Rauh, C.: Model checking – timed UML state machines and collaborations. In: Proc. of 7th International Symposium on Formal Techniques in Real-Time and Fault-Tolerant Systems, Lecture Notes in Computer Science. Volume 2469., Springer (2002) 395–416
30. Kwon, G.: Rewrite rules and operational semantics for model checking UML statecharts. In: Proc. of The Unified Modeling Language (UML2000), Lecture Notes in Computer Science. Volume 1939., Springer (2000) 528–540
31. Larsen, K.G., Pettersson, P., Yi, W.: UPPAAL in a nutshell. International Journal on Software Tools for Technology Transfer **1**(1-2) (1997) 134–152
32. Latella, D., Majzik, I., Massink, M.: Automatic verification of a behavioural subset of UML statechart diagrams using the SPIN model-checker. Formal Aspects of Computer Science **11**(6) (1999) 637–664
33. Latella, D., Majzik, I., Massink, M.: Towards a formal operational semantics of UML statechart diagrams. In: Proc. of 2rd International Conference on Formal Methods for Open Object-Based Distributed Systems. Volume 139., Kluwer (1999)
34. Lilius, J., Paltor, I.: vUML: a tool for verifying UML models. In: Proc. of 14th IEEE International Conference on Automated Software Engineering. (1999) 255–258
35. McMillan, K.L.: Symbolic Model Checking. Kluwer Academic Publishers (1993)
36. Mikk, E., Lakhnech, Y., Siegel, M., Holzmann, G.J.: Implementing statecharts in PROMELA/SPIN. In: Proc. of 2nd Workshop on Industrial-Strength Formal Specification Techniques, IEEE Computer Society (1998) 90–101
37. Moser, L.E., Ramakrishna, Y.S., Kutty, G., Melliar-Smith, P.M., Dillon, L.K.: A graphical environment for the design of concurrent real-time systems. ACM Transactions on Software Engineering and Methodology **6**(1) (1997) 31–79
38. Object Management Group: UML 2.0 OCL Final Adopted Specification. OMG Document ptc/03-10-14, ftp://ftp.omg.org/pub/docs/ptc/03-10-14.pdf (2003)
39. Paltor, I., Lilius, J.: Formalising UML state machines for model checking. In: Proc. of The Unified Modeling Language (UML1999), Lecture Notes in Computer Science. Volume 1723., Springer (1999) 430–445
40. Seshia, S.A., Shyamasundar, R.K., Bhattacharjee, A.K., Dhodapkar, S.D.: A translation of statecharts to Esterel. In: Proc. of World Congress on Formal Methods, Lecture Notes in Computer Science. Volume 1709., Springer (1999) 983–1007
41. Shen, W., Compton, K.J., Huggins, J.: A toolset for supporting UML static and dynamic model checking. In: Proc. of 16th IEEE International Conference on Automated Software Engineering. (2001) 315–318
42. Wasowski, A.: Flattening statecharts without explosions. In: Proc. of the 2004 ACM SIGPLAN/SIGBED conference on Languages, compilers, and tools for embedded systems. (2004) 257–266

A Panel:
Unpaved Road Between Hardware Verification and Software Testing Techniques

Shmuel Ur

IBM Haifa Labs
ur@il.ibm.com

The Haifa verification conference was created to foster assimilation of knowledge and tools between software testing and hardware verification. On the second day of the conference, the tool day, we held a panel discussion on achieving this goal. The panel was moderated by Shmuel Ur, the chair of the first Haifa Verification Conference, who works in the industry and publishes both in software testing and in hardware verification. These were the distinguished panelists:

- Randy Bryant - the dean of the Carnegie Mellon University School of Computer Science and a university professor. Bryant's research focuses on methods for formally verifying digital hardware, and more recently some forms of software. His 1986 paper on symbolic Boolean manipulation using Ordered Binary Decision Diagrams (BDDs) has the highest citation count of any publication in the Citeseer database of computer science literature.
- Andrew Piziali - an industry veteran design verification engineer with 23 years of experience in verifying mainframes, supercomputers, and microprocessors with StorageTek, Amdahl, Evans and Sutherland, Convex Computer, Cyrix, Texas Instruments, Transmeta, Verisity, and Cadence. He is the author of "Functional Verification Coverage Measurement and Analysis" and the co-author of "ESL Design and Verification" together with Grant Martin and Brian Bailey, which will be available in the spring of 2007.
- Gul Agha - a professor of Computer Science and a research professor in Coordinated Science Laboratory at the University of Illinois at Urbana-Champaign. His work on Actors provided an influential model for concurrent computing. Dr. Agha is a Fellow of the IEEE, a Golden Core of the IEEE Computer Society and a former ACM international lecturer. He serves as the editor-in-chief of the ACM Computing Surveys and is the past editor-in-chief of IEEE Concurrency: Parallel, Distributed, and Mobile Computing.
- Avi Ziv - a member of the Simulation-based Verification Technologies department at the IBM Haifa Research Lab. Since joining IBM in 1996, Avi has been involved in many activities related to simulation-based verification, specifically in the area of functional coverage. Currently, he leads projects in functional verification and coverage-directed generation.

Often, hardware design verification and software testing seem to be separate disciplines. Usually, different people work on them in separate companies and conferences. Yet, significant similarities between software development and hardware

E. Bin, A. Ziv, and S. Ur (Eds.): HVC 2006, LNCS 4383, pp. 122–123, 2007.

design exist, and the successful adoption of techniques originally developed for one field for use in the other suggests that these disciplines are related. The panel's goal was to analyze the similarities and differences between hardware verification and software testing and to identify technologies that mature in one field and are ready to cross over. Negative experiences of what did not or will not work are also important as the bent is practical and it is important to know where difficulties lie.

One prominent crossover example is code coverage, which was first developed for software testing and is now commonly used in hardware verification. Another example is the FSM-based test generator, which was developed for the verification of hardware modules and is now successfully employed for software testing. Moreover, some techniques, such as reliability estimation, were developed for hardware, changed and adapted for software, and are now starting to show their usefulness with hardware again.

The panel was very interesting and was followed by lively interaction between the panelists and the audience. Some of the interesting observations included these:

- It is very hard to find people in the software industry who are aware of hardware verification. Indeed, the first question asked, was "Why is it called hardware verification and not hardware testing?" We explained that hardware testing is reserved on the hardware side for testing the hardware itself, where verification is used for the logic. Hardware verification people, on the other hand, are generally familiar with software testing techniques, as after all, they do write software.
- Economics plays an important role in deciding which technique to use. In general, the cost of bugs in hardware is much higher as the product has to be replaced. Therefore, in hardware testing, we try to obtain levels of quality that are unheard of in commercial software. However, the levels of quality demanded of software are rising and people are starting to use techniques such as formal verification, whose advantages are in discovering extreme corner cases.
- The people working in software verification are usually less skilled, and software testing for most people is not a career path. If you are good, you move to development, which means that the tools used in software testing need to be very simple. On the other hand, due to economics, hardware verification has more prestige and people who choose it as a career, so the tools can be more complex.

An Open Source Simulation Model
of Software Development and Testing

Shmuel Ur[1], Elad Yom-Tov[1], and Paul Wernick[2]

[1] IBM Haifa Research Labs, Haifa, 31905, Israel
{ur, yomtov}@il.ibm.com
[2] School of Computer Science, University of Hertfordshire,
College Lane, Hatfield, Herts. AL10 9AB, UK
p.d.wernick@herts.ac.uk

Abstract. This paper describes a new discrete event simulation model built using a mathematical tool (Matlab) to investigate the simulation of the programming and the testing phases of a software development project. In order to show how the model can be used and to provide some preliminary concrete results, we give three examples of how this model can be utilized to examine the effect of adopting different strategies for coding and testing a new software system. Specifically, we provide results of simulation runs intended to simulate the effects on the coding and testing phases of different testing strategies, the adoption of pair programming in an otherwise-unchanged process, and the automation of testing. The model source code is available for downloading at http://qp.research.ibm.com/concurrency_testing, and we invite researchers and practitioners to use and modify the model.

Keywords: Simulation, Software Development, Iterative design, Algorithms, Management, Measurement, Performance, Design, Economics, Reliability, Experimentation, Theory, Verification.

1 Introduction

In many areas of software development, it is difficult to predict the effect of process changes. This is due in large measure to the impact of the scale of real-world development work. Mechanisms that work well in laboratory-sized experiments may or may not scale up to work in industrial-scale developments of large systems.

An example of a mechanism that needs to work well in large-scale development is testing. Current approaches include testing each module as it is completed by the programmers, usually by a separate quality assurance team, formalized testing during programming by the programmers, and the test-first strategy espoused most notably by Beck in eXtreme Programming [1] of writing test harnesses code first and then writing programs specifically to pass those tests. Another approach to managing the resource applied to testing is to automate some or all of the tests, rather than having people run them. Whilst this demands a greater initial investment, subsequent runs are cheaper to perform. The question therefore arises as to when (if ever) the benefits of such an approach outweigh the costs.

E. Bin, A. Ziv, and S. Ur (Eds.): HVC 2006, LNCS 4383, pp. 124–137, 2007.
© Springer-Verlag Berlin Heidelberg 2007

One mechanism for investigating questions such as these is software process *simulation*. Here, an enactable, usually quantified, model is built of a process for software development. This model is then modified to reflect actual and/or proposed process changes, and the results compared with the initial case to determine whether the change seems to improve or degrade performance. We believe that simulation is the most effective way to investigate proposed process changes in large-scale developments; in view of the uncertainty of scaling up small-scale experiments, the only alternative is to conduct development cycles in parallel using each mechanism and compare the results, an approach which is not only costly but also risks introducing confounding factors such as users applying learning from one team to the work of the other. However, the results derived from simulation runs do not carry the same level of certainty as experiments under controlled conditions, in particular because the simulation model is inevitably a simplification of the actual process.

A considerable body of literature describing the simulation of software processes has grown up over time, including a number of journal special issues (see for example [13, 17]). This has included work on software testing and quality assurance such as that of Madachy [9].

To investigate *inter alia* the effects on a software process of different approaches to testing, we have built a new discrete event simulation model using a mathematical tool (Matlab) and used the model to investigate the effect of adopting different strategies for coding and testing new software systems. This paper describes the simulation model itself. Our work also examines the effects of different testing strategies and pair programming on the completion times of the coding and testing phases. The Matlab code of our simulation model is available at http://qp.research.ibm.com/ concurrency_testing. We invite researchers to use and comment on the model, and to publish any improvements they make.

The work presented here shows how simulation-based studies can examine software process behavior in cases where experiments or real-world testing are either difficult or expensive to perform or produce results that cannot be easily generalized. This is especially noted in software activities relating to large systems and/or over many releases of a software product.

One characteristic of much of the published work in software process simulation is that the results of simulation exercises and a description of the model are usually presented but the model is typically not described completely, most often in respect of the omission of the underlying equations or the input data used for the runs presented. This may well be due to the size of the equations and/or data, but it does produce results that are difficult for other workers to check, and in models which researchers find difficulty in critiquing and improving. We have therefore decided to make the code of our model public and easily accessible, not only in the hope that the software testing community will make use of it in process optimization but also to allow other workers to critique it, and, we hope, to modify and improve it.

We regard the simulation model itself as the main contribution of this work. It is explicitly intended as a general-purpose simulation of the coding and testing phases of a software process which can be modified to reflect any required process changes; in this, it is closer in spirit to that of Wernick and Hall [17] than other software process models which have generally been developed to represent a single process environment or a specific process change. We also believe that its usefulness to software engineers is enhanced by it having been written in an environment that is closer to the programming languages with which software developers will be familiar than the specific simulation environments used for other models. The specific results we have obtained so far are of interest, but further validation work is required.

2 The Simulation Model

2.1 Outline of the Model

In this section, we explain our simulation model for the programming phase of a project. We assume the design has been completed and we are simulating iterative cycles for the construction of the program; these cycles continue until the constructed program implements the design.

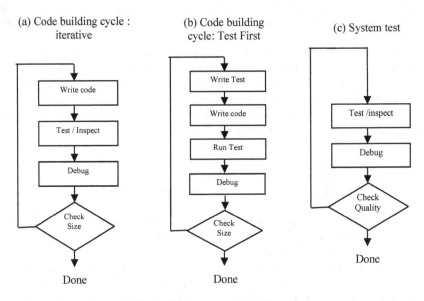

Fig. 1. Simulation model structure

We have designed the simulation model to reflect three phases of code production: code writing, testing, and debugging. First, the programmers develop the project during the code writing phase. Once this has been done, they move onto the test/inspect phase (unit, function or system after all the code is created) where they test and/or inspect the new, and possibly the existing, code. Next, they proceed to the debug/fix phase where they debug and repair all the bugs found during the test/inspect phase. In traditional development methods this cycle repeats until the functionality of the program is complete, as shown in Fig. 1(a). In newer agile methods, the cycle repeats itself many times because each iteration is very short. Once the program is complete, the system test cycles through the test/inspect and debug/fix phases until some pre-defined quality criterion is reached, as shown in Figure 1(c). Generally, this criterion is determined pragmatically and typically reflects less than 100% freedom from bugs. The time dedicated to the code writing and testing phases is predetermined. The time dedicated to debugging depends on the number of bugs found and how long it takes to fix each one.

The Test First approach, depicted in Figure 1(b), results in a slightly different simulation. Here the tests are created first, next the code is developed, and then the tests are executed and the code is debugged. This approach is usually characterized by very short code writing cycles.

The simulation begins with the code writing phase, where objects corresponding to lines of code are actually created. These lines of code may or may not contain bugs; this is determined by a probability parameter. In the test/inspect phase, specific lines are tested/inspected and flaws may be found. In the debug/fix phase, time is spent identifying the bugs related to the flaws and some lines are replaced with new lines, which may, of course, contain new bugs. During the simulation, the program is created and improves hour by hour. In each simulated hour, one of the above activities is carried out, whether adding lines to the program, looking for bugs, or debugging and fixing the code. Each line of code is actually added as a discrete item to the simulation data so that when a specific location in the program is inspected for bugs, only the bugs that were inserted during the code writing phase are found. (We have not simulated the case of an incorrect review in which correct code is marked as a bug and changed.) In addition to explaining the above phases, this section covers the implementation of a bug to provide a more complete understanding of the simulation model.

In the real world and in our model, the more complex the program, the more difficult it is to write, test, inspect, debug, and fix. In our simulation, for the sake of simplicity, we use the size of the code measured in lines of code as a proxy for code complexity and do not take into account the type of code (scientific, GUI, etc.). Type of code would impact on the number of bugs per line, the number of lines written per hour and possibly other parameters. Sometimes code complexity is not the only issue. For example, the time passing between the introduction of the bug and its being found is a major predictor of debug time [15].

Every programming hour, the model adds *#code_line_per_hour* lines to the code base. This is not held as a count of lines; rather, an actual line object is created for every new program line. The number of lines of written code may be impacted by the complexity of the code (down), by the type of code (down or up), and by the programming language. For example, it is possible that GUI code is written at a much faster rate than control code. For each line created, the probability that it contains a bug is the variable *bugs_per_line*. The duration of the code writing phase, which determines the number of lines that are written, is a parameter of the simulation run and is not part of the phase definition.

The test/inspect phase is composed of two distinct sub-phases: test writing and test execution. During test writing a number of tests are created. This number is equal to the length of the phase divided by *time_to_create_test*, corrected for complexity. During the test execution sub-phase, the new tests are executed in order of creation, along with as many old tests as possible. The simulation does not try to optimize the execution of specific new and old tests if there is not enough time, an important field of study in software testing [14]. However, such a module could be added to the simulation and its impact studied. Each test created has a number of parameters, some of which are used to find the lines of code actually tested by these tests. During simulation, for each test there is a percentage of new lines and of old lines covered by it. Another option that is that the test will execute a specific number of tested lines. Of the possible program lines to be tested, some are chosen at random, based on the parameters of the specific simulation run. Another parameter is the execution time per test. Manual tests tend to have shorter creation times and longer execution time, while automated tests have a longer creation time and shorter execution time.

The inspection sub-phase is very simple. The amount of code inspected is governed by the *#lines_reviewed_per_hour* parameter, modified to reflect code complexity. The number of lines reviewed is determined by the length of the phase.

During the debug/fix phase, any flaw found in the test phase is traced to its cause and a bug is found. The debug time is influenced primarily by the duration between the time the bug was put in and the time it was found, corrected for complexity. This is one of the better documented phenomena and is a major reason for the Test First approach [15]. If the bug was found during the review, debug is not necessary because inspection finds root causes.

In the fixing sub-phase a number of lines are modified to correct the bug. The number of lines modified may be influenced by the amount of time the bug was hiding in the code before its discovery. However, because we do not have hard evidence for this value, we have not included it in the simulation. The lines changed are in the vicinity of the bugs and are treated as new code that does not increase the program size. The time it takes to create this new code is *hours_to_fix_bug*.

The time taken to insert, detect, and fix bugs is the heart of the simulation. Each bug is located in a specific line. For simplicity, we ignore multi-line bugs, which are more adept at evading inspection. Each bug has a probability of being discovered by a test, as indicated by *prob_discovered_by_test*, and a probability of being discovered by inspection, as indicated by *prob_discovered_by_inspection*. A bug has a second probability of being discovered by a test when the same test is re-executed. If it is a deterministic bug, this probability is zero or close to it (ignoring random tests). If it is a probabilistic bug (e.g. deadlock), the probability may be higher because the same input (test) might expose the bug, depending on interleaving that is usually beyond the tester's control. This means that if regression testing is undertaken in deterministic code, it rarely finds old bugs (if they become exposed to the test due to code change), and mostly finds bugs introduced by modifications or bug fixes.

2.2 Model Default Values

A common use of a simulation model is to vary one or more parameter values and observe the impact of these changes. To provide a reliable base case from which to construct the investigations, it is first necessary to have well-supported default values for all parameters. These values are based on experimental documentation.

The values we have used for model parameters are as follows:

- *#code_line_per_hour* = 30 [2:207–237]
- *Bugs_per_line* = 0.01 [7]
- *correction_for_time_since_placement* = 1 + (*time_since_ bug*)/2000 – The increase in cost to fix bug due to code written between creation and fixing [3]
- *Hours_to_fix_bug* – base 2, multiply by 2 if a month passed, multiply by 3 if two months passed [15:6–10]

- **Bugs per lines of code after testing** - no default as it is a simulation decision
- **Prob_discovered_by_inspection** = 0.5 : Laitenberger and DeBaud [8] suggest that 70% is achievable; we pessimistically set our rate to 50%.
- **#lines_reviewed_per_hour** = 200 : from [8]; in our experience, these time frames differ greatly, but one hour for 200 lines is reasonable.
- **Cost of testing** = 1.14 hour per one hundred lines to do unit testing. [2: 146]
- **Probability of finding bugs in test** = .5 [15: 6–10]

2.3 Sensitivity Analysis

We have conducted a sensitivity analysis to determine the effect on the base case model of modifying each of the input parameters. This analysis showed that all the parameters cause the expected model output behaviour changes when their values are modified. Our initial expectations that the completion time for the program would increase with increasing the time to fix a bug, with increasing numbers of bugs per line and with greater time required to write tests, were confirmed in simulation runs. We expected the behaviour to be different with the number of lines written per hour. If one writes very few lines per hour then the project time increases as programming takes more time. If one writes many lines, more than can be tested, many of the bugs will be discovered too late and the debugging cost will increase. We expected a 'sweet spot', an optimal value, for the number of lines written per hour, which for our simulation was found around 15 lines per hour as can be seen in Figure 2. The important factor is not the number of lines per hour but

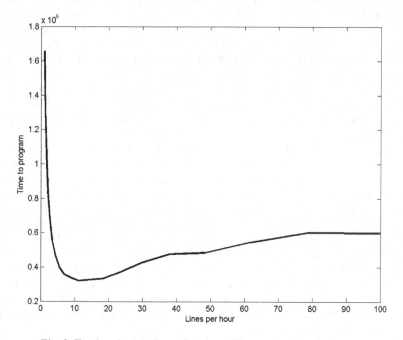

Fig. 2. Total project time as a function of lines programmed per hour

testing keeping pace with coding. If coding becomes more efficient then the testing phase has to become longer to deal with the extra amount of code generated.

3   Sample Simulations

In this section, we describe three scenarios to illustrate the way in which the simulation model can be employed to examine specific issues in software processes.

3.1   Comparing Waterfall, Iterative, and Test First Approaches

In the first simulation, we used the model to determine the optimal length of the coding phase between testing cycles. Many development paradigms are distinguished by this criterion. As our simulation runs the program is built in stages, each comprising a program/test/debug cycle, until the entire program is complete. The system test is then performed until the desired quality is reached. There are 120K lines of code and a desired final bug count of approximately 50. The total bug count is 1200 bugs for all methods, based on a probability of 1/100 that for all methods a bug is created in each line of code.

In our simulation of the traditional waterfall model, all the code is created and then it is tested. Because functions are created and tested before integration, the simulation has long programming phases of 2000 programming hours between test phases. The testing cycles are much shorter in iterative models such as the Rational Unified Process [6]. We simulate this by having programming phases of 400 hours between testing phases. In eXtreme Programming [1] using the Test First approach, tests are written as the first step and the code is tested as soon as it is created.[1] We simulate this approach by testing after every 100 hours of programming. In our simulation, the testing cycle is always 200 hours, divided evenly between the creation of new tests and test execution, regardless of how often it is performed. As a result, in our simulation of eXtreme Programming each testing phase is longer than the programming phase to which it is attached. This division of time is not based on data from the literature but represents a percentage of testing time between 10% and 66%. Our goal is not to claim that one is better than the other, but to show that with proper management, one can optimize the length of the coding phase.

Before running the simulation, we estimated that the 2000 hour programming phase would be too long and result in a very long system test phase. We thought 100 hours (simulating eXtreme Programming) would be too short, as most of the time is spent in testing. Our results showed that with our specific simulation parameters, eXtreme Programming (simulating only the Test First aspects) works best. We believe that the main reason for this result is that the debugging time is shortest when almost no time passes between when the bug is introduced until it is found by a test. In our simulation, we see that the debugging time is indeed very small for extreme programming. This accords with our intuitive reasoning that a developer presented with a bug as they write the code would find it easier to locate and fix. Figure 3 shows the fraction of the project time spent on programming. As expected, this number decreases with time as more time is spent on testing. Also, according to accepted

---

[1] The implications for development timescales of the folding of design work into programming that occurs in extreme programming is not considered in this paper.

wisdom, the smaller the fraction of the time you initially spend on programming and the more you stress quality, the better your project will be. This can be seen when comparing eXtreme Programming with other paradigms. Less time is spent on programming initially but the progress is faster and the project finishes earlier. A counter-intuitive result, which can be seen in the long cycle (2000) line in Figure 3, is that the proportion of time spent on programming rises significantly toward the end of

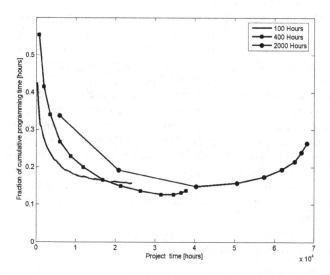

Fig. 3. Fraction of the project spent on programming. Each curve denotes a different length of the programming phase.

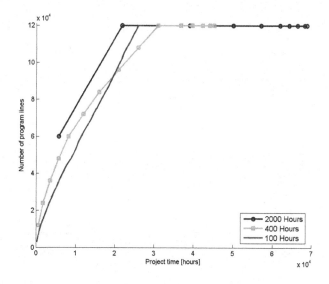

Fig. 4. System size vs. programming time for three approaches to programming. Each curve denotes a different length of the programming phase.

the project. Clearly, when the quality is lower, more time is spent on bug fixing (a programming task) toward the end of the project. Figure 4 shows the time taken to complete the project, in hours. The actual results are:

- Waterfall: 68600 hours to complete, 20800 hours to reach system test
- Iterative: 43800 hours to complete, 30000 hours to reach system test
- Test First: 27300 hours to complete, 26400 hours to reach system test

As expected, with a waterfall process, developers reach the system testing phase faster than in the iterative model; however, the system testing phase is longer and as a result the total time is longer. The unexpected (for some of us) result was that the Test First approach is so effective that not only is the system testing phase very short, but it is actually reached faster than by the iterative process.

Because this simulation runs until the bug count reaches a specified value, it is impossible to compare it with experiments where remaining bugs are counted at the end of the experimental procedure. In an experiment with programmers working under laboratory conditions, George and Williams [4] found that a Test First approach resulted in code that passed 18% more black box tests but took 16% more time. We believe that George and Williams' subjects are likely to have reached the same bug count as the waterfall users in less time. This result is reflected in our simulation, although our simulation shows a greater reduction in time than George and Williams' results might suggest.

3.2 Evaluating Pair Programming

Pair programming, as defined in http://en.wikipedia.org/wiki/Pair_programming, is a practice that requires two software engineers to participate in a combined development effort at one workstation. Each member performs the action the other is

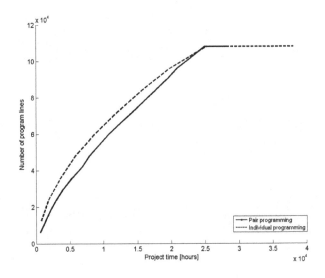

Fig. 5. Program lines vs. programming type for a large project

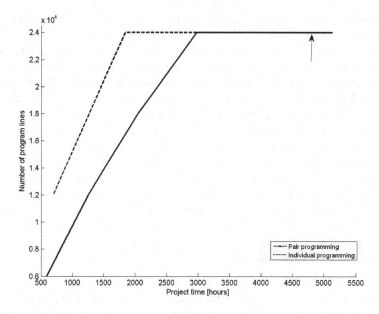

Fig. 6. Program lines vs. programming type for a small project

not currently doing. For example, while one types in unit tests the other thinks about the class that will satisfy the test . The person doing the typing is known as the driver while the person guiding is known as the navigator. It is often suggested that the two partners switch roles at least every half-hour. In this section we would like to show how our simulation model can evaluate the utility of pair programming.

We estimated that in pair programming the code generation rate would be halved, since two people are writing the same amount of code previously written by one person. Studies have been done on the amount of code produced by pairs [18], but the data relate to the productivity of the project, which for us is output and not input. While halving output is rather harsh, we have chosen this number as a lower bound on the basis that, if pair programming with this value is beneficial, it would be even more beneficial with a more optimistic productivity value. We also simulated a reduction in the number of bugs generated since two pairs of eyes are looking for bugs, for which we used a rate of 300/356 suggested by Williams *et al.* [18].

Our simulation showed that the gain or loss in productivity depends on the project size. In larger projects, as shown in Figure 5, careful programming is highly rewarded — not only is the total project time faster but the system test phase is reached earlier due to the decreased amount of debugging. For smaller projects, which have been studied more in the literature (e.g. [18]), there is a productivity cost for pair programming. This can be seen in Figure 6 where the arrow indicates the end of the project for single programmers. Hence, while the jury may still be out on the question of whether pair programming improves productivity for smaller projects, our simulation shows that the advantages are quite clear for larger projects. Our findings differ from those obtained buy Williams *et al.* in small-scale experiments [18], where a gain from adopting pair programming was found even for small projects. It is possible that our simulation of an industrial process differs from the experimental protocol of Williams *et al.* which was based on students' assignments, or results from their the use of student programmers.

Our results suggest that the pros and cons of adopting pair programming for any particular project depends on a number of factors not necessarily captured in small-scale, single cycle experiments such as those of Williams *et al.* [18]. In this particular they parallel the simulation-based work of Wernick and Hall [16]. In the latter case, the effect of adopting pair programming on long-term maintainability of a software system is suggested as an element that needs to be quantified as part of a cost/benefit analysis; here, system size is another aspect to take into account.

Our method of implementing the pair programming paradigm described above can also be viewed as equivalent to early testing, as fewer bugs are introduced. In our simulation, there is a heavy penalty for late debugging, as is consistent with the literature. In conditions where such a heavy penalty is not relevant, the simulation results will be different.

3.3 Evaluating Test Automation

Using our simulation, we have investigated whether it is worthwhile to automate tests. We simulated automated tests as tests that cost five times as much to design, compared with typical industry figures of 3 to 10 [10] but can be executed at minimal human resource cost. We have not allowed for the maintenance cost of automated tests, which can be much higher than for manual tests. In our simulation, when a test is executed more than once, the only bugs it can find are the bugs that were introduced to the code after the previous run (due to bug fixes). Onoma *et al.* [12] observe that the main reason stated for automating testing is to ensure that newly introduced bugs are found as soon as possible after their introduction to the system code.

Our model was modified to simulate the partial automation of testing adopted in test-driven development: "With TDD, all *major* public classes of the system have a corresponding unit test class to test the public interface, that is, the contract of that class ... with other classes (e.g. parameters to method, semantics of method, pre- and post-conditions to method)." ([11]; our emphasis). Automating the tests results in a number of changes that impact on the simulation results, some of them in a non-intuitive way. Creating an automated test takes longer then creating a manual one as programming effort is involved. This means that, since in the simulation the resource allocated to each testing period is fixed, there are initially fewer tests performed on the code.

One surprising result of our simulation runs is that when automated tests are used programming proceeds faster. This is due to the fact that fewer bugs are found because fewer tests are executed and a lower percentage of the time is spent on debugging. However, these bugs still need to be located and fixed before the software is released, so later, during the system tests, more time is spent fixing the bugs. Another obvious trade-off is between running many tests a few times and running fewer tests many times. Usually, one will not choose one extreme. i.e. automating all tests, over the other, but will choose to automate a number of tests and perform the rest manually. Marick [10] states that "The cost of automating a test is best measured by the number of manual tests it prevents you from running and the bugs it will therefore cause you to miss". He also states that "A test is designed for a particular purpose: to see if some aspects of one or more features work. When an automated test that's rerun finds bugs, you should expect it to find ones that seem to have nothing to do with the test's original purpose. Much of the value of an automated test lies in how well it can do that." The cost of developing automated tests suggests that some tests should be automated and some should not. In our model we provide support for the simulation of different mixes of automated and manual tests.

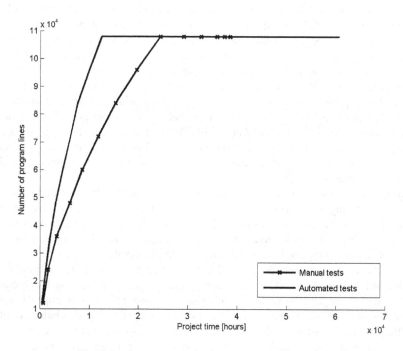

Fig. 7. Performance of automated and manual testing

In the scenario presented in Figure 7, given the parameter values we have used, i.e., an automated test is five times more expansive to write but have no execution cost, we see the benefit gained from automation is outweighed by the fact that fewer tests are initially created; while system test was reached earlier with automated testing (12,500 compared to 24,404 hours) because less unique tests were performed, the project was completed much later (60,622 compared to 38,565 hours).

Maximilien and Williams [11] have reported the results of an industrial case study using pre-written test cases for unit testing. The IBM test-driven development process examined in their report resulted in an error rate reduced by 50% and work completed on time. This was achieved with automated test cases covering 80% of the "important' classes" [11: 566]. A question that needs to be studied is whether the benefits were gained from the automation or from the investment in unit testing. Our simulation points to the latter, and poses a question regarding the use of tools like JUnit and the test automation of unit testing in eXtreme Programming. Is the practice of creating automated tests for unit testing efficient because of, or despite, the automation aspects? Maybe it is even more efficient to do these tests without the automation.

4 Summary

The goal of our work has not been to claim that Test First, pair programming and manual testing are superior to the alternatives; rather it is to show how the open-source simulation model described in this paper may be used to evaluate such claims. The research presented here demonstrates how the model can be used to evaluate software process changes, in this case testing the relative merits of different testing and programming paradigms. Using the simulation, we have obtained results which suggest that even though these approaches are justified in some situations, they may not be valid for all software development projects. For smaller programs, neither Test First nor pair programming seem always to be beneficial; test automation may be preferable when much larger programs are created. These results provide some insight when reading opinions claiming that the results of such process changes are always positive. To generalize on this observation, our simulation model can be used to predict the impact of proposed improvements on project development before these changes are tested in real projects.

Some of our simulation results can be directly attributed to the fact that the cost of finding and fixing a bug rises dramatically when a large amount of code has been written between the introduction of the bug and its discovery. If techniques such as delta debugging [5] which reduce the cost of searching for the bug become more prevalent then current simulation runs will have to be revisited.

From the experiments conducted with our simulation model, we reach a number of conclusions. First, testing early is important; in fact, the Test First approach outperforms other testing strategies. Second, pair programming may or may not improve project timescales, depending on the size of the system being developed. Under simulated conditions, larger systems perform better and smaller systems perform worse than in non-pair programming. Third, automated testing is sometimes over-rated; however, further discussion of this conclusion is beyond the scope of this paper.

5 Future Work

In addition to refining our simulation model and its outputs to reconcile differences from the published results described above, we envisage that our simulation can be extended or amended to address the following:

- The implications of the need to develop test code for automated testing. In modern testing, the testing code is itself a development project. We need to model test creation as a project with its own bugs and costs. This is a fairly natural extension of the model in which two related projects are developed concurrently.
- The effect of adopting from agile methodologies techniques other than the pair programming, automated testing and Test First examples described above.

- Evaluating the effect on software costs of varying the sizes of the components and interface. This would include an examination of definitions of the 'size' of a component more sophisticated than the number of lines of code it contains, reflecting *inter alia* the complexity of the interfaces it uses (including the code behind that interface) and the type of code (e.g. control or GUI) being developed.

References

1. Beck K. *Extreme Programming Explained.* Addison Wesley Professional, 2000.
2. Capers Jones T. *Estimating Software Costs.* McGraw-Hill, 1998.
3. Capers Jones T. *Applied software measurement: assuring productivity and quality.* McGraw-Hill, Inc., New York, NY, USA, 1991.
4. George B. and Williams L.A. An Initial Investigation of Test Driven Development in Industry. Proc. ACM Symposium on Applied Computing (SAC) 2003, March, 2003, Melbourne, FL, USA. ACM, 2003.
5. Holger C. and Zeller A. Locating Causes of Program Failures. Proc. 27th International Conference on Software Engineering (ICSE 2005), St. Louis, Missouri, May 2005.
6. IBM Rational Unified Process: Best practices for software development teams, http://www-128.ibm.com/developerworks/rational/library/253.html, accessed Dec. 2005.
7. Kramer C. (2001) Black Box Software Testing, Section: 7: The Black Box Testing Organization; available at http://testingeducation.org/course_notes/kaner_cem/ac_200108_blackboxtesting/blackboxtesting_07_blackbox_testing_group.pdf, accessed 11 December 2005
8. Laitenberger O, and DeBaud J. An Encompassing Life-Cycle Centric Survey of Software Inspection, report ISERN, 1998, pp. 98-32; Fraunhofer Institute for Experimental Software Engineering.
9. Madachy R.J. *System Dynamics Modeling of an Inspection Based Process.* Proc. International Conference on Software Engineering, 1996
10. Marick B. When should a test be automated? http://www.testing.com/writings/automate.pdf, 1998, accessed 16 December 2005.
11. Maximilien E.M. and Williams L. Assessing test-driven development at IBM; Proceedings of the 25th International Conference on Software Engineering, 2003, p.564– 569.
12. Onoma A.K., Tsai W.T., Poonawala M. and Suganuma H. Regression testing in an industrial environment, Comm. ACM, 41 (5), 1998, pp. 81-86.
13. Raffo D., Harrison W., Kellner M.I., Madachy R., Martin R., Scacchi W. and Wernick P. Guest Editors' Introduction: Special Issue on Software Process Simulation Modelling; J. Systems and Software, 46 (2/3), April 1999
14. Rothermel G. and Harrold M. J. Analyzing Regression Test Selection Techniques. IEEE Transactions on Software Engineering, V.22, no. 8, August 1996, pages 529-551.
15. RTI The Economic Impacts of Inadequate Infrastructure for Software Testing, Final report, May 2002; retrieved from http://www.nist.gov/director/prog-ofc/report02-3.pdf on 21 June 2006.
16. Wernick P. and Hall T. The Impact of Using Pair Programming on System Evolution: a Simulation-based Study; Proc. ICSM, 2004.
17. Wernick P. and Scacchi W. Guest Editors' Introduction: Special Issue on ProSim 2003. Software Process: Improvement and Practice, 9 (2), April-June 2004.
18. Williams L., Kessler R.R. Cunningham W. and Jeffries R. Strengthening the Case for Pair Programming, IEEE Software, 17, 4, July/Aug. 2000, pp. 19-25.

ExpliSAT: Guiding SAT-Based
Software Verification with Explicit States

Sharon Barner[1], Cindy Eisner[1], Ziv Glazberg[1], Daniel Kroening[2],
and Ishai Rabinovitz[3],[*]

[1] IBM Haifa Research Lab
{sharon,eisner,glazberg}@il.ibm.com
[2] ETH Zürich
daniel.kroening@inf.ethz.ch
[3] Mellanox Technologies
ishai@mellanox.co.il

Abstract. We present a hybrid method for software model checking
that combines explicit-state and symbolic techniques. Our method traverses the control flow graph of the program explicitly, and encodes the
data values in a CNF formula, which we solve using a SAT solver. In
order to avoid traversing control flow paths that do not correspond to a
valid execution of the program we introduce the idea of a *representative*
of a control path. We present favorable experimental results, which show
that our method scales well both with regards to the non-deterministic
data and the number of threads.

1 Introduction

In the hardware industry, *model checking* [6] is one of the most commonly used
formal verification techniques. However, while computer programs are just as
error-prone as circuitry, model checking has not yet been adopted by the software industry on a wide scale. Hardware model checkers do not perform well on
software due to the state explosion problem, which is especially acute in software.
Specialized software model checkers such as Spin [13], Zing [1] and VeriSoft [11]
attempt to address this problem. However, most existing software model checkers use explicit-state enumeration, and thus, are unlikely to scale to programs
that use large amounts of data.

In the past, we have applied symbolic methods to the software verification
problem in order to enable the verification of programs with non-trivial amounts
of data [3,4,8,17,9,18]. Other symbolic methods were introduced by NEC [15] and
SLAM [2]. Symbolic model checking handles non-deterministic data efficiently,
whereas explicit-state model checking handles non-deterministic scheduling of
concurrent processes easily using partial order reduction [14]. An additional advantage of explicit-state model checking is that pointer dereferencing is trivial.

---

[*] The work described in this paper was performed while the author was an employee
of the IBM Haifa Research Lab.

E. Bin, A. Ziv, and S. Ur (Eds.): HVC 2006, LNCS 4383, pp. 138–154, 2007.

We present a hybrid explicit-state and SAT-based method for software model checking. Our approach combines the merits of SAT-based symbolic model checking and explicit-state model checking using a hybrid data structure that stores both an explicit state vector and a symbolic CNF formula for the state. JPF [16] implements a similar hybrid approach and uses theorem proving to reason about the symbolic part. Our contribution is a method to guide the symbolic search towards legal program paths, using explicit values and a *representative*. As we show, the use of explicit values and a representative allows optimizations such as the Partial Order Reduction to be used in more cases than the simple hybrid approach of JPF.

Our method verifies invariant properties. We support user-specified assertions and additional implicit properties that must hold in every state, such as "no *NULL* pointer dereference", "no out-of-bounds array access", and "no data race".

Dynamic verification algorithms use sophisticated heuristics for guidance to likely locations of programming errors [10]. These heuristics are applicable for our method as well, as concrete program states are available.

We implemented our hybrid algorithm for concurrent C++ programs in a prototype named ExpliSAT. Our experimental results show that ExpliSAT outperforms state-of-the-art purely explicit or symbolic algorithms, and scales well both with regards to the non-deterministic data and the number of threads.

Related Work. Though most model checkers for software use explicit-state enumeration, e.g., Spin [13], Zing [1], and Verisoft [11], there exist several purely symbolic model checkers. CBMC [17] performs symbolic simulation on sequential programs. It addresses the path-explosion problem by transforming the program into static single assignment (SSA) form [7]. TCBMC [18] is an extension of the algorithm to concurrent programs. In contrast to CBMC, the approach presented in this paper is based on building SSA for single control paths only, which results in significantly smaller SAT instances. In addition, a pre-determined bound on the number of loop iterations or recursion steps is not required.

JPF [16], originally an explicit-state model checker for Java Bytecode, now features a hybrid state representation similar to the one we propose. JPF instruments the code such that it builds a symbolic formula when executed. JPF utilizes a theorem prover for examining the symbolic representation, as opposed to our use of a SAT solver. In JPF, the full symbolic formula is passed to the decision procedure; no attempt is made to reduce its size. JPF tries to avoid exploring non-legal control paths by calling the theorem prover to check whether there exists an execution that follows the path. In contrast, our method of guiding the symbolic search allows us to avoid exploration of non-legal control paths without calling the SAT solver in most cases.

DART [12] integrates symbolic execution into a random test generator. It also replaces symbolic values by explicit values, but only if the solver is unable to handle the symbolic constraint. Explicit values are not used to simplify constraints. Concurrency is not supported in DART but it is supported in its successor, CUTE [19].

Outline. The rest of the paper is organized as follows. Section 2 states the preliminaries. Section 3 shows how to explore only the control paths of the program explicitly while representing all executions symbolically. Section 4 defines the representative and shows how it can be used to guide the search. Section 5 presents our experimental results.

2   Preliminaries and Definitions

We first define the *control flow graph* (CFG), which is an abstract representation of a program. A vertex in a CFG represents a program statement, and there is a designated vertex representing the initial statement of the program. An edge in the CFG represents the ability of the program to change the control location.

For the purpose of this paper, we consider the CFG to be "flat". That is, the CFG considers the whole program as one piece, in which procedure calls are inlined. Therefore the CFG may be infinite. Note that such a CFG spares us the effort of paying special attention to the call stack.

Definition 1 (CFG). *A control flow graph (CFG) is a directed graph $G = \langle V, E, \mu \rangle$ where V is the set of vertices, E is the set of edges, and $\mu \in V$ is the initial vertex.*

We assume that each conditional statement has only one condition, i.e., the vertex v of a conditional statement has an out-degree of exactly 2, and we define the guard of an edge based on the condition of its source. The guard represents the condition that must be satisfied if the program changes its control location by traversing the edge.

Definition 2 ($cond(v)$, $guard(e)$). *Let $cond(v)$ denote the condition of a conditional statement v. For an edge $e = (v, u)$, $guard(e)$ equals true if v is not a conditional statement, $cond(v)$ if the edge is traversed when the condition is satisfied, and $\neg cond(v)$ otherwise.*

Given a concurrent program, we build a CFG representing it using the CFGs of its threads as follows. We denote the CFG of thread t by $G_t = \langle V_t, E_t, \mu_t \rangle$, and the guard labeling function of thread t by $guard_t(e)$. The control flow graph G of the concurrent program is $\langle V, E, \mu \rangle$ where $V = V_1 \times V_2 \times \ldots$, $\mu = (\mu_1, \mu_2, \ldots)$ and E contains edges $(\bar{v}, \bar{u})$ such that only one thread changes its control location. Formally, $(\bar{v}, \bar{u}) \in E$ with $\bar{v} = (v_1, v_2, \ldots)$ and $\bar{u} = (u_1, u_2, \ldots)$ iff $\exists_k.(v_k, u_k) \in E_k \wedge \bigwedge_{i \neq k} v_i = u_i$. The guard of $(\bar{v}, \bar{u})$ is equal to the guard of the thread that makes the transition. If k denotes that thread, then $guard((\bar{v}, \bar{u})) = guard_k((v_k, u_k))$.

Definition 3 (Explicit State). *An explicit state s of the program is a triple $\langle t, v, L \rangle$, where $t \in \mathbb{N}$ denotes the number of threads, $v \in V$ denotes the current control location of each thread (i.e., the vertex in the CFG) and L denotes the valuation of all the variables of the program over their domain. We write $s \models \varphi$ iff the predicate φ evaluates to true if evaluated using L, and $s \not\models \varphi$ otherwise.*

Definition 4 (Kripke Structure of a Program). *Let the CFG of the program be given by the triple $\langle V, E, \mu \rangle$. The* Kripke structure *of that program is the triple $\langle S, I, T \rangle$ where S is the set of explicit states, $I = \{\langle t, v, l \rangle \mid v \in \mu\} \subset S$ is the set of initial states of the program and $T = \{((\langle t_1, v_1, l_1 \rangle, \langle t_2, v_2, l_2 \rangle)) \mid \exists e = (v_1, v_2) \in E \ s.t. \ \langle t_1, v_1, l_1 \rangle \models guard(e)\}$ is the set of transitions between the states.*

Definition 5 (Execution). *An* execution *π of a program is a sequence of explicit states $(s_1, s_2, \ldots, s_n)$ s.t. $s_1 \in I$ and for every $1 \leq i < n. (s_i, s_{i+1}) \in T$. A state s is said to be* reachable *iff there exists an execution π that contains s.*

The property we are interested in is *reachability* of states s that violate a given predicate $p(v)$, where v is the control location of s. As an example, if v is a user-specified assertion with condition x, $p(v)$ is $\neg x$.

Definition 6 (Control Path). *A* control path *c of a program is a path through the CFG of the program, i.e., a finite sequence $(v_1, \ldots, v_n)$ of nodes of the CFG where $v_1 = \mu$ and $\forall_{1 \leq i < n}.(v_i, v_{i+1}) \in E$. The set of control paths is denoted by $\mathcal{C}$. If c is a projection of an execution π on V, we call c a* legal *control path.*

We denote the projection of an execution π onto the CFG by $cp(\pi)$. The execution π is said to follow the control path $cp(\pi)$. There may be many different executions that follow the same control path. They differ only in the data (i.e., the valuation of the variables).

The *Static Single Assignment (SSA)* [7] form is a representation of a program in which every variable is assigned exactly once. Existing variables in the original representation are split into versions. New variables are distinguished from the original name with a subscript such that every assignment has a unique left hand side. In SSA form, the function returning a non-deterministically chosen input $input()$ is replaced by an indexed variable $input_i$, which denotes the value returned by the ith call to the $input()$ function.

CBMC [17] transforms a whole program into SSA. In contrast to that, we only consider the SSA of a control path, which is a much simpler transformation, as a control path is linear whereas a program is branching. The variable x in a particular assignment to x may be indexed differently in different control paths.

Since every variable in the SSA form of a control path is assigned exactly once, it can be considered as a set of constraints that must be satisfied in any execution that follows that control path. We denote the conjunction of the SSA constraints of a control path c by $SSA(c)$.

Definition 7 (Path guard). *The* path guard *of a control path c is denoted by $cpg(c)$ and is the conjunction of the guards of all edges in c given that c is in SSA form:*

$$cpg(v_1, v_2, \ldots, v_n) = \bigwedge_{1 \leq i < n} guard(v_i, v_{i+1}).$$

3   Symbolic Verification Using Explicit CFG Traversal

3.1   The Naïve Hybrid Algorithm

We propose a model checking technique that traverses the abstract representation of the program represented by the CFG, rather than the Kripke structure of the program. That is, we explicitly explore only the control paths and use symbolic methods to cover the various executions.

We define the following equivalence relation over all executions of a program:

Definition 8 (Control equivalent). *Two executions π_1, π_2 are said to be control equivalent, denoted $\pi_1 \sim \pi_2$, iff they follow the same control path, i.e., $cp(\pi_1) = cp(\pi_2)$.*

The equivalence classes that this relation induces serve us in decreasing the size of the software model on which we perform an explicit search. We explicitly traverse each control path in the CFG. Each such control path is a representative for all the executions in the control equivalence class. Note that not every control path in the CFG has an associated execution. We first present a naïve algorithm that ignores this detail, then introduce the technique we use to avoid traversing such control paths.

The naïve algorithm traverses all control paths of the CFG and maintains a CNF encoding of each control path. The encoding is constructed from the SSA form of the path using the constraints given by the guards and the assignments to variables. We use a propositional SAT solver for searching for a satisfying assignment to the encoding of the path and the negation of the property associated with the last control location. We benefit from the fact that SAT-solvers are known to be practically efficient for large number of variables.

```
1.    a = 1;
2.    if (a>0) {
3.        a = input();
4.        if (a ≤ 1) {
5.            c = a+2;
6.            assert(c<3);
7.        }
8.        if (a≤1)
9.            a=2;
10.   else
11.       a=1;
12.   }
```

Fig. 1. A non-deterministic program

```
1.    a₁ = 1;
2.    if (a₁>0) {
3.        a₂ = input₁;
4.        if (a₂ ≤ 1) {
5.            c₁ = a₂+2;
6.            assert(c₁<3);
```

```
1.    a₁ = 1;
2.    if (a₁>0) {
3.        a₂ = input₁;
4.        if (a₂ ≤ 1) {
8.        if (a₂≤1)
10.   else
11.       a₃=1;
```

Fig. 2. The paths π_1 and π_2

If a satisfying assignment is found, there exists an execution that follows the control path and violates the property. The satisfying assignment contains a valuation of the non-deterministic choices made on the control path, and thus, the extraction of a counterexample is straight-forward.

For example, consider the program in Fig. 1. Two possible control paths π_1 and π_2 of this program are shown in their SSA form in Fig. 2. The guards of these two paths are:

$$cpg(\pi_1) \iff (a_1 > 0) \wedge (a_2 \le 1)$$
$$cpg(\pi_2) \iff (a_1 > 0) \wedge \neg(a_2 \le 1)$$

The SSA constraints of these control paths are given by the following two equivalences:

$$SSA(\pi_1) \iff (a_1 = 1) \wedge (a_2 = input_1) \wedge (c_1 = a_2 + 2)$$
$$SSA(\pi_2) \iff (a_1 = 1) \wedge (a_2 = input_1) \wedge (a_3 = 1)$$

Let $c = (v_1, \ldots, v_n)$ be a control path. If there exists a satisfying assignment to $\zeta \equiv cpg(c) \wedge SSA(c) \wedge \neg p(v_n)$, then there exists a reachable state s with control location v_n that violates the property $p(v_n)$. By transforming ζ to CNF, we can use a SAT solver to check if there exists an execution that follows c and violates the property. For example, for π_1:

$$\zeta \equiv (a_1 > 0) \wedge (a_2 \le 1) \wedge$$
$$(a_1 = 1) \wedge (a_2 = input_1) \wedge$$
$$(c_1 = a_2 + 2) \wedge \neg(c_1 < 3)$$

3.2 Simplifying Constraints Using Explicit Values

The naïve algorithm proposed above is improved using the notion of explicit values.

Definition 9 (Explicit Values). *For a given control path c in SSA form, a variable has an* explicit value *if any two executions π_1, π_2 with $\pi_1 \sim \pi_2 \wedge cp(\pi_1) = cp(\pi_2) = c$ assign the same value to this variable. If a variable does not have an explicit value, it has a* symbolic value.

Obviously, if an expression has an explicit value, it can be replaced by a constant during the traversal of the control path. Symbolic values may differ from one execution to the other even if both executions follow the same control path, while explicit values do not differ.

Refer to control path π_1 in Fig. 2. The value of variable a_1 is an explicit value, as every execution that follows this control path assigns 1 to a_1. On the other hand, the value of variable a_2 is symbolic, as the value of a_2 may differ in different executions that follow this control path.

Note that explicit values may depend on non-deterministic choices. In Fig. 3 the value of x depends on $input()$ yet it is explicit in the control path (1, 3, 4),

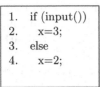

1.	if (input())
2.	x=3;
3.	else
4.	x=2;

1.	x=input()
2.	if (x==3)
3.	y=0;
4.	else
5.	z=6;

Fig. 3. The value of variable x is explicit on the path (1,3,4) even though it depends on non-deterministic data

Fig. 4. The value of variable x is explicit on the path (1,2,3). Syntactically, we approximate it as a symbolic value.

since every execution that follows this path assigns the value 2 to x. Fig. 4 shows another example, in which there exists a control path (1,2,3) on which x is always assigned 3, and thus, has an explicit value.

As identifying whether a value is explicit in a given control path is hard, we make a syntactic, but sound approximation: Values returned by *input()* are symbolic, and values that are a result of an assignment of symbolic values are also symbolic. In any other case, the value is explicit. We denote the set of explicit values for a given control path c by $\mathcal{E}(c)$. In some cases, our approximation classifies explicit values as symbolic. For instance, it classifies x in Fig. 4 as symbolic on the control path (1,2,3). However, it never classifies a symbolic value as explicit.

Definition 10 (Restricted Guards). *Let $e \in E$ denote an edge in the CFG and c denote a control path. We define the restricted guard $guard'(e, c)$ as a function over $e \in E$ and c. If $guard(e)$ has an explicit value in c, then $guard'(e, c)$ is that explicit value, otherwise $guard'(e, c) = guard(e)$. The restricted path guard $cpg'(c)$ is the conjunction of the restricted guards of the edges on $c = (v_1, v_2, \ldots, v_n)$, i.e., $cpg'(c) = \bigwedge_{1 \leq i < n} guard'((v_i, v_{i+1}), c)$.*

Pointers. The value of a pointer is often, at least in part, an explicit value. Though a pointer holds the address of a memory location, which may change from one execution to the other, it conceptually points to an object. Pointers can therefore be seen as a tuple $\langle base, offset \rangle$ where *base* is the base object and *offset* is the offset within that object. The value of a pointer is generally determined in four different ways:

- Explicit address of an object (e.g., operator &): In this case, the value of the pointer is always explicit.
- Memory allocation (e.g., `malloc`): In this case, the pointer may point to any free memory location, hence its value is symbolic. However, since conceptually, the value is a fresh cell location in the heap, we may optimize this and treat its value as an explicit value: the *base* object is given the value of a fresh object that was not used before. This optimization may conceal certain bugs that might occur as a result of accessing an adjacent memory

```
foo( int* p) {
    ...
}
```

```
void main() {
    int a,b;
    foo(&a);
    foo(&b);
}
```

Fig. 5. When examining *foo* procedure on its own, the value of the pointer p is symbolic, and is equivalent to $p = input()$

Fig. 6. When examining the entire program, the value of the pointer p in *foo* is explicit: in the first instance it is the address of a and in the second it is the address of b

location or using values of an already freed memory location. However, since we detect an invalid pointer dereferencing and the use of uninitialized values, this optimization can be used without concealing any bugs. Therefore, the value of a pointer is explicit in this case.

– Non deterministic value (e.g., input to the verified program): both the *base* object and the *offset* have symbolic values.
– Pointer arithmetic (e.g., $p = q + 1$): The *base* value is left unchanged with regards to the original pointer. If it was an explicit value, it remains so. The value of *offset* is explicit only if the original pointer's *offset* value is explicit and the arithmetic calculation uses solely explicit values.

When examining a program from its beginning, as opposed to starting the verification from a procedure with parameters, most pointers are of explicit value. In Figure 5 the value of the pointer p is non-deterministic since the procedure *foo* is examined as a stand-alone function. In Figure 6, the value of p is explicit in each call of the *foo* function. When verifying a complete program, the value of *base* is usually an explicit value. Thus, dereferencing of pointers, which is problematic for most symbolic model checkers, is usually simple using our hybrid state representation. Let b denote the object indicated by *base*. An expression $*p$ with $p = \langle base, offset \rangle$ in which the value of *base* is explicit, can be replaced by b if b is a simple or struct type, and by $b[offset]$ if b is of an array type.

When a pointer has an explicit value, pointer dereferencing is done the same way as in explicit model checking. Otherwise, if its value is symbolic, we may encode its value in the $SSA(c)$, similarly to CBMC [17], or use lazy initialization, as described in JPF [16]. Note that when *base* is explicit, as it is usually the case, both methods are improved, since they take into account only the different possible *offsets* and not all the existing objects.

When computing ζ for verifying a control path, expressions that have an explicit value can be replaced by a constant, as justified by the following lemma. We can use the restricted path guard $cpg'(c)$ (Def. 10) instead of the full path guard $cpg(c)$ (Def. 7).

Lemma 1. *Let $c = (v_1, \ldots, v_n)$ be a control path. There exists a satisfying assignment to $\zeta' \equiv cpg'(c) \wedge SSA(c) \wedge \neg p(v_n)$ iff it also satisfies $\zeta \equiv cpg(c) \wedge SSA(c) \wedge \neg p(v_n)$.*

Continuing our previous example, the guards are simplified as follows:

$$cpg'(\pi_1) \iff (a_2 \leq 1)$$
$$cpg'(\pi_2) \iff \neg(a_2 \leq 1)$$

An additional improvement is that no call to the SAT solver is needed for properties for which $p(v_n)$ is an explicit value. For data intensive programs as well as programs with complicated control graphs, the bring up time of the SAT solver is not always negligible.

Lemma 2. *If the property $p(v_n)$ has an explicit value in the legal control path $c = (v_1, \ldots v_n)$, then there exists a satisfying assignment to $cpg'(c) \wedge SSA(c) \wedge \neg p(v_n)$ iff the explicit value of $p(v_n)$ is false.*

Note that the implicit properties that we add, such as "no data-race", are verified by evaluating a predicate over each state. The naïve algorithm invokes the SAT solver for each location in order to verify these predicates. If the predicate has an explicit value, the SAT solver is not needed.

4   The Path Representative

We introduce the concept of the *path representative*. Path representatives allow us an easy way of filtering out control paths that need not be traversed because they do not have an associated execution path.

Definition 11 (Representative). *Let c be a control path in its SSA form. A representative ρ of a control path is a valuation of all the variables in c such that the guards in the control path are satisfied, i.e., $\rho \models SSA(c) \wedge cpg(c)$. We denote the set of representatives by $\mathcal{R}$.*

Lemma 3. *Let c be a control path in its SSA form. A representative ρ exists for a control path c iff there exists an execution $\pi_r = (s_1, s_2, \ldots, s_n)$ with $cp(\pi_r) = c$.*

The proof makes use of the fact that c is in SSA form, and thus, the last state, s_n, holds the values of all the variables that were assigned at any point during the execution.

In our example in Fig. 1, the path $(1, 2, 3, 4, 8, 9)$ has no representative (because if $a \leq 1$ then 5 and 6 would be on the path as well). Guiding the CFG traversal using a path representative ensures that the traversed path is a legal path. The CFG traversal is guided by the path representative, traversing the control path it follows. Full coverage of the CFG is gained by using a representative of each control equivalence class.

The algorithm we propose is illustrated by means of pseudo code in Fig. 7. The algorithm maintains a hybrid representation $\langle c, \rho \rangle$ of the paths that are

```
// Variables: Priority queue Q ⊆ (C × (R ∪ {⊥}))
// of control paths and path representatives
HYBRIDREACHABILITY(P)
1   Compute initial state c_I
2   Q:={⟨c_I, ⊥⟩};
3   while (Q ≠ ∅)
4       Let ⟨c, ρ⟩ ∈ Q;
5       Q:=Q \ ⟨c, ρ⟩;
6       if ρ = ⊥ then ρ:=GETREPRESENTATIVE(c);
7       if ρ = ⊥ then continue;
8       if CHECKPROPERTY(c, ρ) then return true;
9       Q := Q ∪ GETSUCCESSORS(P, c, ρ);
10  end
11  return false;
```

Fig. 7. High Level Description of the Hybrid Reachability Algorithm

explored. The first component $c \in C$ is a control path. The second part ρ is either a path representative, i.e., a valuation to the state variables, or $\bot$, which denotes the case that the assignment has not yet been computed.

The algorithm uses a priority queue Q of hybrid path representatives that are to be explored. In line 2, the initial state is put into the queue. While the queue is non-empty, a search heuristic removes a hybrid path representative $\langle c, \rho \rangle$ from the queue (lines 4 and 5). The algorithm checks if there is already a representative for c. If $\rho = \bot$, GETREPRESENTATIVE(c) is called to compute a representative for c (line 6). If such a representative does not exist, c is not a legal control path and thus, is not examined (line 7).

In line 8, the algorithm proceeds by calling CHECKPROPERTY. If the property is violated, then a counterexample was found.

Finally, the successors of the last location of c are computed by GETSUCC-ESSORS(P, c, ρ), appended to c, and added into the queue Q (line 9).

The procedure CHECKPROPERTY(c, ρ) determines if the last vertex of the path c is an assertion (Fig. 8). If so, it checks if the condition p of the assertion has an explicit value (line 3). If so, ρ provides the truth value of p for all executions that follow c. If p is symbolic, a SAT solver is used to check if p can be violated (line 6). The formula passed to the SAT solver uses the restricted guard simplified using the explicit values given by ρ.

4.1   Computing the Path Representative

The procedure GETSUCCESSORS(P, c, ρ) computes the successor states of the last state v_n of a given control path $c = (v_1, \ldots, v_n)$. If v_n is not a conditional, the computation of v_{n+1} and a representative ρ' for $(v_1, \ldots, v_n, v_{n+1})$ is straightforward. If v_n contains a non-deterministic choice ι, $\rho'(\iota)$ is simply an arbitrary

CHECKPROPERTY($c \in \mathcal{C}, \rho \in \mathcal{R}$)

```
1    Let c = (v_1, ..., v_n);
2    if v_n = assert(p) then
3          if p ∈ E(c) then
4                if ρ(p) = false then return true;
5          else
6                if IsSATISFIABLE(
7                          cpg'(c) ∧ SSA(c) ∧ ¬p) then
8                      return true;
9          endif
10   endif
11   return false;
```

Fig. 8. Checking assertions using the path representative

but constant value. By choosing one possible value of ι, we maintain a valid representative of the explored control path. Thus, if we have an explicit value for the condition, we can traverse a conditional statement without a call to our SAT solver, as opposed to the call to the theorem prover needed by JPF [16]. However, since we also maintain a symbolic representation of the value of ι, backtracking to v_n, as performed by explicit state model checkers such as SPIN, is not necessary. If the value of ι affects future control decisions, different valuations are examined when other representatives are computed using GETREPRESENTATIVE(c).

If v_n is a conditional, let $v'(\alpha)$ denote the successor of v_n for a given truth value $\alpha \in \{\text{true, false}\}$ of $cond(v_n)$. If $cond(v_n)$ has an explicit value, let $t = \rho(cond(v_n))$ denote that value. The only successor of $\langle c, \rho \rangle$ is $\langle (c, v'(t)), \rho \rangle$.

If $cond(v_n)$ is symbolic, we still compute the truth value t of the guard given by the path representative ρ. Two successors are computed:

1. $\langle (c, v'(t)), \rho \rangle$ corresponds to the branch suggested by the truth assignment made by the representative. Note that ρ is also a representative for $(c, v'(t))$.
2. $\langle (c, v'(\neg t)), \bot \rangle$ corresponds to the other branch. A new representative has to be computed for this control path.

The priority queue $\mathcal{Q}$ should usually give preference to pairs that have a path representative ρ. Only when a pair $\langle c, \bot \rangle$ is chosen, GETREPRESENTATIVE(c) is called to compute a new representative using a SAT solver. If c is not a legal control path GETREPRESENTATIVE(c) returns $\bot$, and c is not explored. When a pair $\langle c, \rho \rangle$ is chosen, the SAT solver is not utilized. The main benefit of using the representative is that in at least half of the cases, we avoid calling GETREPRESENTATIVE(c) and hence avoid utilizing a SAT solver.

The GETREPRESENTATIVE procedure can be improved by using previous representatives as initial partial assignments of the formula of the examined control path. Also note that the GETREPRESENTATIVE procedure is likely to produce a large amount of similar SAT instances, and thus, an incremental SAT solver that preserves previously learnt clauses, when applicable, should be used.

4.2 Concurrency

For concurrent programs, we explore all paths for any order of execution of the statements in the different threads. The number of such executions is typically exponential in the number of program statements. In traditional explicit-state model checking, partial order reductions (POR) are applied to significantly reduce the size of the traversed model. In contrast to other symbolic methods that are unable to apply this reduction, the application of POR is trivial in our hybrid method. Thus, we are able to reduce the size of traversed model without affecting the correctness of the results. POR is usually difficult if there are pointer dereferencing operators in a statement. In contrast, for example, to JPF we often have explicit or at least partially explicit values for pointers, and therefore in many cases can avoid this difficulty.

In contrast to sequential programs, if two control paths c_1, c_2 differ only in the scheduling of the threads, c_1 and c_2 may have the same representative. Thus, when backtracking to a control path c_2 that only differs in its scheduling from another control path c_1 we already traversed, we can use the representative of c_1 instead of computing a new one. This optimization avoids unnecessary calls to the SAT solver. Hence, the path representative does not guide the CFG traversal when the branching of the CFG is the outcome of different possible schedulings.

5 Experimental Results

We have implemented our hybrid algorithm in a prototype named *ExpliSAT*. ExpliSAT utilizes an internal IBM state-of-the-art SAT solver named Mage. ExpliSAT verifies C and the POSIX thread library. ExpliSAT supports heap memory allocation and dynamic thread creation. Like all explicit model checkers, ExpliSAT will not terminate in the case of unbounded recursion. However, unlike symbolic methods in the case of bounded recursion, the user is not required to provide the bound up front. Instead, heuristics may be utilized on-the-fly in order to decide how deep ExpliSAT should explore the unbounded recursion or loop. Of course, in such cases, ExpliSAT does not perform as a model checker, but rather it is simply a bug-hunting tool.

5.1 Case Studies

ExpliSAT was used internally inside IBM to verify several protocols and code segments. In this subsection we review how ExpliSAT is used to improve IBM's products quality.

ExpliSAT examined a complex locking protocol in an industrial middleware software. A prototype of the mechanism was devised, which was verified using

ExpliSAT. The prototype has about 250 lines of code, in which 5 threads exercise the locking mechanism in a non-deterministic order.

ExpliSAT detects a write-write data race in the protocol within approximately 20 seconds. The race results from a subtle definition of the critical section.

ExpliSAT was also used in the verification of communication protocol between three controllers in IBM microcode. This protocol, which is designed for a Linux device driver, should withstand failures of controllers. During a failure of a controller it may exhibit limited Byzantine behavior. The prototype of this protocol has about 400 lines of code, in which 2 controllers pass 6 random messages between them. Two additional processes are used in order to simulate the random failures of the controllers.

ExpliSAT detects that due to a failure of the receiving controller, the sending controller may not be informed that the message was in fact received. Since the sending controller is uncertain that the message was received, it may send a duplicate message. Hence, the protocol should be revised and handle such duplicate messages.

For more information on these two protocols and their verification refer to [5].

An additional verification effort using ExpliSAT was made on synchronization code that was extracted from an IBM random test generator tool. In this code segment, one thread makes a non-deterministic choice which should be passed to all the other threads as well. This process may be repeated several times.

We employed the synchronization code using 4 threads. The threads were allowed to make up to 4 non-deterministic choices. The code segment ExpliSAT examines has about 100 lines.

ExpliSAT verifies that all the threads are synchronized on all the non-deterministic choices. However, it detects a possible deadlock on a specific scheduling. The entire inspection of this code takes ExpliSAT approximately three minutes.

5.2   Artificial Examples

We evaluate the performance benefit of using a path representative using a sequential benchmark. We compare the performance of ExpliSAT when it utilizes a path representative for guiding the CFG traversal with its performance when such guidance is not utilized. As is explained in section 4.2, the path represen-

Table 1. Run time comparison of two versions of the naïve algorithm and ExpliSAT on "Bubble-sort" benchmark. The number of bits in the non-deterministic input is denoted by b, s denotes size of array.

| | Naïve algorithm | | | | | | ExpliSAT | | |
	Late reachability check			Early reachability check					
Benchmark	$b=8$	$b=16$	$b=32$	$b=8$	$b=16$	$b=32$	$b=8$	$b=16$	$b=32$
Bubble-sort $s=3$	0.43s	0.43s	0.56s	2.01s	2.04 s	4.05s	0.60s	0.55s	0.85s
Bubble-sort $s=4$	7.44s	8.43s	12.4s	23.46s	30.37s	43.04 s	5.91s	4.94s	8.59s
Bubble-sort $s=5$	768.33s	885.95s	1708.26s	245.76s	282.98s	458.28s	69.58s	52.89s	90.95s

tative is used to decide what conditional branch to explore, but not for deciding what thread schedule to follow. Hence, we compare the performance of ExpliSAT with the naïve algorithm on a sequential benchmark. The benchmark we use is a sorting algorithm parameterized in the array size.

We compare ExpliSAT with two different versions of the naïve algorithm. In one version, reachability of a state is verified only when a property is examined, i.e., only when reaching an `assert` statement. In this version, the algorithm traverses the entire CFG including all the non-legal control paths. In the second version, the reachability analysis is done at an earlier stage. As soon as a branch in the CFG is encountered, the tool checks feasibility of each of the branches. This version never traverses a non-legal control path. JPF implements such a CFG traversal as well.

As can be seen in Table 1, ExpliSAT scales better than both versions of the naïve algorithm. It is interesting to note that the early reachability analysis is not necessarily better than the late reachability analysis. Using an array size of 4, the late reachability method outperforms the early reachability method. This can be ascribed to the overhead of verifying reachability for every vertex in the CFG. This overhead is worthwhile only if there are a significant number of non-legal paths in the CFG. As an example, this seems to be the case when using array size 5.

Table 2. Run time comparison of Zing and ExpliSAT on three classes of benchmarks. The number of bits in the non-deterministic input is denoted by b. In "Bubble-sort", s denotes size of array, In "Producers", p denotes number of producers and c denotes number of consumers.

Benchmark	Zing					ExpliSAT		
	$b=2$	$b=4$	$b=6$	$b=8$	$b=16$	$b=8$	$b=16$	$b=32$
Bubble-sort $s=3$	1s	3s	277s	>2h	>2h	0.60s	0.55s	0.85s
Bubble-sort $s=4$	1s	58s	>2h	>2h	>2h	5.91s	4.94s	8.59s
Bubble-sort $s=5$	1s	>2h	>2h	>2h	>2h	69.58s	52.89s	90.95s
Producers $p=1$ $c=1$	1s	21s	317s	>2h	>2h	38.38s	41.03s	40.95s
Producers $p=1$ $c=2$	41s	690s	>2h	>2h	>2h	73.38s	78.28s	78.57s
Producers $p=1$ $c=3$	1160s	>2h	>2h	>2h	>2h	130.82s	131.17s	141.24s
Producers $p=2$ $c=2$	18s	230s	>2h	>2h	>2h	0.6s	0.63s	0.65s
Producers $p=2$ $c=3$	443s	>2h	>2h	>2h	>2h	0.66s	0.71s	0.70s
Producers $p=2$ $c=4$	>2h	>2h	>2h	>2h	>2h	0.72s	0.75s	0.75s
Random-Choice	<1s	<1s	<1s	4s	>2h	0.33s	0.34s	0.43s

Using three other code examples, we compare the performance of ExpliSAT with Zing from Microsoft Research [1], a state-of-the-art explicit-state model checker for software. Note that Zing and ExpliSAT are executed on different platforms[1].

The first benchmark is the same as in Table 1. As the number of legal control paths is exponential in the array size, the performance of ExpliSAT deteriorates

---

[1] Zing was executed on Windows while ExpliSAT was executed on Linux. Both were executed on a Pentium 4 with 2 GHz and 1GB of memory.

when the array size is increased. Still, ExpliSAT scales better than Zing on this parameter. The second comparison is a producer-consumer protocol that has a bug in the producer code. Atomicity of the critical section is not enforced, and thus, two producers may overflow the shared buffer. Both ExpliSAT and Zing verify the correctness of the program if only one producer exists, and detect the bug when two producers co-exist. We compare the performance in the number of active consumers and producers. The third program is "Random-choice". This is a program with two threads, where both threads utilize the same function to compute a value. The two threads assert that the same value was computed. Under some rare conditions the computed values are different.

We also compare ExpliSAT and TCBMC [18] (Table 3)[2]. The benchmark program has two threads that sort the same array using the bubble-sort algorithm. Even though atomicity of the critical sections is maintained, for some inputs and a specific scheduling, the threads fail to sort the array correctly. Unlike ExpliSAT, TCBMC requires a bound on the number of context-switches, which is denoted by n. ExpliSAT performs much better than TCBMC. It also scales better in the array size. Though both methods are SAT-based, ExpliSAT performs better since it provides the SAT solver with several small CNF formulas unlike TCBMC which searches a satisfying assignment to one big CNF formula. ExpliSAT allows the SAT solver to slice different literals from each CNF according to the specific clauses this CNF entails. As opposed to TCBMC whose CNF formula encodes all calculations in the program, including those who are irrelevant for finding the bug that exists in the program.

Table 3. Run time comparison of TCBMC and ExpliSAT. The size of the array is denoted by s. The number of bits in the non-deterministic input is denoted by b. The bound on the number of context-switch TCBMC enforces is denoted by n.

Benchmark	TCBMC						ExpliSAT		
	$b=8$		$b=16$		$b=32$		$b=8$	$b=16$	$b=32$
	n=6	n=10	n=6	n=10	n=6	n=10			
Buggy-sort $s=3$	0.4s	0.2s	3.6s	4.0s	20.3s	48.3s	4.68s	4.72s	5.88s
Buggy-sort $s=4$	11.5s	1.3s	14.6s	58.7s	135.2s	323.0s	43.55s	37.01s	44.79s
Buggy-sort $s=5$	71.0s	94.1s	125.7s	3013.0s	1124.0s	> 1h	140.43s	131.86s	154.44s

On all benchmarks, ExpliSAT scales much better than Zing, TCBMC and the two versions of the naïve algorithm in the size of the non-deterministic input. The effect the bit-vector size has on the performance of ExpliSAT is marginal.

6   Conclusion and Future Work

We have presented a novel algorithm for software verification that combines explicit and symbolic methods. Experimental results show that this hybrid representation outperforms both conventional explicit-state model checking and

---

[2] We provide the figures for TCBMC from [18] for reference.

purely symbolic methods. The symbolic part of the representation allows the method to scale with an increasing amount of non-deterministic data, while the explicit state enables powerful search and state-space reduction techniques, such as partial order reduction. In comparison to previous hybrid approaches, our contributions are the concepts of an *explicit value* and a *representative*, which are exploited to reduce the size of the verification conditions as well as the number of calls to the SAT solver. In addition, they allow wider application of explicit techniques such as partial order reduction, for instance, in the case of many pointers.

For future work, we plan to investigate automatic slicing of the formulas according to the assertions, and the merging of control flow paths in order to reduce the number of formulas to be checked. Another promising research direction is to use the proof of unsatisfiability of verification conditions to direct the search towards an error during backtracking.

References

1. T. Andrews, S. Qadeer, S. K. Rajamani, J. Rehof, and Y. Xie. Zing: Exploiting program structure for model checking concurrent software. In *CONCUR*, 2004.
2. T. Ball and S. K. Rajamani. Bebop: A symbolic model checker for boolean programs. In *SPIN*, pages 113–130, 2000.
3. S. Barner, Z. Glazberg, and I. Rabinovitz. Wolf - bug hunter for concurrent software using formal methods. In *CAV*, pages 153–157, 2005.
4. S. Barner and I. Rabinovitz. Effcient symbolic model checking of software using partial disjunctive partitioning. In *CHARME*, pages 35–50, 2003.
5. H. Chockler, E. Farchi, Z. Glazberg, B. Godlin, Y. Nir-Buchbinder, and I. Rabinovitz. Formal verification of concurrent software: two case studies. In *Proceedings of 4th International Workshop on Parallel and Distributed Systems: Testing and Debugging (PADTAD)*, 2006.
6. E. Clarke, O. Grumberg, and D. Peled. *Model Checking*. MIT Press, 1999.
7. R. Cytron, J. Ferrante, B. Rosen, M. Wegman, and F. Zadeck. An efficient method of computing static single assignment form. In *POPL*, pages 25–35. ACM, 1989.
8. C. Eisner. Model checking the garbage collection mechanism of SMV. In *ENTCS*, volume 55. Elsevier Science Publishers, 2001.
9. C. Eisner. Formal verification of software source code through semi-automatic modeling. *Software and Systems Modeling*, 4(1):14–31, February 2005.
10. E. Farchi, Y. Nir, and S. Ur. Concurrent bug patterns and how to test them. In *IPDPS*, page 286b. IEEE, 2003.
11. P. Godefroid. VeriSoft: A tool for the automatic analysis of concurrent reactive software. In *CAV*, pages 476–479. Springer, 1997.
12. P. Godefroid, N. Klarlund, and K. Sen. DART: directed automated random testing. In *PLDI*, pages 213–223. ACM, 2005.
13. G. Holzmann. The model checker SPIN. *IEEE Trans. on Software Engineering*, 23(5):279–295, 1997.
14. G. Holzmann and D. Peled. An improvement in formal verification. In *Proc. Formal Description Techniques, FORTE94*, pages 197–211. Chapman & Hall, 1994.
15. F. Ivancic, Z. Yang, A. Gupta, M. K. Ganai, and P. Ashar. Efficient SAT-based bounded model checking for software verification, 2004.

16. S. Khurshid, C. S. Pasareanu, and W. Visser. Generalized symbolic execution for model checking and testing. In *TACAS*, pages 553–568, 2003.
17. D. Kroening, E. Clarke, and K. Yorav. Behavioral consistency of C and Verilog programs using bounded model checking. In *DAC*, pages 368–371. ACM, 2003.
18. I. Rabinovitz and O. Grumberg. Bounded model checking of concurrent programs. In *CAV*, volume 3576 of *LNCS*, pages 82–97. Springer, 2005.
19. K. Sen and G. Agha. Cute and jcute : Concolic unit testing and explicit path model-checking tools. In *CAV*. *Tool Paper*, 2006.

Evolutionary Testing:
A Case Study

Stella Levin and Amiram Yehudai

School of Computer Science
Tel-Aviv University
stellale@post.tau.ac.il, amiramy@post.tau.ac.il

Abstract. The paper presents a case study of applying genetic algorithms (GAs) to the automatic test data generation problem. We present the basic techniques implemented in our prototype test generation system, whose goal is to get branch coverage of the program under testing. We used our tool to experiment with simple programs, programs that have been used by others for test strategies benchmarking and the UNIX utility uniq. The effectiveness of GA-based testing system is compared with a Random testing system. We found that for simple programs both testing systems work fine, but as the complexity of the program or the complexity of input domain grows, GA-based testing system significantly outperforms Random testing.

Keywords: Software testing, automatic test generation, genetic algorithms.

1   Introduction

Genetic algorithms (GAs) are known to be a robust search method in complex spaces. GAs have been recognized as a suitable techniques for testing software, since, as stated in [9] "Due to the non-linearity of software (if-statements, loops, etc.), the conversion of test problems into optimization tasks usually results in complex, discontinuous, and non-linear search space".

The first work of Xanthakis et al [10] applying GA to test generation problem appeared at 1992. The current fitness function representation was proposed in works of Wegener et al in 2001 and 2002 [11, 12]. More details may be found in a survey by McMinn [1]. We implemented a prototype test generation system based on known techniques. The purpose of our work is to experiment using these techniques with real life programs in order to assess the effectiveness of these techniques.

In [3] there are experimental results on simple programs. We repeat them partially in order to validate our tool, and get similar results: for bubble sort program and greatest common denominator both GA-based testing system and Random testing system work fine; for triangle classification GA-based testing system outperform Random testing.

We further experiment with a string matching program that is known to be used for test strategies benchmark. For this program GA-based testing system outperforms

E. Bin, A. Ziv, and S. Ur (Eds.): HVC 2006, LNCS 4383, pp. 155–165, 2007.

Random testing. In addition, when we vary the input domain complexity, GA-based testing superiority is more significant.

And finally we present results of an experiment with the uniq UNIX utility. For this program GA-based testing system outperforms Random testing even for simple input domain – binary strings. Furthermore, for a more complex input domain – alphabet strings – Random testing becomes impossible - it didn't find a solution for more that 1 day, while GA-based testing system found a solution in about half an hour.

We are not familiar with other works experimenting with the impact of input domain complexity on test generation problem.

2   Genetic Algorithm Search for Testing Problem

2.1   Genetic Algorithm

A Genetic algorithm searches among population of individuals. Every individual codes problem input variables and represents a candidate solution as a vector of *genes*. A *fitness function* is used to classify better solutions. The search starts from generation of random points and every iteration creates new generation. At every generation the fitness of all individuals is evaluated and the next generation is created from the existing one with selection, crossover and mutation operations. These are all probabilistic processes, and have many variations. Selection is a mechanism to choose among the parents to form a new generation. In its simplest form it works as a roulette wheel with slots sized according to fitness, so that a more fit individual has a higher probability to be selected. Crossover just switches genes of parents at a random point. Mutation randomly changes one gene.

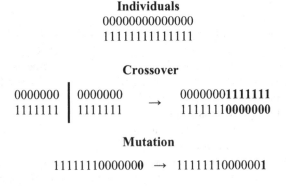

Individuals
00000000000000
11111111111111

Crossover

0000000	0000000		00000001111111
1111111	1111111	→	11111110000000

Mutation

11111110000000   →   11111110000001

Fig. 2.1. Example of GA operations on two individuals

Figure 2.1 presents two individuals with all genes 0 and all genes 1, respectively.

Crossover operation is performed in the middle of the gene vector. Mutation operation is performed on the last bit of the individual. In general case the position of crossover and the position of mutation are chosen randomly.

More about GAs may be read in [5].

2.2 Test Data Generation Problem

We deal with *white-box testing*, when the source code of the program is known.

Every input variable x_i of the program is defined on the set of valid values – the *domain* D_i. The cartesian product of all domains defines the *program domain* D:

$$D = D_1 \times D_2 \times \ldots D_n$$

A program input x is a point in the domain D.

Test data generation aims to find a point in D such that the control flow executes a certain statement in the program called the *target*. In this way we can create a test suite to get some required *coverage* type (e.g. statement coverage).

2.3 Testing Problem as an Optimization Problem

2.3.1 Domain Encoding

Every point in D can be encoded as an individual in GA. The encoding process is dependent on the concrete program input type.

For example let's take the triangle classification program. It takes as input 3 edge lengths and determines if they may form a triangle and if so what type of triangle it is. Let's limit input numbers to be in [0, 15]; Then every input number can be encoded with 4 bits. For example, input 3, 4, 5 is encoded as

0011 0100 0101

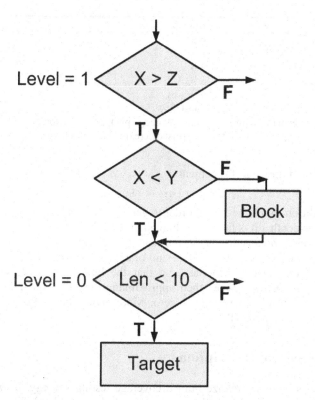

Fig. 2.3.2. Example of control flow with approximation level values on branches

2.3.2 Fitness Function

For a given individual we run the program with the input it encodes and follow the control flow execution. The fitness function should evaluate how close the control flow gets to the target. There may be several control flow paths to the target. The fitness function is defined as in the work of McMinn [1].

A *critical branch* is a branch where the control flow may diverge from a path to the target so that there is no other path to the target.

The *approximation level* of a vertex is the number of critical branches from it to the target minus one.

The control flow example in Figure 2.3.2 the vertex Len<10 has approximation level 0, because it is the last critical branch before the target. The vertex X<Y is not a critical branch, because if control flow doesn't continue via the True outcome of the decision, then there is another path to the target via the False outcome. The vertex X>Z has approximation level 1.

If there are several vertices from which control flow diverges from the path to the target in the same critical branch, then the branch distance is used to determine which one is better. *Branch distance* is equal to zero if the value of the condition in the branch causes to continue the path to the target. Otherwise it is greater than zero and calculated, depending on the operation in the condition, as follows:

Table 2.3.2. Branch distance calculation

Operation	Branch Distance
a>b	b-a
a ≥ b	b-a
a<b	a-b
a ≤ b	a-b
a=b	abs(a-b)
a ≠ b	constant
expr1 or expr2	min(distance(expr1),distance(expr2))
expr1 and expr2	max(distance(expr1),distance(expr2))

For example the following if statement:

```
if (len < 10) ...
```

If the condition should be true in order to get to the target, and if when we run the program we detect that it is false, then branch distance is len − 10.

The value of the branch distance is normalized to [0, 1].

The *Fitness function* is calculated as sum of approximation level (integer part) and normalized distance (fractional part), so that the branch distance can distinguish between two vertices only when their approximation level is equal. The goal of the GA search is to reach fitness equals zero. More about fitness function calculation variations may be read in [1].

3 Testing System Description

In our testing system we realize branch coverage testing strategy. *Branch-coverage testing* requires generating test data to exercise the true and the false outcomes of every decision. More about different strategies may be found in [6]. The testing system must combine static analysis of programs with GA search capabilities. This was done by combining different existing tools, and tailoring them to the task at hand.

3.1 Program Static Analysis

The program under testing is analyzed with the static analysis tool CodeSurfer [7]. We got academic license for it and enjoyed good support. This tool is programmable with scheme as a scripting language. Our scheme script automatically generates command files that are used to follow the execution of the program and to calculate the fitness value as described in 2.3.2. This is performed once per program under testing.

Algorithm 3.1: Definition of dfs-cfg-traverse function

```
Function DFS-CFG-TRAVERSE

Input: vertex, approximation level, outcome
Implicit input: Table of visited critical branches

If the vertex is control point then
    If the vertex is new then
        Add the vertex, level, outcome to the Table
        Increase level
    Else
        If the level is the same as previous
            And outcome is opposite then
            Cancel the vertex entry in the Table
        Else
            Update vertex level, outcome in the Table
            Keep smaller level

Foreach cfg source of the vertex
    DFS-CFG-TRAVERSE source-vertex label level
```

Algorithm 3.1 shows the definition of dfs-cfg-traverse function. It traverses the control flow backward. If the vertex is control statement then we take care on updating approximation level. If traversing gets to unvisited control vertex then the vertex is added to the Table and approximation level is increased. If traversing gets to visited vertex then it keeps smaller approximation level. And finally if it gets twice with opposite outcomes to the same control vertex than it is not critical branch and it entry is cancelled from the Table. For any vertex it calls recursively the dfs-cfg-traverse function with the sources of the vertex in control flow graph.

3.2 GA Search

We use the GA implementation from matlab [8]. Each generation it calls the fitness function with all individuals at once (vectorized fitness function). Our fitness function runs a Perl script and reads back the fitness values and the statistics.

The Perl script manages invocations of the program under testing per each individual. We use GDB [13] to follow the execution of the program. Commands generated by CodeSurfer are used by GDB to calculate fitness and print statistics.

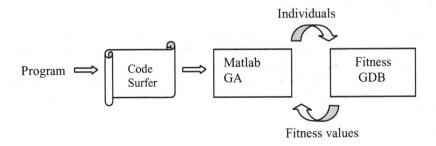

Fig. 3.2. Testing System description

The Random testing system is different from the above only in random creation of individuals.

Example 3.2.1: Line 20 of the triangle classification program code

```
20      if (i+j <= k)
```

As an example, consider the if statement in example 3.2.1. Its fitness is calculated with the GDB command shown in example 3.2.2. This code is created by the scheme script for CodeSurfer. The break point on the line 20 is set and commands cmds_37 are executed automatically when the break point is reached. First the notification that the flow gets to target 37 and condition value are printed. Then approximation level equal one is printed. And finally branch distance is calculated and printed.

Example 3.2.2: GDB commands for target on line 20

```
break 20
commands
cmds_37
end
define cmds_37
printf "TARGET %d %d \n", 37, (i+j <= k)
set $app_level=1
print $app_level
if ((i + j) > (k))
set $val = ((i + j)-(k))
abs $val
set $x37 = $abs_v
else
set $x37 = 0
end
print $x37
cont
end
```

4   Experimental Results

For experiments we take simple programs as bubble sort and greatest common denominator, also programs that are known to be used for test strategies benchmark ([4]) such as triangle classification and string matching, and finally a real program - UNIX utility uniq.

The goal of all the experiments is to get branch coverage of the program. The only exception is the uniq program, where the goal is to cover one single target. We don't use the whole input domain of the programs, but rather take a part of it sufficient to satisfy coverage requirement.

GA-based testing system and random testing system differ in the test data generation process but share the same mechanism to follow program execution. We compare 5 successive attempts of the GA testing system to cover the program with 5 successive attempts of the Random testing system. We compare the following parameters: number of invocations of original program under testing and percent of coverage that is collected as a part of statistics in GA search.

Usually GA search uses 20 individuals, unless mentioned explicitly in the experiment description. This is why 20 is the minimal number of invocations received by GA testing system, because it needs to test at least the first generation.

Random testing system generates randomly input for the program. It runs the program per each target using target specific GDB command file and determines if the target is covered. Therefore a minimal number of executions of the Random testing system is as a number of targets. It may be less than number of targets if there are targets that are covered on the way to other targets.

The testing system may follow the execution to the specific target and record other targets covered on the way. Therefore the testing system is invoked separately for every target, except the targets already covered on the way to others.

4.1   Triangle Classification

The Triangle classification program code is taken from work of Schatz et al [3]. The input of the program is 3 numbers – triangle edge lengths. The program determines if these edges may form a triangle and if so what type of triangle it is.

The Input domain: 3 integer numbers from [-10, 20]. The program checks that the input values are not negative, therefore in order to cover this target negative values are needed.

The most difficult target was the condition to satisfy an isosceles triangle.

Table 4.1. Triangle classification program testing

Testing	1	2	3	4	5	Avrg
GA	2040	3820	1360	1080	2360	**2132**
Random	18880	19520	22240	14240	24000	**19776**

Both testing systems get 100% coverage. Five successive attempt of GA testing system requires on average 2132 invocations while random testing requires 19776 invocations (about 9 times more).

4.2 Bubble Sort

Given a list of integers it returns a sorted list.

Both testing systems get 100% coverage with minimal number of invocations: 20 for GA testing and 3 for Random testing (as the number of targets in the program).

4.3 Greatest Common Denominator

The program takes as input 2 integers from [1, 100] and returns the greatest common denominator. Both testing systems get 100% coverage with minimal number of invocations: 20 for GA testing and 3 for Random testing (as the number of targets in the program).

4.4 String Matching

The string matching program is taken from work of Rad [4], where he used it not for evolutionary testing. Given a string and a pattern it returns the start position of the pattern in the string. String is over the alphabet a..z. It checks different boundary conditions - when the length of the string or the pattern is larger than some maximal length, when the length is 0, when the pattern is longer than the string.

Coding of input domain: every individual encodes the length of the string followed by numbers representing the string characters, and then similarly for the pattern. We enable variety in length in order to get coverage also for boundary conditions.

4.4.1 Small String and Pattern Lengths
The first experiment is for an input string with maximal length equals 8 and a pattern with maximal length equals 3. Both systems get 100% coverage. The GA system requires on average 54 invocations while the random system requires on average 220 (4 times more) (See Figure 4.4.1 in the next page).

Table 4.4.1. String matching testing with small length

Testing	1	2	3	4	5	6	7	8	9	10	Avrg
GA	40	60	40	40	140	40	40	40	60	40	**54**
Random	150	330	156	366	126	210	162	492	114	90	**220**

4.4.2 Large String and Pattern Lengths
The second experiment is for an input string with length 25 and a pattern with length 10. Both systems get 100% coverage. GA system requires in average 178 invocations when random requires in average 2680 (15 times more).

Increasing string and pattern length by a factor of 3 resulted in increased number of invocation by a factor of 3 for GA testing, and a factor of 12 for random testing. This indicates that GA scales much better than Random testing.

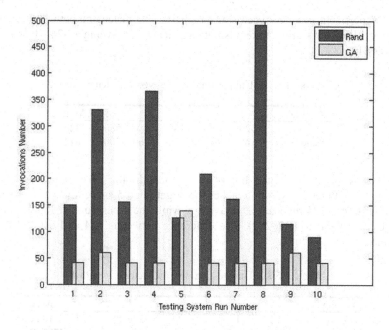

Fig. 4.4.1. The number of invocations for GA testing vs. Random testing, for the string matching program with short strings and patterns

Table 4.4.2 String matching testing with larger length

Testing	1	2	3	4	5	6	7	8	9	10	Avrg
GA	180	100	200	160	260	300	120	180	120	160	**178**
Random	4590	5040	2766	654	2070	738	3294	2442	2748	2460	**2680**

4.5 Uniq UNIX Utility

Uniq is a UNIX utility which, when fed a text file, outputs the file with adjacent identical lines collapsed to one [14].

The goal of the experiment is to find input with identical adjacent lines in order to satisfy the condition of collapsing lines, i.e. it searches input data for one specific target. We restrict the input domain to files with two lines only.

Coding of input domain: every individual is a vector of numbers. Each number is translated to a character. The first half of the vector forms the first line. The second half of the vector forms the second line.

4.5.1 Binary Strings

In this experiment the numbers in the vector are binary. For example individual: 10101110010100110001 is translated to the file with two lines:
    1010111001
    0100110001

One experiment is for bit vector of length 20. The difference between GA testing system and Random testing system is not significant, GA averages 324 while Random averages 612.

Table 4.5.1.1. Uniq testing with bit vector of length 20

Testing	1	2	3	4	5	Avrg
GA	320	160	180	380	580	**324**
Random	540	640	20	1160	700	**612**

Another experiment is for bit vector of length 40. GA population has 40 individuals. Both testing system reaches the target in all 5 successive runs. GA testing system requires 1424 invocations in average while the 4 best runs of Random require 240000 (the average is 478288). The difference between 1424 and 240000 is about 168 times.

Table 4.5.1.2. Uniq testing with bit vector of length 40

Testing	1	2	3	4	5	Avrg
GA	1520	1240	520	3200	640	**1424**
Random	223440	517600	196240	22720	1431440	**478288**

4.5.2 Alphabet String

In this experiment the numbers in the vector are integers. They are mapped to [0, 25] interval and the resulting character code is the code of 'a' plus the mapped number. GA population has 50 individuals. GA testing system requires on average 14900 invocations. Random testing system didn't find a solution in any attempt with 1000000 invocations.

Table 4.5.2. Uniq testing with alphabet string of length 20

Testing	1	2	3	4	5	Avrg
GA	15600	7200	16050	12850	22800	14900
Random	-	-	-	-	-	-

5 Conclusions

Our work aims to evaluate the applicability of GA testing to various types of software. The initial results presented in this paper are encouraging. Our experiments show that for simple programs both GA-based testing system and Random testing system work fine, but as the complexity of the program or the complexity of input domain grows, GA-based testing system significantly outperforms Random testing. Both testing systems are based on randomness; therefore variance in performance is understandable, as in table 4.5.1.1 attempt number 3. But the average result is demonstrative.

GA testing requires some preparatory work. To get the testing system to work on new example we need to write a script to translate individual genes of GA search to program input. This means that GA testing is worthwhile if the improvement over Random testing is significant. The GA system as presented has one important limitation: The conditions in control flow statements must be side-effect free.

We intend to continue to examine more types of programs, with the aim to better classify programs for which GA testing is applicable and superior to other techniques.

References

1. P. McMinn. Search-based software testing: A survey. *Software Testing, Verification and Reliability*, 14(2): 105-156, 2004/6.
2. R. Ferguson and B. Korel. The chaining approach for software test data generation. *ACM Transactions on Software Engineering and Methodology*, 5(1): 63-86, 1996
3. G. McGraw, C. Michael, and M. Schatz. Generating software test data by evolution. *IEEE Transactions on Software Engineering*, 27(12):1085-1110, 2001.
4. Soroush Karimi Rad. *Can structural test adequacy criteria be used to predict the quality of generated invariants?* MSc thesis, University of Antwerp, 2005
5. David E. Goldberg: Genetic *Algorithms in Search, Optimization and Machine Learning* Kluwer Academic Publishers, Boston, MA, 1989.
6. Mark Roper: *Software Testing* McGraw-Hill, 1994
7. Codesurfer, http:// www.grammatech.com/products/codesurfer, last visited July 2006
8. http://www.mathtools.net/MATLAB/Genetic_algorithms, last visited July 2006
9. H. Sthamer, J. Wegener and A. Baresel: Using Evolutionary Testing to improve Efficiency and Quality in Software Testing. In *Proceedings of the 2nd Asia-Pacific Conference on Software Testing Analysis and Review (AsiaSTAR)*, July 2002. 22-24th July.
10. S. Xanthakis, C. Ellis, C. Skourlas, A. Le Gall, S. Katsikas, and K. Karapoulios. Application of genetic algorithms to software testing (Application des algorithmes g_en_etiques au test des logiciels). In *5th International Conference on Software Engineering and its Applications*, pages 625-636, Toulouse, France, 1992.
11. J. Wegener, K. Buhr, and H. Pohlheim: Automatic test data generation for structural testing of embedded software systems by evolutionary testing. In *Proceedings of the Genetic and Evolutionary Computation Conference (GECCO 2002)*, pages 1233-1240, New York, USA, 2002. Morgan Kaufmann.
12. J. Wegener, A. Baresel, and H. Sthamer: Evolutionary test environment for automatic structural testing. *Information and Software Technology*, 43(14):841-854, 2001
13. GDB, The GNU Source-Level Debugger http://www.fismat.umich.mx/mn1/gdb/ gdb_toc.html, last visited July 2006
14. Wikipedia, Uniq http://en.wikipedia.org/wiki/Uniq, last visited November 2006

A Race-Detection and Flipping Algorithm for Automated Testing of Multi-threaded Programs

Koushik Sen[1] and Gul Agha[2]

[1] University of California Berkeley, USA
ksen@cs.berkeley.edu
[2] University of Illinois at Urbana-Champaign, USA
agha@cs.uiuc.edu

Abstract. Testing concurrent programs that accept data inputs is notoriously hard because, besides the large number of possible data inputs, nondeterminism results in an exponentially large number of interleavings of concurrent events. In order to efficiently test shared-memory multi-threaded programs, we develop an algorithm based on race-detection and flipping and illustrate how it can be combined with concolic execution (a simultaneous symbolic and concrete execution method) to test multi-threaded programs with data inputs. The goal of our algorithm is to minimize redundant executions while ensuring that all reachable statements in a program are executed. To achieve this, our algorithm explores all distinct causal structures of a multi-threaded program (i.e., the partial order among events generated during an execution). Because our algorithm is based on race-detection, it enables us to report potential data races and deadlocks. We have implemented our algorithm in a tool called jCUTE. We describe the results of applying jCUTE to real-world multi-threaded Java applications and libraries. In particular, we discovered several undocumented potential concurrency-related bugs in the widely used Java collection framework distributed with the Sun Microsystems' JDK 1.4.

1 Introduction

Testing programs is generally hard because of the large number of possible inputs to a program. Testing concurrent programs is notoriously harder because of the exponentially large number of possible interleavings of concurrent events. Many of these interleavings share the same causal structure (also called the *partial order*), and thus are equivalent with respect to finding bugs in a given program. Techniques for avoiding such redundant executions are called *partial order reduction* [20,11,5].

A number of approaches [6,4,2,1] to testing concurrent programs assume that the data inputs are from a small finite domain. These approaches rely on exhaustively executing the program for all possible inputs and perform a partial order reduction to reduce the search space. The problem with these approaches is that it is hard to scale them – the input set is often too large.

E. Bin, A. Ziv, and S. Ur (Eds.): HVC 2006, LNCS 4383, pp. 166–182, 2007.

A second approach is to execute a program symbolically in a customized virtual machine which supports partial order reduction [8,21]. This requires checking satisfiability of complex constraints (corresponding to every branch point in a program). Unfortunately, checking such satisfiability may be undecidable or computationally intractable. Moreover, in concurrent programs, partial order reduction for symbolic execution requires computing the dependency relations between memory accesses in a program. Because it involves alias analysis, such a computation is often conservative resulting in extra dependencies. For these reasons, large numbers of unreachable branches may be explored, often causing many warnings for bugs that could never occur in an actual execution.

Our approach is to extend *concolic testing*, which combines concrete and symbolic execution by using one to guide the other [15,7,13]. The idea behind concolic testing is to use symbolic execution to generate inputs that direct a program to alternate paths, and to use the concrete execution to guide the symbolic execution along a concrete path, and replace symbolic values (variables) by concrete values if the symbolic state is too complex to be handled by a constraint solver.

To systematically test multithreaded programs, we propose a new algorithm called the *race-detection and flipping algorithm* and combine this algorithm with concolic testing. The algorithm works as follows. For a given concrete execution, at runtime, we determine the partial order relation or the *exact* race conditions (both data race and lock race) between the various events in the execution path. Subsequently, we systematically re-order or permute the events involved in these races by generating new thread schedules as well as generate new test inputs. This way we explore one representative from each partial order. The result is an efficient testing algorithm for concurrent programs which, at the cost of missing some potential bugs, avoids the problem of false warnings.

We have implemented the algorithm in a tool, called jCUTE, for testing Java programs.[1] Apart from detecting assertion violations and uncaught exceptions, jCUTE reports all data race conditions and deadlock states encountered during the process of testing.

We provide some case studies to illustrate the utility of our approach. In our first case study, we tested the thread-safe Java Collection framework provided with the Sun Microsystems' Java 1.4. Surprisingly, we discovered several previously unknown data races, deadlocks, uncaught exceptions, and an infinite loop in this widely used library. All of them are potential bugs related to multithreaded execution. In our second case study, we tested several small to medium sized concurrent Java programs used as case studies for evaluating NASA's Java PathFinder and KSU's Bandera tool. In all those programs, our tool discovered bugs which had previously been found by model-checking *manually abstracted* versions of the programs–of course, in our case without abstracting the program. In the last two case studies, we detected well-known security attacks in the concurrent implementation of the Needham-Schroeder and the TMN protocols.

---

[1] Available at http://osl.cs.uiuc.edu/~ksen/cute/

The contributions of this paper are as follows:

- We describe a new algorithm, called *race-detection and flipping algorithm*, for efficiently exploring all non-equivalent executions of a shared-memory multi-threaded program with no data input.
- We apply a tool based on our method to real world case studies. The results show that our method can efficiently detect data races, deadlocks and other bugs in a multi-threaded program.

Due to space limitations, we skip the description of the concolic testing and the details about how to combine concolic testing and the race-detection and flipping algorithm. The description of concolic testing can be found in [7,15] and the details of the combination can be found in [12].

The outline of the rest of the paper is as follows. In Section 2, we use an example to give an overview of the race-detection and flipping algorithm combined with concolic testing. In Section 3, we describe the execution model that we assume for the purpose of describing our the race-detection and flipping algorithm. In Section 4, we describe the race-detection and flipping algorithm. Section 5 describes four case studies. In Section 6, we discuss related work.

2   Overview of Our Approach

In concolic testing our goal is to generate data inputs and schedules that would exercise all feasible executions paths of a program. Our algorithm for concolic testing uses concrete values as well as symbolic values for the inputs, and executes a program both concretely and symbolically. The symbolic execution is similar to the traditional symbolic execution [9], except that jCUTE follows the path that the concrete execution takes. During the course of the execution, it collects the constraints over the symbolic values at each branch point (i.e., the *symbolic constraints*). At the end of the execution, the algorithm has computed a sequence of symbolic constraints corresponding to each branch point. We call the conjunction of these constraints a *path constraint*. Observe that all input values that satisfy a given path constraint will explore the same execution path, provided that we follow the same thread schedule.

Apart from collecting symbolic constraints, the algorithm also computes the race condition between various events in the execution of a program, where, informally, an event represents the execution of a statement in the program by a thread. We say that two events are in a *race* if the following three conditions hold: they are events belonging to different threads, they access (i.e. read, write, lock, or unlock) the same memory location without holding a common lock, and the order of the happening of the events can be permuted by changing the schedule of the threads. The race conditions are computed by analyzing the concrete execution of the program with the help of dynamic vector clocks for multithreaded programs (dynamic vector clock algorithm was introduced in [17] for predictive monitoring of multi-threaded programs.)

The algorithm first generates a random input and a schedule which specifies the order of the execution of threads. Then the algorithm does the following in a loop: it executes the code with the generated input and the schedule. At the same time the algorithm computes the race conditions between various events as well as the symbolic constraints. It backtracks and generates a new schedule or a new input and executes the program again. It continues until it has explored all possible distinct execution paths using a depth-first search strategy. The choice of new inputs and schedules is made in one of the following two ways:

1. The algorithm picks a constraint from the symbolic constraints that were collected along the execution path and negates the constraint to define a new path constraint. The algorithm then finds, if possible, some concrete values that satisfy the new path constraint. These values are used as input for the next execution.
2. The algorithm picks two events which are in a race and generates a new schedule that at the point where the first event happened, the execution of the thread involved in the first event is *postponed* or *delayed* as much as possible. This ensures that the events involved in the race get *flipped* or re-ordered when the program is executed with the new schedule. The new schedule is used for the next execution.

We illustrate how jCUTE performs concolic testing along with race-detection and flipping using the sample program P in Figure 1. The program has two threads t_1 and t_2, a shared integer variable x, and an integer variable z which receives an input from the external environment at the beginning of the program. Each statement in the program is labeled. The program reaches the ERROR statement in thread t_2 if the input to the program is 1 (i.e., z gets the value 1) and if the program executes the statements in the following order: $(t_2, 1)(t_1, 1)(t_2, 2)(t_2, 3)$, where each event, represented by a tuple of the form (t, l), in the sequence denotes that the thread t executes the statement labeled l.

```
                        x is a shared variable
                        z = input();

    Thread t₁
                                Thread t₂

      1:   x = 3;
                                  1:   x = 2;
                                  2:   if (2*z + 1 == x)
                                  3:       ERROR;
```

Fig. 1. A Simple Shared-Memory Multi-Threaded Program

jCUTE first generates a random input for z and executes P with a default schedule. Without loss of generality, the default schedule always picks the thread which is enabled and which has the lowest index. Thus, the first execution of P is $(t_1, 1)(t_2, 1)(t_2, 2)$. Let z_0 be the symbolic value of z at the beginning of the execution. jCUTE collects the constraints from the predicates of the branches executed in this path. For this execution, jCUTE generates the path constraint $\langle 2 * z_0 + 1! = 2 \rangle$. jCUTE also decides that there is a race condition between the first and the second event because both the events access the same variable x in different threads without holding a common lock and one of the accesses is a write of x.

Following the depth-first search strategy, jCUTE picks the only constraint $2 * z_0 + 1! = 2$, negates it, and tries to solve the negated constraint $2 * z_0 + 1 = 2$. This has no solution. Therefore, jCUTE backtracks and generates a schedule such that the next execution becomes $(t_2, 1)(t_2, 2)(t_1, 1)$ (here the thread involved in the first event of the race in the previous execution is delayed as much as possible). This execution re-orders the events involved in the race in the previous execution.

During the above execution, jCUTE generates the path constraint $\langle 2 * z_0 + 1! = 2 \rangle$ and computes that there is a race between the second and the third events. Since the negated constraint $2 * z_0 + 1 = 2$ cannot be solved, jCUTE backtracks and generates a schedule such that the next execution becomes $(t_2, 1)(t_1, 1)(t_2, 2)$. This execution re-orders the events involved in the race in the previous execution.

In the above execution, jCUTE generates the path constraint $\langle 2 * z_0 + 1! = 3 \rangle$. jCUTE solves the negated constraint $2 * z_0 + 1 = 3$ to obtain $z_0 = 1$. In the next execution, it follows the same schedule as the previous execution. However, jCUTE starts the execution with the input variable z set to 1 which is the value of z that jCUTE computed by solving the constraint. The resultant execution becomes $(t_2, 1)(t_1, 1)(t_2, 2)(t_2, 3)$ which hits the ERROR statement of the program.

3   Execution Model

We assume that programs under test are written in a shared-memory multi-threaded imperative programming language such as Java. Such a program consists of a finite set of *threads*, which communicate by reading or writing shared variables, or by acquiring or releasing locks. Each thread executes a sequence of deterministic statements. Without loss of generality, we assume that the execution of a statement by a thread can perform at most one shared-memory operation–this can be achieved by splitting complex statements into a sequence of simple statements. We also assume that the execution of each thread terminates.[2]

A program supports mutual exclusion by using locks.[3] A thread suspends its execution if it tries to acquire a lock which is already acquired by another

---

[2] In practice, this can be enforced by limiting the number of execution steps.

[3] Due to space limit, we do not describe how to handle other synchronization constructs. In our implementation, we handle all synchronization primitives of Java. We express wait as a sequence of lock release and acquire actions. A join operation on a parent thread is *sequentially related* to the termination event of the child thread. Handling of message-passing primitives were discussed in [13].

thread. Normal execution of the thread resumes when the lock is released by the other thread. We assume that the acquire and release of locks take place in a nested fashion as in Java. Locks are assumed to be *re-entrant*: if a thread already holds a lock on a shared variable, then an acquire of the lock on the same variable by the same thread does not deadlock. When the execution of a thread terminates, all the locks held by the thread are released. For technical simplicity, we assume that the set of memory locations that can be locked or unlocked is disjoint from the set of memory locations that can be read or written. We assume a sequentially consistent memory model.

We fix a multi-threaded program P. The execution of each statement in P is an event. Note that a statement may involve access to a shared memory location. We represent an event as (t, l, a), where l is the label of the statement executed by thread t and a is the type of shared memory access in the statement. If the execution of the statement accesses a shared memory location, then $a = \mathbf{r}$ if the access is a read, $a = \mathbf{w}$ if the access is a write, $a = \mathbf{l}$ if the access is a lock, and $a = \mathbf{u}$ if the access is an unlock; otherwise, $a = \bot$. If the execution of a fork statement labeled l by a thread t creates a new thread t', then we get two events: $(t, l, \bot)$ representing the fork event on the thread t and $(t', \bot, \bot)$ representing the creation of the new thread. Thus the event $(t', \bot, \bot)$ represents the first event of any newly created thread t'. We use the term *access* to represent a read, a write, a lock, or an unlock of a shared memory location. We use the term *update* to represent a write, a lock, or an unlock of a shared memory location. We call an event

- a *fork event*, if the event is of the form $(t, l, \bot)$ and l is the label of a fork statement,
- a *new thread event*, if the event is of the form $(t, \bot, \bot)$,
- a *read*, a *write*, a *lock*, an *unlock*, an *access*, or an *update event*, if the event reads, writes, locks, unlocks, accesses, or updates a memory location, respectively,
- an *internal event*, if the event is not a fork event, a new thread event, or an access event.

An execution of P can be seen as a *sequence of events*. We call such a sequence an *execution path*. Note that the execution of P on several inputs may result in the same execution path. Let $\mathbf{Ex}(P)$ be the set of all feasible execution paths exhibited by the program P on all possible inputs and all possible choices by the scheduler.

If we view each event in an execution path as a node, then $\mathbf{Ex}(P)$ can be seen as a tree. Such a tree is called the *computation tree* of a program. The goal of our testing method for concurrent programs is to systematically explore a minimum possible subset of the execution paths of $\mathbf{Ex}(P)$ such that if a statement of P is reachable by a thread for some input and some schedule, the subset must contain an execution path in which that statement is executed. To achieve this, we abstract an execution path in terms of a partial order relation called *causal relation*. Any partial order represents a set of equivalent execution paths. In our testing algorithm, the goal is to exactly explore one execution path corresponding to each partial order. However, in the actual algorithm, we are able to guarantee that at least one—though *not* at most one—execution path corresponding to each partial order is explored if a program has no data input. We next define the various binary relations that we use to define a partial order.

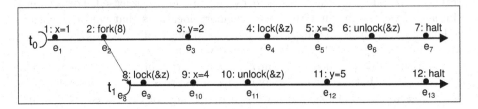

Fig. 2. Time increases from left to right. $e_3 \parallel e_{10}$, $e_9 \prec e_4$, $e_{10} \nprec e_5$, $e_3 \prec e_{12}$, $e_1 \nprec e_{10}$, $e_1 \preccurlyeq e_{10}$, $e_1 \preccurlyeq e_{12}$, $e_1 \lhd e_9$, $e_3 \lhd e_4$, $e_3 \Updownarrow e_{12}$, etc.

In an execution path $\tau \in \mathbf{Ex}(P)$, any two events $e = (t_i, l_i, a_i)$ and $e' = (t_j, l_j, a_j)$ appearing in τ are *sequentially related* (denoted by $e \lhd e'$) iff:

1. $e = e'$, or
2. $t_i = t_j$ and e appears before e' in τ, or
3. $t_i \neq t_j$, t_i created the thread t_j, and e appears before e'' in τ, where e'' is the fork event on t_i creating the thread t_j, or
4. there exists an event e'' in τ such that $e \lhd e''$ and $e'' \lhd e'$.

Thus $\lhd$ is a partial order relation. We say $e \Updownarrow e'$ iff $e \ntriangleleft e'$ and $e' \ntriangleleft e$.

In an execution path $\tau \in \mathbf{Ex}(P)$, any two events $e = (t_i, l_i, a_i)$ and $e' = (t_j, l_j, a_j)$ appearing in τ are *shared-memory access precedence related* (denoted by $e <_m e'$) iff:

1. e appears before e' in τ, and
2. e and e' both access the same memory location m, and
3. one of them is an update of m.

In the above definition, it is worth remembering that the memory locations that can be locked or unlocked are disjoint from the memory locations that can be read or written. Therefore, if $e <_m e'$ and e (or e') is a lock or unlock of m, then the e' (or e) is also a lock or unlock of m. Similarly, if $e <_m e'$ and e (or e') is a write of m, then the e' (or e) is a read or write of m.

Given the definition of the sequential relation and the shared-memory access precedence relation, we can define another relation, called *causal relation*, as follows. In an execution path $\tau \in \mathbf{Ex}(P)$, any two events $e = (t_i, l_i, a_i)$ and $e' = (t_j, l_j, a_j)$ appearing in τ are *causally related* (denoted by $e \preccurlyeq e'$) iff:

1. $e \lhd e'$, or
2. $e <_m e'$ for some shared-memory location m, or
3. there exists e'' such that $e \preccurlyeq e''$ and $e'' \preccurlyeq e'$.

The causal relation is a partial-order relation. We say that $e \parallel e'$ iff $e \not\preceq e'$ and $e' \not\preceq e$. If $e \preceq e'$, then we say e *causally precedes* e'.

We next define a relation $\prec$, called *race relation*, that captures the race condition between two events. We say that any two events $e = (t_i, l_i, a_i)$ and $e' = (t_j, l_j, a_j)$ are *race related* (denoted by $e \prec e'$) iff

1. $e \updownarrow e'$,
2. if e is a lock event and e'' is the corresponding unlock event, then $e'' <_m e'$ and there exists no e_1 such that $e_1 \neq e''$, $e_1 \neq e'$, $e'' \preceq e_1$, and $e_1 \preceq e'$, and
3. if e is a read or a write event, then $e <_m e'$ and there exists no e_1 such that $e_1 \neq e$, $e_1 \neq e'$, $e \preceq e_1$, and $e_1 \preceq e'$.

If two events in an execution path are related by $\prec$, then there exists an immediate *race* (data race or lock race) between the two events. Therefore, we call $\prec$ a *race* relation.

Figure 2 gives an example of the various relations defined above.

Given two execution paths τ and τ' in $\mathbf{Ex}(P)$, we say that τ and τ' are *causally equivalent*, denoted by $\tau \equiv_\preceq \tau'$, iff τ and τ' have the same set of events and they are linearizations of the same $\preceq$ relation. We use $[\tau]_{\equiv_\preceq}$ to denote the set of all executions in $\mathbf{Ex}$ that are equivalent to τ.

We define *a representative set of executions* $\mathbf{REx} \subseteq \mathbf{Ex}$ as a set that contains exactly one candidate from each equivalence class $[\tau]_{\equiv_\preceq}$ for all $\tau \in \mathbf{Ex}$. Formally, $\mathbf{REx}$ is a set such that following properties hold:

1. $\mathbf{REx} \subseteq \mathbf{Ex}$,
2. $\mathbf{Ex} = \bigcup_{\tau \in \mathbf{REx}} [\tau]_{\equiv_\preceq}$, and
3. for all $\tau, \tau' \in \mathbf{REx}$, it is the case that $\tau \not\equiv_\preceq \tau'$.

The following result shows that a systematic and automatic exploration of each element in $\mathbf{REx}$ is sufficient for testing.

Proposition 1. *If a statement is reachable in a program P for some input and schedule, then there exists a $\tau \in \mathbf{REx}$ such that the statement is executed in τ.*

The proof of this proposition is as follows. If a statement is reachable then there exists an execution τ in $\mathbf{Ex}$ such that the execution τ executes the statement. By the definition of $\equiv_\preceq$, any execution in $[\tau]_{\equiv_\preceq}$ executes the statement. Hence, the execution in $\mathbf{REx}$ that is equivalent to τ executes the statement.

The race-detection and flipping algorithm tries to explore all paths in a superset of $\mathbf{REx}(P)$ and a small subset of $\mathbf{Ex}(P)$. A key observation that guides our testing algorithm is that if two events are sequentially related then their happening order cannot be permuted by changing the schedule of the threads. However, if the two events are race related, then their happening order can be permuted by modifying the schedule. In our algorithm, we systematically permute or flip the race relation between various events by generating new schedules one by one.

4   The Race-Detection and Flipping Algorithm

We next describe the race-detection and flipping algorithm. For simplicity of exposition, we assume that a program under test has no data input. As illustrated in Section 2, a combination of race-detection and flipping algorithm and concolic testing can be used to systematically test a shared-memory multi-threaded program with data inputs. In the interest of space, this paper does not discuss the details of the combined method–the details can be found in [12].

```
global var τ = ε; // the empty sequence

//input: P is the program to test
test_program(P)
    while testing not completed
        execute_program(P)

execute_program(P)
    execute_prefix(P, τ);
    while there is an enabled thread
        execute the next statement of the lowest indexed enabled thread in P
            to generate the event e;
        race(τ) = false;
        postponed(τ) = ∅;
        append e to τ;
        if ∃e' ∈ τ such that e' ⋖ e
            let τ = τ₁e'τ₂ in race(τ₁) = true;
    // end of the while loop
    if there is an active thread
        print ''Error: found deadlock'';
    generate_next_schedule();

// modifies τ
generate_next_schedule()
    if ∃e such that τ == τ₁eτ₂ and backtrackable(τ₁) and
        there is no e' such that τ == τ₁'e'τ₂' and |τ₁| < |τ₁'| and backtrackable(τ₁')
        race(τ₁) = false;
        let (t, _, _) = e in add t to postponed(τ₁);
        let t = smallest indexed thread in enabled(τ₁)\ postponed(τ₁) in τ = τ₁(t, _, _);
    else
        testing completed;

backtrackable(τ₁) =
    race(τ₁) ==true and |enabled(τ₁)\postponed(τ₁)| > 1
```

Fig. 3. The Race-Detection and Flipping Algorithm

The race-detection and flipping algorithm is given in Figure 3. Recall that $\mathrm{Ex}(P)$ is the set of all feasible execution paths that can be exhibited by the program P. Similarly, $\mathrm{REx}(P)$ is a set that contains exactly one candidate from each equivalence class of feasible execution paths of P. $test\_program(P)$ repeatedly executes the program P with different schedules until all paths in a $\mathrm{REx}(P)$ have been explored. Given two sequences of events τ and τ', we let $\tau\tau'$ denote the concatenation of the two sequences. Similarly, given a sequence of events τ

and an event e, we let τe to denote the concatenation of the sequence and the event. Let ϵ be the empty sequence. A sequence of events is called a *prefix*, if it is the prefix of a feasible execution path. The global variable τ keeps track of the execution path for each execution of P. At the end of each execution, τ is appropriately truncated so that a depth-first search of the computation tree takes place. *execute_prefix*(P, τ) executes the program from the beginning until the sequence of events generated by the execution is equal to the prefix τ. Since an execution path is solely determined by the sequence of threads that are executed in the path, from now onwards we will ignore the second and the third components of a tuple representing an event. Thus $(t, \_, \_)$ represents an event on the thread t. With every prefix τ, we associate a set, denoted by *postponed*(τ). Moreover, with every prefix τ, we associate a boolean flag, denoted by *race*(τ). *enabled*(τ) returns the set of threads that are enabled after executing the prefix τ. *enabled*$(\tau)\backslash$*postponed*(τ) represents the set of threads that are enabled but not postponed after executing τ.

In each execution of P during the testing process, P is first partly executed so that it follows the prefix τ computed in the previous execution. Then P is executed with the default schedule, where the lowest indexed enabled thread is always chosen. If $\tau = \tau'e$ before the start of an execution, then the execution path and the previous execution path has the same prefix τ'. In an execution path τ, for any prefix τ' of τ, we set *race*(τ') to **true**, if there exist e, τ_1, e', and τ_2 such that $\tau = \tau'e\tau_1 e'\tau_2$ and $e \prec e'$. The algorithm computes the $\prec$ relation at runtime using the dynamic vector clock algorithm [16,12]. We omit the vector clock update procedures in the pseudo-code of the race-detection and flipping algorithm to keep the description simple. Setting *race*(τ') to **true** flags that in a subsequent execution, we must postpone the execution of e after the prefix τ' so that we may explore a possibly non-equivalent execution path. At the end of an execution, if τ_1 is the longest prefix of the current execution path τ such that *race*(τ_1) is set to **true** and $|$*enabled*$(\tau_1)\backslash$*postponed*$(\tau_1)| > 1$, we generate a new schedule by truncating τ to $\tau_1 e$, where e is an event of a thread t that has not been scheduled after τ_1 in any previous execution.

The following result holds for the race-detection and flipping algorithm.

Theorem 1. *If* $Ex'(P)$ *is the set of the execution paths that are explored by the race-detection and flipping algorithm, then there is a set* $REx(P)$ *such that* $REx(P) \subseteq Ex'(P) \subseteq Ex(P)$.

The proof of the above theorem can be found in [12].

5   Case Studies

For Java, we have implemented the combination of the race-detection and the flipping algorithm and concolic testing. The tool is called jCUTE. The details of the implementation can be found in the tool paper [14].

We use two sets of case studies to illustrate the effectiveness of jCUTE in finding potential bugs. The experiments were run on a 2.0 GHz Pentium M processor laptop with 1 GB RAM running Windows XP.

5.1   Java 1.4 Collection Library

We tested the thread-safe Collection framework implemented as part of the java.util package of the standard Java library provided by Sun Microsystems. A number of data structures provided by the package java.util are claimed as thread-safe in the Java API documentation. This implies that the library should provide the ability to safely manipulate multiple objects of these data structures simultaneously in multiple threads. No explicit locking of the objects should be required to safely manipulate the objects. More specifically, multiple invocation of methods on the objects of these data structures by multiple threads must be equivalent to a sequence of serial invocation of the same methods on the same objects by a single thread.

We chose this library as a case study primarily to evaluate the effectiveness of our jCUTE tool. As Sun Microsystems' Java is widely used, we did not expect to find potential bugs. We found several previously undocumented data races, deadlocks, uncaught exceptions, and an infinite loop in the library. Note that, although the number of potential bugs is high, these bugs are all caused by a couple of problematic design patterns used in the implementation.

Experimental Setup. The java.util provides a set of classes implementing thread-safe Collection data structures. A few of them are ArrayList, LinkedList, Vector, HashSet, LinkedHashSet, TreeSet, HashMap, TreeMap, etc. The Vector class is synchronized by implementation. For the other classes, one needs to call the static functions such as Collections.synchronizedList, Collections.synchronizedSet, etc., to get a synchronized or thread-safe object backed by a non-synchronized object of the class. To setup the testing process we wrote a multithreaded test driver for each such thread-safe class. The test driver starts by creating two empty objects of the class. The test driver also creates and starts a set of threads, where each thread executes a different method of either of the two objects concurrently. The invocation of the methods strictly follows the contract provided in the Java API documentation. We created two objects because some of the methods, such as containsAll, takes as an argument an object of the same type. For such methods, we call the method on one object and pass the other object as an argument. Note that more sophisticated test drivers can be written.

The arguments to the different methods are provided as input to the program. If a class is thread-safe, then there should be no error if the test-driver is executed with any possible interleaving of the threads and any input. However, jCUTE discovered data races, deadlocks, uncaught exceptions, and an infinite loop in these classes. Note that in each case jCUTE found no such error if methods are invoked in a single thread. As such the bugs detected in the Java Collection library are *concurrency related*.

The summary of the results is given in the Table 1. Here We present a simple scenario under which the infinite loop happens. The test driver first creates two synchronized linked lists by calling

```
List l1 = Collections.synchronizedList(new LinkedList());
List l2 = Collections.synchronizedList(new LinkedList());
l1.add(null);
l2.add(null);
```

The test driver then concurrently allows a new thread to invoke `l1.clear()` and another new thread to invoke `l2.containsAll(l1)`. jCUTE discovered an interleaving of the two threads that resulted in an infinite loop. However, the program never goes into infinite loop if the methods are invoked in any order by a single thread. jCUTE also provided a trace of the buggy execution. This helped us to detect the cause of the bug. The cause of the bug is as follows. The method `containsAll` holds the lock on `l2` throughout its execution. However, it acquires the lock on `l1` whenever it calls a method of `l1`. The method `clear` always holds the lock on `l1`. In the trace, we found that the first thread executes the statements

```
modCount++;
header.next = header.previous = header;
```

of the method `l1.clear()` and then there is a context switch before the execution of the statement `size=0;` by the first thread. The other thread starts executing the method `containsAll` by initializing an iterator on `l1` without holding a lock on `l1`. Since the field `size` of `l1` is not set to 0, the iterator assumes that `l1` still has one element. The iterator consumes the element and increments the field `nextIndex` to 1. Then a context switch occurs and the first thread sets `size` of `l1` to 0 and completes its execution. Then the other thread starts looping over the iterator. In each iteration `nextIndex` is incremented. The iteration continues if the method `hasNext` of the iterator returns true. Unfortunately, the method `hasNext` performs the check `nextIndex != size;` rather than checking `nextIndex < size;`. Since `size` is 0 and `nextIndex` is greater than 0, `hasNext` always returns true and hence the loop never terminates. Note that this infinite loop should not be confused with the infinite loop in the following wrongly coded sequential program commonly found in the literature.

```
List l = new LinkedList(); l.add(l); System.out.println(l);
```

Table 1. Results for testing synchronized Collection classes of JDK 1.4

Name	Run time in seconds	# of Paths	# of Threads	# of Functions Tested	# of data races/deadlocks/ infinite loops/exceptions
Vector	5519	20000	5	16	1/9/0/2
ArrayList	6811	20000	5	16	3/9/0/3
LinkedList	4401	11523	5	15	3/3/1/1
LinkedHashSet	7303	20000	5	20	3/9/0/2
TreeSet	7333	20000	5	26	4/9/0/2
HashSet	7449	20000	5	20	19/9/0/2

5.2   NASA's Java Pathfinder's Case Studies

In [10], several case studies have been carried out using Java PathFinder and Bandera. These case studies involve several small to medium-sized multithreaded Java programs; thus they provide a good suite to evaluate jCUTE. The programs include RemoteAgent, a Java version of a component of an embedded spacecraft-control application, Pipeline, a framework for implementing multi-threaded staged calculations, RWVSN, Doug Lea's framework for reader writer synchronization, DEOS, a Java version of the scheduler from a real-time executive for avionics systems, BoundedBuffer, a Java implementation of multi-threaded bounded buffer, NestedMonitor, a semaphore based implementation of bounded buffer, and ReplicatedWorkers, a parameterizable job scheduler. Details about these programs can be found in [10]. We also considered a distributed sorting implementation used in [8]. This implementation involves both concurrency and complex data inputs.

We used jCUTE to test these programs. Since most of these programs are designed to run in an infinite loop, we bounded our search to a finite depth. jCUTE discovered known concurrency related errors in RemoteAgent, DEOS, BoundedBuffer, NestedMonitor, and the distributed sorting implementation and seeded bugs in Pipeline, RWVSN, and ReplicatedWorkers. The summary of the results is given in the Table 2. In each case, we stopped at the first error. Note the although the running time of our experiments is many times smaller than that in [10,8], we are also using a much faster machine.

It is worth mentioning that we tested the *un-abstracted version* of these programs rather than requiring a programmer to manually provide abstract interpretations as in [10]. This is possible with jCUTE because jCUTE tries to explore distinct paths of a program rather than exploring distinct states. Obviously, this means that we cannot prove a program correct if the program has infinite length paths. Java PathFinder and Bandera can verify a program in such cases if the state space of the abstracted program is finite.

Table 2. Java PathFinder's Case Studies (un-abstracted)

Name	Run time in seconds	# of Paths	# of Threads	Lines of Code	# of Bugs Found data races/deadlocks/ assertions/exceptions
BoundedBuffer	11.41	43	9	127	0/1/0/0
NestedMonitor	0.46	2	3	214	0/1/0/0
Pipeline	0.70	3	5	103	1/0/1/0
RemoteAgent	0.45	2	3	55	1/1/0/0
RWVSN	2.19	8	5	590	1/0/1/0
ReplicatedWorkers	0.34	1	5	954	0/0/1/0
DEOS	35.23	111	6	1443	0/0/1/0

6   Related Work

Bruening [1] first proposed a technique for *dynamic partial order reduction*, called ExitBlock-RW algorithm, to systematically test multithreaded programs. They used two sets, *delayed set* and *enabled set*, similar to the sets *postponed* and $T_{enabled}$ in our algorithm, to enumerate meaningful schedules by re-ordering dependent atomic blocks. However, they assume that the program under test follows a consistent mutual-exclusion discipline using locks. The dynamic partial order reduction technique proposed by Carver and Lei [2] guarantees that exactly one interleaving for each partial order is explored. However, the approach involves storing schedules that have not been yet explored; this can become a memory bottleneck.

More recently, dynamic partial order reduction proposed by Flanagan and Godefroid [4] removes the memory bottleneck in [2] at the cost of possibly exploring more than one interleaving for each partial order. This technique uses dynamically constructed *persistent sets* and *sleep sets* [5] to prune the search space. The key difference between the DPOR algorithm in [4] and our race-detection and flipping algorithm is that,for every choice point, the DPOR algorithm in [4] uses a persistent set and we use a postponed set. These two sets can be different at a choice point. For example, for the 3-threaded program in Figure 4, if the first execution path is $(t_1, 1, \mathbf{w})(t_2, 2, \mathbf{w})(t_3, 3, \mathbf{w})$, then at the first choice point denoting the initial state of the program, the persistent set is $\{t_1, t_3\}$; whereas, at the same choice point, the postponed set is $\{t_1\}$. (Apart from scheduling the thread t_1, the race-detection and flipping algorithm also schedules the thread t_2 at the first choice point.) Note that the DPOR algorithm in [4] picks the elements of a persistent set by using a complex forward lookup algorithm. In contrast, we *simply* put the current scheduled thread to the postponed set at a choice point.

t_1 :	t_2 :	t_3 :
1: x = 1;	2: y = 4;	3: x = 2;

Fig. 4. A Three-Threaded Program

Moreover, the implementation in [4] considers two read accesses to the same memory location by different threads to be dependent. Thus for the 3-threaded program in Figure 5, the implementation described in [4] would explore six interleavings. We remove the redundancy associated with this assumption by using a more general notion of race and its detection using dynamic vector clock algorithm. As such, for the above example, we will explore only one interleaving. Note that none of the previous descriptions of the above dynamic partial order reduction techniques have handled programs which have inputs.

t_1 :	t_2 :	t_3 :
1: lv1 = x;	2: lv2 = x;	3: if (x > 0) 4: ERROR;

Fig. 5. Another Three-Threaded Program

In [13] concolic testing has been extended to test asynchronous message-passing Java programs written using a Java Actor library. Shared memory systems can be modeled as asynchronous message passing systems by associating a thread with every memory location. Reads and writes of a memory location can be modeled as asynchronous messages to the thread associated with the memory location. However, this particular model would treat both reads and writes similarly. Hence, the algorithm in [13] would explore many redundant executions. For example, for the 2-threaded program $t_1 : x = 1; x = 2; t_2 : y = 3; x = 4;$, the algorithm in [13] would explore six interleavings. Our algorithm assumes that two reads are not in race and thus would explore only three interleavings of the program.

In a similar independent work [18], Siegel et al. uses a combination of symbolic execution and static partial order reduction to check if a parallel numerical program is equivalent to a simpler sequential version of the program. However, their main emphasis is in symbolic execution of numerical programs with floating points, rather than programs with pointers and data-structures. Therefore, static partial order reduction proves effective in their approach.

Model checking tools [19,3] based on static analysis have been developed, which can detect bugs in concurrent programs. These tools employ partial order reduction techniques to reduce search space. The partial order reduction depends on detection of thread-local memory locations and patterns of lock acquisition and release.

7   Conclusion

We presented an efficient algorithm for testing multithreaded programs. A pure symbolic execution based testing algorithm for concurrent programs may end up exploring redundant execution paths having the same partial order. This is because optimal partial order reduction requires accurate knowledge of dependency relation; such knowledge may not be computable due to inaccuracies of alias analysis during symbolic execution. On the other hand, a pure concrete execution based testing algorithm for concurrent programs requires the exploration of all partial orders for all possible inputs. This may not scale up if the domain of inputs is large. Our algorithm addresses the limitations of both these approaches by extending concolic testing with the race-detection and flipping algorithm. The concrete execution of concolic testing helps to resolve aliases exactly at runtime. As a result we get the exact dependency or causal relation among the events. The symbolic execution helps to generate a small set of inputs from a large domain of inputs through constraint solving. Therefore, we believe that concolic execution combined with the race-detection and flipping algorithm is an attractive technique to test concurrent programs.

Acknowledgment

We would like to thank Ras Bodik, Timo Latvala, Darko Marinov, Grigore Roşu, and Mahesh Viswanathan for useful discussions and comments. This work is supported in part by the ONR Grant N00014-02-1-0715, the NSF Grant NSF CNS 05-09321. The work was done primarily while the first author was at the University of Illinois at Urbana Champaign.

References

1. D. Bruening. Systematic testing of multithreaded Java programs. Master's thesis, MIT, 1999.
2. R. H. Carver and Y. Lei. A general model for reachability testing of concurrent programs. In *6th International Conference on Formal Engineering Methods (ICFEM'04)*, volume 3308 of *LNCS*, pages 76–98, 2004.
3. J. Corbett, M. B. Dwyer, J. Hatcliff, C. S. Pasareanu, Robby, S. Laubach, and H. Zheng. Bandera : Extracting Finite-state Models from Java Source Code. In *Proc. of ICSE'00: International Conference on Software Engineering*, Limerich, Ireland, June 2000. ACM Press.
4. C. Flanagan and P. Godefroid. Dynamic partial-order reduction for model checking software. In *Proc. of the 32nd Symposium on Principles of Programming Languages (POPL'05)*, pages 110–121, 2005.
5. P. Godefroid. *Partial-Order Methods for the Verification of Concurrent Systems – An Approach to the State-Explosion Problem*, volume 1032 of *LNCS*. Springer-Verlag, 1996.
6. P. Godefroid. Model Checking for Programming Languages using VeriSoft. In *24th ACM Symposium on Principles of Programming Languages*, pages 174–186, 1997.
7. P. Godefroid, N. Klarlund, and K. Sen. DART: Directed automated random testing. In *Proc. of the ACM SIGPLAN 2005 Conference on Programming Language Design and Implementation (PLDI)*, 2005.
8. S. Khurshid, C. S. Pasareanu, and W. Visser. Generalized symbolic execution for model checking and testing. In *Proc. 9th Int. Conf. on TACAS*, pages 553–568, 2003.
9. J. C. King. Symbolic Execution and Program Testing. *Communications of the ACM*, 19(7):385–394, 1976.
10. C. S. Pasareanu, M. B. Dwyer, and W. Visser. Finding feasible abstract counter-examples. *International Journal on Software Tools for Technology Transfer (STTT'03)*, 5(1):34–48, 2003.
11. D. Peled. All from one, one for all: on model checking using representatives. In *5th Conference on Computer Aided Verification*, pages 409–423, 1993.
12. K. Sen. *Scalable Automated Methods for Dynamic Program Analysis*. PhD thesis, University of Illinois at Urbana-Champaign, June 2006.
13. K. Sen and G. Agha. Automated systematic testing of open distributed programs. In *International Conference on Fundamental Approaches to Software Engineering (FASE'06)*, LNCS (To appear), 2006.
14. K. Sen and G. Agha. CUTE and jCUTE : Concolic unit testing and explicit path model-checking tools. In *Computer Aided Verification (CAV'06)*, LNCS, 2006. (To Appear).
15. K. Sen, D. Marinov, and G. Agha. CUTE: A concolic unit testing engine for C. In *5th joint meeting of the European Software Engineering Conference and ACM SIG-SOFT Symposium on the Foundations of Software Engineering (ESEC/FSE'05)*. ACM, 2005.
16. K. Sen, G. Roşu, and G. Agha. Runtime Safety Analysis of Multithreaded Programs. In *9th European Software Engineering Conference and 11th ACM SIGSOFT International Symposium on the Foundations of Software Engineering (ESEC/FSE'03)*, pages 337–346. ACM, 2003.
17. K. Sen, G. Roşu, and G. Agha. Online efficient predictive safety analysis of multithreaded programs. *International Journal on Software Technology and Tools Transfer*, 2006.

18. S. F. Siegel, A. Mironova, G. S. Avrunin, and L. A. Clarke. Using model checking with symbolic execution to verify parallel numerical programs. Technical Report UM-CS-2005-15, University of Massachusetts Department of Computer Science, 2005.
19. S. D. Stoller. Model-Checking Multi-Threaded Distributed Java Programs. In *Proc. of SPIN'00: SPIN Model Checking and Software Verification*, volume 1885 of *LNCS*, pages 224–244. Springer, 2000.
20. A. Valmari. Stubborn sets for reduced state space generation. In *10th Conference on Applications and Theory of Petri Nets*, pages 491–515, 1991.
21. W. Visser, C. Pasareanu, and S. Khurshid. Test Input Generation with Java PathFinder. In *Proceedings of ACM SIGSOFT ISSTA'04*, pages 97–107, 2004.

Explaining Intermittent Concurrent Bugs by Minimizing Scheduling Noise

Yaniv Eytani and Timo Latvala[*]

Department of Computer Science, University of Illinois at Urbana-Champaign, USA
yeytani2@uiuc.edu, tlatvala@uiuc.edu

Abstract. A noise maker is a tool for testing multi-threaded programs. It seeds shared memory accesses and synchronization events (concurrent events) with conditional context switches and timeouts during runtime, in order to increase the likelihood that a concurrent bug manifests itself. However, an instrumented program with many seeded events may not be useful for debugging; events have been seeded all over the source code and provide almost no information regarding the bug. We argue that for many bug patterns only a few relevant context switches are critical for the bug. Based on the observation that bugs involve only a small set of critical events, we develop a randomized algorithm to reduce the scheduling noise and discover these events related to the bug. To evaluate the effectiveness of our approach, we experiment with debugging of industrial code, known open source code software, and programs representing known concurrent bugs. Our results demonstrate that this simple technique is in many cases very powerful, and significantly helps the user locating and understanding concurrent bugs.

Keywords: Concurrent debugging, testing, scheduling noise, Java.

1 Introduction

The increasing popularity of Java concurrent programming, both on the client and the server side, has brought to the forefront the issue of concurrent defects analysis. Concurrent defects such as unintentional race conditions and deadlocks are very common, yet are very difficult to uncover. As a result, such bugs often remain undetected and are discovered only after product deployment, when it is expensive to correct them. The reason it is hard to detect these concurrent defects is that for a given functional test, the size of the set of possible interleavings can be unbounded. It is not possible to test them all. Only a fraction of the interleavings actually produce concurrent faults.

The large interleaving space is not the only factor affecting the problem of debugging multi-threaded programs. Tests that reveal faults run under environmental conditions that are different from the ones found in the debugging stage. Consequently, faults are not necessarily repeatable. Once a fault is detected,

---

[*] Supported by the Academy of Finland (project 109539) and the Emil Aaltonen Foundation.

E. Bin, A. Ziv, and S. Ur (Eds.): HVC 2006, LNCS 4383, pp. 183–197, 2007.

extensive efforts must be invested in recreating the conditions under which it occurred. When these are finally recreated, the debugging itself may mask the bug (the probe effect). For example, adding debugging printing may change timing conditions and mask a concurrent bug.

Previous work showed that inducing different timing scenarios through the addition of scheduling perturbations [1,2,3] increases the likelihood of concurrent bugs being discovered. This is based on seeding scheduling noise during program execution by instrumenting the program with conditional synchronization primitives (such as yield(),wait() or sleep()). These primitives are performed with a given probability, and they trigger context switches or timeouts during the execution of the program. The seeded program is more likely to execute different interleavings, and therefore trigger bugs in the program. Inducing scheduling noise helps triggering bugs, but a program with many seeded events (or even the trace of the run) does not help pinpointing the bug nor understanding the reason why the program fails.

In this work we take a test generation based approach for finding the root causes of race related bugs in concurrent programs. We argue that in practice concurrent bugs are small, i.e. they do not require many context switches or timeouts to manifest. Similarly, we observe that scheduling preconditions for reaching concurrent bugs are also simple: bugs do not usually depend on complex interleavings for reaching the relevant events. Consequently, finding a minimal set of seeded events that generates interleavings manifesting a bug can be very helpful in the debugging process. The small set of seeded locations are very likely related to scheduling permutations leading to the bug.

We present a simple black-box and randomized algorithm for automatically minimizing scheduling noise (assuming that the correct test result is known a-priori). Our approach has many benefits. It is lightweight and runs on the byte code of the program; it does not require complex symbolic analysis or using computationally intensive solvers. The bug is not guaranteed to occur every time the test is run with the minimal set of seeded locations, but it will occur with a reasonably high probability. Hence, our approach eliminates the need for deterministic replay or other heavy logging infrastructure.

We have implemented the noise reduction algorithm as a prototype tool. We have evaluated our approach by experimenting with different types of examples taken from various sources: real industrial code, known open source code, Java runtime libraries, and programs used to evaluate testing and verification tools at NASA. The experiments show that the locations found by our tool are very helpful for pinpointing the root causes of the bug. We also describe the lessons learned by working with a large set of programs with different bug patterns. Our experience shows that in many cases it is possible to explain the scenarios leading to the bug by quickly examining the seeded locations and the program's control flow. Our work is done in the context of the Java programming language. However, we believe that the approach is generally applicable to other languages and threading libraries (e.g. C++ and POSIX).

2   Concurrent Bug Patterns

In this section we present the common bug patterns that are being studied in the academic literature and/or have been found in real code, and are scheduling dependent. These types of bugs usually occur when the programmer conceives the possible interleavings as a subset of the interleavings the Java semantics actually allows [4]. For example, a programmer may assume that a scheduler will always perform two sequential statements in the source code without context switches interrupting the execution. This may be the case in a certain running environment; however, it is not guaranteed by the Java semantics. Two of the most investigated bug types are (i) deadlocks, and (ii) data races and atomicity violations. We briefly describe previous research on these.

Work on race detection and atomicity has long traditions (for example [5]). Savage [6] defines a data race as two accesses to a shared variable by different threads, at least one of which is a write, with no mechanism used to prevent simultaneous access. As a result, different runs of the same program with the same input might change the sequence of the values a program variable had during the run. Atomicity [7] is a common higher-level correctness requirement that expresses non-interference between concurrently executed code blocks. A code block is atomic, if every execution of the program is equivalent to an execution in which that code block is executed without being interleaved with actions of other threads. High-level races [8] can informally be described as when two concurrent threads have conflicting views accessing a set V of shared variables: the two threads access variables in V but at least one of the threads does not access V atomically. Programmers can make false assumptions of the program state due to the view inconsistency.

Deadlocks are usually divided into two types: resource and communication deadlocks. Resource deadlocks arise when processes compete for access to exclusive resources. A process which requests resources must wait until it acquires all the requested resources before it can proceed with its computation. A set of processes is resource deadlocked if each process in the set requests a resource held by another process in the set, forming a cycle of lock requests. Communication deadlocks are conceptually different since the processes involved do not necessarily share resources. However, the difference between the two types of deadlocks is fairly superficial. In communication deadlocks, messages can be seen as the resources for which processes wait.

There are certain programming language constructs in Java that are usually associated with the different types of concurrent bugs described above. In Java threads can communicate via shared objects by calling methods on those objects. In order to avoid data races in these situations, objects can be locked using the `synchronized` statement, or by declaring methods on the shared objects synchronized, which is equivalent. Java provides the `wait()` and `notify()` primitives in support for user controlled interleaving between threads. While the `synchronized` primitive is the main source of resource deadlocks in Java, the `wait()` and `notify()` primitives are the main source of communication deadlocks. For example, a lost `notify()` (or a lost signal) is a common cause of blocked threads in programs that use condition variables [4,9]. A `notify()` is lost, if it is called before the thread it should wake up actually calls `wait()`. As a result, the notify has no effect and when that thread does call `wait()`, it may wait forever. In addition, a lost `notify()` may induce other control errors depending on the logical design of the program.

The presence of a concurrent bug in a program can be intimately related to the data state of the program (see [7]). It may also be dependent on the input data. However, we believe that focusing on purely race related bugs is very beneficial and practical. Bugs that are caused by the scheduling nondeterminism of concurrency continues to attract research interest as demonstrated above. We believe that bugs that require very complex interactions are not interesting in many real-life scenarios: the cumulative probability that exactly the right data input is combined with a very complex sequence that occurs exactly in the right order is very small, even if the system is run for extended periods.

2.1   Concurrent Bugs Are Small

Recent taxonomies of concurrent bugs have been presented in [4,9,10,11]. Analyzing these, we observe that a concurrent bug manifests when a few concurrent events occur in a specific order. We can thus identify a concurrent bug with that set of concurrent events. The set of events that constitute the concurrent bug involves events from different threads. A context switch is required before or after some of the events for the bug to manifest itself. For a set of events to expose the concurrent bug, it is best that no other switches occur in other locations in the sequence. Redundant context switches hide the underlying reason for the bug.

The number of events related to a bug (which intuitively corresponds to a measure of the size of a concurrent bug) is usually small. This is supported by the above mentioned studies of concurrent bug patterns, research on data races [6], atomicity [7], and stale values [12]; recent research on techniques such as context-bounded model checking [13,14] and concurrent coverage models [15,16]. All suggest that concurrent bugs are usually composed of a small number of interacting relevant events and a specific ordering for the events.

Even though both deadlocks and high-level races can theoretically involve any number of threads, in practice the number of threads needed to trigger a bug tends to be small [8,17,18]. The initial deadlock detection algorithm of Havelund [17], used for testing NASA software, only works for interactions between two threads, and it was extended to several threads only recently [19]. Furthermore, our own experience when compiling a benchmark of multi-threaded Java programs [20] also supports the notion that bugs found in real code tend to be small.

3   Seeding Noise

The nondeterministic nature of Java program execution is controlled by the scheduling mechanism of Java threads. An execution behavior of a thread schedule can be characterized by the order of shared variable accesses and synchronization events [21], referred to as events in this paper. Finding concurrent bugs is very much about finding schedules of the concurrent threads that trigger the bug. Running a test several times will might not reveal a bug because of the deterministic nature of the underlying scheduler: repeating the test will not in most cases produce a new interleaving of the test.

Model checkers try to exhaustively explore all schedules (interleavings), and are therefore always guaranteed to find the bug if it exists, provided that the model checker does not run out of resources. The systematic and exhaustive nature of model checkers is attractive, but it limits their scalability. *Noise making* [1,2] is a technique that is more scalable but less systematic. The scheduler of the underlying machine can be influenced by performing a conditional seeding of events. Calls to a scheduling function are inserted at selected points in the program under test. The scheduling function either does nothing or causes a context switch with a certain probability. However, the noise makers themselves do not report results; rather, they strive to make the tests fail. Noise makers rely on the tests to trigger assertions or other mechanisms for detecting that a test has failed. We explain the technique in more detail below.

A scheduling function works by inserting a scheduling primitive, or a combination of such primitives, that may cause context switches, timeout, or delay a set of events. An example of a seeding primitive is Java's `yield()` instruction. It will probably cause the current thread to give up the CPU and to be transferred to the end of the ready threads queue. The thread will be scheduled to some processing unit when it reaches the head of the queue. Intuitively, a `yield()` can be seen as a directive for a possible transfer of control from one thread to another. As a result of the seeding process, each time a functional test is run, it will produce a potentially different interleaving.

An important property of noise making is the probabilistic completeness property: if all relevant locations are seeded, there is a sequence of choices by the scheduling function for each reachable deadlock and assertion violation [1]. Thus, there is a non-zero probability of finding a buggy interleaving by testing the seeded program, even if the probability of finding it by testing the original program in the same runtime environment is zero due to the particular thread scheduler in that runtime environment. We only assume that the thread scheduler is fair.

4   Explaining Intermittent Concurrent Bugs

Previous work [22] shows that conditional seeding of critical events can increase the likelihood that a bug is either masked or revealed. Most bugs require that a context switch occurs at a specific location. For example, a program with an erroneous data race may exhibit the bug only if the two competing threads read or write the variable in question in a certain order. However, in many cases the underlying scheduler will work deterministically. Thus, a context switch will not occur between two given consecutive statements in one thread. A seeding event that triggers the bug may re-create the bug frequently and therefore pinpoint a statement where an atomicity violation occurs in the source code. Instrumenting the

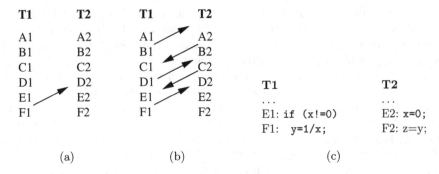

Fig. 1. Sample execution traces

program with many seeded events does not aid debugging: events that have been seeded all over the source code provide almost no information regarding the location of the atomicity violation. In addition, different seeded events can interact with each other in ways that will make it hard for the programmer to correlate the behavior leading to the bug manifesting itself with the seeded events.

Figure 1 illustrates the difference between many and few seeded events. In Fig. 1(a) and Fig. 1(b) two execution traces are depicted, both of them leading to a concurrent bug manifesting. We can examine the traces in a black box manner, where we record the events occurring but do not attribute any semantic meaning to the corresponding statements in the source code. The arrows in Fig. 1 represent context switches occurring between the two threads. By examining the trace in Fig. 1(a) we can observe that the bug probably occurs due to events E1 and F1 executing in a non-atomic manner, even with out understanding the semantic meaning of these events. Fig. 1(b) does allow us to correlate the bugs with a specific seeding, but it forces us to review the source code thoroughly in order to locate the bug. By examining the relevant parts of the source code in Fig. 1(c), we can see that the bug can be easily explained by context switching at E1.

Deterministically finding a small set of seeded events that triggers the bug may be hard. A context switch at the wrong time can cancel the effect of a necessary switch, effectively masking the bug. To illustrate this point, consider the simple program in Fig. 2. The program is similar in nature to the program in Fig. 1(c). In this example the two threads acquire two locks in a symmetric manner. Context switching at the right points can cause the program to deadlock. If thread 1 executes first, the deadlock can occur if a context is switch is triggered after the first statement; thread 1 would regain control after thread 2 has acquired lock b. The situation is symmetric if thread 2 would have been executed first. A context switch between acquiring the locks in one thread is a necessary precondition for the bug to manifest. However, two context switches may cancel each other, thus effectively masking the bug by allowing one of the threads to to complete the

T1	T2
...	...
E1: lock(a);	E2: lock(b);
F1: lock(b);	F2: lock(a);

Fig. 2. Simple deadlocking concurrent program with two threads

locking sequence before the other thread. By seeding events near the lock()-statements, the deadlock would manifest itself after executing the program a few times. Although the interactions between events occurring in a program affect how exactly a bug manifests, the probability for performing the right set of switches is still high. This is illustrated in our example in Fig. 2, where there is a simple even/odd symmetry of context switching for reaching the lock()-statements from different threads.

In addition to events where seeding affects the likelihood that a bug manifests, there also exist events for which conditional seeding does not affect whether the bug is revealed or not. Such "neutral" events can be dependent on the context of an execution. A trivial example is any event reached after the bug has already occurred. The neutral events can usually be removed. Given a functional test, we can nicely de-couple the conditions for a bug to manifest into (i) reaching a usually simple scheduling precondition, and (ii) executing some events relevant to the bug in a given order. For example, in Fig. 1(c) the precondition is that event E1 happens before event E2. If we start from thread 1, an arbitrary even number of context switches is required before reaching E1 and E2. These context switches can be safely removed to simplify the trace as long as the scheduling precondition invariant is maintained. This, however, implies that such switches cannot be removed in a completely deterministic way without a-priori knowledge about the semantics of the programs. Hence, a number of changes in the scheduling preconditions, such as executing a certain thread first, should not severely affect the likelihood of occurrence of the bug as long as the interactions between different seeded events are small. This motivates our use of a simple randomized algorithm to reduce the number of seeded events, as described in the next section.

5   An Algorithm for Minimizing Noise

Once a concurrent bug has occurred, we would like to locate a small set of related seeded events. Based on our observations above, randomly selecting a small set of events should be a good strategy. However, we do not know the number of required good events. This problem can be overcome by using an iterative approach. The general strategy we use is the following. We repeatedly run the program and iteratively create a smaller hypotheses for the correct set of seeded events. As the first set we will choose a set of seeded events that caused the bug to manifest itself. To obtain a smaller set, we apply noise to a randomly selected subset of these and check if the bug still manifests itself. If the bug still

```
1    I = SubsetOfConcurrentEvents(Program)
2    (s, done) = new_s(I, s, done)
3    I' = RandomSubset(I, s)
4    while(¬done) :
5        Run the noise maker with noise only on concurrent events in I'
6        if (there was a concurrent bug in the last run):
7            I = I'
8            (s, done) = new_s(I, s, done)
9            I' = RandomSubset(I, s)
10   Print I as explanation for bug
```

Fig. 3. Algorithm for minimizing noise

occurs for the subset of events, we conclude that the subset is related to the bug and repeat the process recursively on that subset.

A set of good events that are known to cause the bug to manifest itself are called the initial events (I). This set is known to be related to the concurrent bug and is used as our base hypothesis. We can create I by using previously proposed methods; these could be heuristics related to highly contended variables [3], non-uniform seeding [22], or uniform seeding techniques [2,1]. Using the set of initial events I, we start minimizing the set of events. There are several possible strategies for selecting a new set of events. We could randomly select a subset I' of I and then run the program repeatedly with the new set of seeded events. If a large enough fraction (defined by a parameter) of the runs causes the bug to manifest, we accept this set of events as the new set. A much simpler strategy is to choose a new subset of events I' every run. Usually a simple strategy like randomly choosing half of the events works well. When running the program, the seeded synchronization primitives cause random context switches and timeouts at events in I'. We check whether the concurrent bug has manifested after the program is run. If the concurrent bug occurs, we replace I with I' and apply the same procedure again. In this paper we have used the latter strategy to minimize noise.

In the pseudo-code in Fig. 3, the function $new\_s(I, s, done)$ decides whether we have reached a fixpoint and how large the next subset should be. The function also decides whether we have reached a fixpoint and should not try to minimize I' further. In practice, the algorithm stops when a set with a small number of seeded events (1-3, pre-defined by a parameter) are found or we cannot find a smaller set where the bug manifests with high probability. After the algorithm has stopped, the resulting events are identified by their program location, method scope and variable name, and then presented to the user.

With this simple approach, reproducibility of bugs is likely but not guaranteed. Guaranteed reproducibility requires a capture-and-replay mechanism. Note that choosing a small set of seeded events can be seen as a special case of partial replay [2] that was shown to work well in practice.

6   Experimental Results

We have implemented the noise minimization algorithm as a prototype tool. Our implementation interfaces with ConTest's instrumentation engine [2]. This eases implementation and allows us to focus on the noise minimization algorithm. Although our implementation works with Java, we see no reason why it could not be interfaced with e.g. the POSIX pthreads library.

To evaluate our approach we tested the algorithm on a set of programs of various types taken from various sources: real industrial code, known open source code, Java runtime libraries, programs used to evaluate testing and verification tools at NASA, and programs from a multi-threaded benchmark consisting of implementations of known bug patterns [23]. In what follows we provide detailed explanations for four of the programs. The program sizes range from around 200 to 1200 lines of code. In order to create an initial set of seeded events we used the approach suggested in [22]. We seeded a random subset of variables until the bug first manifested. We then used the set of seeded locations as the objective of our noise reduction algorithm. Our experience is not limited to the big examples described here. The results below are representative of our experience with the tool.

Tomcat Logger. Tomcat is a popular open source Java application server. It can be used to generate dynamic web content that can access databases and other resources. The bug we explored in Tomcat logger occurs because of a race on a static variable in the class org.apache.tomcat.util.log.SystemLogHandler. The class has a static variable, `reuse`, which represents a stack that is shared between different threads. In the method `startCapture()` (see Fig. 4) there is an obvious race between the function calls `reuse.empty()` and `reuse.pop()`. If a context switch occurs just after the `if`-statement, another thread can empty `reuse`, causing an EmptyStack-exception at `reuse.pop()`.

Our algorithm pinpoints the bug and reports that context switching after the `if` is an important location for the bug. Understanding the bug with this information is fairly straight-forward as the race condition between `reuse.empty()` and `reuse.pop()` is fairly obvious. To fix the error the `if`-block should be enclosed with a `synchronized` block.

Crawler. Crawler is a web crawling algorithm embedded in an IBM product and is implemented using a "worker thread" design pattern. For the experiment we used a skeleton of the program previously used internally at IBM for testing. This was still 1200 lines of code spread over 19 classes (for more details see [2]).

The crawler algorithm contains two concurrent bugs known to us. The first is a race condition bug that triggers a null pointer exception. A shared variable `connection` is manipulated carelessly in the `finish()` method of the Worker class. The method has the following line:

```
if(connection ! = null) connection.setStopFlag( );
```

If the `connection` variable is not null and after that a context switch occurs, the connection variable might be set to null by another thread. Should this happen before `connection.setStopFlag()` is executed, a null pointer exception is

```
public static void startCapture() {
  ...
  if (!reuse.empty()) {
    log=(CaptureLog) reuse.pop();
  } else {
    log=new CaptureLog();
  }
  ...
}
```

Fig. 4. Skeleton for buggy method in Tomcat

thrown. To fix this bug, the above statement should be executed within an appropriate `synchronized` block so that the execution of the block would be atomic.

The set of locations that our algorithm returns are after the `if`-block above, and the place in the code of the Worker class where the variable `connection` is set to null. This makes explaining the bug very simple. Understanding the bug without the locations provided by our algorithm is fairly challenging. Crawler has more than 40 variables, which makes locating the bug manually very hard.

The second bug in Crawler is a deadlock reported in [3]. Applying the algorithm shows that when seeding delay to locations in the `waitForConnection()` function the deadlock occurs. Since the code itself contains some printings for debugging, explaining the bug from an execution trace if fairly simple. When a thread is seeded with a delay near the end of the run, the function `finish()` executes before the `waitForConnection()` function. This leads to the program not terminating.

Java Collection Library. The Java Collection library provides containers that should be thread safe. Although the library has been extensively tested, Sen and Agha [24] report several race related errors in the library.

The `ArrayList` class has a race related error that can trigger an uncaught `ConcurrentModificationException` exception. The bug occurs in a simple scenario only involving two threads. Two synchronized lists l1 and l2 are created, and a single object is added to each list. If the two threads concurrently call the functions `l1.add(new Object())` and `l2.containsAll(l1)`, certain interleavings of the threads will cause a race on the field `modCount` of the `ArrayList` class. The result is the uncaught exception. The program never throws the exception if the methods are invoked in any order by a single thread. Our algorithm pinpointed the non-atomic segment between the assignments of `modCount` when `l2.containsAll(l1)` creates an iterator for l1 that records `modCount`, and a call to an `hasNext()` function that checks `modCount` to be of the same value. Examining the trace, we notice that `add()` increments this field between calling the constructor of the iterator and the invocation of the `hasNext()` function, and thus causes the exception. We were able to debug similar bug patterns in other Java runtime libraries such as `LinkedList`.

Concurrent Readers, Exclusive Writing. This code is one of the examples used to test the Java PathFinder model checking tool developed by NASA. It includes an intentionally buggy implementation of the concurrent readers, exclusive writer scenario [25]. In this scenario the implementation should guarantee that several readers can read the database concurrently. Writes should be exclusive so that only the single writer has access to the database. The bug in the implementation causes non-atomicity in the write() function. Seeding noise helps trigger the bug, because it triggers context switches in the write() function that did not occur when normally executing the program. However, the noise does not pinpoint the exact location of the bug although it reveals the non-atomicity of the write() function. This is because the bug causes an error in the control flow, and noise making can only identify the symptom, non-atomicity, in this case. However, given the symptom and by examining the control flow of the program it is possible to detect the defect.

7   Related Work

Static analysis tools of various types [11] as well as formal analysis tools [26,13,27], are also being developed to detect faults. Static technologies are being used to generate information that other technologies may find useful, such as a list of program statements from which there can be no thread switch [28] (single thread executing). Tools used for replay and partial replay [21,2] are necessary for debugging and contain technology that is useful for testing. Other tools that present specific and interesting views of the interleaving space to help analyze both coverage and performance include [29,30].

A different approach is taken by a set of tools called noise makers, which increase the likelihood of bug discovery by inducing different timing scenarios through the addition of scheduling perturbations [1,2,3]. If done with care, the seeding technique only creates correct interleavings and does not interfere with replay algorithms [2]. Biased heuristics based on coverage information were shown to increase the probability that the concurrent defect is uncovered compared to unbiased seeding [3]. Most previous research on noise making generally used a white box approach. In [1], static analysis was suggested for use in detecting the locations where thread switches will help reveal bug patterns. In [2], noise-making decisions were made based on coverage information. Experiments carried out in [3] showed that focusing on the locations related to variables one-at-a-time will improve the probability of finding bugs.

Recent work [22] explored the theory and practice of deciding where in the program to induce thread switches. It proposed a model and static classification of seeding to be of good, bad or neutral for placing thread switches according to their effect on the probability of the bug manifesting itself. The work in [31] formulated noise making as a search problem. It used a genetic algorithm as the search method. It applied some of the insights presented here to define a fitness function that allows it to converge to a small set of good seeded events.

Noise minimization can naturally be compared to work on the delta debugging technique [32], which extracts differences between failing and successful test cases and their executions. The original delta-debugging work applied to test inputs only, but was later extended to minimize differences in thread interleavings [33]. Our method is an improvement w.r.t. delta debugging in several ways. First, inducing different thread schedules using delta debugging may require a replay mechanism, which has inherent limitations. Second, delta debugging assumes that no thread switch can disable the bug. This assumption may be sufficient for debugging purposes where one can assume that a failing schedule only contains events that either cause the bug or are indifferent to it. However, a context switch may sometimes alternate between being good, bad or neutral in its effect on manifesting the bug. By taking a probabilistic test generation approach our method avoids these problems. Thus, we believe that our approach is simpler but can still be seen as a more general one.

8   Lessons Learned and Conclusions

Generating random scheduling noise is an effective way of triggering concurrent bugs. Precisely located scheduling noise can be very helpful in locating and understanding bugs. Our simple approach using noise minimization efficiently finds a set of locations related to the bug automatically. In our evaluation of the algorithm, the locations provided by our algorithm proved to be very helpful for understanding the bug. Simplicity is one of the key strengths of our approach. It is black-box and requires no complex logging infrastructure such as replay.

In what follows, we further describe the lessons learned while applying this method. We also base our discussion on our work on the multi-threaded benchmark [20]. One of the assumptions of this work was that programmers usually assume that small-size code blocks are atomic; hence they sometimes avoid forcing correct synchronization for shared variables in such code blocks. A second assumption was that once noise is applied in the correct location, the concurrent bug manifests itself. Since the non-atomic code blocks are relatively small, it will facilitate localizing the bug.

When examining the code and the bugs, we found that concurrent code is generally written in a very concise way. The relevant code blocks are small, and the seeded events are indeed very indicative of the statements related to the bug. Many of the bugs involve the issue of control, e.g. an if-statement guarding access to a shared variable. We found that in this scenario the guarding if tends to be very close to the protected variable. This scenario also exists in the case of condition variables, where wait() or notify() are usually guarded with if-statements.

In order to explain the bugs, we found two simple trace reviewing methods to be effective. The first is to observe where the first access to a shared variable takes place after the seeded events of that type. We also found that looking at the methods where seeding occurs provides a reasonable high level description of the bug scenario. This was also helpful for reasoning about some of the bugs where the control flow error was not related directly with the race, or when the bug involved actual timeouts that changed the order of the methods being executed.

Our approach has some limitations. The first limitation is caused by the fact that our algorithm converges to a small number of locations in the source code. This means that if several bugs share the same assertion violation, the algorithm will converge to only one of them. However, this is not a severe limitation as a common practice in debugging is to fix one bug at a time [34]. Another limitation is that our algorithm is dependent on seeding the correct events to localize the scheduling noise. However, this is true only for intermittent bugs that do not appear without applying noise.

Previous work [3,22] shows that variables tend to be good functional abstractions of a subset of the program's events. Often it is beneficial to treat all events before or after a shared variable access as a single event of a larger granularity. We believe that there are other useful functional abstractions, such as methods and possibly classes, that may act in a similar manner. For example, in the deadlock in Crawler scheduling noise determines the order of two methods, regardless of at which locations it is applied. Knowing that we need to seed an event in a method, instead of seeding of a few different statements in the method, will provide more information to the programmer. In addition, we also believe it may be beneficial to identify events where seeding masks the bug. This step should provide additional information useful for debugging and allow us to reason about the interaction of events in the program, without inspecting the actual semantics of the program. This can also allow us to deal with bugs occurring frequently or without applying noise.

Acknowledgements. The first author is indebted to Eitan Farchi, Shmuel Ur and Yosi Ben Asher for their guidance on this research direction and early discussions on the subject. We thank Rajesh Kumar, Feng Chen and Koushik Sen for their help during the preparation of the paper.

References

1. Stoller, S.D.: Testing concurrent Java programs using randomized scheduling. In: Proceedings of the Second Workshop on Runtime Verification (RV). Volume 70(4) of Electronic Notes in Theoretical Computer Science., Elsevier (2002)

2. Edelstein, O., Farchi, E., Nir, Y., Ratsaby, G., Ur, S.: Multithreaded Java program test generation. IBM Systems Journal **41** (2002) 111–125

3. Ben-Asher, Y., Eytani, Y., Farchi, E.: Heuristics for finding concurrent bugs. In: International Parallel and Distributed Processing Symposium, IPDPS 2003, PADTAD Workshop. (2003)

4. Farchi, E., Nir, Y., Ur, S.: Concurrent bug patterns and how to test them. [35] 286

5. Netzer, R., Miller, B.: Detecting data races in parallel program executions. In: Advances in Languages and Compilers for Parallel Computing, 1990 Workshop, Irvine, Calif., Cambridge, Mass.: MIT Press (1990) 109–129

6. Savage, S., Burrows, M., Nelson, G., Sobalvarro, P., Anderson, T.: Eraser: a dynamic data race detector for multithreaded programs. ACM Transactions on Computer Systems (TOCS) **15** (1997) 391–411

7. Flanagan, C., Freund, S.N.: Atomizer: A dynamic atomicity checker for multithreaded programs. In: 31'st ACM SIGPLAN Symposium on Principles of Programming Languages (POPL). (2004)

8. Artho, C., Havelund, K., Biere, A.: High-level data races. In: VVEIS'03, The First International Workshop on Verification and Validation of Enterprise Information Systems, Angers, France. (2003)

9. Long, B., Strooper, P.A.: A classification of concurrency failures in Java components. [35] 287

10. Hallal, H., Alikacem, E., Tunney, W.P., Boroday, S., Petrenko, A.: Antipattern-based detection of deficiencies in Java multithreaded software. In: QSIC, IEEE Computer Society (2004) 258–267

11. Hovemeyer, D., Pugh, W.: Finding bugs is easy. SIGPLAN Notices **39** (2004) 92–106

12. Artho, C., Havelund, K., Biere, A.: Using block-local atomicity to detect stale-value concurrency errors. In Wang, F., ed.: ATVA. Volume 3299 of Lecture Notes in Computer Science., Springer (2004) 150–164

13. Rabinovitz, I., Grumberg, O.: Bounded model checking of concurrent programs. In Etessami, K., Rajamani, S.K., eds.: CAV. Volume 3576 of Lecture Notes in Computer Science., Springer (2005) 82–97

14. Qadeer, S., Rehof, J.: Context-bounded model checking of concurrent software. In Halbwachs, N., Zuck, L.D., eds.: TACAS. Volume 3440 of Lecture Notes in Computer Science., Springer (2005) 93–107

15. Bron, A., Farchi, E., Magid, Y., Nir, Y., Ur, S.: Applications of synchronization coverage. In Pingali, K., Yelick, K.A., Grimshaw, A.S., eds.: PPOPP, ACM (2005) 206–212

16. Tasiran, S., Elmas, T., Bolukbasi, G., Keremoglu, M.E.: A novel test coverage metric for concurrently-accessed software components. In Grieskamp, W., Weise, C., eds.: FATES. Volume 3997 of Lecture Notes in Computer Science., Springer (2005) 62–71

17. Havelund, K.: Using runtime analysis to guide model checking of Java programs. In Havelund, K., Penix, J., Visser, W., eds.: SPIN. Volume 1885 of Lecture Notes in Computer Science., Springer (2000) 245–264

18. Artho, C., Biere, A.: Applying static analysis to large-scale, multi-threaded Java programs. In: Australian Software Engineering Conference, IEEE Computer Society (2001) 68–75

19. Bensalem, S., Havelund, K.: Dynamic deadlock analysis of multi-threaded programs. In: Parallel and Distributed Systems: Testing and Debugging 2005 (PADTAD'05). Volume 3875 of Lecture Notes in Computer Science., Springer (2006) 208–223

20. Eytani, Y., Ur, S.: Compiling a benchmark of documented multi-threaded bugs. In: IPDPS, IEEE Computer Society (2004)

21. Choi, J.D., Srinivasan, H.: Deterministic replay of Java multithreaded applications. In: Proceedings of the SIGMETRICS Symposium on Parallel and Distributed Tools, Welches, Oregon (1998) 48–59

22. Ben-Asher, Y., Eytani, Y., Farchi, E., Ur, S.: Producing scheduling that causes concurrent programs to fail. Technical Report UIUCDCS-R-2006-2684, University of Illinois at Urbana-Champaign (2006)

23. Eytani, Y., Havelund, K., Stoller, S., Ur, S.: Toward a framework and benchmark for testing tools for multi-threaded programs. Concurrency and Computation: Practice and Experience (to appear)

24. Sen, K., Agha, G.: jCUTE: Automated testing of multithreaded programs using race-detection and flipping. Technical Report UIUCDCS-R-2006-2676, University of Illinois at Urbana-Champaign (2006)

25. Pasareanu, C.S., Dwyer, M.B., Visser, W.: Finding feasible abstract counter-examples. STTT **5** (2003) 34–48

26. Visser, W., Havelund, K., Brat, G.P., Park, S., Lerda, F.: Model checking programs. Autom. Softw. Eng. **10** (2003) 203–232

27. Corbett, J.C., Dwyer, M., Hatcliff, J., Pasareanu, C., Robby, Laubach, S., Zheng, H.: Bandera: Extracting finite-state models from Java source code. In: Proc. 22nd International Conference on Software Engineering (ICSE), ACM Press (2000)

28. Choi, J.D., Gupta, M., Serrano, M., Sreedhar, V., Midkiff, S.: Escape analysis for Java. In: Proc. ACM Conference on Object-Oriented Programming, Systems, Languages and Applications (OOPSLA). (1999)

29. Cheer-Sun Yang, A.S., Pollock, L.: All-du-path coverage for parallel programs. ACM SigSoft International Symposium on Software Testing and Analysis **23** (1998) 153–162

30. Havelund, K., Pressburger, T.: Model checking Java programs using Java PathFinder. International Journal on Software Tools for Technology Transfer, STTT **2** (2000)

31. Eytani, Y.: Concurrent Java test generation as a search problem. In: Fifth Workshop on Runtime Verification, Edinburgh, UK (2005)

32. Zeller, A., Hildebrandt, R.: Simplifying and isolating failure-inducing input. IEEE Trans. Software Eng. **28** (2002) 183–200

33. Choi, J.D., Zeller, A.: Isolating failure-inducing thread schedules. In: ISSTA. (2002) 210–220

34. Liblit, B., Aiken, A., Zheng, A., Jordan, M.I. In: ACM SIGPLAN Conference on Programming Language Design and Implementation, ACM (2003) 141–154

35. 17th International Parallel and Distributed Processing Symposium (IPDPS 2003), 22-26 April 2003, Nice, France, CD-ROM/Abstracts Proceedings. In: IPDPS, IEEE Computer Society (2003)

Testing the Machine in the World

Michael Jackson

The Open University & Newcastle University
jacksonma@acm.org

A central aim of software testing is assurance of functional correctness and dependability. For many software-intensive systems, including administrative, embedded, enterprise and communication systems, functional correctness means achieving the desired effects in the physical world, and dependability means dependability of those effects. For example, an administrative system for a lending library is required to ensure that only members can borrow books; that a member who has reserved a book and has been notified that the book is now available for collection in the library will not find that it has been lent to another member; that the catalogue gives reliable information about what is currently on the shelves, and so on. Similarly, a system to control a lift must ensure that the lift comes when summoned and takes the user to the desired floor; that the building manager can specify service priorities in terms of express lifts and time-dependent needs such as rush hours at the beginning and end of the working day; and that failure of the mechanical equipment does not endanger life.

The Machine, the World, and the Requirement

Functional correctness of such systems means that their *requirements* in the world are satisfied by a cooperation between the *machine*, which is the software executing on the computer, and the physical *problem world* itself. To demonstrate satisfaction it is necessary to formulate and reason about three distinct subjects. First, the requirements themselves, describing the desired effects in the world. Second, the specified behaviour of the computer at its interface with the problem world. Third, the given properties of the problem world on which the computer behaviour can rely to satisfy the requirement. These three are related by an entailment: if a computer with the specified behaviour is installed in a world with the given properties as described, then the requirement will be satisfied. For example: the computer behaviour is specified in terms of input and output ports at which it can switch the motor on and off and set its polarity, monitor the request buttons and the floor sensors, and so on; it is a given problem world property that a user wishing to summon the lift will press a request button, that if the motor is on and its polarity is set upwards then the lift rises in its shaft, and that when the lift is at the home position at a floor the corresponding sensor is on; and it is a requirement that when the lift is summoned it comes to the floor.

In a software-intensive system the problem world is inherently non-formal. We must reason about it to assure ourselves and our customers that the requirements will be satisfied, but this reasoning is always fragile. We reason on the basis of abstractions that are inevitably imperfect in the sense that we can never absolutely

E. Bin, A. Ziv, and S. Ur (Eds.): HVC 2006, LNCS 4383, pp. 198–203, 2007.

exclude all possibility of a counterexample to any formal assertion about the world: no bound can be set to the considerations that may affect the truth of a formal assertion. Further, the problem world, unlike an abstract mathematical world, will typically exhibit autonomous, and easily neglected, state changes: library members may change their names, or become bankrupt, or emigrate or die, and the books may be lost or destroyed; users who have requested the lift may change their mind and walk away, or may place an obstruction between the lift doors while they go back and forth between the open lift and their office. A functionally correct and dependable software-intensive system must find a way to deal adequately with all these evident obstacles to reliable formal reasoning.

The World Can Not Be Avoided

It may, therefore, seem attractive to eliminate the messy non-formal world from our consideration as software engineers. Can we not treat our task simply as the development of software to satisfy a formal specification of the computer's behaviour at its interface with the problem world, leaving the messy non-formality of the world outside our *cordon sanitaire*? This was the view of Dijkstra, who regarded the specification as a 'logical firewall' between the non-formal concerns of the world outside and the formal task of program development. [1]

Unfortunately this neat division is not possible for a software-intensive system. Specification of the computer behaviour to be evoked by the software will make little sense when divorced from a clear description of the given properties of the problem world and of the effects that the system must produce there. To understand the stipulation that when line 17 goes high the computer must set line 23 low we must talk in terms of the meaning of line 17—that a request button has been pressed on floor 3—and of line 23—that the motor polarity is being set to upwards—and of the association that the problem world and the system requirement impose between these otherwise unrelated phenomena. In other words, we must reason, as before, about the requirements, problem world properties, and computer specification.

Decomposition into Subproblems

The complexity of the system and its problem world demands mastering by decomposition. An appropriate form of decomposition is to decompose the original *problem* into *subproblems*. Like the original problem, each subproblem has a requirement, a machine, and a problem world. For example, the lift control problem may be decomposed into three subproblems. The first, the service subproblem, provides lift service according to the priorities currently established by the building manager; the second, the display subproblem, maintains a display in the ground floor lobby showing the position of each lift and the outstanding service requests; the third, the safety subproblem, monitors the equipment and, on detecting a fault, applies the emergency brake that prevents an uncontrolled free fall of the lift car to the bottom of the shaft. Each subproblem is concerned only with certain parts of the original problem world. For example, the service subproblem is not concerned with the emergency brake or with the lobby display; and the safety subproblem is not concerned with the display or with the request buttons. Further decomposition will be needed. For example, the lift service subproblem must be decomposed into an editing subproblem, in which the building manager edits a representation of the scheduling priorities, and a scheduling subproblem, in which the latest edit priorities are used to govern decisions about lift dispatch.

Normal Design and Subproblem Concerns

This kind of decomposition is based on two complementary principles. First, each subproblem captures a coherent and intelligible subfunction of the system, where a subfunction can often be loosely identified with a feature. Second, each subproblem matches a recognised problem pattern. For example, editing the priority rules is a problem of the same general kind as a simple text or graphics editor. There is an analogy here, between subproblems identified in this way and the familiar components of a physical system such as a motor car. This decomposition is typical of what Vincenti [2] calls *normal design*: "The engineer engaged in such design knows at the outset how the device in question works, what are its customary features, and that, if properly designed along such lines, it has a good likelihood of accomplishing the desired task." A vital characteristic of normal design is that the unbounded potential difficulties posed by the problem world are brought under a good degree of control by accumulated experience. The engineering community knows what concerns must be addressed to obtain a dependable product, and those concerns are addressed partly by the standard normal design itself, and partly by the practice of normal design in which the engineers pay explicit attention to the concerns that have proved important in the past. Departure from normal design norms is a recipe for failure—sometimes catastrophic, as in the famous collapse of the Tacoma Narrows Bridge [3].

An example of such concerns in a component of a software-intensive system is the *initialisation concern*. The need for initialisation of program variables is well known, and schemes have been developed to ensure that failure due to accessing an uninitialised variable can be reliably avoided. A similar concern applies to the relationship between a software component and its problem world. When the lift control program begins execution, for example, it may be necessary to ensure that the lift car is at the ground floor with the doors open. Or, alternatively, it may be possible for the software to detect the state of the problem world and to adjust its own initial behaviour accordingly. There are many variations on this theme. What matters is that the developers must be aware of the concern and know how to address it adequately.

Subproblems as System Components

If we regard subproblems as system components we must recognise that they do not interact solely within the machine. On the contrary, much of their interaction takes place through the medium of the problem world itself, as one component affects the state of a part of the problem world that it shares with another subproblem. These interactions in the problem world give rise to the need for explicit attention to subproblem composition and to the composition concerns that accompany it. For example execution of two subproblems that share a part of the problem world must be controlled to obtain an appropriate interleaving: the newly edited representation of the lift scheduling priorities must at some point be adopted by the lift service subproblem. A very different example is the possibility of requirement conflict. The safety subproblem may determine that the mechanical equipment has developed a fault, that the emergency brake must be applied, and that the motor must be switched off and held off; the lift service subproblem may at the very same time determine that there is a service request for which the lift must be sent to a certain floor, and that the motor must therefore be switched on. The conflict must, of course, be resolved by a consideration of the relative precedence of the two requirements, and the chosen precedence must be implemented in the composed system. Another example of a composition concern is the need to ensure that failure of a non-critical function—possibly by erroneous design or programming of the software—cannot cause failure of a critical function. The lobby display subproblem, however badly, or even perversely, implemented, must not be able to obstruct correct functioning of the safety subproblem.

A Different View of Functional Correctness

These composition concerns compel us to consider a different, and more nuanced, notion of functional correctness. In place of the single simplistic entailment relating machine specification, given properties of the problem world, and requirement, we have a corresponding entailment for each subproblem, along with the need to compose and reconcile the different views of the problem world that have been adopted for each individual subproblem. For the lift service subproblem the mechanical equipment is fault-free; but for the safety subproblem it is potentially faulty. For the lobby display the lift movement is autonomous, but for the lift service it is the object of control. A comprehensive universal description of the problem world properties, accommodating the point of view of every subproblem, would be intractably complex and obscure. We are compelled to retain the view of the whole problem and its world as an assemblage of components, locating our view of each component in its place in the structure of interactions induced by our addressing of the manifold composition concerns.

The unbounded richness of the problem world precludes a fully comprehensive enumeration of all possible subproblem interactions. But it is useful to recognise two general interaction categories, somewhat in the spirit of the treatment of feature interactions in telecommunication systems. Some *positive interactions* must be reliably realised by the implemented system. For example, the lift service subproblem must use the newest edited version of the priority rules, and the lobby display subproblem must recognise that the outstanding requests for a floor have been serviced exactly when the lift service subproblem has indeed caused the lift to visit that floor and to permit the requesting users to enter or leave the lift car. These positive interactions are, in general, readily identifiable. But there is also a set of potential *negative interactions*, in which the interaction of two subproblems causes undesired and even catastrophic effects. For example, it is imaginable that the changeover from an older to a newly edited version of the priority rules might be able to deadlock the lift service problem. Such negative interactions, of which there are potentially an unbounded number, must be identified and addressed by the application of normal design practices, in which are embodied the lessons learned by long experience.

Some Implications for Software Testing

Ultimately, functional testing of a software-intensive system must take place when the software has been installed in the problem world. Nothing less can bridge the gap that is opened up between the non-formal nature of the problem world and the formal—or quasi-formal—world of a well-engineered computer executing software written in a well-defined programming language under a reliable operating system. But of course such full integration testing is very expensive, and may sometimes be literally impossible. So, for this reason alone, it is certainly necessary to conduct smaller and cheaper unit tests, substituting simulation for the relevant parts of the real problem world.

Since different subproblems typically take different views of the parts of the problem world they have in common, the problem world simulation must embody different properties according to the subproblem under test. One simulation of the problem world cannot be enough.

Another reason for unit testing is the need to decompose the system function into subfunctions in order to reduce the number of test cases needed. The hope here is that the decomposed subfunctions, once tested, can be reassembled in a compositional fashion. That is, that if subfunction A and subfunction B are both known to be correct, then their composition into a combined function A+B must be correct. In its naïve form this hope is too optimistic. Even if the interactions between the subproblem software parts within the computer can be fully mastered, their interactions through the medium of the problem world parts they share are potentially more problematical. The sad story of the de Havilland Comet 1 aircraft showed the difficulty clearly. The aircraft body had been fully tested for behaviour under compression and decompression; and it had been fully tested for behaviour under flexing and torsional stress: both tests showed that the fuselage design fully met its objectives in each respect. But it had never been tested for both simultaneously, and in practice the combination of both kinds of stress was a major contributor to the aircraft's failure in flight.

Testing is, from one point of view, a searching process, in which faults potentially leading to failures are sought. The search should, ideally, be conducted in the light of the richest possible knowledge of how faults come about and hence where they are likely to be found. To take a very simple example from program coding, it is well-known that programmers are prone to write the assignment operator '=' in place of the equality condition '=='; so a code inspection should search specifically for such errors. In the same way, in a software-intensive system, such knowledge is the fruit of the experience embodied in normal design. To know that subproblems of a particular class raise an initialisation or identities concern, or that a particular subproblem composition raises a switching or interleaving concern, is to know that testing should explicitly search for failure to address those specific concerns in an adequate fashion.

References

[1] E W Dijkstra; On the Cruelty of really Teaching Computer Science; CACM 32,12, December 1989, pp1398-1404.

[2] W G Vincenti; What Engineers Know and How They Know It; Johns Hopkins University Press, 1993.

[3] C Michael Holloway; From Bridges and Rockets; Lessons for Software Systems; Proceedings of the 17th International System Safety Conference, 1999.

Choosing a Test Modeling Language: A Survey

Alan Hartman[1], Mika Katara[2], and Sergey Olvovsky[1]

[1] IBM Haifa Labs, Mt. Carmel Campus
Haifa 31905, Israel
{hartman,olvovsky}@il.ibm.com
[2] Tampere University of Technology, Institute of Software Systems
P.O. Box 553, FI-33101 Tampere, Finland
mika.katara@tut.fi

Abstract. Deployment of model-based testing involves many difficulties that have slowed down its industrial adoption. The leap from traditional scripted testing to model-based testing seems as hard as moving from manual to automatic test execution. Two key factors in the deployment are the language used to define the test models, and the language used for defining the test objectives. Based on our experience, we survey the different types of languages and sketch solutions based on different approaches, considering the testing organization, the system under test, etc. The types of languages we cover include among others domain-specific, test-specific as well as generic design languages. We note that there are no best practices, but provide general guidelines for various cases.

1 Introduction

A common view in the software development community is that there is a need to raise the level of abstraction from a code-centric view to a model-driven one. In Model-Driven Development (MDD), behavioral and structural models are treated as first class entities that are used to generate code automatically. However, there is an ongoing debate whether to use generic modeling languages (GMLs) or domain-specific (DSMLs) ones. GMLs, such as UML, are advocated by the OMG's Model-Driven Architecture (MDA) [1] initiative and others. DSMLs are gaining popularity through industrial success stories that report huge improvements in productivity [2], and the growing availability of tooling support for DSMLs.

Unfortunately, this debate has not yet reached the area of testing. Based on our experience from the model-based testing of industrial systems developed using code-centric practices, we think that the same debate needs to be extended to cover testing. Moreover, another equally important and related question is whether to model tests using a design language or a test-specific language. In this respect, the driving force of the MDD community seems to be the ability to generate applications, while test generation has been somewhat neglected. This is in contrast with the new developments in the more traditional software development process areas. In these, Test-Driven Development and other approaches deeply rooted in testing are seen to increase productivity.

E. Bin, A. Ziv, and S. Ur (Eds.): HVC 2006, LNCS 4383, pp. 204–218, 2007.
© Springer-Verlag Berlin Heidelberg 2007

From the viewpoint of black-box testing, the reasons for choosing between the different types of test modeling languages may differ significantly from those relevant to application and document generation. We believe the main differences to be:

1. Developers generally need to introduce details of the target platform and other implementation specifics – while testers may often disregard these aspects during modeling.
2. Test models may focus more on "user experience" and system boundary – as opposed to the need to model precise internal system behavior by developers.
3. Developers usually have a better command of high level generic design languages, e.g. UML or SDL – whereas testers are better versed in the language of user experience and requirements documentation.

In model-based testing, tests are generated automatically from models that describe the behavior of the system under test (SUT) from a perspective of testing. The usual goal is to make the SUT fail the test in order to find defects.

Even if we build the most sophisticated model-based test automation system, there are still great difficulties in deploying the methodology and the tools (see, for instance [3,4]). In fact, based on our experience, the leap from traditional scripted testing to model-based testing seems as hard as moving from manual to automatic test execution.

Two key factors in the deployment of model-based testing are the language used to define the test models, and the language used for defining the test objectives. The test models describe the behavior of the SUT, whereas the test objectives describe the behavior expected from the test generation software. Whether visual or textual, these languages are used for the interaction between the test automation system and its user. In many cases, we can translate existing test artifacts to test models ([5]), but even in this case, the aforementioned languages play an important intermediate role. There are also other languages used for defining test execution directives, or test set ups, but we consider these somewhat less important from the deployment point of view.

In this survey we discuss types of test modeling languages to be used in order to deploy model-based testing practices. The best answer is context-sensitive, but we try to develop some guidelines for choosing between different approaches. Since there is no clear division between the different language types, but rather a wide spectrum, we concentrate on design vs. test-specific, as well as generic vs. domain-specific languages.

The remainder of this paper is structured as follows. We briefly present the theory and practice of model-based testing in Section 2. In Section 3, we discuss the differences between using a design language vs. a testing language for test modeling. The discussion is continued in Section 4 concerning DSMLs and GMLs. Section 5 contains further considerations on the subject from other points of view. Finally, Section 6 presents some guidelines for decision making, and Section 7 draws some conclusions.

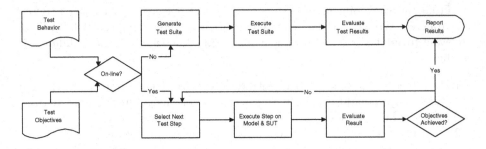

Fig. 1. MBT process: on-line vs. off-line testing

2   Model-Based Testing

In this section we briefly review the theory and practice of model-based software testing, and its role in model-driven development.

2.1   Model-Based vs. Model-Driven Testing

In principal, any form of software testing can be seen as model based. The tester always forms a mental model of the system under test before engaging in activities such as test case design. The term Model Based Testing (MBT) is applicable when these mental models are documented and subsequently used to generate tests, or to evaluate their results. The term Model Driven Testing (MDT) has also been used frequently. Our interpretation of MDT is that it refers to a particular style of model-based testing, inspired by the OMG's Model Driven Architecture (MDA) initiative. The underlying principles behind MDA (and hence MDT) are the separation between platform specific and platform independent aspects of the software, and the use of automated transformations to pass between different levels of abstraction. In model-driven testing, this means that the testing model is independent of the testing platform, and that a transformation is used to pass from platform independent test cases to platform specific ones.

2.2   On-Line vs. Off-Line Testing

Model-based testing involves the following key activities: modeling the behavior of the SUT, describing the test objectives, generating the test cases (using input from the behavioral model and test objectives), running the test cases on the SUT, and evaluating the test results to decide whether the testing is complete. These activities are depicted in the upper part of Figure 1. Alternatively, especially when testing reactive systems, we may choose to execute the test steps once they are generated as depicted in the lower part of Figure 1. In this so-called on-line testing approach, test cases and suites are implicit and testing is seen as a game [6] between the MBT tool and the SUT. To differentiate between these two alternatives, the former scheme is referred to as off-line testing.

The choice between these two approaches also affects the tool architecture. In the on-line case, the test generation software is connected to the SUT using an adapter that constantly translates inputs and outputs between the test automation system and the SUT. In the off-line case, the test cases (or suites) are generated first and, often after a translation or transformation, are executed at the SUT. An example of a tool implementing both approaches is Spec Explorer, which is currently used by several Microsoft product groups on a daily basis [7].

2.3   Behavioral Modeling

This paper discusses the choice of appropriate languages to enable the aforementioned activities, and therefore focuses on languages that are used to describe SUT behavior and test objectives. Behavioral models can take many forms: diagrams (e.g., UML state diagrams), grammars, tables (e.g., decision tables), control flow graphs, and others. They have two main functions: to describe the set of stimuli that can be applied to the SUT in any given situation and to describe the possible responses to those stimuli. Models which do not describe the responses can still be useful for test generation. However, if an oracle is not supplied, the success or failure of a test case must be determined by other means.

Behavioral models for testing may be at different levels of abstraction. In the most extreme case, test engineers will re-implement the entire SUT independently in order to have an accurate test oracle. This is usually prohibitively expensive. On the other hand, when the SUT is developed using a purely model-driven approach, and the testing model simply reuses the implementation model, the only part of the system being tested is the model transformation and not the system itself. Model-based testing usually falls between these two extremes, with a behavioral model at a higher level of abstraction than the implementation, but with significant portions of the testing model developed independently of the design models.

When there is a significant difference between the abstraction level of the behavioral model and the SUT, there is a need to describe the transformation between abstract test cases and concrete test scripts at the implementation level. This paper does not deal with transformation languages, but we note that this is often a significant issue in the success or failure of model-based testing.

2.4   Test Objectives

Test objectives are often formulated in natural language; however, where test generation is automated, the test objectives are required inputs for test generation algorithms. The test objectives may be couched in terms of the model (model coverage), the implementation (code coverage), user experience (usage profiling, use cases), or combinations thereof. Some of the early attempts at model-based testing failed due to the complexity of defining test objectives for a given automation system.

The objectives may be described in a variety of ways. These reflect both the variability of the objectives themselves and the varying sophistication level of the users of model-based testing systems. In order to test compliance with a complex requirement, the test engineer may be required to generate a long sequence of related inputs with complicated constraints. Test objectives of this kind are usually referred to as test purposes, and can be formally specified, for instance, as sequence diagrams or state machines (TGV [8] and AGEDIS [9]). Less specific test objectives may be expressed as coverage requirements on the model as in Testmaster [10] and GOTCHA [11], on the input combinations as in Modelware [12], or on other aspects of the test suite or on-line test execution trace. Some tools take a very simplistic approach to the description of test objectives and offer the engineer a choice of testing "levels", with higher levels generating more test cases and greater coverage while not involving the engineer in the details of specifying objectives.

3   Design vs. Test-Specific Languages

The section covers the use of a design language for test modeling, and goes on to discuss the benefits of using a test-specific language.

3.1   Using a Design Language

When using a design language, such as UML or SDL, for test modeling – there are certain distinct advantages. Many tool vendors offer modeling tools for these languages. In the case of UML, for instance, its visual notation has become an industry-standard for software design.

Another advantage of the popularity of the language is the availability of qualified people for designing the models. Some best practices have already developed around testing with UML, and some of these are codified into the UML Testing Profile [13]. Moreover, consultation services are readily available.

A key step in any model-based testing methodology is the validation (e.g., formal inspection) of the test model by the developers and other application stakeholders. This is a vital step in resolving specification ambiguities and synchronizing the understanding of the requirements. Thus, it is important for developers to understand test models. A UML-based modeling language will employ a vocabulary and approach that is native and easy to understand for software developers and will obviate their need to study unfamiliar DSMLs.

The disadvantage of these languages and the supporting tools lies in the fact that they are usually much more complex to learn and use than the alternatives. Practitioners often complain about the perceived need to perform system design twice – once for development and once for testing.

An example of adaptation and use of a design language can be found in the AGEDIS project reports [9]. While the experiment reports found many positives, all noted the complexity of the solution and the counter-intuitive modeling.

3.2   Using a Test-Specific Language

Using a test-specific language can ease the deployment of the model-based approach, because testers do not need to learn UML or any other language whose main purpose is not the support of testing activities.

TTCN-3 [14] is an example of a test-specific language that has been defined solely for the purposes of test specification. Although the language concepts are mostly inherited from the scripted protocol testing domain, the language maybe suitable for expressing high level test models. Distinct advantages also include the ability to specify tests both in textual and visual notations as well as the close relationship with the UML Testing Profile. However, also in this case, one should be careful to avoid the aforementioned problem of performing the system design twice. There is a choice of tools that execute the specification by interpreting the TTCN-3 code or by compiling it into some programming language.

In addition, different tool vendors have defined languages to be used with their tools. Such languages are optimized for the tool at hand, and can be supported by advanced editors and other utilities that ease the learning curve. These languages are often proprietary, which increases risks of their adaptation. However, in many cases they can still be used for model-based testing in conjunction with a higher-level specification language and a source-to-source compiler.

4   Domain-Specific vs. Generic Language

Next, we compare domain-specific and generic approaches to test modeling.

4.1   Domain-Specific Languages

Due to the context-sensitive nature of testing, domain-specific approaches offer many attractive advantages. The basic idea of using a domain-specific solution is to introduce a language solely for the purpose of test modeling in the particular domain at hand. This way, it is possible to tailor the modeling language for the needs of the testers in this domain.

In most cases, there are no commercial tools available for modeling and generating tests in a particular domain, and custom made tools are needed. Firstly, there needs to be a test design tool for modeling the tests using the domain-specific language. Secondly, a translator (a compiler or an interpreter) is needed from the language to the underlying test execution environment. Development of such tools does not need to start from scratch; there are tools available for developing domain-specific modeling environments, such as MetaEdit+ [15] or XMFMosaic [16]. In principle, such tools may mitigate many of the risks and difficulties associated with DSMLs. However, we have not found reports on the use of such tools for testing.

Alternatively, a domain-specific layer of abstraction can be built on top of an MBT tool that uses a generic language. This means developing a translator from the domain-specific language to the generic one. As in any development of a source-to-source translator, the difficulty of this task depends on the differences between the input and output languages.

As an example of the domain-specific approach, consider a DSML for testing mobile phones through a graphical user interface (GUI) [17]. The purpose of the DSML is to model the behavior of the phone user at a high level of abstraction. The language consists of so-called action words [18], such as "send an SMS", "answer a call", and "add a new contact". The action words are used as transition labels in test models given as LTSs (Labeled Transition Systems, i.e., simple finite state machines). Because the underlying test automation system operates at a lower level of abstraction, each action word is implemented by a sequence of so-called keywords, which correspond to key strokes on the phone's keyboard. A keyword sequence implementing an action word is given in a separate LTS. The component LTSs are composed automatically to obtain a final test model, which in turn is used for generating the actual tests on-line through a commercially available generic test automation system. Test objectives are stated using LTSs, in conjunction with a textual coverage language in the top tier of the 3-tier test model architecture [19].

Another, quite different, DSML-based approach is HOTTest [20] used for testing database applications. There, tests are specified using a textual language, based on the Haskell functional programming language. The textual test model is first translated to an extended finite state machine from which the actual tests are generated. It's argued that the strong type system of the modeling language makes it easier to introduce domain knowledge and capture domain-specific requirements than using more conventional model-based testing approaches.

Genesys-Pro [21] is an example that uses DSMLs for testing areas other than software. IBM uses this proprietary approach for verifying processor designs. The tests are specified in test templates defined by an XML schema. The Genesys-Pro test generator uses a constraint solver to create test cases after translating the test template into a set of equational constraints. It has been reported that it takes an experienced engineer from two to six months to learn to utilize the full capabilities of the language. However, novice users can exploit the tool with minimal learning time to create basic scenarios. Compared to their previous approach, fewer defects escape into silicon despite the increased complexity of the design.

4.2   Generic Modeling Languages

One of the advantages of using a generic test modeling language is the possibility of model-based testing practitioners to move between different domains while still enjoing similar modeling experiences. The look and feel and the basic (e.g. UML-based) terminology will remain the same across different domains.

To support domain-specific modeling, UML provides a standard extension mechanism called "profiles". Profiles are collections of stereotypes, tagged values and constraints usually defined as Object Constraint Language (OCL) expressions that can be defined to support modeling concepts found in different domains. Depending on the profile, the result can be fundamentally different from the plain UML. There are several predefined profiles freely available from OMG, including the aforementioned Testing Profile.

Although a generic approach should liberate us from any specific tool, in practice, there are problems with exchanging models between tools. Moreover, not all tools handle profiles (and possible conflicts between different profiles) in standard ways, so we may be shackled to a specific tool capable of processing the needed profiles.

Another problem with using profiles is that while they support incorporating the concepts of the problem domain into the test models, they lack the ability to hide unnecessary details. That is, when stereotyping a UML class to encapsulate test data, we should be able to forget everything we know about classes, methods, attributes, visibility etc. and concentrate on defining the test data. However, even though we can define constraints to hide the superfluous details, the user interface of the tool is not usually customizable to the same extent. The menus remain cluttered with options having nothing to do with the task of defining test data. This makes the work of the tester unnecessarily complex. Depending on the background of the testing personnel, these kinds of usability problems can hamper the deployment of a generic approach significantly.

An additional problem manifests itself when the domain is hard to define through a UML profile. There are cases where defining stereotypes and tags is simply not sufficent to describe the target environment. Extending UML through other means is not frequently supported by UML tools and can hardly be supported by any infrastructure developed for previous UML profile-based solutions. This problem may be either very hard or impossible to solve. Moreover, some previously unseen interoperability problems could surface later.

Yet another issue is the SUT adapter/translator needed in generic solutions. It is a software component that handles the transfer and translation of messages between the test execution system and the SUT. Because the generic tools are designed to work with any kind of SUT, they need to be adapted when deployed in a new context. Depending of the type of the SUT, this component can be very simple or more complex. In any case, it needs to be developed before the test execution can be started and maintained as any other piece of software. There do exist tool-specific adapters for certain domains, and there is work on generic adapters for TTCN-3 [22]. However, the effort needed to develop this component should be considered before choosing a generic tool.

On the application and document generation side of MDD, there is active research to bridge the gap between DSMLs and UML profiles that will most probably enchance model-based testing. For example, one interesting approach [23] uses metamodels for defining translations between the two types of models.

5   Further Considerations

In this section, we cover additional aspects concerning the choice of a test modeling language.

5.1 Visual vs. Textual Languages

The question of whether to use visual or textual languages for test modeling is somewhat orthogonal to the previous discussion, and is a matter of personal background and taste of the testers. On the one hand, most testers would probably prefer a visual language for understanding a model. Model inspections and reviews – especially the ones where both testers and designers are present – are much easier with visual models. On the other hand, textual languages can be very productive in test creation [20]. Another example of a textual language used in industrial settings is Gotcha Definition Language, supported by the Gotcha tool [11]. When developing large models with visual languages, one has to utilize the abstraction and encapsulation mechanisms effectively in order to avoid cluttering the models. Modular development may be easier with a textual language, at least for testers with some programming experience.

It is usually much harder to provide validation and simulation support for visual models. Hence, debugging and refactoring may often be easier in the case of textual languages. A language like TTCN-3, offering both types of notations with a mapping between the two, is viewed as the best solution in this respect.

There are also vast libraries of free and open source software, that facilitate testing with Java, Python, or Perl. However, since these languages have not been designed for modeling as such, the level of abstraction may be too low. If, for instance, it takes several lines of code to model a test event, there is practically no difference with traditional test scripting from the modeler's point of view. A better approach might be to use an existing programming language that has been extended to support model-based testing such as in [24].

5.2 Commercial vs. In-House vs. Open-Source Tools

In principle, the domain-specific approach does not rely on commercially available tools as much as the generic approach. However, custom-made tool solutions are often considered more risky than generic ones. This is especially true when you need to decide on starting development of a new tool for a domain-specific language before having any experience in the approach. On the other hand, a well-known vendor of a commercial tool can become a reliable partner providing support for many years – but prove to be too costly in the long term.

Custom made tools demand a heavy upfront investment, which is only justified when they are used in numerous consecutive projects, for example in a product family development. This could also tie the organization to a specific partner used for tool development. An alternative is to develop an in-house tool. However, many testing organizations lack such competencies or prefer concentrating on their core business. Moreover, if the domain changes, the organization has to be prepared to maintain the language and the associated tools. Depending on the organization, this might be infeasible without outside help.

Naturally, the quality of the tools is always an issue; without industry-strength tools, it is easy to fail in deployment, even with the best possible language. There is a much lower level of competition in domain-specific test tool market than in the one for generic tools. Consequently, the organization has to make a careful choice regarding the tool maker. We see that in many cases, the best solution is an open-source tool, supported by a critical mass of organizations and individuals with similar needs.

5.3 Proprietary vs. Standard Language

If an organization that uses a standard language, such as UML, SDL, or TTCN-3, wishes to move to another tool, (e.g., for licensing or new functionality reason) it should be possible to preserve the investment in existing models due to the standard nature of language. Thus, a standards-based approach for test modeling provides freedom in the choice of tools.

Another example of benefits gained by using standard languages is the TTCN-3 SIP Test Suite [25] for testing the SIP protocol [26]. SIP, the Session Initiation Protocol, is a signaling protocol for Internet services, such as conferencing, telephony, presence, events notification and instant messaging. By utilizing a standard test suite for conformance testing of a protocol implementation, many interoperability and other problems can be resolved in the early phases of developing SIP protocol implementations. Without using a standard testing language, it would be very difficult to benefit from the standard test suite.

However, since one size rarely fits all, a custom made proprietary solution might be more favorable because of the anticipated improvements in productivity. If the testing organization owns the proprietary language, which is often the case with DSMLs, it can govern the language and the associated tools without outside interference. On the other hand, if the language is owned by some other organization, possibly a partner, a joint understanding about the development of the language and the tools is needed.

6 Pitfalls and Solution Considerations

SUTs are not equal with regards to testing difficulty. In the simplest case, there are test interfaces designed to make testing easier. In a more difficult case, test execution has to be done through a GUI, using text recognition, to convert bitmap characters to text strings. There is also a vast difference in testing control vs. data intensive systems, concurrent vs. single threaded ones, or deterministic vs. non-deterministic ones. Obviously, it is impossible to develop best practices covering all the different SUT types.

The decision to select a language should be based on business objectives. We believe that the major consideration is to weigh the trade-offs between the solution's long-term risks and development/adoption costs against the ease-of-use, provided by that solution. In the following section, we cover some pitfalls and solutions for the less obvious long-term risk factors.

6.1   Testing Solution Language and Tooling Choice Pitfalls

The pitfalls we identified concerning language and tooling choice:

Domain slippage. Over time, the domain that requires testing may change, standards on which it is based may evolve and new technologies may appear. The changes may not be drastic enough to demand a totally new solution. Even worse, they may be gradual, requiring constant updates to the modeling language. DSMLs present a higher risk, since they are specific to the addressed problems.

Underestimating effort needed in language definition. As domain-specific languages gain popularity for application generation, there is a danger that such a solution may be adapted for testing leading to low solution quality. Designing a language is a difficult task that needs expert knowledge and should not be underestimated.

Language ownership. If the adopting organization does not own the language definition, it may find over time that the language changed in ways that are not compatible with the organization's goals. While it is not a problem in itself, since the organization already owns the required tools, it may create significant difficulties. For example, support for existing tools may be discontinued, hiring may become a problem, acquiring new licenses may be impossible, etc. Language definition ownership and the use of GMLs can reduce the risk. Proprietary standards owned by tool vendors are high risk.

Tool lock-in. Dependence on a specific tool may become a problem. Support costs may skyrocket, new licenses may become extremely expensive and tool vendors may become less responsive to the organization's needs – e.g. support of new features in future releases. The problem remains more severe for DSMLs, even though proprietary storage formats and the absence of export capabilities for some GMLs may cause similar problems.

Development process change. A change in the development process may make the chosen testing tools extremely inappropriate. For example, adopting automatic workflow systems to handle bug tracking, requirements management and version control – all bundled together to achieve traceability – may require tools that can work within the process management system. Small vendors (or internal solutions) often present higher risk.

Unsustainable vendors. Many systems need to be maintained and supported for decades. A small vendor (or even a large one) may become unavailable for support or tool/language updates over the years. The choice of non-standard DSMLs, and small vendors (whose customer base won't be large enough to provide migration paths by competitors) increase the risk.

Solution complexity. Many MBT solutions are technologically complex when compared to traditional testing approaches. The organization might not be able to find professionals with the required background, nor educate a large enough number of its own testers. The problem might well remain hidden until the market for software developers heats up. In such a case, top testers often move on to development positions and the organization may find itself unable to substitute them. GMLs and design languages are more risky due to their higher complexity.

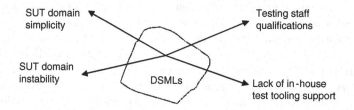

Fig. 2. DSML vs. generic solution

6.2 Solution Guidelines for Different Organization and Project Types

Figure 2 summarizes our view on the strengths of the DSML approach, which is perceived to challenge the more generic approaches. DSMLs are good in capturing complex domains, and require only domain skills from their users. However, in-house tool support is probably needed and problems can occur in case of domain changes. If the domain is simple and the required skills exist in the testing staff, a more generic solution may be more favorable. Such an approach is seen more robust in the case of domain changes. In addition, tools and the associated services can be bought from third parties.

Below, we provide some general guidelines that take into consideration different factors. The guidelines are listed in the order of importance but should not be considered to be mutually exclusive:

– An organization lacking the infrastructure to develop and support tools in-house and is possibly unable to educate testers: *Reliable large vendor solution, GML and probably test-specific language.* We believe that the existence (or lack thereof) of an in-house team to develop/support testing solutions is possibly the single most important factor in choosing a solution. Good support becomes paramount, domain slippage can cause high costs when handled by external tool vendors (DSML risk), language evolution may render an external DSML solution unusable, and external education and support for testers mean that an easy to use language (test specific) is preferable.
– An organization that is either developing point-in-time solutions for many domains (e.g., services or outsourcing), or has a wide range of products in different domains: *GML.* The first case means that the high risk of adopting new solutions (DSML) is repeated for each new project, and the cost is not amortized over long term/multiple projects. GML, on the other hand, means a stable testing methodology and the reuse of tester's expertise. The second case means that GML solutions allow easy reassignment of testers between testing teams, without requiring re-education.
– Big, long term projects in a stable domain (e.g. Air Traffic Management Systems, systems for government services, defense or financial organizations): *An in-house solution*, with a DSML, test-specific and possibly even internally owned language. A second (but worse) alternative is a widely accepted

public standard language with either an open source solution or a set of implementations by different vendors. Preventing vendor lock-in is extremely important in this case, both due to possibly escalating costs, and the risk of loss of tool/language support over the project lifecycle. This is best addressed, by an in-house solution, but can be prevented by adopting a widely accepted language. However, domain slippage and language evolution are better addressed by an in-house solution. An additional justification for an in-house solution is that projects of this type are usually run by a large organization that has the skills and resources needed to run a language definition/maintenance project. An investment in a DSML development could be amortized over the long life cycle of the project. The investment in a test-specific language, as well as dedicating a testing team to exclusively support the project for years, limits the risk and improves the quality of these (often safety critical) systems. Thus, specialization of the personnel is not an issue. Ownership of the language is preferable and its cost (in hiring language definition experts) acceptable because the language should support the project needs for a long term. An organization may benefit from publicizing the language and making it a de-facto industry standard in the area.

– An organization using developers for component/functional/system testing: *Design language*. Lower education costs for testers, who are already familiar with the language and only need to learn the new tools, easier buy in by these "testers", and less opposition to perform testing tasks (which are often disliked by developers).

– An organization lacking advanced testers: *Test-specific language*. An organization like this will struggle to adopt MBT in any case. It should be carefully considered whether a more conventional solution would serve the business goals better or not. To succeed the organization must adopt easy-to-use tools and languages that can be mastered by its personnel.

– An organization that uses domain experts to create testing scenarios: *DSML*. Reduces the education costs and increases the chances that domain experts will be ready to create testing scenarios. These experts are often either scientists or expert engineers, and are usually not keen on participating in testing-related activities. The choice will also decrease the time they spend on the activities, and reduces the high cost of these specialists.

– An organization that relies on internal experts to adopt/provide and internally support best practice solutions (e.g., advanced start-up companies): *Open source tools*, standardized or internally created languages (likely DSMLs). Open source gives you the possibility to make necessary changes to the tools when needed. Experts in testing tools (as in other areas of computer sciences) often prefer the flexibility of open source solutions and the ability to both provide their solution to a wide community and cooperate with other experts in their day-to-day work. Such experts are hard to find and expensive to hire. They are usually motivated not just by high compensation (they can find employment anywhere), but mainly by their work definition. Thus, open source and open solutions are usually preferable, since this keeps these people satisfied and makes them more efficient.

7   Conclusions

In this paper we discussed the choice between different types of languages for test modeling. We also provided some guidelines to help in the decision between the alternatives. We believe this decision may have far-reaching consequences in the deployment of model-based practices to a testing organization.

As noted by the authors of [27], there are no best practices in software testing. When selecting between different types of languages, the right choice depends on various aspects. If, for instance, two different organizations need to use common languages and tools for testing, the choice of a test modeling language may be governed by numerous reasons that are less than obvious.

Public case studies on deployments using various approaches are needed. However, since testing organizations, and especially tool vendors, are usually not willing to share their experiences in unsuccessful projects, the published evaluations are presumably biased towards success stories. References to successful deployments are important, but because of the context-sensitive nature of the problem, they should not be over-emphasized in decision making. Thus, we think that the debate between the different approaches needs to be continued.

Acknowledgments

The work of the first and third author was partially supported by the MODEL-WARE project. MODELWARE is a project co-funded by the European Commission under the "Information Society Technologies" Sixth Framework Programme (2002-2006). Information included in this document reflects only the authors' views. The European Community is not liable for any use that may be made of the information contained herein. The work of the second author was partially funded by Nokia Foundation.

References

1. OMG: Model Driven Architecture. Available at http://www.omg.org/mda/ (2006)
2. Domain-Specific Modeling Forum: DSM case studies and examples. Available at http://www.dsmforum.org/cases.html (2006)
3. Robinson, H.: Obstacles and opportunities for model-based testing in an industrial software environment. In: Proceedings of the 1st European Conference on Model-Driven Software Engineering, Nuremberg, Germany (2003) 118–127
4. Baker, P., Loh, S., Weil, F.: Model-driven engineering in a large industrial context – Motorola case study. In: Proceedings of MoDELS 2005. Number 3713 in Lecture Notes in Computer Science. Springer (2005) 476–491
5. Hartman, A., Kirshin, A., Olvovsky, S.: Model driven testing – as an infrastructure for custom made solutions. In: Proceedings of the 4th Workshop on System Testing and Validation (STV'06), Potsdam, Germany (2006)
6. Nachmanson, L., Veanes, M., Schulte, W., Tillmann, N., Grieskamp, W.: Optimal strategies for testing nondeterministic systems. In: ISSTA'04: Proceedings of the 2004 ACM SIGSOFT International Symposium on Software Testing and Analysis, Boston, MA, USA, ACM (2004) 55–64

7. Campbell, C., Grieskamp, W., Nachmanson, L., Schulte, W., Tillmann, N., Veanes, M.: Testing concurrent object-oriented systems with Spec Explorer. In: Proceedings of Formal Methods 2005. Number 3582 in Lecture Notes in Computer Science. Springer (2005) 542–547

8. Jard, C., Jéron, T.: TGV: theory, principles and algorithms – a tool for the automatic synthesis of conformance test cases for non-deterministic reactive systems. STTT **7** (2005) 297–315

9. Hartman, A.: AGEDIS project final report. Available at `http://www.agedis.de/documents/d423_3/FinalPublicReport(D1.6).PDF` (2004)

10. Apfelbaum, L., Doyle, J.: Model based testing. Software Quality Week (1997)

11. Farchi, E., Hartman, A., Pinter, S.: Using a model-based test generator to test for standard conformance. IBM Systems Journal **41** (2002) 89–110

12. Modelware: Modelware project homepage. Available at `http://www.modelware-ist.org` (2006)

13. OMG: UML Testing Profile. Available at `http://www.omg.org/technology/documents/formal/test_profile.htm` (2006)

14. ETSI: TTCN-3 homepage. Available at `http://www.ttcn-3.org` (2006)

15. MetaCase: MetaEdit+ homepage. Available at `http://www.metacase.com` (2006)

16. Xactium: XMFMosaic homepage. Available at `http://www.xactium.com` (2006)

17. Katara, M., Kervinen, A., Maunumaa, M., Pääkkönen, T., Satama, M.: Towards deploying model-based testing with a domain-specific modeling approach. In: Proceedings of TAIC PART - Testing: Academic & Industrial Conference, Windsor, UK, IEEE Computer Society (2006) 81–89

18. Buwalda, H.: Action figures. STQE Magazine, March/April 2003 (2003) 42–47

19. Kervinen, A., Maunumaa, M., Katara, M.: Controlling testing using three-tier model architecture. In: Proceedings of the Second Workshop on Model Based Testing (MBT 2006), ENTCS **164(4)** (2006) 53–66

20. Sinha, A., Smidts, C.: HOTTest: A model-based test design technique for enhanced testing of domain-specific applications. ACM Trans. Softw. Eng. Methodol. **15** (2006) 242–278

21. Behm, M., Ludden, J., Lichtenstein, Y., Rimon, M., Vinov, M.: Industrial experience with test generation languages for processor verification. In: Proceedings of the 41st Annual conference on Design Automation (DAC-04), San Diego, CA, USA, ACM (2004) 36–40

22. Hyrkkänen, A.: General purpose SUT adapter for TTCN-3. Master's thesis, Tampere University of Technology, Department of Information Technology (2005)

23. Abouzahra, A., Bézivin, J., Didonet Del Fabro, M., Jouault, F.: A practical approach to bridging domain specific languages with UML profiles. In: Proceedings of the Best Practices for Model Driven Software Development at OOPSLA'05, San Diego, California, USA (2005)

24. UniTesK: UniTesK tools homepage. Available at `http://www.unitesk.com` (2006)

25. ETSI: Conformance test specification for SIP – part 3: Abstract test suite (TTCN-3 code). Available at `http://portal.etsi.org/docbox/EC_Files/EC_Files/ts_10202703v030101p0.zip` (2003)

26. IETF: IETF RFC 3261 – SIP: Session Initiation Protocol. Available at `http://www.ietf.org/rfc/rfc3261.txt` (2002)

27. Kaner, C., Bach, J., Pettichord, B.: Lessons Learned in Software Testing. Wiley (2001)

Making Model-Based Testing More Agile:
A Use Case Driven Approach

Mika Katara and Antti Kervinen

Tampere University of Technology
Institute of Software Systems
P.O. Box 553, FI-33101 Tampere, Finland
firstname.lastname@tut.fi

Abstract. We address the problem of misalignment of artifacts developed in agile software development projects and those required by model-based test generation tools. Our solution is domain specific and relies on the existence of domain experts to design the test models. The testers interface the test generation systems with use cases that are converted into sequences of so called action words corresponding to user events at a high level of abstraction. To support this scheme, we introduce a coverage language and an algorithm for automatic test generation.

1 Introduction

Agile software development practices are rapidly gaining wide popularity. From the testing point of view, this can be seen as a step forward since testing is no longer seen as the last and the least respected phase of software development projects. Instead, tests are driving the development, and automated tests are replacing some design artifacts and documents. However, finding the balance between agile and plan-driven development is a difficult managerial task that needs to be made on a case-by-case basis [1].

Agile methods are lifting the status of testing by advocating automated unit and acceptance tests. However, conventional tests are limited in their ability to find defects. Test cases are scripted as linear and static sequences that help in regression testing but may prove inadequate in their coverage and maintainability. On the other hand, tests generated automatically from models can introduce the necessary variance in tested behavior or data for better coverage. Moreover, thanks to the higher level of abstraction, the maintenance of test models can be easier than test cases crafted by hand.

However, there is a mismatch between the artifacts needed in automatic test generation and those usually created in agile development projects. The models created in the latter are rarely detailed enough to be used as the basis for generating tests, since precise modeling is not seen to add any value [2]. An easy answer to this problem would be to use model-based test generation only when detailed models and heavy documentation are produced in any case, for example, in projects developing safety-critical systems.

We think that model-based testing needs to be adapted to make it more suitable for agile projects by developing highly automated and user-friendly tools. There are opportunities to introduce model-based practices to increase test coverage especially when quality is essential, for instance in development of high-volume consumer products.

E. Bin, A. Ziv, and S. Ur (Eds.): HVC 2006, LNCS 4383, pp. 219–234, 2007.

Furthermore, the importance of maintainability and reusability of artifacts grows when working in a setting such as product family development. However, the right balance should be found between what should be modeled and what should not.

In our previous work [3,4,5] we have introduced a methodology for model-based graphical user interface (GUI) testing in the context of Symbian S60. Symbian S60 is an operating system and a GUI platform for mobile devices, such as smart phones, that has over 50 million installations [6]. Our methodology is built around a *domain-specific modeling language* consisting of so called *action words* and *keywords* [7,8] that describe user actions at a high level of abstraction as well as their lower-level implementations, respectively. Action words are used as transition labels in labeled transition systems (LTSs) modeling the behavior of the user of the phone. They are refined to sequences of keywords with an automatic model transformation. For example, an action word for taking a picture with the phone is translated to the sequence of key strokes that conduct the action on the system under test (SUT).

Based on our experiences with the prototype implementation of our testing tools, the biggest obstacles in the practical use of our methodology concern the creation of the action word model. Moreover, even though the domain-specific language can help domain-experts without programming skills to build models, there is no clear picture on the relationship between the models created for testing, and other artifacts, especially the requirements and design documents. Another related question is about requirements coverage: "How can we know when some requirement has been covered by the generated tests?"

In this paper, we tackle the above problems. Agile development should be supported by easy-to-use tools that can show immediate added value, for instance, by finding serious defects. Thus, our approach is highly automated in a way that all the complexity associated with model-based test generation is hidden from the tester. To achieve the high level of automation, the approach is domain-specific. However, a similar approach can be developed also for other domains.

In more detail, we build our solution on use cases. Since our domain is quite restricted, experts can handle the actual test modeling while testers define test objectives based on use cases. On the one hand, use cases should be familiar to most system level testers. On the other hand, use cases can help us to solve one re-occurring problem in model-based testing, i.e., how to restrict the set of generated tests.

The structure of the remainder of the paper is as follows. In Section 2 we introduce the background of the work. Our contributions on adapting model-based testing to agile development are presented in Section 3. This includes the definition of an improved coverage language that can be used in use case driven testing and the associated algorithm for test generation. Related work is presented in Section 4 and Section 5 concludes the paper with some final remarks.

2   Background

To present the background of our work briefly, we first review the role of requirements in agile software development. Second, we describe our domain-specific test automation methodology including the so-called 3-tier test model architecture [4].

2.1 Role of Requirements in Agile Development

Requirements form the foundation upon which the entire system is built. One of the most import roles of testing is to validate that the system meets its requirements. However, we see the role of requirements in agile development quite different from conventional plan-driven projects. In the latter case requirements are documented in the beginning of the project. Any changes to requirements in later stages of the development should be avoided, due to the high costs involved in rework. In the former case, changes to requirements are considered to be inevitable. In XP [9] for instance, simple descriptions of requirements are documented as "user stories" that are used mainly for release planning. The actual implementation should be based on the face-to-face interaction with the customer or the end user. While the costs of changes can also be high in agile development, the increased customer satisfaction is seen as more important and also more cost effective in the course of the whole project.

Agile Modeling [2] is an extension to more code-centric agile methods, such as XP. It suggests developing models that can help to design and document the implementation, quite similarly to plan-driven approaches but emphasizing certain agile principles and light weight. Requirements can be captured using UML like diagrams or simple textual format, for instance.

Use cases are one of the most popular methods of capturing requirements in industrial projects. Whether textual or visual, they can be written with various levels of formality, depending on the criticality of the system under development. However, in Agile Modeling, the use cases should contain just enough information to communicate the idea and no more. Instead of developing all the use cases in the beginning, it is suggested that they should be defined in iterations and refined incrementally when needed just like other artifacts developed during the project.

The definition of a use case varies in the literature. Here we will use the informal use case format, as defined in [2]. It includes three elements: name, identifier and the basic course of action, which is a sequence of event descriptions corresponding to the high-level interaction between the user and the system. We will use the following informal use case as a running example:

Name: Alice asks Bob to meet for lunch
Identifier: UC1
Basic course of action:

1. Alice sends Bob an SMS asking him to meet for lunch.
2. Bob replies by sending a multimedia message containing a picture of a bumper taken at a traffic jam and a text "I will call you when I'll get there".
3. After a while, Bob calls to Alice, but she is talking to Carol so the line is busy.
4. After a few minutes Alice calls back to Bob and they agree to meet at the cafeteria.

All use cases are not equally important. In order to cope with this, some risk-based testing practices [10] should be deployed: the use cases must be prioritized based on some formal risk analysis or customer intuition. From the testing point of view, the source of the priority is less important; what is important is that the tests should be executed in the priority order. This way it can be ensured that at least the most important

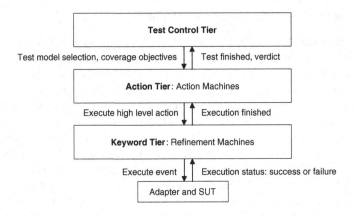

Fig. 1. 3-tier model architecture

risks have been covered if testing needs to be discontinued for some reason. However, because there is always a risk that the risk analysis has been done poorly, it is suggested to aim at covering each use case at least in some detail.

2.2 Domain-Specific Test Modeling

Our approach to domain-specific test modeling using keywords and action words is built around the 3-tier model architecture, consisting of *control*, *action* and *refinement machines* each in its own tier (see Figure 1). The machines are LTSs that model the behavior of the user of the SUT. In order to support testing of different products of the same product family, a high-level functionality is separated from the GUI events. This facilitates the reuse of action machines with SUTs that support the same operations on different kind of GUIs. Refinement machines in the Keyword tier are used for refining the action words in action machines to sequences of executable events in the GUI of the SUT. To obtain an executable test model, we compose action machines with their corresponding refinement machines, i.e., the machines on the two lowest tiers in the model architecture.

For execution, we use an *on-line* approach, i.e., we run tests as we generate them. The tests are executed using a commercial Windows GUI test automation tool running on a PC and an adapter tool connecting the PC to the SUT. A separate log file is used for re-running the test when, for example, debugging.

In the following, the three tiers are presented (see [4] for more details).

Keyword tier. In Figure 2 Camera$_{RM}$ is a refinement machine for a Camera application. In its initial state (the filled circle) the machine refines high level actions for starting the application (awStartCam) and for verifying that the application is running (awVerifyCam).

Keywords are used for generating input events to the SUT as well as making observations on the SUT. A test oracle is encoded in the model. During the test run, execution of a keyword always either succeeds or fails. For example, executing kwVerifyText 'Camera' succeeds if string "Camera" is found on the display and fails otherwise. Sometimes

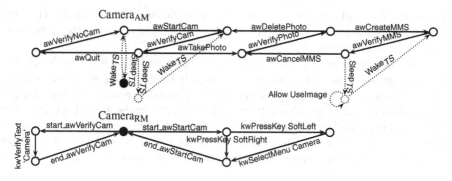

Fig. 2. Action machine and refinement machine

failure is allowed or even required. Allowed results are expressed in the labels of transitions; an error is found if the status of an execution does not match any of these.

In a test model library, the keyword tier consists of a number of machines refining several action words. Each of the refinement machines interacts only with one action machine. Usually, the refinement corresponds to a simple macro expansion: an action word is always implemented with the same sequence of keywords. However, in some cases the sequence may vary depending on the action words executed earlier. For example, the keyword implementation of "activate Camera application" could be different, depending on whether or not the application is already running in the background.

Action tier. Action machines model concurrently running applications. The machines contain action words whose executions can be interleaved to the extent defined in this tier. In a Symbian S60 GUI context, it is sufficient to define few dozens of keywords. However, the number of action words is required to be much higher.

Interleaving the executions of the action machines is an essential part of our domain-specific modeling approach. Symbian S60 applications should always be interruptible: user actions, alarms, received phone calls and messages may stop the ordinary execution of the application at any time. Obviously, it is hard for developers to ensure that applications behave well in every case. The number of cases that should be tested is far beyond the capabilities of conventional testing methods, whether automated or not. To facilitate the creation of test models where the action machines are automatically interleaved, the concepts of running and sleeping action machines have been introduced.

There are two kinds of states in action machines: running and sleeping states. An action word can be executed only when the corresponding machine is running, i.e., it is in a running state. The interleaving mechanisms guarantee that there is always exactly one action machine in a running state. In the beginning of a test run, the running action machine is a special task switcher.

Camera$_{AM}$ in Figure 2 is a simple action machine for testing the Camera application. The machine tests the following functionality: starting the camera application (awStartCam), taking a picture (awTakePhoto), and creating a multimedia message containing the picture (awCreateMMS). The three dotted states are sleeping states, the leftmost of which is the initial state. The application is started when the machine wakes up for the first time. After that, it is verified that the application actually started. Then, the test guidance algorithm makes a choice between taking a photo, quitting the application, and entering a sleeping state.

At this tier, there are two communication mechanisms between the machines. The first one controls which action machine is currently running using primitives $Sleep_{TS}$, $Wake_{TS}$, $Sleep_{App}$ and $Wake_{App}$. These represent putting to sleep and waking up an application with a task switcher (TS) or directly within another application (App). The other mechanism is for exchanging information on shared resources between the machines: there are primitives for requesting (Req) and giving permissions (Allow). The former can be executed only between running states and the latter between sleeping states.

Test control tier. The test control tier is used for defining which test models to use and what kind of tests to run in which order. Naturally, there are different needs depending on whether we are performing a quick test in conjunction with a continuous integration [11] cycle or chasing the cause for some randomly appearing strange behavior.

We have initially identified three different testing "modes" that should be supported in an agile project. Firstly, smoke tests are needed for verifying that a build has been successful. Such verification step can be included in the test run for each continuous integration build, for instance. However, we do not restrict to a static sequence of tests such as in conventional test automation. Instead, we may set limits on the duration of the test and explore the test model on a breadth-first fashion within those limits.

Secondly, we need to be able to cover certain requirements. Goals for testing projects are often set in terms of requirements coverage; for example, at least requirements R1, R2 and R4 should be tested. Thirdly, we would like to do serious bug hunting. In this case our primary motivation is not to cover certain requirements or to stop within five minutes. Instead, we try to find as many defects as possible. However, requirements can be used to guide the test generation also in this mode. Furthermore, the coverage data obtained in the previous test could be used to avoid retesting the same paths again.

It is also in this tier where we define which machines are composed into an executable test model. Obviously, composing all the machines is usually not necessary. In cases where we use requirements to limit the test generation, we include in the composite model only those machines that are needed to cover the requirements. However, in smoke testing mode, the machines required to be composed should be explicitly stated: machines for the Camera, Messaging and Telephony applications, for example. Moreover, within the Symbian S60 domain, the task switcher machine is always included in the executable test model. Since the state-space explosion can occur when composing test models by interleaving executions of a number of machines, instead of generating the composite test model at once, we do the parallel composition on the fly.

3   From Informal Use Cases to Model-Based Tests

This section presents the process of use case driven test generation in conjunction with the associated coverage language and test generation algorithm.

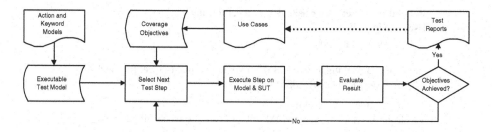

Fig. 3. Use case driven testing

3.1   Use Case Driven Testing

Organizations developing software in an agile manner prefer testing tools that are easy to use, can find defects effectively, and integrate seamlessly with the agile processes. In the following we will concentrate on the first and the last of these requirements. Firstly, the sophisticated algorithms etc. should be hidden as much as possible from the tool users. Secondly, the input of the tools should be something that is produced in the project anyway.

We think that it is hard to get average testers to build test models. Thus, we developed a visual and easy-to-grasp domain-specific language comprising LTSs and action words. However, in a strict domain such as ours, the test models themselves could be developed by a third party. Alternatively, the adapting organization could train one or two dedicated experts to build test models using requirements, design documents, etc. In both cases, the basic test model library consisting of the fundamental models, such as machines for calling, contacts, calendar and camera in our case, may be developed with a reasonable effort. Moreover, the library could be extended incrementally based on the new requirements to be tested.

We suggest that the testers should primarily interact with the test automation system through coverage objectives that drive the test generation. To achieve this, we must link the informal use cases to coverage objectives and define test generation algorithms based on the objectives. Moreover, there should be a clear mapping between the use cases and the tests; testers need to be able to report test coverage in terms of use cases. This scheme is depicted in Figure 3.

As discussed in Section 2.1, we make the following assumptions about the requirements used as input to the test automation:

1. The requirements are stated as informal use cases including a name, an identifier and the basic course of actions.
2. The uses cases have been prioritized, for instance, based on a risk analysis.

The tester maps the events listed in the basic course of actions to action words. For instance, a spreadsheet can be used to list the action words corresponding to each event. As discussed above, if there are no predefined action words corresponding to some event, the test model library needs to be extended with new models. For traceability and

Related use case: Alice asks Bob to meet for lunch
Use case identifier: UC1
Action word sequence:

1. Alice.Messaging.awCreateSMS "Would you like to meet for lunch?"
2. Bob.Messaging.awReadSMS

3. Bob.Camera.awTakePhoto
4. Bob.Messaging.awCreateMMS "I will call you when I'll get there"
5. Alice.Messaging.awReadMMS

6. Alice.Contacts.awSelectCarol
7. Carol.Telephone.awAnswerCall
8. Bob.Contacts.awSelectAlice
9. Bob.Contacts.awVerifyBusy
10. Carol.Telephone.awHangUp

11. Alice.Contacts.awSelectBob
12. Bob.Telephone.awAnswerCall
13. Bob.Telephone.awHangUp

Fig. 4. An action word sequence based on use case UC1

comprehensibility, the action word sequence is annotated with the use case name and identifier. The priority affects the test guidance, so it must be stated as well.

Based on the above, our running example would result in the action word sequence presented in Figure 4. The action words are chosen from a model consisting of three actors: Alice, Bob, and Carol. When running in the requirements coverage mode, for instance, the sequence in Figure 4 can be automatically expanded based on the models referenced in the names of the action words. An expanded sequence is presented in Figure 5. From the intermediate steps the tester can make sure that there is a sensible way to execute the sequence in the model.

1. Alice.Messaging.awCreateSMS Msg_1
    Alice.Messaging.awVerifySMS
    Alice.Messaging.awOpenRecipientList
    Alice.Messaging.awChooseBob
    Alice.Messaging.awSendSMS
2. Bob.Messaging.awReadSMS

    Bob.Camera.awStartCam
    Bob.Camera.awVerifyCam
3. Bob.Camera.awTakePhoto
4. Bob.Messaging.awCreateMMS Msg_2
    Bob.Messaging.awVerifyMMS
    Bob.Messaging.awOpenRecipientList
    Bob.Messaging.awChooseAlice
    Bob.Messaging.awSendMMS
5. Alice.Messaging.awReadMMS

    Alice.Contacts.awOpenAddressBook
6. Alice.Contacts.awSelectCarol
    Alice.Contacts.awDialSelected
7. Carol.Telephone.awAnswerCall
    Bob.Contacts.awOpenAddressBook
8. Bob.Contacts.awSelectAlice
    Bob.Contacts.awDialSelected
9. Bob.Contacts.awVerifyBusy
10. Carol.Telephone.awHangUp

    Alice.Contacts.awOpenAddressBook
11. Alice.Contacts.awSelectBob
    Alice.Contacts.awDialSelected
12. Bob.Telephone.awAnswerCall
13. Bob.Telephone.awHangUp

Fig. 5. A detailed action word sequence generated from the model

3.2 Coverage Language

The action word sequences are processed further using the coverage language that will be introduced next. The design of the language has been guided by the following principles:

1. *Syntax should be concise and readable.*
2. *Elements can be required to be covered in a free order or in some specific order.*
3. *There can be alternative coverage criteria.*
4. *Criteria can relate to both test environment and test model.* A test criterion can be fulfilled, for example, if the test run has already taken too long, if some resources in the test system are running low, or if some elements in the test model are covered in sufficient detail.
5. *Execution paths in the test model must not be restricted by the language.* We keep the roles of the coverage criteria and the test model separate. The test model (alone) specifies what can be tested, whereas the coverage criteria specifies the stopping condition for test runs.

A coverage criterion (CC) is either an elementary criterion (EC) or a combination of two other coverage criteria:

$$CC = EC \,|\, (CC\,(\textbf{and}\,|\,\textbf{or}\,|\,\textbf{then})\,CC)$$

The operators that combine the criteria have the following meaning

and requires that both coverage criteria are fulfilled in any order and or simultaneously. (Design principle 2, free order.)

or requires that at least either one of the criteria is fulfilled. (Design principle 3.)

then requires that the second criterion is fulfilled after the first one. (Design principle 2, a specific order.)

Note that A **then** B does not require that B must not be fulfilled before A, it only requires that B is fulfilled (possibly again) after fulfilling A. The reasons for this will be elaborated at the end of the section.

Elementary criteria consist of two parts, a query and a requirement for the return value of the query:

$$EC = Req \textbf{ for } Query$$
$$Req = (\textbf{every}\,|\,\textbf{any})\,\textbf{value} \geq n$$
$$Query = (\textbf{actions}\,|\,\textbf{states}\,|\,\textbf{transitions}\,|\,\textbf{sysvars})\,regexps$$

The query part of an elementary criterion returns a set of item-value pairs. The items are actions, states, transitions or test system variables. While the first three items relate to the test model, the test system variables give access to time and date, amount of free memory in the SUT and the number of executed actions, for instance. There is an item-value pair for every item that matches any regular expression in the query.

The meaning of the value associated with an item depends on the type of the item. For actions, states and transitions we use the number of times the item has been executed (actions and transitions) or visited (states) during the test run. For system variables it is natural to choose the value of the variable to occur in the pair.

There are two quantifications for the values in the return value set. Either *every* or *any* value is required to satisfy the condition. Once the requirement is met, the elementary criteria is fulfilled.

We often use the coverage language for setting coverage requirements based on the action word sequences. For that purpose, we define a short-hand notation (design principle 1). If the requirement part of a query is omitted, it defaults to "**every value** ≥ 1" or "**any value** ≥ 1" depending on whether or not the type of items is given in the plural form. For example, the requirement that SendMMMessage and SendShortMessage are tested after making a call can be written as follows:

$$\textbf{action } \texttt{MakeCall} \textbf{ then actions } \texttt{Send.*Message}$$

which is a short-hand notation for

> **any value** ≥ 1 **for actions** MakeCall
> **then**
> **every value** ≥ 1 **for actions** Send.*Message

The use case of our running example would be converted to the following coverage language sentence simply by adding "**action**" in front of every action word and joining the results with "**then**":

> | | **action** | Alice.Messaging.awCreateSMS |
> |--------|------------|------------------------------|
> | **then** | **action** | Bob.Messaging.awReadSMS |
> | **then** | **action** | Bob.Camera.awTakePhoto |
> | **then** | **action** | Bob.Messaging.awCreateMMS |
> | **then** | **action** | Alice.Messaging.awReadMMS |
> | **then** | **action** | Alice.Contacts.awSelectCarol |
> | **then** | **action** | Carol.Telephone.awAnswerCall |
> | **then** | **action** | Bob.Contacts.awSelectAlice |
> | **then** | **action** | Bob.Contacts.awVerifyBusy |
> | **then** | **action** | Carol.Telephone.awHangUp |
> | **then** | **action** | Alice.Contacts.awSelectBob |
> | **then** | **action** | Bob.Telephone.awAnswerCall |
> | **then** | **action** | Bob.Telephone.awHangUp |

The data in the use case (the messages "Would you like to meet for lunch?", "I will call you when I'll get there") is stored in a separate table which is used as a data source in the test run.

Coverage requirements can also be built from a number of use cases. Both **and** and **then** operators are sensible choices for joining the requirements obtained from the use cases. However, depending on the guidance algorithm, they may result in very different test runs. But before we can show why, we have to show how the operators affect the evaluation of the coverage criteria.

Next we define an evaluation function f that maps coverage criteria to real numbers from zero to one. The number describes the extent to which the criterion has been fulfilled, number one meaning that the criterion has been completely fulfilled. The evaluation function is defined using function E, which evaluates an elementary criterion to a real number, and three $\mathbb{R} \times \mathbb{R} \to \mathbb{R}$ functions. The three functions are T for evaluating **and**, S for **or**, and R for **then**:

$$f(EC) = E(EC)$$
$$f(A \textbf{ and } B) = T(f(A), f(B))$$
$$f(A \textbf{ or } B) = S(f(A), f(B))$$
$$f(A \textbf{ then } B) = R(f(A), f(B))$$

Let us first consider function E for elementary criteria. Once an elementary criteria EC has been fulfilled, $E(EC) = 1$. Defining that otherwise $E(EC) = 0$ would be easy and it would not contradict the semantics. However, the evaluation would not give any hint for test guidance algorithms about smaller advances in the coverage. When the search depth of the guidance algorithms is bounded, or a best-first [12] search is used, a more fine-grained evaluation is useful.

Of course, it is not always possible to give more detailed information than 0 and 1. For instance, if a coverage requirement requires that a single state in the test model has been visited at least once, we are clearly dealing with 0 or 1 value. On the other hand, a requirement that every action in a set of actions is executed at least once can be thought to be one step closer to the fulfillment every time a new action in the set is executed. More generally, consider criterion EC that sets an upper limit to a monotonically growing query value. $E(EC)$ evaluates closer to 1 every time the result of the query grows, reaching 1 when the result reaches the limit.

Based on this, we define E as follows for elementary criterion $EC = Req$ **for** $Query$:

$$E(EC) = \begin{cases} min(n, max(Query))/n & \text{if } Req \text{ is } \textbf{any value} \geq n \\ avg\_w\_ulimit(Query, n) & \text{if } Req \text{ is } \textbf{every value} \geq n \end{cases}$$

where avg_w_ulimit is the average of values returned by the query so that values greater than n are replaced by n. Thus $E(\textbf{every value} \geq 1 \textbf{ for actions } a\ b) = 0.5$ when a has been executed three times and b has not been executed.

Next, we define the evaluation function so that logically equivalent coverage criteria produce equal values. That is, the evaluation function respects the idempotence (1.x), symmetry (2.x), associativity (3.x) and distributivity (4.x) laws presented in Table 1.

A basic result for norms in fuzzy logic [13] says that the only functions that satisfy the properties x.1 and x.2 in Table 1 are the following:

$$f(A \textbf{ and } B) = T(A, B) = min(f(A), f(B))$$
$$f(A \textbf{ or } B) = S(A, B) = max(f(A), f(B))$$

When T and S are defined as above, the following R satisfies properties 4.3 and 4.4:

$$f(A \textbf{ then } B) = R(A, B) = \frac{f(A) + f(B_{\text{after A}})}{2}$$

Where $B_{\text{after A}}$ denotes coverage requirement B whose covering does not start until A has been covered. Therefore, $f(B_{\text{after A}}) = 0$ if $f(A) < 1$.

Table 1. Equal coverage criteria

$$f(A \text{ and } A) = f(A) \tag{1.1}$$
$$f(A \text{ or } A) = f(A) \tag{1.2}$$
$$f(A \text{ and } B) = f(B \text{ and } A) \tag{2.1}$$
$$f(A \text{ or } B) = f(B \text{ or } A) \tag{2.2}$$
$$f((A \text{ and } B) \text{ and } C) = f(A \text{ and } (B \text{ and } C)) \tag{3.1}$$
$$f((A \text{ or } B) \text{ or } C) = f(A \text{ or } (B \text{ or } C)) \tag{3.2}$$
$$f(A \text{ and } (B \text{ or } C)) = f((A \text{ and } B) \text{ or } (A \text{ and } C)) \tag{4.1}$$
$$f(A \text{ or } (B \text{ and } C)) = f((A \text{ or } B) \text{ and } (A \text{ or } C)) \tag{4.2}$$
$$f(A \text{ then } (B \text{ and } C)) = f((A \text{ then } B) \text{ and } (A \text{ then } C)) \tag{4.3}$$
$$f(A \text{ then } (B \text{ or } C)) = f((A \text{ then } B) \text{ or } (A \text{ then } C)) \tag{4.4}$$

Let us now get back to the two possible ways to join use cases to a single coverage requirement. Assume that we have converted two use cases to coverage requirements CC_{UC1} and CC_{UC2}. They can both be tested at once by combining them to the requirement "CC_{UC1} **and** CC_{UC2}" or "CC_{UC1} **then** CC_{UC2}". Our test guidance algorithm is a greedy bounded-depth search, which will be presented in the following subsection. Here it is enough to know that the algorithm chooses the path of at most length d (the search depth) where the value evaluated for the coverage requirement is maximal. Using the **then** operator to combine the requirements implies a test run where the first use case is fulfilled before the second. But if the use cases are combined with the **and** operator, it would result in a test run where the execution of the use cases advances roughly side-by-side. Thus, we suggest combining the use cases with the same priority using **and** and use cases with different priorities with **then**.

We have excluded the negation "**not**" in the language because of the design principle 5. Consider the following (false) example which would state that making a phone call should be tested without sending an email at any point of the test run:

action MakeCall **and not action** SendEmailMessage

The negation would provide a way to restrict the behavior of the test model. Therefore, the language would not anymore state the coverage criteria; it would also change the test model. This would break the separation between the roles of the test model and the coverage language (design principle 5). The same applies also to many other operators that we considered. For example, stating that something should be tested strictly before something else is tested breaks the same principle. This is the reason for the limitations of our "**then**" operator.

In the language, there is a nice property obtained from the design principle 5 together with our requirement that the initial states of test models are reachable from every other state of the models. Consider finite sets of coverage criteria that can be fulfilled in the same test model and that talk only about the model elements (actions, states and transitions), not system variables. Every new criterion build by combining the criteria in any set with **and**, **or** and **then** operators can also be fulfilled in the same test model. This gives the testers the freedom to choose any combination of valid coverage criteria to define the stopping condition for the test run.

NextStep(s : state, $depth$: integer, c : coverage requirement)
1 **if** $depth = 0$ **or** $s.outTransitions() = \emptyset$ **or** $c.getRate() = 1$ **then return** ($c.getRate()$, {})
2 $best\_rate = 0$; $best\_transitions = \{\}$
3 **for each** $t \in s.outTransitions()$ **do**
4      $c.push()$
5      $c.markExecuted(t)$
6      $(new_rate, dont_care) = $ **NextStep**($t.destinationState()$, $depth - 1, c$)
7      $c.pop()$
8   **if** $new\_rate > best\_rate$ **then** $best\_rate = new\_rate$; $best\_transitions = \{t\}$
9   **if** $new\_rate = best\_rate$ **then** $best\_transitions = best\_transitions \cup \{t\}$
10 **end for**
11 **return** ($best\_rate$, $best\_transitions$)

Fig. 6. An on-line test guidance algorithm using the coverage requirements

3.3   Using Coverage Language in Test Generation

Next, we will present a simple algorithm that can be used in test generation. First, let us describe briefly the data structure that we use for storing and evaluating coverage requirements in our on-line test generation algorithms.

Parsing a coverage requirement results in a tree where leaf nodes represent elementary requirements and the other nodes the operators **and**, **or** and **then**. Every node implements *markExecuted(transition)* method. **And** and **or** nodes pass the calls to all children, **then** nodes pass the call to the first child that has not been fulfilled yet (see the definition for the R function), and leaf nodes update their item execution tables. The tables, indexed by the queried items, store the number of executions/visitations of each item.

All nodes also offer *push()* and *pop()* methods whose calls are always passed through the tree to the leaf nodes. The leaf nodes either push or pop the current execution tables to or from their table stacks. Push and pop methods allow guidance algorithms to store the current coverage data, evaluate how the coverage would change if some transitions were executed, and finally restore the data.

Lastly, there is *getRate()* method which returns the fulfillment rate of the requirement represented by the node and its children. Non-leaf nodes calculate the rate by asking first the rates of their child nodes and then using T, S or R function, depending on the operator of the node. Leaf nodes evaluate the value with the E function.

The NextStep function, presented in Figure 6, can be used as a core of the test generation algorithms. Three parameters are given to the function: a state from which the step should be taken, the maximum search depth in which the algorithm has to make the decision, and the coverage requirement, that is, the root node of the tree. The function returns a pair: the best rate that is achievable in the given number of steps (search depth) and the set of transitions leaving the given state. Any of those transitions can be executed to achieve the coverage rate in the given number of steps.

For simplicity, we did not take into account in NextStep that the SUT may force the execution of certain transitions in some states. Instead, we assumed that the suggested transition can always be executed. If this is not the case, one can use the expectation value for the fulfillment rate in place of *getRate()* (for details, see "state evaluation" in [14]).

4   Related Work

The idea of using use cases (or sequence diagrams) to drive test generation is not new. In addition, it has been suggested to use more expressive formalisms, such as state machines [15,16]. Traceability between requirements and model-based tests has also been studied before. For instance, Bouquet et al. present an approach in [17] where the idea is to annotate the model used for test generation with requirement information. The formal model is tagged with identifiers of the requirements allowing model coverage to be stated in terms of requirements. This allows automatic generation of a traceability matrix showing relations between the requirements and the generated test suite.

We have tackled these issues from a slightly different angle. In a restricted domain such as ours, test modeling can be assigned to some internal experts or third parties. Then, the primary task of the test automation engineer is to transform use cases to sequences of predefined actions words. The action words correspond to concepts familiar to testers in the particular domain, thus facilitating the translation. Our generation algorithms use the action word sequences as coverage objectives. Moreover, a test run produces a test log that can be used for generating reports based on requirements coverage.

In formal verification, the properties concerning models are commonly stated in terms of temporal logics such as LTL [18] and CTL [19]. This approach has been adopted also for test generation in model-based testing, for example in [20]. We defined a simpler and less expressive language for coverage for two reasons. Firstly, using temporal logics require skills not too often available in testing projects. Secondly, the strength of logics is great enough to change (restrict) the behavior of the test model: fulfilling a criterion can require that something is not tested. What we gained is that coverage requirements cannot conflict.

5   Conclusions

In this paper we have introduced an approach to adapting model-based testing practices in organizations developing software using agile processes. Such organizations are often reluctant to develop detailed models needed in most other approaches. Our approach is based on a domain-specific methodology that entails high-level of automation. The test models are developed incrementally by internal experts or third parties, and the informal uses cases are used to drive the test generation. This involves simple translation from the events listed in the use cases to actions words used in the high-level test models. Such action words describe the abstract behavior that is implemented by lower-level keyword models in the test model library.

We have also defined a test coverage language used in producing coverage objectives from the sequences of action words. The language supports different kinds of testing modes such as requirements coverage, bug hunting, or smoke testing. In the first two modes, the coverage objectives obtained from the use cases are used as input to the test generation algorithm.

We are currently implementing a tool set supporting our scheme. The future work includes conducting industrial case studies to assess the overall approach as well as investigating the defect-finding capability of the presented heuristic. Moreover, since model-based tests include complex behavior, some of the defects can be very hard to reproduce. Towards this end we must explore different possibilities to ease debugging.

Acknowledgments

The authors would like to thank the anonymous reviewers for their helpful comments.

References

1. Boehm, B., Turner, R.: Balancing Agility and Discipline: A Guide for the Perplexed. Addison Wesley (2004)
2. Ambler, S.W.: Agile modeling homepage. Available at http://www.agilemodeling.com (2006)
3. Kervinen, A., Maunumaa, M., Pääkkönen, T., Katara, M.: Model-based testing through a GUI. In: Proceedings of the 5th International Workshop on Formal Approaches to Testing of Software (FATES 2005), Edinburgh, Scotland, UK, Number 3997 in LNCS, Springer (2006) 16–31
4. Kervinen, A., Maunumaa, M., Katara, M.: Controlling testing using three-tier model architecture. In: Proceedings of the Second Workshop on Model Based Testing (MBT 2006), ENTCS **164(4)** (2006) 53–66
5. Katara, M., Kervinen, A., Maunumaa, M., Pääkkönen, T., Satama, M.: Towards deploying model-based testing with a domain-specific modeling approach. In: Proceedings of TAIC PART - Testing: Academic & Industrial Conference, Windsor, UK, IEEE Computer Society (2006) 81–89
6. S60: Symbian S60 homepage. Available at http://www.s60.com (2006)
7. Fewster, M., Graham, D.: Software Test Automation. Addison–Wesley (1999)
8. Buwalda, H.: Action figures. STQE Magazine, March/April 2003 (2003) 42–47
9. Wells, D.: Extreme programming: a gentle introduction. Available at http://www.extremeprogramming.org (2006)
10. Craig, R.D., Jaskiel, S.P.: Systematic Software Testing. Artech House (2002)
11. Fowler, M.: Continuous integration. Available at http://www.martinfowler.com/articles/continuousIntegration.html (2006)
12. Russel, S., Norvig, P.: Artifical Intelligence. Prentice-Hall (1995)
13. Klement, E.P., Mesiar, R., Pap, E.: Triangular Norms. Springer (2000)
14. Kervinen, A., Virolainen, P.: Heuristics for faster error detection with automated black box testing. In: Proceedings of the Workshop on Model Based Testing (MBT 2004), ENTCS **111** (2005) 53–71
15. Jard, C., Jéron, T.: TGV: theory, principles and algorithms – a tool for the automatic synthesis of conformance test cases for non-deterministic reactive systems. STTT **7** (2005) 297–315
16. AGEDIS Consortium: AGEDIS project homepage. Available at http://www.agedis.de/ (2004)
17. Bouquet, F., Jaffuel, E., Legeard, B., Peureux, F., Utting, M.: Requirements traceability in automated test generation – application to smart card software validation. In: Proceedings of ICSE 2005 Workshop on Advances in Model-Based Software Testing (A-MOST), ACM (2005)

18. Pnueli, A.: Temporal semantics of concurrent programs. In: Proceedings of the 18th IEEE Symposium on the Foundations of Computer Science, IEEE Computer Society (1977) 46–57
19. Clarke, E.M., Emerson, E.A.: Design and synthesis of synchronization skeletons using branching time temporal logic. In: Workshop on Logic in Programs. Number 131 in LNCS, Springer (1981) 52–71
20. Hong, H.S., Lee, I., Sokolsky, O., Ural, H.: A temporal logic based coverage theory of test coverage and generation. In: Tools and Algorithms for the Construction and Analysis of Systems: 8th International Conference (TACAS 2002). Number 2280 in LNCS, Springer (2002) 327–339

Author Index

Lecture Notes in Computer Science

For information about Vols. 1–4291

please contact your bookseller or Springer

Vol. 4340: R. Prodan, T. Fahringer, Grid Computing. XXIII, 317 pages. 2007.

Vol. 4339: E. Ayguadé, G. Baumgartner, J. Ramanujam, P. Sadayappan (Eds.), Languages and Compilers for Parallel Computing. XI, 476 pages. 2006.

Vol. 4338: P. Kalra, S. Peleg (Eds.), Computer Vision, Graphics and Image Processing. XV, 965 pages. 2006.

Vol. 4337: S. Arun-Kumar, N. Garg (Eds.), FSTTCS 2006: Foundations of Software Technology and Theoretical Computer Science. XIII, 430 pages. 2006.

Vol. 4335: S.A. Brueckner, S. Hassas, M. Jelasity, D. Yamins (Eds.), Engineering Self-Organising Systems. XII, 212 pages. 2007. (Sublibrary LNAI).

Vol. 4334: B. Beckert, R. Hähnle, P.H. Schmitt (Eds.), Verification of Object-Oriented Software. XXIX, 658 pages. 2007. (Sublibrary LNAI).

Vol. 4333: U. Reimer, D. Karagiannis (Eds.), Practical Aspects of Knowledge Management. XII, 338 pages. 2006. (Sublibrary LNAI).

Vol. 4332: A. Bagchi, V. Atluri (Eds.), Information Systems Security. XV, 382 pages. 2006.

Vol. 4331: G. Min, B. Di Martino, L.T. Yang, M. Guo, G. Ruenger (Eds.), Frontiers of High Performance Computing and Networking – ISPA 2006 Workshops. XXXVII, 1141 pages. 2006.

Vol. 4330: M. Guo, L.T. Yang, B. Di Martino, H.P. Zima, J. Dongarra, F. Tang (Eds.), Parallel and Distributed Processing and Applications. XVIII, 953 pages. 2006.

Vol. 4329: R. Barua, T. Lange (Eds.), Progress in Cryptology - INDOCRYPT 2006. X, 454 pages. 2006.

Vol. 4328: D. Penkler, M. Reitenspiess, F. Tam (Eds.), Service Availability. X, 289 pages. 2006.

Vol. 4327: M. Baldoni, U. Endriss (Eds.), Declarative Agent Languages and Technologies IV. VIII, 257 pages. 2006. (Sublibrary LNAI).

Vol. 4326: S. Göbel, R. Malkewitz, I. Iurgel (Eds.), Technologies for Interactive Digital Storytelling and Entertainment. X, 384 pages. 2006.

Vol. 4325: J. Cao, I. Stojmenovic, X. Jia, S.K. Das (Eds.), Mobile Ad-hoc and Sensor Networks. XIX, 887 pages. 2006.

Vol. 4323: G. Doherty, A. Blandford (Eds.), Interactive Systems. XI, 269 pages. 2007.

Vol. 4320: R. Gotzhein, R. Reed (Eds.), System Analysis and Modeling: Language Profiles. X, 229 pages. 2006.

Vol. 4319: L.-W. Chang, W.-N. Lie (Eds.), Advances in Image and Video Technology. XXVI, 1347 pages. 2006.

Vol. 4318: H. Lipmaa, M. Yung, D. Lin (Eds.), Information Security and Cryptology. XI, 305 pages. 2006.

Vol. 4317: S.K. Madria, K.T. Claypool, R. Kannan, P. Uppuluri, M.M. Gore (Eds.), Distributed Computing and Internet Technology. XIX, 466 pages. 2006.

Vol. 4316: M.M. Dalkilic, S. Kim, J. Yang (Eds.), Data Mining and Bioinformatics. VIII, 197 pages. 2006. (Sublibrary LNBI).

Vol. 4314: C. Freksa, M. Kohlhase, K. Schill (Eds.), KI 2006: Advances in Artificial Intelligence. XII, 458 pages. 2007. (Sublibrary LNAI).

Vol. 4313: T. Margaria, B. Steffen (Eds.), Leveraging Applications of Formal Methods. IX, 197 pages. 2006.

Vol. 4312: S. Sugimoto, J. Hunter, A. Rauber, A. Morishima (Eds.), Digital Libraries: Achievements, Challenges and Opportunities. XVIII, 571 pages. 2006.

Vol. 4311: K. Cho, P. Jacquet (Eds.), Technologies for Advanced Heterogeneous Networks II. XI, 253 pages. 2006.

Vol. 4309: P. Inverardi, M. Jazayeri (Eds.), Software Engineering Education in the Modern Age. VIII, 207 pages. 2006.

Vol. 4308: S. Chaudhuri, S.R. Das, H.S. Paul, S. Tirthapura (Eds.), Distributed Computing and Networking. XIX, 608 pages. 2006.

Vol. 4307: P. Ning, S. Qing, N. Li (Eds.), Information and Communications Security. XIV, 558 pages. 2006.

Vol. 4306: Y. Avrithis, Y. Kompatsiaris, S. Staab, N.E. O'Connor (Eds.), Semantic Multimedia. XII, 241 pages. 2006.

Vol. 4305: A.A. Shvartsman (Ed.), Principles of Distributed Systems. XIII, 441 pages. 2006.

Vol. 4304: A. Sattar, B.-H. Kang (Eds.), AI 2006: Advances in Artificial Intelligence. XXVII, 1303 pages. 2006. (Sublibrary LNAI).

Vol. 4303: A. Hoffmann, B.-H. Kang, D. Richards, S. Tsumoto (Eds.), Advances in Knowledge Acquisition and Management. XI, 259 pages. 2006. (Sublibrary LNAI).

Vol. 4302: J. Domingo-Ferrer, L. Franconi (Eds.), Privacy in Statistical Databases. XI, 383 pages. 2006.

Vol. 4301: D. Pointcheval, Y. Mu, K. Chen (Eds.), Cryptology and Network Security. XIII, 381 pages. 2006.

Vol. 4300: Y.Q. Shi (Ed.), Transactions on Data Hiding and Multimedia Security I. IX, 139 pages. 2006.

Vol. 4299: S. Renals, S. Bengio, J.G. Fiscus (Eds.), Machine Learning for Multimodal Interaction. XII, 470 pages. 2006.

Vol. 4297: Y. Robert, M. Parashar, R. Badrinath, V.K. Prasanna (Eds.), High Performance Computing - HiPC 2006. XXIV, 642 pages. 2006.

Vol. 4296: M.S. Rhee, B. Lee (Eds.), Information Security and Cryptology – ICISC 2006. XIII, 358 pages. 2006.

Vol. 4295: J.D. Carswell, T. Tezuka (Eds.), Web and Wireless Geographical Information Systems. XI, 269 pages. 2006.

Vol. 4294: A. Dan, W. Lamersdorf (Eds.), Service-Oriented Computing – ICSOC 2006. XIX, 653 pages. 2006.

Vol. 4293: A. Gelbukh, C.A. Reyes-Garcia (Eds.), MICAI 2006: Advances in Artificial Intelligence. XXVIII, 1232 pages. 2006. (Sublibrary LNAI).

Vol. 4292: G. Bebis, R. Boyle, B. Parvin, D. Koracin, P. Remagnino, A. Nefian, G. Meenakshisundaram, V. Pascucci, J. Zara, J. Molineros, H. Theisel, T. Malzbender (Eds.), Advances in Visual Computing, Part II. XXXII, 906 pages. 2006.